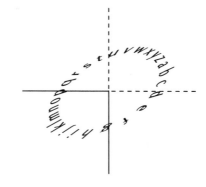

teach yourself...

Word 6 for Windows

by
Mike Lottridge and Vicky Stevens

Copyright © 1993 by MIS:Press
a subsidiary of Henry Holt and Company, Inc.
115 West 18th Street
New York, New York, 10011

First Edition—1993

ISBN 1-55828-324-2

Printed in the United States of America.

10 9 8 7 6 5 4 3 2 1

MIS:Press books are available at special discounts for bulk purchases for sales promotions, premiums, fund-raising, or educational use. Special editions or book excerpts can also be created to specification.

For details contact: Special Sales Director
MIS:Press
a subsidiary of Henry Holt and Company, Inc.
115 West 18th Street
New York, New York 10011

Trademarks

Throughout this book, trademarked names are used. Rather than put a trademark symbol after every occurrence of a trademarked name, we used the names in an editorial fashion only, and to the benefit of the trademark owner, with no intention of infringement of the trademark. Where such designations appear in this book, they have been printed with initial caps.

Acknowledgements

Anyone who credits only the authors for the work that goes into a book has never had an inside peek at what it takes to get to press.

We would like to thank Steve Berkowitz, our Publisher, for offering us this opportunity.

Judy Brief, our Development Editor (or birthing coach) through this process, has worked tirelessly to coordinate everything with everyone, all the time, while keeping her sense of humor.

Dawn Erdos, our copy editor, caught *everything* that we (and the spelling- and grammar-checking software) missed in our rush to get it all done NOW.

Laura Specht, our Production Editor, is truly a pro at handling complex layout issues.

Amy Carley, our Associate Production Editor, did an excellent job of cleaning up files and making sure that editing changes went where they were supposed to go.

Xanadu and Bastet, our feline companions, made sure we understood that sometimes you leave the PC long enough to eat, sleep, and play. We thank them.

Finally, Vicky and Mike thank each other.

Table of Contents

Chapter 9: Using Microsoft Draw and WordArt

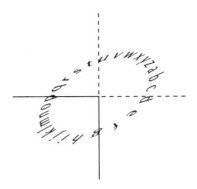

Introduction

A long time ago (but it seems like yesterday), we became technical writers. We typed our documents, using a text processing program "on a dumb terminal hanging off a mainframe." Formatting was nonexistent. We did what we could with the equal sign (as a double underline for level-one headings), the hyphen character (as a single underline for level-two headings), and quotation marks (for miscellaneous anything else). Bold? Italic? Forget it. Uppercase letters had to suffice.

Then our company really went high tech and bought us a state-of-the-art text composer. Great. We had to code every little formatting item, even for simple things such as underlining words. Stop in the middle of typing a sentence, turn on the macro for underlining, type the words to be underlined, and turn off the underlining macro. Of course, we forgot to turn off the code, and the remainder of the entire document was underlined. What a mess! Not only that, we had to walk three miles barefoot in the snow at midnight to get a printout...Okay, we're starting to exaggerate a little, but you get the picture.

It doesn't have to be that way anymore. Microsoft's Word 6 for Windows makes creating any kind of document easy, usually quick, and often fun. This book will help you become a confident Word 6 user. It will introduce you to many of Word's powerful, but easy-to-use features so you can develop professional-quality personal and business documents.

What This Book Teaches

Teach Yourself Word 6 for Windows gets you started in Word's environment and shows you, step by step, how to progress from basic tasks such as setting up a document and formatting to making templates, drawing, and working with online forms. This book also introduces you to some of Word's more complex features such as Graph, Equation Editor, Mail Merge, and macros. In short, this book teaches about most of Word's important features and helps you gain the confidence you need to progress logically from a basic user to a power user.

The tutorials, along with the work files on the disk, teach you how to edit a document, design styles, create a template, and make an online form. By the time you are done, you will have experience with many of the features that help you become an expert user.

Chapter 1

Mastering the Word for Windows Environment explains the Word workplace, how to navigate in it, and how to use the tools in the work area. You'll learn about the Standard toolbar, the Formatting toolbar, the Ruler, the Borders and Shading toolbar, and the Status bar. This chapter also explains the page views and how to use them, quick navigation, and use of the Clipboard for cutting, copying, and pasting text.

Chapter 2

Setting Up a Word Document shows you how to set up all the elements of a Word document. You will learn about page setup, section breaks, page breaks, headers and footer, footnotes, annotations, and bookmarks.

Chapter 3

Formatting Characters and Words shows you multiple ways to apply and change the look of the font you use. You will learn multiple ways to apply attributes, such as bold, italic, underlines, hidden text, and superscript and subscript text characters.

The chapter also covers use of hyphens, nonbreaking spaces, character spacing, copying and repeating formats, and working with special characters and symbols.

Chapter 4

Formatting Paragraphs and Objects explains the use of line spacing, tabs, indentations, paragraph alignment, numbered and bulleted lists, tables, columns and borders.

Chapter 5

Formatting Tutorials provides two structured lessons for applying formatting to text. You can use the text on the disk to format a letter and a business proposal.

Chapter 6

Creating a Template shows you how to define styles, based on the formatting you apply, and how to create a new template that you can use for similar documents.

Chapter 7

Tables of Contents and Indexes shows you how to build and generate tables of contents, lists, and indexes in much less time than it takes to generate them manually.

Chapter 8

Forms and Tables teaches you how to develop an online form that can save you hours of time. Instead of performing repetitive typing and revising, you can design a form one time and use form fields to change only the information you need for each use. This chapter also teaches you how to use Word's powerful table feature. You can present information in tables quickly and easily and then change the columns, rows, and individual cells as you need, using drag and drop and dialog boxes.

Chapter 9

Microsoft Draw and WordArt show you how to use Word's powerful graphic capabilities. The chapter explains how to use the tools for drawing objects and

capabilities. The chapter explains how to use the tools for drawing objects and modifying them as you need. In addition, you will learn how to import graphics from other applications. This chapter also teaches you how to use WordArt to insert text that you shape into a variety of graphic designs.

Chapter 10

Using Microsoft Graph shows you how to create many different types of graphic characters from numerical data, making the presentation of numeric data far more interesting.

Chapter 11

The Equation Editor teaches you how to enter and customize equations for simple to complex mathematical expressions.

Chapter 12

Saving Time with Macros teaches you how to automate and simplify repetitive operations by saving them as macros that you can run with a few keystrokes.

Chapter 13

Using Mail Merge shows you how to create your own mailing lists, form letters, and form documents.

What You Need to Know First

The exercises in this book assume that you know how to use your computer, and that you are familiar with Microsoft Window's functions such as selecting, using a mouse, and using pull-down menus. You also need to understand active windows, and how to open, save, and close a file from the File menu, which is standard in Windows.

What You Need to Use This Book

This book assumes that you have Microsoft Windows and the Word 6.0 for Windows package. It also assumes that you have installed the package.

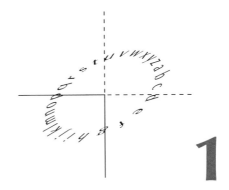

1

Mastering the Word for Windows Environment

In this chapter you learn about the working environment in Word for Windows, and some navigation methods for working in a document, including:

- the Title bar
- the Menu bar
- the Standard toolbar
- the Formatting toolbar
- the Borders and Shading toolbar
- the ruler
- the workplace
- the Status bar
- the insertion point
- text selection
- page views
- the Clipboard
- the Find command
- the Go To command

Learning all of the ways you can move around a document will help you become a more efficient (and more powerful) user. Word provides an interface that gives you a variety of ways to choose options, select and change text, and move from one area to another. Many users find that they never stick to just one method of moving around a document. After they learn all of the navigation techniques, they just do whatever seems right for the moment.

The Overall Word Work Area

When you start Word for Windows, the program displays the default work area, which is the *workplace*. This area is the foundation on which you can build many document types, using all of Word's features. Also, when you start Word, it displays a document window with a default name of Document 1. If you open an existing file, Word displays its name in the Title bar, as shown in Figure 1.1. The following sections describe the parts of the work area.

The Title Bar

The Title bar shows the document name. Word assigns your document a temporary name until you save it with the name you choose. The leftmost area of this bar contains the button for the Application Control menu, which you click to display commands that let you size and move the Word window, switch to other applications, and close Word. The rightmost area of this bar shows the minimize and restore buttons that you click to either fill the screen with Word, or shrink Word to an icon.

Figure 1.1

The Menu Bar

You use the Menu bar to choose all commands while working in Word. The leftmost area of the bar contains the button for the Document Control menu, which displays the commands for restoring a document window to its previous size, moving, sizing, minimizing, maximizing, closing the document window, and switching to another window.

Figure 1.2

The Standard Toolbar

The Standard toolbar lets mouse users quickly access some of Word's commands without having to use a pull-down menu. The following table describes the Standard toolbar options, and gives hints for using each one. Word 6 allows you to see the function of each button of the toolbar. Simply point to a button with the mouse pointer for an instant description.

Figure 1.3

Table 1.1   Standard Toolbar Options and Descriptions

Tool		Description
New		Opens a new document, named Document *N*, where *N* equals the number Word assigns. The document has the default settings. You name the document when you save it.
Open		Displays the Open dialog box, which lets you type the name of a document to open or select one.
Save		Saves the active document. If you have several documents open, make them active, one at a time, to save them. If you have not named the active document, Word displays the Save As dialog box when you select Save.
Print		Prints the active document.
Print preview		Displays the document in print preview mode so you can see how it looks before printing.
Spelling		Checks the spelling of all words in your document or any selected word or line. You can check spelling from any point in a document. Word checks from the insertion point to the end and then asks if you want it to check from the beginning. If anything is selected, it checks the selection. If *nothing* is selected, it starts at the insertion point and goes to the end. For

more information on insertion, please see "Moving the Insertion Point," later in this chapter. Word flags any word that it does not recognize and allows you to ignore the word, change it, ignore or change all identical entries, or to enter it in a custom list. Note: Choose custom additions judiciously. If you enter the wrong spelling of a word by accident, Word ignores the mis-spelled word in the future, unless you change the dictionary.

Cut Removes the selected text or object and places it on the Clipboard, where you cannot see it in the work area. If you cut another item and place it on the Clipboard, then you lose the first one you cut. Always paste the text or object in the Clipboard before you cut another one.

Copy Copies the selected text or object and places it on the Clipboard, where you cannot see it in the work area. If you copy another item and place it on the Clipboard, then you lose the first one you copied. Always paste the text or object in the Clipboard before you copy another one.

Paste Inserts whatever is stored on the Clipboard at the location of the insertion point. You can paste the text or object multiple times until you cut or copy another item to the Clipboard.

Copy formatting Lets you use the mouse to copy the last formatting (for example, bold) applied to text. Click the button, and when the cursor becomes a paintbrush, "brush" it across the text to which you want to apply the formatting, then release it.

Undo Reverses the last action you performed. Click the **Down Arrow** to display a history list of all actions you've performed since opening the document. From this list, you can reverse actions. You can drag down the list to select as many *sequential* items to undo as you wish.

Redo Repeats the last action you performed. Click the **Down Arrow** to display a history list of all actions you've performed since opening the document. From this list, you can redo actions. You can drag down the list to select as many sequential items to redo as you wish.

Automatic format Automatically formats a document with a format predefined in Word.

Enter AutoText Inserts text you've defined as AutoText. You must first define the AutoText by typing a name for the entry and clicking the **AutoText** button. Then to insert the text, you choose **AutoText** from the Edit menu to display the list from which you can select AutoText names.

Table	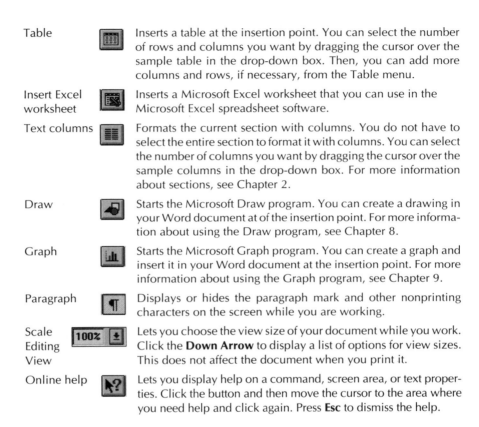	Inserts a table at the insertion point. You can select the number of rows and columns you want by dragging the cursor over the sample table in the drop-down box. Then, you can add more columns and rows, if necessary, from the Table menu.
Insert Excel worksheet		Inserts a Microsoft Excel worksheet that you can use in the Microsoft Excel spreadsheet software.
Text columns		Formats the current section with columns. You do not have to select the entire section to format it with columns. You can select the number of columns you want by dragging the cursor over the sample columns in the drop-down box. For more information about sections, see Chapter 2.
Draw		Starts the Microsoft Draw program. You can create a drawing in your Word document at of the insertion point. For more information about using the Draw program, see Chapter 8.
Graph		Starts the Microsoft Graph program. You can create a graph and insert it in your Word document at the insertion point. For more information about using the Graph program, see Chapter 9.
Paragraph		Displays or hides the paragraph mark and other nonprinting characters on the screen while you are working.
Scale Editing View		Lets you choose the view size of your document while you work. Click the **Down Arrow** to display a list of options for view sizes. This does not affect the document when you print it.
Online help		Lets you display help on a command, screen area, or text properties. Click the button and then move the cursor to the area where you need help and click again. Press **Esc** to dismiss the help.

The Formatting Toolbar

The Formatting toolbar contains quick formatting options.

The three leftmost options (from left to right) let you apply styles, fonts, and font point sizes. Click on the down arrows beside the options to select them.

Figure 1.4

The next three options let you apply bold, italic, and underline attributes to characters, words, or paragraphs.

The next four options let you apply text alignment for left, centered, right, and block (right justified). Right=right–justified; Block=justified both right and left, and padded with spaces.

The last four options let you apply consecutive numbers or bullets to paragraphs to create numbered or bulleted lists, move selected indented paragraphs to the previous default tab stop, and indent selected paragraphs right to the next tab stop. The last option button on the right is for displaying or hiding the Borders toolbar.

The Borders Toolbar

Using the Borders toolbar, you can add a border or shading to a selected paragraph. The toolbar includes some of the simplest types of borders you might use in a document, and it is the quickest way to add them. For example, if you are working in a technical document, and you want to give your reader a warning, you can select the warning paragraph and apply a box around it to make it stand out.

Figure 1.5

To display the Borders toolbar, click the last button on the Formatting toolbar. It looks like a window pane.

The leftmost box on the Borders toolbar shows the line width of the border. You can choose very thin hairline-style borders or thick, bold borders. Table 1.2 explains the seven options Word gives you for adding a border to text or objects.

Table 1.2   Border Options

Tool		Description	·
Border above	▢	Adds a border to the top of a paragraph, table cell, or frame. The border will match the paragraph width. To shorten the border, you must make the paragraph indentations narrower. To do this, select the paragraph and move the markers on the ruler to the width you want. The border will be as high as the paragraph, cell, or frame.	

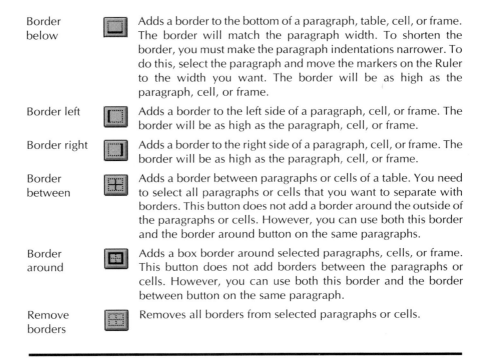

Border below		Adds a border to the bottom of a paragraph, table, cell, or frame. The border will match the paragraph width. To shorten the border, you must make the paragraph indentations narrower. To do this, select the paragraph and move the markers on the Ruler to the width you want. The border will be as high as the paragraph, cell, or frame.
Border left		Adds a border to the left side of a paragraph, cell, or frame. The border will be as high as the paragraph, cell, or frame.
Border right		Adds a border to the right side of a paragraph, cell, or frame. The border will be as high as the paragraph, cell, or frame.
Border between		Adds a border between paragraphs or cells of a table. You need to select all paragraphs or cells that you want to separate with borders. This button does not add a border around the outside of the paragraphs or cells. However, you can use both this border and the border around button on the same paragraphs.
Border around		Adds a box border around selected paragraphs, cells, or frame. This button does not add borders between the paragraphs or cells. However, you can use both this border and the border between button on the same paragraph.
Remove borders		Removes all borders from selected paragraphs or cells.

The last area on the Borders toolbar lets you add shading to a paragraph block or a table cell or frame. Click the **Down Arrow** and choose the percentage you want to use.

If you plan to shade an area that will contain text, choose a lower percentage of shade so that the reader can distinguish the text from the shading without straining the eyes. Twenty to 30% is usually a good choice.

N O T E

The Horizontal Ruler

The Ruler (shown in Figure 1.6 on the next page) lets you change paragraph indentations, margins, and column widths for text and tables. To display or hide the ruler, choose **Ruler** from the View menu. For more information, see Chapter 4, *Formatting Paragraphs and Objects*.

Figure 1.6

 Most tasks you can do from the Standard toolbars, Formatting toolbar, and Ruler can also be done by choosing commands and options from the Menu bar. However, the opposite is not true.

N O T E

The Workplace

The *workplace* is where you type text, use all formatting features, and open other windows. To open another document in a window, choose **Open** from the File menu, (**Alt-F**, **O**) and open a document. You can view and work between the two documents by choosing **Arrange All** from the Window menu (**Alt-W**, **A**). Only the window in which you are working is active.

The workplace also includes the vertical and horizontal scroll bars that let you move around in the document. For more information about using the scroll bars, see "Using the Mouse to Move the Insertion Point" later in this chapter.

The Status Bar

The Status bar, located on the bottom of your screen, displays the page number, section number, the number of pages in the document, the insertion point position from the top of the page, the line and column numbers, the time, the status of keys on your keyboard, and whether you are recording macros or have a revision marking turned on.

You cannot type anything in the Status bar.

Figure 1.7

Selecting Units of Text

Selecting text means that you highlight it so that it is displayed in reverse video (generally, light text on a dark background). After you select text or an item, you can perform actions on the entire block of selected text, such as cutting and pasting, copying, and deleting. You can select text in Word with the keyboard or the mouse.

Using the Mouse

You can select with the mouse by holding down the left mouse button and dragging the mouse pointer over the area you want to select. Or you can use the Selection bar—the unmarked area that runs vertically down the left side of the document's window. Table 1.3 lists steps to select whole units of text with the mouse.

Table 1.3   Selecting Text Using the Mouse

To select	Do this
A word	Double-click on the word.
A sentence	Hold down **Ctrl** and click anywhere in the sentence.
A line of text, regardless of whether it is a sentence	Position the pointer in the Selection bar, point to the line, and click. (The Selection bar is an unmarked area on the left side of the window were you can select text with a mouse.)
Lines of text, regardless of whether they are sentences	You can select multiple lines by dragging in the selection bar beside the lines.
A paragraph	Position the pointer in the Selection bar, point to the paragraph and double-click. You can select multiple paragraphs by dragging in the Selection bar beside them.
An entire document	Hold down **Ctrl** and click anywhere in the Selection bar.

It's easy to go a little too far when you select text with the mouse. If you do, you don't have to cancel and start over. Position the insertion point where you want the selection to begin, move the pointer to where you want it to end, then hold down **Shift** and click to select everything in between.

N O T E

Using the Keyboard

If you don't have a mouse, or simply prefer using the keyboard, you can use key sequences to select text.

Table 1.4   Selecting Text Using the Keyboard

To select this unit	Press this key sequence
One character to the right	**Shift-Right Arrow**
To the end of a word	**Ctrl-Shift-Right Arrow**
To the beginning of a word	**Ctrl-Shift-Left Arrow**
To the end of a line	**Shift-End**
To the beginning of a line	**Shift-Home**
One line down	**Shift-Down Arrow**
One line up	**Shift-Up Arrow**
To the end of a paragraph	**Ctrl-Shift-Down Arrow**
To the beginning of a paragraph	**Ctrl-Shift-Up Arrow**
An entire table	**Alt-5** (on the keypad) (NumLock *OFF*)
One screen down	**Shift-Page Down**
One screen up	**Shift-Page Up**
To the end of a document	**Ctrl-Shift-End**
To the beginning of a document	**Ctrl-Shift-Home**
An entire document	**Ctrl-A** or **Ctrl-5** (on the keypad) (NumLock *OFF*)

If you press **Del** while text is selected, *you delete everything that is selected.* If you accidentally delete the text, choose **Undo** from the Edit menu (**Alt-E**, **U**) to restore it before you do anything else. You may also N O T E choose **Ctrl-Z** to undo.

Page Views

Word's page views help you get a better idea of how the pieces of a document are coming together. There are five ways that you can view your document while you are working:

◆ Normal

◆ Outline

- Page Layout
- Master Document
- Full Screen
- Print Preview

You choose Normal, Outline, Page Layout, Master Document, and Full Screen views from the View menu. However, you choose Print Preview from the File menu. You use each view for a different purpose, and you will probably find each type useful during the development of any document. All view modes, except for Print Preview, allow you to reduce and enlarge the view, and edit just as you would in the normal size.

Normal View

Normal is Word's default view. Usually, you will do most of your work in this view, where you can perform all typing, editing, and formatting, including styles, fonts, and spacing. You can open other panes, such as headers and footers, in Normal view. Also, you can open and work in more than one document (for example, cutting and pasting text from one document to another). When you add a header or footer, you must be in Normal view; however, when you close the header or footer pane, you can look at your document in another view.

If you are not working in Normal view, and you want to be, choose **Normal** from the View menu (**Alt-V**, **N**).

Outline View

Outline view (**Alt-V**, **O**) is much more than just another view mode in Word. In addition to allowing you to look at the structure of your document, it lets you reorganize topics with a few simple steps.

Outline view is particularly useful if you designate headings within a template (a .DOT file containing styles you can apply to format text). When you switch to Outline view, all headings and paragraphs are marked with symbols that show whether there is subordinate text and point out body text. If you move a heading, all text associated with that heading moves with it.

Figure 1.8 on the next page shows the Outline view for a section of a chapter. Notice the bar above the outline. You can choose to display from one to nine levels or all levels of headings and text in your document.

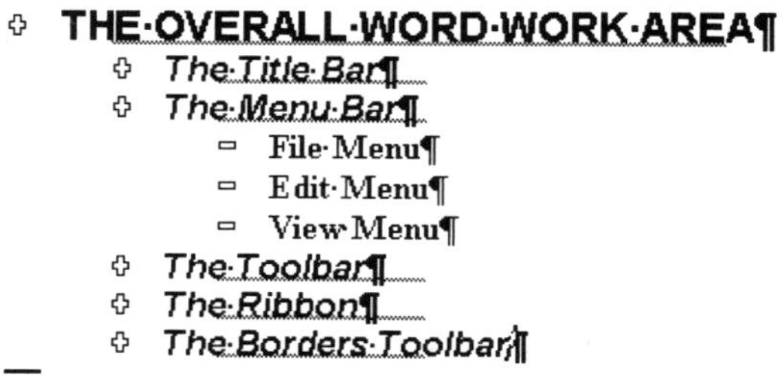

⇩ **THE·OVERALL·WORD·WORK·AREA¶**
   ⇩ *The·Title·Bar¶*
   ⇩ *The·Menu·Bar¶*
     ▫ **File·Menu¶**
     ▫ **Edit·Menu¶**
     ▫ **View·Menu¶**
   ⇩ *The·Toolbar¶*
   ⇩ *The·Ribbon¶*
   ⇩ *The·Borders·Toolbar¶*

Figure 1.8

The following table describes the symbols you see in Outline mode.

Table 1.5   Outline Mode Symbols

This symbol	Indicates
⇩	There is subtext associated with the heading.
▫	There is no subtext associated with the heading.
▫	Body (or paragraph) text.

You use the buttons on the Outline bar (above the view area) to reorganize information. Table 1.6 shows how to use these buttons. They are described from left to right as they appear on the Outline bar.

Table 1.6   Outline Bar Buttons

Select this button	To do this
Right Arrow (**Alt-Shift-Right Arrow**)	Move a selection down one level.
Left Arrow (**Alt-Shift-Left Arrow**)	Move a selection up one level.
Up Arrow (**Alt-Shift-Up Arrow**)	Move a selection above the preceding heading.

Down Arrow (**Alt-Shift-Down Arrow**)	Move a selection below the preceding heading.
Right Arrow with shadow (**Alt-Shift** with NumLock *OFF*)	Convert a heading to body text.
Plus sign (**Alt-Shift-+**)	Expand subheadings or body text under a heading.
Minus sign (**Alt-Shift--**)	Collapse subheadings or body text under a heading.
1 through 9 (**Alt-Shift-1 through 9**)	Display headings up to nine levels.
All(**Alt-Shift-A**)	Show all headings and text.

Master Document

Master Document View lets you see a long document that is made up of subdocuments. This view shows an outline of the current document *and* the subdocuments. You can open any subdocument. If you switch to Normal view, each subdocument is a section of the master document. See your Word manual for information about managing long documents. This feature is one that you will use more after you learn the basics of Word 6.

Page Layout View

Page Layout view can help you save a lot of time and paper. Instead of printing your document to see how the parts look together, you can see how the page is laid out before you print. Choose **Page Layout** from the View menu (**Alt-V**, **P**). This view is particularly useful if you are building a document that has multiple formatting elements, for example, headers, footers, columnar text, and graphics. However, line numbers and lines between columns are not available in Page Layout view. The illustration on the next page in Figure 1.9 shows a page in Page Layout view, with the Zoom Whole Page option applied to reduce it. While you cannot read the text, you can see how the overall page will look when you print it. A discussion of enlarging and reducing documents is included in this section.

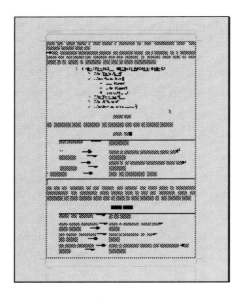

Figure 1.9

Page Layout View versus Normal View

While you are working in Page Layout view, you can edit and format your document much like you can in Normal view. However, there are a few things that you cannot do in Page Layout view that you can do in Normal view, and vice versa. For example, in Normal view, you cannot drag a framed item to another position on the page, but Page Layout view allows it. You can also adjust headers and footers in Page Layout view without having to open the header or footer pane.

You will probably find it easier to make most formatting changes while working at 100 % of the size of the document, instead of at 50 or 200%. The 100 % size is the one in which most people are accustomed to typing N O T E and formatting.

When you scroll in Normal view, you can scroll to the bottom of one page and continue scrolling so the bottom of one page and the top of the next are both displayed at one time. However, in Page Layout view, when you scroll past the bottom of a page, Word displays the top of the next page on the screen. It is impossible to see the bottom of one page and the top of another at the same time.

Page Layout view also allows you to display dotted lines around the different blocks of text or graphics on a page. This is particularly useful in pointing out how text and graphics are positioned. If you have a page with a header, text, a graphic, and a footer, Word draws a dotted line around each of the elements. To display the dotted lines, choose **Options** from the Tools menu (**Alt-T, O**). Then, select the **View** category and select the **Text Boundaries** check box under Show Text With.

You need to be in Page Layout before you choose **Options**, or this option will not be present.

You can see that the zero mark on the ruler on top of the workspace is not aligned with the left margin in Page Layout view. This is because the zero mark aligns with the left document margin.

N O T E

Print Preview

The Print Preview feature, like Page Layout, lets you see how your document will look when you print it. However, Print Preview can show you any elements you added to the printable area, whereas Page Layout cannot always show elements that you placed outside of the margins. Additionally, Print Preview can display two whole pages at a time, as shown in Figure 1.10.

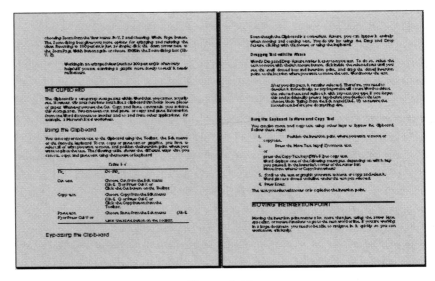

Figure 1.10

To invoke Print Preview, choose **Print Preview** from the File menu (**Alt-F**, **V**). The four options across the top of the screen allow you to print the document, magnify the document, display only one page, display multiple pages, display the document at a smaller or larger size, display the Ruler, shrink to fit on a smaller page, display a full screen, close the Page Layout view without printing, or get help.

If you are working with a document that has landscape orientation, you might find it easier to reduce the page size further.

Making Adjustments in Print Preview

Word lets you edit text and move the margins in Print Preview.

To edit text in Print Preview, perform these steps:

1. In Print Preview, scroll to the page you want to edit.
2. Position the mouse pointer over the area you want to edit, and click the left mouse button. The mouse pointer now looks like a magnifying glass.
3. Click the **Magnifier** button (second from the left) to restore the original mouse pointer and change the document as you want.
4. Choose one of the following options:

To	Do this
Restore the original magnification	Click the **Magnifier** button, and click in the document.
Print the document	Click the **Print** button.
Exit from Print Preview	Click the **Close** button.

To move margins in Print Preview, perform these steps:

1. Click the **View Ruler** button (fifth button from the right) to display the Ruler.
2. Do one of the following:

To	Do this
Move the left or right page margin	Click the **View Ruler** button, and drag a margin boundary on the horizontal ruler.
Move the top or bottom page margin	Click the **View Ruler** button, and drag a margin boundary on the vertical ruler.

Reducing and Enlarging Page Views

You can display a full-page view by clicking down arrow next to the Page View Percentage button (second from the right) from the Standard toolbar, or by choosing **Zoom** from the View menu (**Alt-V, Z**) and clicking on the **Whole Page** button. The Zoom dialog box gives you more options for enlarging and reducing the view. Returning to 100% is just as simple: Click **100** in the Zoom To box.

Working in an enlarged view (such as 200%) is often very helpful if you are examining a graphic more closely to see if it needs refinement.

N O T E

The Clipboard

The Clipboard is a temporary storage area within Word that you cannot actually see. However, this area functions much like a clipboard that holds loose pieces of paper. Whenever you use the Cut, Copy, and Paste commands, you activate this storage area. You can even cut and paste or copy and paste information from one Word document to another, and to and from other applications, such as a Microsoft Excel worksheet.

Using the Clipboard

You can copy or move text to the Clipboard using the Standard toolbar, the Edit menu, or from the keyboard. To cut, copy, or paste text or graphics, you have to select all of what you want to move, and position the insertion point where you want to place the text. Table 1.7 shows the different ways that you can cut, copy, and paste text using the mouse or keyboard.

Table 1.7   Cut, Copy, and Paste Actions Using the Mouse or Keyboard

To	Do this
Cut text	Choose **Cut** from the Edit menu (**Alt-E, T**), or press **Ctrl-X**, or click the **Cut** button on the Standard toolbar.

What the oh difference

Copy text	Choose **Copy** from the Edit menu (**Alt-E**, **C**), or press **Ctrl-C**, or click the **Copy** button from the Standard toolbar.
Paste text	Choose **Paste** from the Edit menu (**Alt-E**, **P**), or press **Ctrl-V**, or click the **Paste** button on the Standard toolbar.

Bypassing the Clipboard with Drag-and-Drop

Even though the Clipboard is a convenient feature, you can bypass it entirely when moving and copying text. You do this by using the Drag-and-Drop feature, clicking with the mouse, or using the keyboard.

Dragging Text with the Mouse

Word's Drag-and-Drop feature makes it easy to move text. To do so, select the text you want to move with the left mouse button, then *hold down* the left mouse button inside the selected area until you see the small dotted box appear near the bottom of the mouse pointer. Then drag the dotted insertion point to the location where you want to move the text. When you release the mouse button, Word moves the text.

N O T E

After you drag text, it remains selected. Therefore, you need to deselect it immediately, as any keystroke causes Word to delete the selected text and replaces it with any text you type. If you forget this and accidentally press a key before you deselect the text, choose **Undo Typing** from the Edit menu (**Alt-E**, **U**) to restore the moved text *before* you do anything else.

Using the Keyboard to Move and Copy Text

You can also move and copy text, using other keys to bypass the Clipboard. Follow these steps:

1. Select the text you want to move or copy.

2. Press the **Move Text** key (**F2**) to move text, or press the **Copy Text** key (**Shift-F2**) to copy text. Word displays one of the following messages (depending on which key you pressed) in the lower-left corner of the Status bar:

   `Move to where?` or `Copy to where?`

3. Move the insertion point where you want to move or copy. Word places a dotted underline under the text you selected.

4. Press **Enter**.

The text you selected moves or is copied to the insertion point.

Moving the Insertion Point

Moving the insertion point means a lot more than just using the Arrow keys, Spacebar, or mouse functions to go to the next word or line. If you are working in a large document, you need to be able to navigate in it quickly so you can work more efficiently.

Using the Keyboard to Move the Insertion Point

Even if you become a die-hard mouse user, you need to know all of the quick ways you can move around using keystrokes. Table 1.8 shows you which key or key combination to use to move the insertion point.

Table 1.8   Key Combinations

To move the insertion point	Press
Back one character	**Left Arrow**
Forward one character	**Right Arrow**
Up one line	**Up Arrow**
Down one line	**Down Arrow**
To the previous word	**Ctrl-Left Arrow**
To the next word	**Ctrl-Right Arrow**
To the beginning of the line	**Home**
To the end of the line	**End**
Up one paragraph	**Ctrl-Up Arrow**
Down one paragraph	**Ctrl-Down Arrow**
To the window's first character	**Ctrl-Pg Up**
To the window's last character	**Ctrl-Pg Dn**
To the previous window	**Pg Up**
To the next window	**Pg Dn**

| To the beginning of the document | **Ctrl-Home** |
| To the end of the document | **Ctrl-End** |

Using the Mouse to Move Through the Document

Word's scroll bars allow you to use the mouse to move vertically and horizontally through your documents.

The Vertical Scroll Bar and Box

The vertical scroll box, on the rightmost side of the work area, (shown at left) lets you see your relative position in the document. If you move the box near the top of the bar, you are closer to the beginning of the document. If you move the box near the bottom of the bar, you are closer to the end of whatever amount of information you have entered. The distance that the scroll box moves is relative to the length of your document. The longer your document, the less the scroll box moves when you click above or below it.

Table 1.9 shows where to click the mouse button to move to certain places in your document.

Table 1.9   Vertical Scroll Options

To scroll here	Do this
Up one line	Click on the **Up Arrow** one time.
Down one line	Click on the **Down Arrow** one time.
Up one window	Click on the scroll bar above the scroll box one time.
Down one window	Click on the scroll bar below the scroll box one time.
To any position you choose	Hold down the mouse button and scroll up or down.

The Horizontal Scroll Bar and Box

The horizontal scroll box, at the bottom of the work area, lets you see the position of the page on which you are working. Scrolling left takes you toward the left margin; scrolling right takes you toward the right margin. This feature is particularly helpful if you are working on a multiple-column document or on a document with wide margins and a longer line length.

Table 1.10 shows where to click the mouse to move to certain places on your page.

Table 1.10 Horizontal Scroll Options

To scroll	Do this
Left a few columns	Click on the **Left Arrow**.
Right a few columns	Click on the **Right Arrow**.
Left into the margin	Hold down **Shift** and click on the **Left Arrow**.
One window to the left	Click on the scroll bar left of the scroll box.
One window to the right	Click on the scroll bar right of the scroll box.
To any position you choose	Hold down the mouse button and drag the scroll box left or right.

Moving the Insertion Point to the Previous Location

Word lets you move the insertion point to the last location where you performed an action in a document. Even if you save and close a document, then open it again, you can move the insertion point where it was when you last saved the document.

To move to the point where the last action took place, press **Shift-F5**.

You can only move back to three prior insertion point locations. For example, if you delete a word, go to the next line and type a word, and save the document, you can press the key sequence to go back where you saved, then where you typed, and finally where you deleted the word. If you press **Shift-F5** a fourth time, the insertion point moves where it was before you first pressed this key sequence.

N O T E

Using the Find Command

The Find command from the Edit menu (**Alt-E**, **F**) lets you search for a string of characters.

You can enter a maximum of 255 characters in the Find What box. As you type, the text scrolls horizontally in the box.

Figure 1.11

There are several options for finding text:

Table 1.11

Select this option	To
Match Case	Find words that have certain uppercase and lowercase letters. For example, in Figure 1.11, Word would find *needle in haystack*, but not *Needle in Haystack* or NEEDLE IN HAYSTACK.
Find Whole Words Only	Find whole separate words in the document. For example, Word would find the word *text*, but would not stop at *context*.
Use Pattern Matching	Use wild cards such as * and ? to find words that match search criteria. For example, use s*t to find sit, sat, seat, sent, or s?t to find sit, set, and sat.
Sounds Like	Find words that are spelled differently, but sound alike such as *roam* and *Rome*.
Search	Search for words either up or down (backward or forward) from your current position. You can also search the entire document, forward and backward from the insertion point.
No Formatting	Find a word or phrase, regardless of its format.
Format	Search for the particular font, language, style, and paragraph that you indicate.

Special	Search for any type of special characters, such as paragraph marks and tabs, that are represented by special codes. For example, you could use this feature to replace all double tabs with single tabs. To search for double characters, click on the list twice, selecting the special character each time.
Find Next	Find the next occurrence of the text.
Cancel	Find no text. Return to the text and edit it.
Replace	Open the Replace dialog box where you can enter the text, format, and special characters that you want to replace with the text you find.

Using the Go To Command

The Go To command lets you move quickly to any point in your document. You won't have to scroll through the document to find the location where you need to work. You can find a page, section line, footnote, endnote, annotation, bookmark, field table graphic, equation, or object. For example, if you need to find a footnote, you simply tell Word the number and it will find the footnote for you.

1. From the Edit menu, choose **Go To** (**Alt-E, G**). Word displays the Go To dialog box.

2. In the Go To What box, select the item type you want to find.

3. Do one of the following:

To	Do this
Move to a specific location	Type the name or number of the item in the Enter box and choose **Go To**. For example, to go to a specific bookmark, type the bookmark name. Notice that the Enter box changes, depending on whether the item you need to find needs a name or a number.
Move to the next or previous occurrence of the item	Type nothing in the Enter box and choose **Next** or **Previous**.

4. When you finish, choose **Close**.

Summary

Now you know some of the basics of working in Word, including how to navigate in a document; how to use the Menu bar, the Standard toolbar, the Formatting toolbar, and the Ruler; and how to view a document. In the next chapter you learn to use some of the powerful features that help you to easily create complex and professional-looking documents every time.

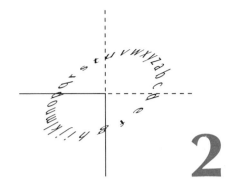

2

Setting Up a Word Document

T his chapter explains the optional "peripheral" pieces that give your Word document a more professional look. These are the elements you set up in addition to the body of text. They include:

- page setup
- section breaks
- page breaks
- page numbers
- headers and footers
- footnotes
- annotations
- bookmarks
- file attachments

When you open a new document in Word, you see toolbars and the workspace on which you can begin working. However, underneath this facade lie the powerful features you can use to create a very complex, professional-quality document with a minimum of headaches and frustration.

Page Setup

You can choose your page settings at any time while you are working in a document. However, if you use this feature as soon as you open your document, you will know the exact length and look of your document as you work. You can prevent a lot of reworking if you organize your document with the correct page setup. (A document that is five pages long at the standard settings may turn out to be seven or eight pages when you convert to a smaller page or change the margins.)

Word's default template, Normal, assumes that you are working on an 8.5-by-11-inch page with top and bottom margins of 1 inch, left and right margins of 1.25 inches, and no gutter. This is acceptable for a variety of documents. In fact, most manuscripts, professional papers, proposals, and preprinted forms work best in the standard paper size. However, if you are building a document that will be printed on a different size of paper (such as this book), you need to use the Page Setup feature to set the corresponding margins, page orientation, and paper source or printing setup.

See Chapter 6 for more information about templates.

Setting Margins

To set up the margins, orientation, or paper source for printing, choose **File** from the menu bar, and select **Page Setup** (**Alt-F**, **U**). Word displays the Page Setup dialog box, with the default margin options displayed.

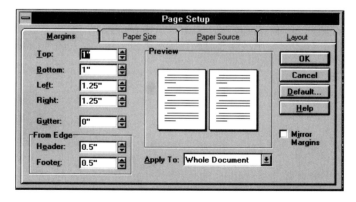

Figure 2.1

Margin settings affect the headers and footers in a document. If headers and footers are several lines long, Word automatically adjusts the top and bottom margins. To prevent Word from making that adjustment, type a minus sign in front of the top or bottom margin setting. If you do this, however, you can have a header that overlaps the text, and you will need to have less information in the header or footer.

N O T E

If you have not used a gutter before, it is an extra space in the margin to allow for binding. If you are working on a document that will not be bound, then leave the gutter width at zero.

The Mirror Margins option is for documents that will be printed on both sides of the paper. Word automatically adjusts your margin settings to accommodate facing pages. The inside margins are the same width on both pages, and the outside margins are the same width. If you choose to have a gutter, that space is also added to the inside margin.

The Apply To option lets you apply the margin setup either to the whole document or forward from the point where you are working.

The Preview box shows a sample layout for all changes that you make in this dialog box.

Even after you set your margins, you can place information so that it prints in the margin. By default, Word prints page numbers, headers, and footers in the margins. You can set an indentation for headings and text to print them in the margins, where you can also place graphics. See Chapter 4, *Formatting Paragraphs and Objects*, for more information about placing text and graphics in the margins.

N O T E

Setting the Page Size and Orientation

The Page Setup dialog box also allows you to set up the size, orientation, and layout of your page. At the top of the dialog box, press **S** or click the button for **Size and Orientation** to display the following option boxes:

The Paper Size option gives you choices based on paper sizes that your printer can use. The Custom option in the list lets you set the page size of your choice and is generally used for nonstandard paper sizes. Word assumes you will be printing on the paper size you enter, even if you print on letter-size or legal-size paper. For

Figure 2.2

example, if you set up your page to be 10-by-15 inches, and you are printing on 8.5-by-11-inch paper, then the text and graphics will "run off" the page.

Orientation refers to portrait or landscape. Use *portrait orientation* if you want the reader to hold the page with the short edge at the top; use *landscape orientation* if you want the reader to hold the page sideways, with the long edge at the top.

The Apply To option (to the right of the Paper Size options) works the same way it does for the margin setup. You can apply the settings to the whole document or from the insertion point forward.

Setting the Paper Source

When you choose paper source settings in the Page Setup dialog box (**Alt-P**), as shown in Figure 2.3, your printer defaults to that paper source when you print the document.

Figure 2.3

If your printer has only one tray, then use the default option of Default Tray. If you have a standard 8.5-by-11 inch tray and another tray that holds a different size, then choose the tray holding the paper on which you want to print. You can also set up a document so that the first page prints from a different tray than the other pages. For example, you can have an envelope print first from its tray, and then the remainder of the document from the tray you choose in the Other Pages box.

The Page Setup Default Option

The Default option lets you use any settings you choose for one document as defaults for any documents based on the template in which you are working.

Word displays this dialog box shown in Figure 2.4 if you choose **Default**.

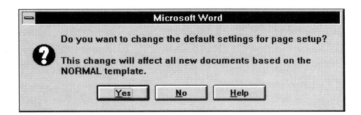

Figure 2.4

Think for a minute before you choose **Yes**, because all documents you construct in the template style will have *these* default settings. You will have to go back and change the template again to use Word's defaults.

Section Breaks

The section break options are available from the Page Setup dialog box (**Alt-F, U**), where you also choose the page margins, size, and source.

You can divide a single document into as many sections as you need. For example, if your document happens to be a book, you can divide each chapter and retain its formatting using the section break. However, a section can be as small as a short paragraph. If you are working in a document that needs to have the same formatting, headers, and footers throughout, you probably do not need to add any section breaks.

How the Section Break Works

A section break contains all of the formatting that you add to the section, for example, margins, headers and footers, and page-numbering options. When you add a section break, Word assumes that you will continue using the same section formatting that you have been using. However, when you change the formatting for the new section, the formatting for the previous section remains intact. When you insert the section break, you can force Word to start numbering a section with a specified line number. The section-break line does not print on the page.

Adding a Section Break

To add a section break, position the insertion point where you want to add the break. From the Insert menu, choose **Break** (**Alt-I**, **B**) to display the Break dialog box. Choose the appropriate option in the Section Break area. (See the following section for information about Page Break options.)

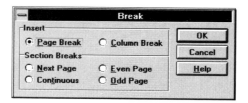

Figure 2.5

Table 2.1   Break Options

Select	To
Next Page	Creates a page on which the section will begin.
Continuous	Start a section immediately following the previous one. Word does not insert a page break for a continuous option. Use this option if you want sections to have no page break in between.
Even Page	Start the section on the next even-numbered page. Therefore, if you are working on an even page when you choose the Even Page option, Word adds an odd page before it starts the new section.
Odd Page	Start the section on the next odd-numbered page. Therefore, if you are working on an odd page when you choose the Odd Page option, Word adds an even page before it starts the new section.

Figure 2.6 shows a page that has two sections on the same page: a one-column section and a three-column section.

One-Column Section

This is a section that uses the default settings of the Manual 1 template. The margins are the same for body text as they are for a heading 2. The text is one-column wide. A section break follows. After the section break is a completely different format. Any work done in a section uses the formatting and setup specifically for that section.

Three-Column Section

This section is completely different than the previous one but it appears on the same page. This section is set up in three columns like a newsletter might be. The section mark above stored the text above the break. Although this section bears no resemblance to the one above it, the change was very simple. There is a section break above and below this text. You can insert text and graphics and edit in this section just as in any others, as long as the inserted object will fit.

Figure 2.6

If you are working in a default one-column section, and you want to produce the preceding layout, perform these steps:

1. At the end of the first section, press **Enter** and type the heading "Three-Column Section."

If the heading is longer than one column, and you want to stretch it across the three columns, don't put it in the three-column section. If you do, Word will force it into a column and it might not look good.

N O T E

2. Press **Enter** again, and from the Insert menu, choose **Break (Alt-I, B)**.

3. Under Section Breaks, choose **Continuous**. Word adds the End of Section break (which does not print).

4. From the Format menu, choose **Columns (Alt-O, C)**. Word displays the Columns dialog box.

5. Choose three columns, with 2 points of space between each column.

6. When you finish adding everything you want in the three-column section, insert another continuous page break and continue working.

Page Breaks

Word inserts page breaks automatically; however, there are a few ways that you can break the pages wherever you choose.

Automatic or "Soft" Page Breaks

Word repaginates in the background to break pages automatically every time you enter a full page of text or graphics. This is a *soft* page break, meaning that no matter how much text or formatting you add or delete, Word adjusts the break as necessary. The soft page breaks are based on the page setup of your document, which was explained in the previous section. The soft page break is indicated by a "loose" dotted line (the dots are far apart) that extends across your screen.

Turning Off Repagination

You can turn off the automatic repagination by choosing **Options** from the Tools menu (**Alt-T**, **O**), and turning off **Background Repagination** in the General category. Even if you do turn off this option, Word still repaginates every time you print, view in page layout or print preview, repaginate, or generate an index or table of contents. However, Word does not repaginate while you are typing or editing.

Inserting a "Hard" Page Break

Word lets you insert a page break anywhere you want. This is called a *hard* page break. No matter how Word readjusts page breaks, the hard page break never moves. This is particularly useful if you want to keep certain blocks or text and graphics together. For example, you would not want a page to break so that a heading is the last thing on one page and the text for the heading is on the next.

To insert a page break, position the insertion point where you want to start a page. Then, press **Ctrl-Enter** or press **Alt-I**, **B** and choose **Page Break**. The hard page break is indicated by a "tight" dotted line that extends across your screen.

Using Paragraph Formatting to Break a Page

The Format Paragraph command (**Alt-O**, **P**) gives you four options in the Text Flow dialog box for controlling page breaks. They are described in the following sections.

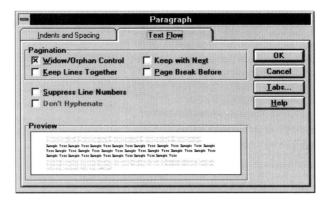

Figure 2.7

The Widow/Orphan Control Option

A *widow* is a single line at the top of a page. An *orphan* is a single line at the bottom of a page. Widows and orphans in your document can make it unattractive and difficult to read. Select this option to have word automatically check each page to prevent widow and orphan lines.

The Keep Lines Together Option

There may be times when you want to keep all of a single paragraph together on a page to prevent Word from breaking it with a page break. The Keep Lines Together option keeps all lines in a paragraph together, regardless of its length. If the whole paragraph does not fit on the page where it starts, Word moves it to the beginning of the next page.

The Page Break Before Option

Word lets you insert a page break before a graphic or text that you would rather have printed at the top of the next page.

To insert a page break before a paragraph or heading, position the insertion point in the paragraph in which you want to start a page. Press **Alt-O**, **P** or choose **Paragraph** from the Format menu. Then, choose **Page Break Before** in the Pagination box.

The Keep With Next Option

You can keep two paragraphs together on a page and ensure they are never separated by a page break by using the Keep With Next option. One of the paragraphs might be a heading or a graphic.

To keep two paragraphs together, position the insertion point in the paragraph that you want to keep with the next paragraph. Press **Alt-O**, **P** or choose **Paragraph** from the Format menu. Then, choose **Keep With Next** in the Pagination box.

N O T E

For related information about pagination, see Chapter 3, *Formatting Characters and Words.*

Numbering Pages

Word gives you several methods for numbering pages. You can choose:

- ◆ The style and placement of page numbers.
- ◆ Whether you want numbers on all pages except the first.
- ◆ Whether to add chapter-page numbers.
- ◆ Whether to add additional text with the page number.

Style and Placement

You can use any font that you use in text for your page numbers, and you have the option of applying them in Arabic or Roman numerals (uppercase and lowercase), and letters (uppercase and lowercase). Also, you can choose whether to have page numbers in the header or footer and where in the header or footer you want them to print.

Numbering All Pages Except the First

Sometimes you might not want to have a page number on the first page of a document. For example, if your first page is a cover or title page, you generally don't need to number it. You can begin numbering with the second page, and you can choose if you want that page to be numbered 1 or 2. (See "Creating a Header or Footer" later in this chapter for more information.)

Follow these steps to add page numbers for all pages except the first to headers or footers:

1. From the Insert menu, choose **Page Numbers** (**Alt-I, U**). Word displays the Page Numbers dialog box.

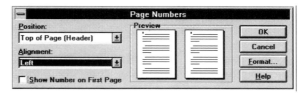

Figure 2.8

2. Uncheck the **Show Number on First Page** option.
3. Choose the position and alignment of page numbers.
4. Click **Format**. Word displays the Page Number Format dialog box.

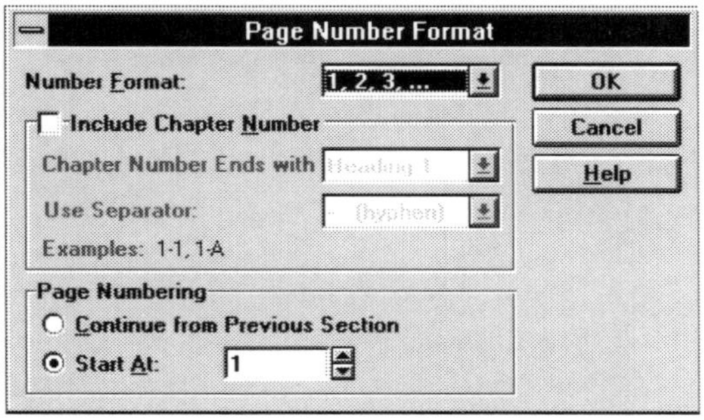

Figure 2.9

5. Select the Number Format you want from the drop-down list.
6. Choose **OK**.

At this point, you can also choose whether to include the chapter number with the page number, select a separator between the two, and select whether to continue the page numbering without a break in numbers from the previous section. Word prints page numbers in the format that you choose. However, you cannot see them in Normal view.

If you want to change the font for page numbers, open the header or footer, select the page number, and choose a font and point size. This changes the font for all page numbers in the section. (See Chapter 3, *Formatting Characters and Words*, for more information.) You can also define your header or footer as a style and add it to a template. (See Chapter 6, *Creating a Template*, for more information.)

N O T E

You can also add page numbers to your document by choosing the **Page Number** button from the Header and Footer toolbar. See "Creating Headers and Foots" later in this chapter for more information.

Numbering All Pages, Including the First

If you are constructing a document that does not have a cover page or another type of unnumbered page, follow these instructions to have Word number all pages:

1. From the Insert menu, choose **Page Numbers (Alt-I, U)**. Word displays the Page Numbers dialog box.
2. Select **Show Number on first Page**.
3. Choose **OK**.

Inserting Chapter–Page Numbers

If you are working in a document that has multiple chapters, you can show a chapter–page number, for example, 3–4 for Chapter 3, page 4. If you want to show chapter–page numbers in the index or Table of Contents, then you must set up chapter-page numbers in the chapter itself. (See Chapter 7, *Tables of Contents and Indexes*, for related information.)

N O T E

Before you set up chapter–page numbers you must format the chapter headings with one of the nine built-in headings packaged with Word. From the Format menu, choose **Heading Numbering (Alt-O, H)**, and select a style for numbering chapter headings. If you have several chapters in one document, then you also need to insert a section break at the beginning of each chapter.

Follow these steps to set up chapter-page numbers:

1. Apply a style to your chapter heading that you will not use for any other heading in your document. For example, if you apply Heading 1 from the style sheet you are working in, then use Heading 2 for the first heading for text in your document.

2. From the Insert menu, choose **Page Numbers (Alt-I, U)**. Word displays the Page Numbers dialog box.

3. Choose **Format**.

4. Choose **Include Chapter Number**.

5. In the Chapter Number Starts With box, select the heading style you applied to the chapter heading.

6. In the Use Separator box, select the character you want to use to separate the chapter from the page number.

7. Choose **OK**.

Now when you print your document, the chapter numbers show the chapter number, a separator, and the page number, for example 1–2.

An en dash (–) is the standard separator between chapter and page numbers. An em dash (—) is usually too wide and a hyphen (-) is too narrow.

N O T E

Headers and Footers

Adding headers and footers to your document is an easy process, and they can be as simple as just adding a page number, or as elaborate as adding a graphic or logo. Word places header text within the top margin and footer text within the bottom margin.

If you specify a margin in your page setup that is too small for the header or footer you design, Word adjusts the margin to accommodate the design.

Generally, headers and footers are repeated throughout a document, with the first page as an exception. However, Word allows you a lot of choices for using them.

Creating a Header or Footer

Word never automatically creates a header or footer. It is up to you to decide whether you want to add one or whether you want to add page numbers to either. One issue to consider is the document size. If someone drops a large, unnumbered document, it can be nightmarish to try to get the pages in the correct order again.

To create a header or footer, choose **Header and Footer** from the View menu (**Alt-V, H**). Word displays the Header/Footer dialog box where you can choose options from the toolbar. The Header and Footer default depends on where the insertion point is.

Figure 2.10

Whether you choose add a header or footer, Word displays the same toolbar in document window. The only difference is that the top line of the window shows whether a header or footer is open.

Table 2.2

Choose this button	To
	Switch between the display of the header and the footer. Note: You can also use the vertical scroll bar to switch between the header and the footer.
	Display the header or footer in the next section of the document if there is one.
	Display the header or footer in the previous section of the document if there is one.
	Make the header or footer (depending on which you are using) the same as the one in the previous section.

⊞	Insert a page number in the header or footer (depending on which one you are using).
	Insert the date in the header or footer (depending on which one you are using). Note: Make sure the date on your computer is correct.
	Insert the time in the header or footer (depending on which one you are using). Note: Make sure the time on your computer is correct.
	Display the Page Setup dialog box where you can change the page setup of selected sections.
	Display or hide the document text while you are working in a header or footer.

You type the information that you want to add in the box, and format it the same way you format any other text. See Chapter 3 and Chapter 4 for more information about formatting text. You can also define your headers and footers as styles. Refer to Chapter 5, *Formatting Tutorials*, for more information about defining styles.

By default, Word places the header .5 inch from the top edge of the page, however you can enter another measurement in the Margins in the Page Setup dialog box (**Alt-F**, **U**).

Creating Different Headers or Footers in One Document

In any document that has multiple sections, you might want to have different headers or footers for each section. For example, you might want to show the chapter number and name for each chapter in a book. If that's the case, you often will not need to show the header on the first page of the chapter. (Notice that in this book, the first page of each chapter does not have a header. It doesn't need one because the chapter title is on the first page.)

Creating a Different First Page

Follow the steps on the next page to create a different header or footer for the first page in your document, or in your section if you have multiple sections.

1. From the View menu, choose **Header and Footer** (**Alt-V, H**).

2. On the toolbar, click the **Page Setup** button.

3. Select **Layout**, if it is not selected already.

4. In the Headers and Footers box, select **Different First Page**, and choose **OK**.

5. On the toolbar, click the **Show Next** or **Show Previous** button to move to the first page header or footer in the document or section.

6. Type the text you want for the first page. If you do not want a header or footer on the first page do not type anything.

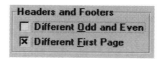

Figure 2.11

Figure 2.12

7. Click the **Show Next** button, and the **Switch between Header and Footer** button to move to the header or footer area.

8. Type the text for the header or footer you want to appear in the remainder of the document or section.

9. Click **Close** to return to the document.

Creating Headers or Footers for Odd and Even Pages

If your document has multiple chapters, is printed on both sides, and bound, it is likely that you will need to show the document name on one header or footer (usually the even header), and the chapter or section name on the other (usually the odd header).

1. From the View menu, choose **Header and Footer** (**Alt-V, H**).

2. On the toolbar, click the **Page Setup** button.

3. Select **Layout**.

4. In the Headers and Footers box, select **Different Odd and Even**, and choose **OK**.

If your headers or footers are connected, Word applies the option to the whole document.

N O T E

5. Click the **Show Previous** button or the **Show Next** button to move to an even header or footer.

6. Type the text you want to appear in the header or footer for each even-numbered (left side) page.

7. Click the **Show Next** button to move to the odd header or footer.

8. Type the text you want to appear in the header or footer for each odd-numbered (right side) page.

9. Click **Close** to return to the document.

Creating Different Headers or Footers for Each Section

If you want to divide your document into multiple sections, and you want each section to have a different header or footer, you must define headers or footers within each section. If you don't, Word applies the header or footer you define in one section to *all* sections because all headers and footers are connected initially.

You must break the connection between the headers or footers it you want to created unique headers or footers for each section. You simply click the **Same As Previous** button on the Header and Footer toolbar.

To create different headers or footers in the same document:

1. Position the insertion point in the section where you want to create a different header or footer.

2. From the View menu, choose **Header and Footer (Alt-V, H)**.

3. Click the **Same As Previous** button on the toolbar to disconnect the headers and footers in the section from the previous section.

4. Type the text you want to appear in the section.

Word also inserts this header or footer in all sections following the current one. To create different headers and footers in following sections, open each section and repeat steps 1 through 4.

N O T E

5. Click **Close** to display the document text.

To reconnect a header or footer:

1. Position the insertion point in the section where you want to create a different header or footer.

2. From the View menu, choose **Header and Footer** (**Alt-V, H**).

3. Click the **Same As Previous** button on the toolbar to reconnect the headers and footers.

4. Word asks you to confirm that you want to delete the current header or footer and connect to the preceding header or footer. Choose **Yes**.

5. Click **Close** to display the document text.

Numbering Pages Consecutively in Headers and Footers

If your document has only one section, Word automatically numbers pages consecutively when you add page numbers. However, if you want to have consecutive page numbers in a document with multiple sections, you choose *to have the numbering* in the Page Number Format dialog box or the Header and Footer dialog box. Then, you choose *how to number the pages* in the Page Numbering dialog box.

Follow these steps in *each* section of your document:

1. From the Insert menu, choose **Page Numbers** (**Alt-I, U**).

2. Click **Format**.

3. Choose **Continue from Previous Section** to begin numbering the section where the last section left off.

Figure 2.13

For example, if the last page number in section 1 is 54, the first page number of section 2 will be 55. If the last page of the previous section ends with an odd number, Word skips an even page number to leave a blank page, and begins the next section with an odd number. For example, if the last page of section 1 ends with 55, the first page number of section 2 will be 57.

Creating Nonconsecutive Page Numbers in Headers and Footers

Word lets you choose to number pages differently in the headers and footers in each section of your document.

Follow these steps in each section of your document:

1. From the Insert menu, choose **Page Numbers** (**Alt-I**, **U**).
2. Click **Format**, and choose **Start At**.

The Start At option allows you to enter a page number on which you want the section to start. You can enter any number, regardless of the sequence of page numbers in other sections. You use this option in conjunction with the page-numbering icon (#) inside the header or footer window. See "Numbering Pages" earlier in this chapter for more information about page numbering.

You can readjust the position of your headers and footers in Page Layout view without having to open the separate panes. For more information about Page Layout view, see the section "Page Views" in Chapter 1.

N O T E

Adding Footnotes and Endnotes

When typing documents on a typewriter or in many other word processing programs, it is difficult to add footnotes. The spacing at the bottom of the page has to be perfect, and if you type one line too many, you must retype the page, delete or move a line, or let the page look very crowded at the bottom. If you're compiling a list of endnotes, you have to keep track of all of them, and then type each one at the end. Either of these tasks can be the most difficult to handle with working in a long document.

Word makes this whole process very easy. It lets you add footnotes and endnotes in a manner that is similar to the way you add a header or footer. Word opens a pane at the bottom of the workspace where you can add, format, and edit footnote text. You don't have to set options for spacing because Word automatically adjusts the area to accommodate the footnote. There is no line limit: You can make the footnote as long as you want.

Reference Marks

Word places a reference mark in your document so you can see where you added a footnote or endnote. The default mark is a number encircled by a faint dotted line.

You can customize the footnote or endnote mark, using characters that are more meaningful to you. The following procedures include steps for changing the default reference mark.

To add a footnote to a document, follow these steps:

1. Position the insertion point where you want Word to display the reference mark.

2. From the Insert menu, choose **Footnote** (**Alt-I**, **N**). Word displays the Footnote and Endnote dialog box.

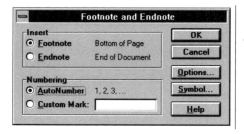

Figure 2.14

3. Choose **Footnote** or **Endnote**, depending on the one you need.

4. To have Word number the footnotes or endnotes automatically, choose **AutoNumber** or to choose a reference mark that you prefer, choose **Custom Mark** and enter a character, or click **Symbol** and select the one you want.

5. Choose **OK**. Word inserts a reference mark at the insertion point and opens the footnote or endnote pane.

6.   Type your footnote or endnote, and click **Close** to return to the document.

Positioning Footnotes

While the traditional placement of footnotes is at the bottom of a page, Word also lets you choose to print them beneath the text anywhere on the page. You can place endnotes at the end of the section or the end of the document.

You choose the footnote position by choosing the **Options** button from the Footnote and Endnote dialog box shown in the previous procedure (**Alt-I**, **N**).

Viewing Footnotes and Endnotes

There are two ways to view footnotes and endnotes in normal or page layout view:

- ◆ Double-click a reference mark, or
- ◆ Choose **Footnotes** from the View menu (**Alt-V**, **F**).

In Normal view, Word displays the note pane and moves the insertion point to the note text that corresponds to the selected reference mark.

In Page Layout view, you can double-click the vertical scroll bar to view the note area.

Editing Footnotes and Endnotes

Word lets you edit footnote and endnote text as it does any other kind of text. You can apply all kinds of fonts and styles. Also, you can move or copy a footnote or endnote. The note consists of two parts: the reference mark and the note text. When you edit a note, you do it in the same pane where you input footnotes.

You cannot change a reference mark in the document window. You must make that change through the Footnote and Endnote dialog boxes.

N O T E

For more details about moving, copying, and deleting footnotes and endnotes, see your *Microsoft Word for Windows User's Guide.*

Annotations and Revision Marks

When you are working on a document, you may find that you often need to revise it and make notes about the information you add or change. Sometimes, you might want to make reminders to yourself about things you want to change, but you would rather not have them printed. Also, if multiple people are working on one document, each needs a way to make individual comments and identify them later.

Word gives you the means for annotating the text and adding marks to show where you added, changed, or deleted text or graphics.

Annotating a Document

An annotation has two parts: the annotation mark and the annotation text. The annotation mark is the initials of the author and the number of the annotation. This is a very important feature because if multiple authors work on a document, then you can easily see who added the pieces of material. The annotation is added to the text so you can see it on the screen, but Word formats it as hidden text, and does not print it unless you choose to print hidden text.

As with footnotes, Word opens a separate pane in which you enter the annotation text. That text does not become part of the document. However, the mark is displayed in the text so you can see what you have annotated.

Follow these steps to annotate your document:

1. Position the insertion point where you want to annotate the text.

2. From the Insert menu, choose **Annotation** (**Alt-I**, **A**). Word adds the annotation mark ([VS1], for example) where you positioned the insertion point, and opens the Annotations window.

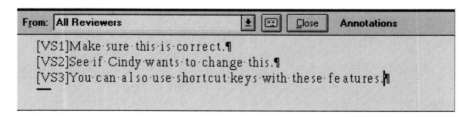

Figure 2.15

The From list shows names or group names of users annotating the document.

3. Enter the text for the annotation in the pane.

4. Choose **Close** to close the pane.

If you share a computer with multiple authors, you should have Word insert the correct initials for each author. With the document open, choose **Options** from the Tools menu and select the **User Info** tab to enter the correct initials.

You can work in a Word document while the pane is open by clicking in the pane where you want to work.

N O T E

Editing Annotations

You can edit the annotations by choosing **Annotations** from the View menu (**Alt-V**, **A**) and entering more text, or selecting existing text and typing over it.

You can also copy an annotation and its reference mark into the text if you want. Use the cut and paste methods described in "The Clipboard" in Chapter 1, *Mastering the Word for Windows Environment.*

You can define annotation text and marks as styles that you can apply automatically. See Chapter 6, *Creating a Template*, for information about defining styles.

SHORTCUT

Finding Annotations

Word's Go To command makes it easy for you to find annotation marks in your document. Follow these steps to find annotations:

1. From the Edit menu, choose **Go To** (**Alt-E**, **G**) or **F5**. Word displays the Go To dialog.

2. Select **Annotation**.

3. Type the annotation name in the Enter box and choose **Go To**.

Securing a Document

If you are using Word on a network or in a technical environment, it is quite possible that multiple authors will share responsibility for a document. If that is the case, it is very important that an author does not overwrite another author's text without permission.

Word lets you lock the document so that other authors cannot alter it, but they can add annotations for future updating. Follow these steps to lock the document:

1. From the File menu, choose **Save As (Alt-F, A)** or press **F12**. Word displays the Save As dialog box.

2. Choose **Options**. Word displays the Save tab in the Options dialog box.

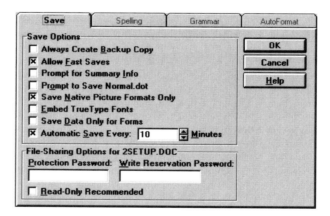

Figure 2.16

3. In the Protection Password box, enter a password of up to 16 characters and choose **OK**.

4. To prevent other users from saving changes to a document, type a password in the Write Reservation Password box and confirm it.

The next time anyone tries to open the document, Word prompts for the document password.

Printing Annotations

Although annotations do not show up in the text, you can have Word print them if you set the correct printing options.

Printing the Annotation and the Document

To print annotations along with the document, follow these steps:

1. From the File menu, choose **Print** (**Alt-F**, **P**). Word displays the standard Print dialog box.

2. Choose **Options**, and select **Annotations** in the Include with Document box.

3. Choose **OK** to close the Options dialog box.

4. Choose **OK** to print the document and annotations.

Revision Marks

Revision marks let you see not only what you changed in the last revision, but how you changed it. Word marks only the paragraphs that you changed, and shows added, deleted, replaced, and moved text. You can choose the character formatting for showing new text, the placement of the revision bars, and whether the bars appear in the text. However, Word marks all deleted text with the strikethrough character formatting.

When you finish revising a document, you can use the Compare Versions command to see the differences in two versions of it. You can also choose to accept or undo the changes when you finish working on a document.

Turning Revision Marking On or Off

Follow these steps to start revision marking:

1. Open a document that you want to edit.

2. From the Tools menu, choose **Revision** (**Alt-T**, **V**). Word displays the Revision Marks dialog box, shown in Figure 2.17 on the next page.

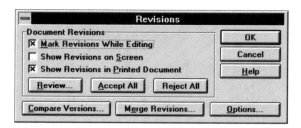

Figure 2.17

3. Select **Mark Revisions While Editing**. If you want to stop marking revisions, clear the check box.

4. Choose **Options**. Word displays the Revisions tab in the Options dialog box.

5. Select the options you want, and choose **OK**.

Any time you add text, Word displays and prints it in the character format you chose. The following illustration shows a revision mark and some added and deleted text.

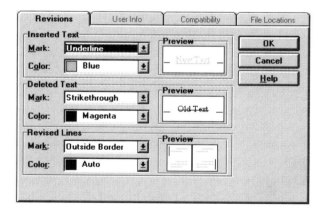

Figure 2.18

Word displays the letters *MRK* in the status bar at the bottom of your work area when you use this feature.

N O T E

Comparing Versions

If you want to see the differences in a document from one version to the next, you can use the Compare Versions command from the Revisions dialog box (**Alt-T**, **V**). This feature lets you choose to have Word mark the changes in the current document compared to a previous version of the same document. When you do this, Word formats the characters added to the previous version with the formatting style you chose for revision marking. If you did not choose a specific style, Word displays the text with underlining.

To compare versions, follow these steps:

1. From the Tools menu, choose **Revisions**. From the Revisions dialog box, choose **Compare Versions** (**Alt-T**, **U**).

2. Type the name the name of the former version of the document into the Original File Name box or select the name of the document, using the File Name and Directories lists.

3. Choose **OK**.

Searching for Revisions

While working in a document, you can search for any revisions you have made. Follow these steps to search for the revision marks.

1. Open the document (if it is not open already).

2. From the Tools menu, choose **Revision**s (**Alt-T**, **V**).

3. Choose **Review**. Word displays the Review Revisions dialog box.

4. Click **Find** to review the revisions one at a time.

5. Choose **OK** when you finish.

Accepting and Undoing Revisions

If you choose to mark revisions in a document, you can later accept or undo the changes and remove the marks and revision bars.

Accepting Revisions

To accept all revisions you've made, follow these steps:

1. Select the text that has revisions you want to keep.

If you do not select specific blocks or sections of text, Word assumes you want to accept revisions for the entire document.

NOTE

2. From the Tools menu, choose **Revision Marks** (**Alt-T**, **V**).

3. Choose **Accept All**.

If you have not selected text, Word asks if you want to accept all revisions. If you choose **Yes**, Word deletes any text marked for deletion and deletes all revision marks for the document. If you choose **No**, Word displays the Revision Marks dialog box again.

Undoing Revisions

If you do not like the revisions you have made to a document, you can undo them. To undo revisions, follow these steps:

1. Select the text that has revisions you want to undo.

If you do not select specific blocks or sections of text, Word assumes you want to undo revisions for the entire document.

NOTE

2. From the Tools menu, choose **Revisions** (**Alt-T**, **V**). Word displays the Revisions box.

3. Choose **Reject All**.

If you have not selected text, Word asks if you want to reject all revisions. If you choose **Yes**, Word removes all revisions, revision marks, and bars from the document. If you choose **No**, Word returns to the Revision Marks dialog box.

Bookmarks

There may be times when you want to find something in your document quickly. For example, if you insert a reference to another chapter in a book you're writing, you may want to be able to find that reference so you can update it if you change the chapter number or title later.

Word's bookmark function lets you perform something as simple as locating a place, or as sophisticated as updating linked text. You can also insert marked text into another document and mark numbers in a calculation and insert the result in your document. (Refer to the documentation provided with your software for more information about using bookmarks for linked text and calculations.)

Additionally, you can create cross-references to other information. Word allows up to 450 bookmarks in any document.

Word does not print the bookmark nor does it display it on the screen. The Bookmark function serves to let you find other text or elements.

Inserting a Bookmark

To insert a bookmark in your document, follow these steps:

1. Position the insertion point where you want to insert a bookmark.

    You have two options:

    - ◆ Position the insertion point in the location if you want only to be able to find this location again, or
    - ◆ Select text that you want to mark and be able to find again.

2. From the Edit menu, choose **Bookmark (Alt-E, B)** to display the Bookmark dialog box.

3. In the Bookmark Name box, type a name (from 1 to 40 characters) for the bookmark. The bookmark name must begin with a letter. The name must be only letters or numbers and the underscore character as shown in Figure 2.19. You cannot add spaces.

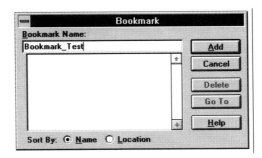

Figure 2.19

4. Choose **Add**.

Finding Your Bookmarks

After you've inserted bookmarks in your document, you can use them to locate the text or areas you need to find. Follow these steps to locate a bookmark:

1. From the Edit menu, choose **Bookmark (Alt-E, B)** or use **Go To (F5)**. Word lists the bookmark names is alphabetic order. To sort bookmark names by their location in the document, select **Location**.

2. Type or select the name of the bookmark you want to find.

3. Choose **Go To**. Word scrolls to the area or text that is marked, and keeps the Bookmark dialog box open so that you can find other bookmarks if you want.

4. When you finish, choose **Close**.

Cross-References

Suppose you are building a long document and in most chapters you refer your reader to related information in other chapters. Your reader will have an easier time finding the information if you include a page number. With a lot of other word processing and desktop publishing packages, the page number reference feature is nonexistent. Since maintaining this construction throughout drafts and revisions could be a nightmare without automation such as Word's, most authors and editors never include that helpful page number in a reference.

Follow these steps to create a cross-reference with a page number:

1. In your document, type the introductory text that you want to use to begin a cross-reference. For example, you might want to use "See also."

2. From the Insert menu, choose **Cross-reference (Alt-I, R)**. Word displays the Cross-reference dialog box, shown in Figure 2.20.

3. In the Reference Type box, select the type of item you want to refer to, for example **Figure**.

4. In the Insert Reference To box, select the type of information about that item you want Word to insert in the document, for example, **Page Number**.

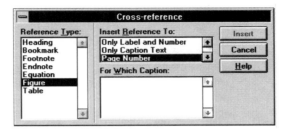

Figure 2.20

5. In the For Which box, select the specific item you want to refer to. For example, if you choose **Figure** in the Reference Type box, and the document has 20 figures, select the figure you want to refer to.

6. Choose **Insert**. Word keeps the Cross-reference dialog box open so you can add information. Position the insertion point in the document to type additional text. When you finish typing, click in the dialog box and repeat steps 3 through 6.

7. Choose **Close** when you are done.

Now your reader will be able to find additional information about a topic very easily. Word keeps track of the correct page number; you don't have to worry about providing the page number yourself, no matter how many times you revise your drafts.

N O T E

Summary

In this chapter you learned how to set up a Word document's margins and page layout, how to add page and section breaks to your document, and how to use more sophisticated features, such as headers and footers, footnotes, bookmarks, and annotations. The next three chapters show you how to improve the appearance of a document by formatting it, and how to add columns, tables, and some simple graphic elements to your document.

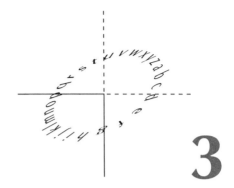

3

Formatting Characters and Words

This chapter shows you a variety of ways to apply and change formats for characters and words (which you can also apply to whole paragraphs if you want). Word's features for formatting characters allow you to:

- change fonts
- apply attributes (such as bold, italic, and underline)
- change point size
- choose letter spacing
- insert special symbols

How To Add and Change Character Attributes

Table 3.1 shows how you can quickly change the appearance of characters. Most table entries show multiple ways of changing the characters. What may seem easiest for a die-hard mouse user may seem more cumbersome for someone who prefers the keyboard. You may find that you prefer a variety of ways for applying formats to characters.

 Remember that you must select the text you want to format before you can format anything.

NOTE

Table 3.1   Character Attributes

To add this formatting	Do this
Bold	Choose **B** from the Formatting toolbar or press **Alt-O**, **F** and choose **Bold** or press **Ctrl-B**.
Italics	Choose **I** from the Formatting toolbar or press **Alt-O**, **F** and choose **Italics** or press **Ctrl-I**.
Underline	Choose **U** from the Formatting toolbar or press **Alt-O**, **F** and choose **Underline** or press **Ctrl-U.**
Word underline	Press **Ctrl-Shift-W**. (Word underline does not underline the spaces between words.) You can also choose this in the Font dialog box (**Alt-O**, **F**).
Double underline	Press **Ctrl-Shift-D** or press **Alt-O**, **F** and choose **Double Underline.**
Small caps	Press **Ctrl-Shift-K**. This option displays characters in all capitals, but the ones that would be lowercase are in a smaller point size. You can also choose this in the Font dialog box (**Alt-O**, **F**).
All caps	Press **Ctrl-Shift-A**. You can also choose this in the Font dialog box (**Alt-O**, **F**).
Hidden text	Press **Alt-O**, **F** and choose **Hidden Text.** You can see hidden text on the screen, but it does not print, and Word does not leave blank spaces where the hidden text resides. This feature is particularly useful when you are adding index entries. Note that you won't see the

	hidden text unless you have non-printing characters and choose the **Show/Hide Paragraph** button on the Standard toolbar.
Font change	Click the **Down Arrow** beside the font box on the Formatting toolbar and choose a font or press **Alt-O, F**, click the **Down Arrow** next to the font box, and choose a font or Type the font name in the font box.
Point size change	Click the down arrow beside the point size box on the Formatting toolbar, and choose a point size or type the point size in the point size box.
Next larger size	**Ctrl->**
Next smaller size	**Ctrl-<**
Up one point	**Ctrl-]**
Down one point	**Ctrl-[**
Superscript and subscript	Press **Alt-O, F** and choose **Superscript** or **Subscript** from the Superscript or Subscript option. Word automatically calculates the number of points to raise or drop the text. You generally use superscript and subscript text in mathematical equations. Trademark symbols are usually in superscript format. (Refer to Chapter 11, *The Equation Editor,* for more information about using this formatting in equations.)

Clearing A Format

You clear a format the same way you add it, but you do not have to use the same method. For example, if you apply the bold format from the Formatting toolbar, you can remove it by selecting the text and choosing **Bold** from the toolbar again, or pressing **Ctrl-B**.

Using Hyphens

Word's special hyphens control paragraph line breaks. You use these when you want to keep hyphenated words from breaking at the end of a line. You can see that these hyphens look different on the screen; however, when you print your document, they look like normal, typed hyphens. Table 3.2 explains the differences in the nonbreaking hyphens.

Table 3.2   Nonbreaking Hyphens

Use this type of hyphen	For
Normal hyphen (-)	Any word that you would normally hyphenate to keep it grammatically correct, such as a compound word, no matter where it falls in the paragraph line.
Optional hyphen (**Ctrl-(-)**)	Indicating where you want Word to hyphenate a word that falls at the end of a line.
Nonbreaking hyphen (**Ctrl-Shift-(-)**)	Words that have hyphens you do not want to break at the end of a line. Business letters and most technical documents look better and are easier to read when you use nonbreaking hyphens. Additionally, there are some words, particularly hyphenated proper nouns (such as Peg Daigle-Riley), that you should not allow Word to break. When you use this hyphen, Word keeps the hyphenated work or words together.

Using the Hyphenation Feature

You can choose to have Word hyphenate words in your document. However, most of the time you should reserve hyphenation for documents with narrow columns or for justified text. There is really no need to hyphenate your document more than one time, and usually it's best to wait until you finish constructing it so your line breaks will be logical, and the text smoothes out the right margin.

Follow these steps to have Word hyphenate your document:

1. From the Tools menu, choose **Hyphenation (Alt-T, H)**. Word displays the Hyphenation dialog box.

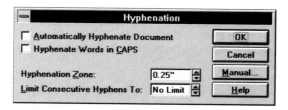

Figure 3.1

2. Choose how you want Word to hyphenate from the options in Table 3.3.

Table 3.3   Hyphenation Options

To	Do this
Let Word hyphenate the entire document automatically	Select **Automatically Hyphenate Document.**
Allow hyphenation of capitalized words	Select **Hyphenate Words in CAPS.**
Choose less ragged right margin and more hyphenation	Decrease the measurement in the Hyphenation Zone box, which is the amount of hyphenation you choose. The smaller the measurement, the more words are hyphenated.
Choose more ragged right margin and less hyphenation	Increase the measurement in the Hyphenation Zone box.
Limit the number of consecutive lines that can be hyphenated	Select the limit you want in the Limit Number of Consecutive Hyphens To box.
Have Word highlight each word in the document that can be hyphenated, and suggest hyphenation	Select **Manual**. This is useful in preventing hyphenation of names, which is generally not acceptable in most publications. Also, use this if you want to hyphenate only *selected* text.

3. After you select all options, choose **OK**.

Word begins hyphenating. If you choose **Manual**, then Word enters Page Layout view and displays each hyphenated word. You can choose **Yes** and change the hyphenation point, choose **No** for no hyphenation, or stop hyphenating from that point on. Word returns to Normal view.

Dashes

Word lets you use many special characters in your document, but two of the most commonly used in personal and business writing are the *en dash* and the *em dash*. These two dashes are often used incorrectly. The most often made mistakes are to use a single hyphen instead of the en dash, and a double hyphen instead of an em dash. Word makes it easy for you to apply the correct one, but here you will also learn when to use each one appropriately.

The En Dash

You generally use the en dash (–) to show a range of numbers, to show a range of pages, as a minus sign, and as a separator between a chapter and page number. The en dash is always as wide as the capital N in the font you are using. Therefore, it can be slightly different in each font you use in your document.

To apply the en dash:

◆ Position the insertion point where you want the en dash to appear, press **Alt-I, S**, and select the en dash from the Symbol dialog box. Choose **Insert** and **Close**. Word inserts the en dash, or

◆ Position the insertion point where you want the en dash to appear, press **Alt-I, S**, click the **Special Characters** tab, select **en dash** from the list, and press **Insert**.

The Em Dash

The em dash (—) shows a change of thought or perhaps sets off a parenthetical phrase in writing. See your favorite English grammar text book for a complete explanation.

To apply the em dash:

◆ Position the insertion point where you want the em dash to appear, press **Alt-I, S**, and select the **em dash** from the Symbol dialog box. Choose **Insert** and **Close**. Word inserts the em dash, or

◆ Position the insertion point where you want the em dash to appear, press **Alt-I, S**, click the **Special Characters** tab, select **em dash** from the list, and click **Insert**.

 You might have to spend a little time searching for these dashes in the Symbol dialog box. The em dash will look about twice as wide as the en dash on the screen. The two might be several lines apart. Some decorative fonts might not use the dashes.

N O T E

Nonbreaking Spaces

The functionality of the nonbreaking space is like that of the nonbreaking hyphen. This is often called a *hard space*. Use this space when you do not want Word to break a line between two words. Examples for this usage are a person's name—it is generally unacceptable to break a first name from a surname in text. To insert a nonbreaking space, press **Ctrl-Shift-Spacebar**.

Character Spacing

When you type normal text in Word, it applies default spacing similar to the text you are reading. Many people are comfortable and familiar with this spacing. However, you can change the spacing of the letters to something you find more appropriate or pleasing. Printers call this *kerning*. The amount you choose to kern letters may depend on the type of font you choose. Some fonts look better when you adjust the spacing. The following examples show differences in text with different spacing.

- ◆ Helvetica. This is the default spacing.
- ◆ Helvetica. This is condensed spacing.
- ◆ Helvetica. This is expanded spacing.

Follow these steps to kern text:

1. Select the characters you want to format, or place the insertion point where you want to enter new text and start the new spacing.

2. From the Format menu, choose **Font** (**Alt-O**, **F**). Word displays the Font dialog box shown in Figure 3.2.

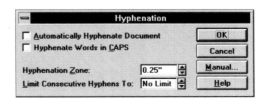

Figure 3.2

3. Click the **Character Spacing** tab.

4. In the Spacing text box, click the **Down Arrow** and choose **Expanded** to *increase* spacing, or choose **Condensed** to *decrease* spacing.

5. Type or select a number in the By box to change the default spacing.

You can adjust the spacing in tenth-of-a-point increments.

N O T E

6. Choose **OK**.

In general, save kerning for decorative or special text. Most of us were taught to read with "normal" spacing, which we find more pleasing for regular text.

N O T E

If you decide to change kerned text back to normal text, select the **Normal** option under Spacing in the Character dialog box.

You can also raise or lower the text by choosing either of those options in the Position text box.

Saving Time Repeating And Copying Formats

Word offers a powerful capability for repeating and copying any formatting. This can save you a lot of time and keystrokes when you are working in a long document or one that requires complex formatting.

Using the Mouse or Keyboard to Repeat Formatting

To repeat a formatting procedure, you must reapply the formatting immediately after you finish. Word "remembers" only the last formatting that you have done, for example, if you made some text bold or italic.

Follow these steps:

1. After formatting: Select the text to which you want to apply the format, or place the insertion point where you want to start the new format.
2. From the Edit menu, choose **Repeat Formatting (Alt-E, R)** or press **F4**.

Using the Mouse to Copy Formatting

You can use the mouse and the Brush button to copy formatting that you have just applied. When you do this, you can apply the formatting to another area of the document, or into another open document.

Follow these steps:

1. Select the word or character containing the formatting you want to copy.
2. Choose the **Brush** button from the toolbar.
3. Select the word or character to which you want to apply the formatting. Word applies the last formatting you chose.

Symbols And Special Characters

Many documents require special symbols or characters that a keyboard does not provide, but sometimes it's just fun to include some special characters to make a border or use as bullets.

Most fonts come with a set of symbol characters. Word provides symbols for the fonts included with the package. To display the Symbol font, choose **Symbol** from the Insert menu (**Alt-I, S**).

The Symbol font includes all of the Greek alphabet plus other characters defined by the American National Standards Institute (ANSI). It's easy to use the Symbol font characters, and you can apply most other character formatting to them.

Follow these steps to add a symbol or special character:

1. Position the insertion point where you want to insert the special character.
2. From the Insert menu, choose **Symbol (Alt-I, S)**. Word displays the Symbols dialog box, shown in Figure 3.3 on the next page.
3. Click the **Symbols** tab if it is not displayed.

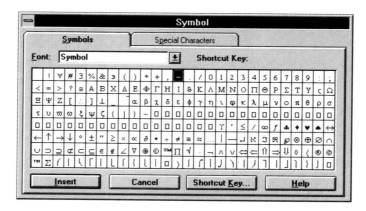

Figure 3.3

4. In the Font box, select the font that contains the character, or type the font name, and then click anywhere in the set of characters to display the font.

5. Select the character. You can:

   ◆ Click the character and choose **Insert**.

   ◆ Double-click the character.

   ◆ Select the character with Arrow keys and press **Enter**.

   Word inserts the symbol.

If you know the name of the special character you need to use, click the **Special Characters** tab from the Symbols dialog box, select the character type from the list, and choose **Insert**.

N O T E

Working With Hidden Characters

Word gives you the option of hiding or displaying text and special characters while you work. Some examples of text you might want to hide include index entries, table of contents entries, and other field codes. You may need to display the hidden text while you are working, and then hide it when you are ready to print. In fact, you always need to hide table of contents and index entries before you generate a Table of Contents or an Index for your document. Otherwise, your document will have incorrect page numbering.

Follow these steps to format hidden text:

1. Select the characters you want to format as hidden, or position the insertion point where you want to type hidden text.
2. Press **Ctrl-Shift-H**, or from the Format menu, choose **Font (Alt-O, F)**. Word displays the Font dialog box.
3. Select the **Hidden** check box and choose **OK**.

The text you select or the text you type is in the hidden format. If you choose the Hidden option or the All option in the View category of the dialog box (from the Tools menu), Word inserts a dotted underline to indicate hidden text.

Hiding and Displaying Hidden Text

Follow these steps to hide or display hidden text:

1. From the Tools menu, choose **Options (Alt-T, O)**.
2. Click the **View** tab.
3. Under Nonprinting Characters:
    -   Display hidden text by *selecting* either the **Hidden Text** or **All** check boxes, or
    -   Hide text by *deselecting* both the **Hidden Text** and **All** check boxes.
4. Choose **OK**.

Rather than performing steps 1-3 above, it is even easier to click the Paragraph button on the toolbar. You use the option only if you don't want to see all the hidden characters.

SHORTCUT

Summary

In this chapter, you learned how to change the appearance of the text in your document by using fonts, adding attributes, kerning, and using special symbols. The next chapter shows you more ways to format and organize your document by aligning text and by adding lists, columns, tables, and borders to your document.

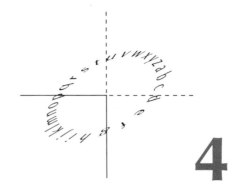

Formatting Paragraphs and Objects

4

This chapter discusses formatting features using each of these elements:

- line spacing
- tabs
- indentations
- alignment
- numbers and bullets
- lists
- automatic formatting

Formatting whole paragraphs in Word is generally no more complicated than formatting a single character. Word makes it very easy to change multiple paragraphs or even whole documents with just a few commands. In many documents, a paragraph is simply a series of sentences separated by a line from other paragraphs. In Word and in this chapter, however, *paragraph* refers to any amount of text and objects, such as graphics, that fall between two paragraph marks.

Like the character formatting features, you can format paragraphs using Word's variety of formatting methods, including the commands from the Format menu, the Formatting toolbar, the Ruler, the Toolbar, the Style Gallery, and shortcut keys.

Some of the more basic information is covered first, and formatting with desktop publishing features is covered later in the chapter.

Paragraph Marks

Most of the time while you are formatting, you will probably want to display paragraph marks in your document so you can see exactly where they are. To display the marks, click the **Show/Hide Paragraph** button on the toolbar. You use the same button to display or hide the paragraph and other formatting marks.

Aligning Paragraphs

There are four ways to align paragraphs in a document. You can:

- ◆ Use the Paragraph dialog box.
- ◆ Use the Formatting toolbar.
- ◆ Assign a shortcut key sequence to a paragraph style.
- ◆ Define the aligned text as a style and apply the style to any other paragraphs.

(See Chapters 5 and 6 for more information about defining styles.)

When you align a paragraph, it does not mean that you change the margins. It means that you place the paragraph somewhere in relation to the margins.

N O T E

Using the Paragraph Dialog Box

Follow these steps to align paragraphs using the Paragraph dialog box:

1. Select the paragraphs to align or position the insertion point where you want the alignment to begin.

2. From the Format menu, choose **Paragraph** (**Alt-O**, **P**). Word displays the Paragraph dialog box, with the Indents and Spacing tab selected.

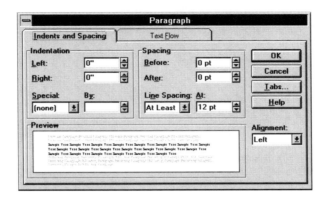

Figure 4.1

3. From the Alignment box, select one of the options in Table 4.1

Table 4.1 Alignment Options

Select	To do this
Left	Aligns the paragraph or object with the left margin or paragraph indent. The right edge will be *ragged,* which means that there is no alignment on the right side. (Information about indenting paragraphs is included later in this chapter.)
Centered	Aligns each line of the paragraph between the left and right margins or indents. This creates paragraphs that are ragged on the left and on the right.
Right	Aligns the paragraph or object with the right margin or paragraph indent. The left edge will be ragged, which means that there is no alignment on the left side.
Justified	Aligns paragraph text so that both the left and right margins have a straight edge, creating blocks. Use this option judiciously because it can create white "rivers" of space in the text, which can make reading difficult.

This is left-aligned text.

This is centered text.

This is right-aligned text.

This is justified text. If this text is on a line that is shorter than the paragraph width, it will remain aligned left. For longer lines of text and paragraphs, Word breaks the line at the most logical place. If you turn on hyphenation, Word breaks individual words to break the line.

Using the Formatting Toolbar

If you have a mouse, using the Formatting toolbar makes paragraph alignment much quicker. Follow these steps to align using the Formatting toolbar:

1. Select the paragraphs to align or position the insertion point where you want the alignment to begin.

2. From the Formatting toolbar, choose the **Left**, **Centered**, **Right**, or **Justify Alignment** button.

NOTE

For more information about the functions of the Formatting toolbar, see Chapter 1, *Mastering the Word for Windows Environment*.

Using Shortcut Keys

Word also gives you the option of aligning text using shortcut keys. To use shortcut keys, select the paragraphs to align or position the insertion point where you want the alignment to begin and use one of the key combinations in Table 4.2.

Table 4.2   Shortcut Keys for Alignment

Alignment	Shortcut keys
Left	**Ctrl-L**
Center	**Ctrl-E**
Right	**Ctrl-R**
Justified	**Ctrl-J**

Indenting

Indentations play an important role in giving your document the look you want it to have. Your document will look much more finished if special information, such as quoted material, is indented differently than the normal text. The indenting functions are similar to the alignment functions, and you have several methods from which to choose. You can use the Paragraph dialog box, the Standard toolbar, the Ruler, and default tab stops.

Using the Paragraph Dialog Box

Follow these steps to indent paragraphs using the Paragraph dialog box:

1. Select the paragraphs to indent or position the insertion point where you want the indentation to begin.

2. From the Format menu, choose **Paragraph** (**Alt-O**, **P**). Word displays the Paragraph dialog box.

3. Do one or both of these:

   ◆ Under Indentation, in either the Left box or Right box, type or select the distance from the left or right margin that you want to indent the paragraphs, or

   ◆ To indent the first line of each paragraph differently from the rest of the paragraph, under Special, select **First Line** and type or select in the By box the distance from the left indent that you want the first line to begin.

4. Choose **OK**.

The paragraph now has the indentations you chose.

Using the Ruler

The Ruler provides an excellent way for you to see exactly where you set indentations as you work. You can indent paragraphs without using commands and keystrokes. Before you start, notice the triangular indent markers on the Ruler as shown in Figure 4.2 on the next page. You use these to set indentations on the left and right sides of the paragraph.

Figure 4.2

Notice the triangle on the left, the inverted triangle above it, and the small square below. You can move the two triangles together or separately.

1. Select the paragraphs to indent or position the insertion point where you want the indentation to begin.

2. Perform one of the actions in Table 4.3 to achieve the indentations you want.

Table 4.3   Indentation Options

To	Do this
Indent all lines in a document	Press **Ctrl-A** to select the entire document. Then click the square, hold down the mouse button, and drag to the left or right as you want.
Indent all lines in the selected paragraph	Click the square, hold down the mouse button, and drag to the left or right as you want.
Indent all lines except the first line in the selected paragraph	Click the lower triangle, hold down the mouse button, and drag to the left or right. This creates a *hanging* indentation if you move all lines except the first to the right. Hanging indentation is described later in this section.
Indent only the first line in a selected paragraph	Click the upper triangle, hold down the mouse button, and drag to the left or right.
Move the lines on the right margin for a selected paragraph	Click the triangle on the right and move it left or right as you want.
Move the lines on the right margin for the entire document	Press **Ctrl-A** to select the entire document. Click the triangle, hold down the mouse button, and drag to the left or right as you want.

Using the Formatting Toolbar

The Formatting toolbar gives you two indentation choices: Indent and Unindent. Each time you select a paragraph and click the Indent button, Word moves the paragraph to the next tab stop. The Unindent button moves the selected paragraph back one tab stop each time you click.

Figure 4.3

Follow these steps to indent paragraphs using the Formatting toolbar:

1. Select the paragraphs to indent or position the insertion point where you want the indentation to begin.
2. Click the **Indent** button on the Formatting toolbar. To unindent, select the text, and click the **Unindent** button.

Using Shortcut Keys

Follow these steps to indent paragraphs using shortcut keys:

1. Select the paragraphs to indent or position the insertion point where you want the indentation to begin.
2. Follow one of the steps in Table 4.4.

Table 4.4   Shortcut Keys for Indentation

To	Press
Indent left to the first tab stop	**Ctrl-M**
Remove the last indentation	**Ctrl-Shift-M**
Create a hanging indentation to the first tab stop	**Ctrl-T**
Remove a hanging indentation	**Ctrl-Shift-T**

Setting Hanging Indents

A *hanging indent* means that the first line of text is left aligned and the other lines are indented or "hang" from the first line. Most of the time, you will use hanging indents in formatting lists and bibliographies. The following examples show hanging indents. You can use the Formatting toolbar, Paragraph dialog box, the Ruler, or shortcut keys to create hanging indents. The following examples show hanging indents. The first shows a hanging indent in a bulleted list item. The second shows a bibliographic reference.

- This is an example of a hanging indent in a bulleted list. All lines after the first one are indented and "hang" from the first line to align with the text instead of the bullet, making the bulleted text easier to read|

Figure 4.4

Stevens, Vicky. *Begging Your Editor for a Few More Days: Tips and Tricks.* Software Publications, Portland 1993

Figure 4.5

Using the Formatting Toolbar

Use the Formatting toolbar when you want to add bulleted and numbered lists. Word creates the hanging indent automatically. Follow these steps to create a hanging indent using the Formatting toolbar:

1. Select the paragraph to which you want to add bullets or numbering.

2. Click the **Numbered List** button to number the list, or click the **Bulleted List** button to give the list bullets.

Word inserts a number or a bullet in front of the paragraph and adjusts the lines with a hanging indent under the first line.

If you decide to change the bulleted or numbered item back to plain paragraph text, select it, choose **Bullets and Numbering** from the Format menu (**Alt-O**, **N**) and choose **Remove** from the Bulleted tab or the Numbered tab, depending on which you have selected.

Using the Paragraph Dialog Box

This method is for text only, and for when you want to use precise measurements for indenting. Follow these steps to set hanging indents using the Paragraph dialog box:

1. Select the paragraphs to indent or position the insertion point where you want the indentation to begin.

2. From the Format menu, choose **Paragraph (Alt-O, P)**. Word displays the Paragraph dialog box.

3. Click the **Indents and Spacing** tab.

4. In the Left box under Indentation, type or select the distance from the left margin that you want to indent the first line.

5. Under Special, select **Hanging**, and in the By box, type or select the measurement from the left that you want to indent all lines beneath the first line, as shown in Figure 4.6.

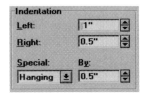

Figure 4.6

Watch the Preview box. Word changes the diagram as you change the measurement.

6. Choose **OK**.

Word applies the indentation.

Using the Ruler

Follow these steps to set a hanging indent using the left marker on the Ruler:

1. Select the paragraphs to indent or position the insertion point where you want the first line to begin.

2. On the Ruler, drag the bottom part of the left marker to where you want to begin all lines but the first. You can move the top triangle to move the first line. Word applies the hanging indent.

Using the Shortcut Key

You can set a hanging indent very quickly using the shortcut key sequence. Follow these steps:

1. Select the paragraphs to indent.

2. Press **Ctrl-T**.

Word indents all lines except the first to the first default or custom set tab. Each time you press the key sequence, the lines move to the next tab stop. To reverse the hanging indent, press **Ctrl-Shift-T**.

Setting Negative Indentations

If you have never used a negative indentation, it may sound unusual. However, this is an excellent feature to use if you have text, headings, or illustrations that you need to place outside of the margin area on the left or right. The following illustration shows a heading that has negative indents. Notice the position of the heading compared to the zero position on the ruler in Figure 4.7.

A Negative Indentation

This sample shows a heading with a negative intation above regular text.

Figure 4.7

Follow these steps to set a negative indentation:

1. Select the paragraphs you want to indent negatively, or position the insertion point where you want the formatting to begin.

2. From the Format menu, choose **Paragraph (Alt-O, P)**. Word displays the Paragraph dialog box.

3. Click the **Indents and Spacing** tab.

4. In the Left box, type or select a number.

5. In the Special box, select **Hanging**, and in the By box, type or select the amount of difference you want between the first line and the other lines. Watch the Preview box. Word changes the diagram as you change the measurement.

6. Choose **OK**.

Word places the text or object in the margin.

Nesting Paragraphs and Items in Lists

There may be times when you need to nest paragraphs under paragraphs or lists under lists. In paragraph text, you would normally nest a paragraph of quoted text. Follow these steps to nest a paragraph or list:

1. Select the paragraph.
2. Click the **Indent** button on the Formatting toolbar or press **Ctrl-M**.

Word moves the paragraph to the next tab stop on the right each time you click or press the keys.

Tabs

It is easy to set and use tabs in Word. Word provides default tab stops at every .5-inch interval; however, you can choose any custom settings you want. Traditionally, authors and typists used the tab stops when typing tables. In Word, you won't need to do that because you can use the table function (described later in this chapter). However, you will still find the need to use tabs in some documents. You can set tabs using the Ruler, the Tabs dialog box, or shortcut keys.

Word does not display the tab characters unless you choose to have them displayed. Follow these steps to display the tab characters:

1. From the Toolbar, choose the **Show/Hide Paragraph** button on the far right, or from the Tools menu, choose **Options (Alt-T, O)**. Word displays the Options dialog box.
2. Click the **View** tab.
3. Under Nonprinting Characters, select **Tab Characters**.
4. Choose **OK**.

Word displays the tab characters.

Using the Ruler

Using the Ruler is the quickest way to set and move tabs. If you want to use ruler measurement, you don't have to figure any adjustments.

1. Select the paragraphs where you want to set or change tab stops.
2. Click the **Tab Alignment** button at the far left of the Ruler until you see the type of tab you want.

Table 4.5   Tab Alignment Buttons

To set tab stops	Click this tab alignment button
Left aligned	⌊
Centered	⊥
Right aligned	⌟
Decimal	⊥

3. Click on the Ruler. Wherever you click, Word inserts a tab stop.

NOTE   Each tab stop can have a different alignment; they do not have to match.

Using the Tab Dialog Box

Using the Tab dialog box from the Tab command gives you more flexibility in setting custom tabs. The command also lets you choose whether to use a tab stop leader character like you see in many tables of contents. Also, you can clear all custom tabs and restore the default tabs with just a few keystrokes.

Follow these steps to set tabs, using precise measurements, in the Tab dialog box:

1. Select the paragraphs to which you want to add tabs or position the insertion point where you want the formatting to begin.
2. From the Format menu, choose **Tabs** (**Alt-O**, **T**). Word displays the Tabs dialog box.

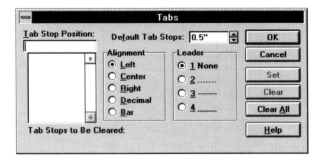

Figure 4.8

3. In the Tab Stop Position box, type the precise measurement and abbreviation for where you want the tab. Do not add a space between the two. (For example, type **2pi** for two picas of space.)

Table 4.6   Tab Measurements

For this measurement	Use this abbreviation
Centimeters	cm
Inches	in
Picas	pi
Points	pt

4. In the Alignment box, select the alignment for the tabs: Left, Center, Right, Decimal, or Bar.

5. In the Leader box, select whether to have a leader (a character that prints within the tabbed area), and the type: None, Periods, Hyphens, or Underscore.

6. Choose **Set**.

7. Repeat steps 3 through 6 for each tab stop you want to set.

8. Choose **OK** when you finish setting tab stops.

You can set all tab stops without closing the dialog box.

Changing Your Tab Stops

If you decide you don't like the tab stops you've set, you can change them easily, using this procedure:

1. Display the Tabs dialog box as described earlier.
2. In the Tab Position box, select or type the position of the tab stop you want to change.
3. Select the alignment you want the tabs to have (and a leader if appropriate).
4. Choose **Set**.

You can remove all other formatting, including tab stops by selecting the text and pressing **Ctrl-Q**. The formatting reverts to the style in which the paragraph was originally defined.

Removing Tab Stops

You can clear a single tab stop, or you can clear all tabs in a document.

1. Select the paragraphs where you want to clear a tab stop.
2. Do one of the following:
   - ◆ Drag the tab marker off the Ruler, or
   - ◆ In the Tabs dialog box, choose **Clear** to clear one tab stop or choose **Clear All** to clear all tab stops in the paragraph. Choose **OK**.

Line Spacing

The right amount of line spacing is crucial for a printed document. Word, like most desktop publishing packages, uses the *point* measurement. There are 72 points in an inch. Too many or too few points of spacing between lines makes text difficult to read. Word's default line spacing for normal text is the single line of space. However, you can change the line spacing to suit your needs.

You can choose to have different line spacing in different parts of the document just as you can for Word's other formatting elements. Word also automatically adjusts the line spacing for the size and type of font you use. This prevents lines from running together or being too far apart. When you choose fonts and line spacing for a document, ask someone else to read the information to make sure that it is easy to read.

To adjust line spacing, choose **Paragraph** from the Format menu (**Alt-O, P**). If you want, you can press **Enter** to add as many lines of space as you need, but generally, you work more efficiently and improve the quality of your document if you define the line spacing for the task at hand. Also, if you add lines with the Enter key and then adjust line spacing for the whole document with the Format command, you might have a lot of extra lines of space, which are actually blank paragraphs.

Adjusting Line Spacing

Follow these steps to adjust line spacing in a document:

1. Select the paragraphs you want to adjust.

2. From the Format menu, choose **Paragraph** (**Alt-O, P**).

3. In the Line Spacing box, select one of the following options:

Figure 4.9

Table 4.7 Line Spacing Options

Select this option	To set
Single	Single-line spacing. Word increases spacing by one line, based on the font type and size you choose. This is the same single spacing that a typewriter uses.
1.5 lines	One-and-a-half line spacing. Word increases spacing by one and a-half lines, based on the font type and size you choose. This is the same line-and-a-half line spacing that a typewriter uses.
Double	Double-line spacing. Word increases spacing by two lines, based on the font type and size you choose. This is the same double-line spacing that a typewriter uses.
At least	A minimum amount of line spacing that you want Word to insert to accommodate fonts or graphics. When you select

	this option, enter the minimum amount of space you want Word to insert between lines in the At box.
Exactly	Fixed line spacing that Word does not adjust. Use this option judiciously because you might cut off text or graphics that does not fit. When you select this option, enter the amount of space you want Word to insert between lines in the At box.
Multiple	Multiple line spacing. When you select this option, you type the number by which to multiply single-line spacing. For example, type **3** if you want Word to add three lines of space instead of one.

N O T E   If you ever import a graphic, and it looks as though only a line or two is copied in the document, select the portion that you can see, and choose the **Multiple** option. Then enter a number, such as 10, in the At box. If that is too much or too little to display the graphic, you can readjust as necessary.

4. Choose **OK**.

Paragraph Spacing

Defining paragraph spacing helps you give your documents a more professional, typeset look, and makes them easier to read. You add space before and after paragraphs, titles, headings, graphics, lists, and tables. Saving before or after spacing in a style can save you a lot of time in formatting. These are some other benefits of adjusting before and after spacing:

◆ You can use points or decimal fractions to fine-tune spacing.

◆ You can make the document more eye-pleasing and easy to read.

◆ You can move any element to which you have applied the spacing, and the spacing moves with the element.

◆ The spacing remains consistent no matter what fonts you use.

◆ When you print the page, Word ignores space before a heading so that the top margin remains intact.

Setting Before and After Spacing

Follow these steps to add space before, after, or both:

1. Select the paragraphs to which you want to add space before or after.

2. From the Format menu, choose **Paragraph (Alt-O, P)**. Word displays the Paragraph dialog box.

3. Click the **Indents and Spacing** tab.

4. Under Spacing, in the Before and After boxes, type or select the measurements you want.

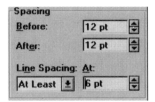

Figure 4.10

5. Choose **OK**.

Word applies the spacing to the paragraphs.

You can change the line spacing in Word's predefined templates if you find it more convenient. See the formatting tutorials in Chapter 5, *Formatting Tutorials*, for more information about changing and defining styles.

N O T E

Deciding Where to Add Paragraph Spacing

Table 4.8 on the next page provides guidelines you might use to decide which areas of your document need line spacing additions or adjustment.

Table 4.8   Paragraph Spacing Suggestions

For this element	Add space
Paragraph text	Before.
A paragraph, such as quoted text, that needs special separation from other paragraph text	Before and after the special paragraph.
Headings	Before and after the heading, but add more space before than after, since a heading needs to be closer to the text it precedes than the text it follows.
Notes, tips, shortcuts, and warnings	Before and after in equal amounts to make sure the information stands out.
Artwork, photographs, and tables	Before and after, usually equal amount.

Lists

In professional documents, especially technical ones, you will probably need to show a lot of information in lists. Word's powerful feature for bulleted and numbered lists makes it easy to format them. In addition, Word can renumber lists automatically if you add or delete items. This can save you a tremendous amount of time over making the changes manually.

You have two ways to format and work with lists:

◆ Using the Bullet and Number buttons on the Formatting toolbar.
◆ Using the Bullets and Numbering dialog box from the Format command.

Using the Formatting Toolbar

The Formatting toolbar provides the quickest way to add bullets or numbers to an existing paragraph. You need only to select a paragraph, and click the button in Figure 4.11 for a numbered item, or the button in Figure 4.12 for a bulleted item.

If you have not selected a paragraph, Word adds a bullet or number to the paragraph where you left the insertion point. You can add a bullet or number to more

Figure 4.11   Figure 4.12

than one paragraph at a time by selecting all of the paragraphs you want to change. Word adds a bullet or number to every paragraph you selected.

When you choose the **Numbered List** button, Word automatically checks to see if you have formatted the previous paragraph with numbering. If you have, it uses the same numbering style as that paragraph and adds 1 to the number. You can change the bullet and numbering style with the Bullets and Numbering dialog box.

Using the Bullets and Numbering Dialog Box

The Bullets and Numbering dialog box gives you more formatting options than the toolbar does. You can choose a different size and shape of bullet and six different options for numbering.

Adding and Changing Bullets

Follow these steps to add bullets to paragraphs:

1. Select the paragraphs to which you want to add bullets.

2. From the Format menu, choose **Bullets and Numbering (Alt-O, N)**. Word displays the Bullets and Numbering dialog box, with six default bullet styles from which you can choose.

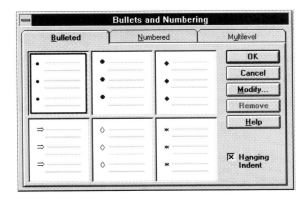

Figure 4.13

3. Choose the bullet style you need, and choose **OK**.

If you don't want to use the default styles, choose **Modify**. Word lets you change the bullet style's point size and spacing. Clicking **Bullets** displays the symbol template for the font you are working in. From there you can choose any symbol you like.

Adding and Changing Numbers

Follow these steps to add numbers to paragraphs:

1. Select the paragraphs to which you want to add numbers.
2. From the Format menu, choose **Bullets and Numbering (Alt-O, N)**.
3. Click the **Numbered** tab. Word displays the Numbered dialog box, with six default styles you can choose from.
4. Choose the options you need, and choose **OK**.

If you don't want to use the default styles, choose **Modify**. Word lets you change the style of the numbered list.

Creating Multi-Level Lists

Some documents you create might require you to use multi-level lists, that is lists that multiple levels of indented information. Word allows you have a maximum of nine levels for any document. Follow these steps:

1. From the Format menu, choose **Bullets and Numbering (Alt-O, N)**.
2. Select the **Multilevel** tab.
3. Choose **OK**.
4. Type the list.
5. To demote selected items, click the **Increase Indent** button on the Formatting toolbar.

To promote selected items, click the **Decrease Indent** button on the Formatting toolbar.

Adding More Paragraphs to a Numbered List

If you convert a series of paragraphs into a numbered list, and decide to add more items between two of them, Word renumbers the list automatically each time you press **Enter**. For example, if you have a list of four numbered steps, and you press **Return** after step 2, the new paragraph is numbered step 3, and steps 3 and 4 becomes steps 4 and 5.

Removing Bullets and Numbers

If you decide you want your paragraphs to have no bullets or numbers after you have added them, you can remove them just as easily as you added them. If you add either, you can remove them immediately by choosing **Undo** from the Edit menu (**Alt-E, U**).

Follow these steps to remove bullets or numbers using the Bullets and Numbering dialog box:

1. Select the paragraphs that have the bullets or numbers.
2. From the Format menu, choose **Bullets and Numbering** (**Alt-O, N**).
3. Select the **Bullets** tab to remove bullets or select the **Numbered** tab to remove numbers.
4. Clear the **Hanging Indent By** check box if you want to remove hanging indent formatting.
5. Choose **Remove**.

Word reformats the paragraphs.

Sorting Lists

Did you ever type a perfect alphabetic or numbered list of items, only to discover that you left out a few? Word makes it easy to sort a list alphabetically, numerically, or by date. If you need to add items to your list, you don't have to retype any of your work, using this feature.

There a few things you need to keep in mind when sorting a list:

◆ Items beginning with punctuation symbols will be at the top of the list. Numbered items come next, and alphabetic entries come last.

◆ Uppercase letters are placed before lowercase letters.

◆ Alphabetic entries are sorted by subsequent characters, as you would find in an index.

◆ If you have two identical entries, Word evaluates the subsequent entries specified in the Then By options in the Sort Text dialog box.

Follow these steps:

1. Select the text you want to sort.

2. From the Table menu, choose **Sort Text (Alt-A, T)**.

3. Depending on what and how you need to sort, do one or more of the following:
   - ◆ To prevent sorting the list's heading along with its items, select **Header Row** under the My List Has options.
   - ◆ Under Sort By, select a field number or name. You can sort by as many as three criteria.
   - ◆ In the Type box, select the type of information to be sorted: text, number, or date.
   - ◆ To change a field separator, choose **Options**, and type or select the separator you want. Choose **OK**.

4. Choose **OK** to begin sorting.

Formatting Text with AutoFormat

Until now in this chapter, you've learned only about formatting text manually. It's very important to learn how to apply formatting from the menu commands, and dialog boxes because you learn about the foundation of Word's formatting capabilities. This helps you to understand what Word does to your documents when you apply automatic formatting. Plus, it helps you to appreciate all the quick ways you can format as you become a power user.

You use AutoFormat after you've typed a document. This is an excellent feature for those who would rather get all the text together first and worry about formatting later. However, you still need to review Word's changes to your document to make sure you like all the changes.

Follow these steps to format all the paragraphs of your document automatically:

1. Open a document.

2. Position the insertion point anywhere in the document.

3. From the Format menu, choose **AutoFormat (Alt-O, A)**. Word analyzes the text and applies styles from the template your document is formatted in. This might take a minute or two for a large document. Then Word displays the AutoFormat dialog box.

Figure 4.14

4. Click on **Review Changes**.

5. In the Review AutoFormat dialog box, click the **Find** buttons to move forward and backward through the document to review each change individually. Word displays in the Description box details about each change it made to your document.

6. For any change that you do not want to keep in the document, click **Reject**. Click **Close** when you finish reviewing.

7. To accept all changes or all the changes you did not reject during your review, click **Accept**, or to reject all changes Word made to your document, click **Reject All**.

At this point, you might want to choose another template and use AutoFormat again. You can also Undo the last change you rejected by choosing **Undo Last**.

Selecting a Different Template for Automatic Formatting

If you reject all changes after using the AutoFormat feature, and you want to apply automatic formatting from a different template, choose **Style Gallery** from the AutoFormat dialog box. From there, you can select another template from the Template box. Word reformats and gives you the option of rejecting or accepting changes as described in the previous procedure.

Columns

You can format a document, a section, or a paragraph in multiple columns if you choose. However, you must designate the multiple-column area (no matter how short) as a section by adding a section break. This type of formatting does not require you to use the Table command. (For simple columns, you might prefer setting up a table. See Chapter 8 for more information.)

The column feature sets up your section like a newspaper layout. To view the layout as you work, you need to use Page View. Normal view displays the text in the correct column width, however, it shows a single column.

Follow these steps to create a multiple-column layout using the mouse:

1. Choose **Page Layout** from the View menu (**Alt-V**, **P**)
2. Make sure the Standard toolbar is displayed (**Alt-V**, **T**).
3. Insert a section break above the area you want to put in columns (**Alt-I**, **B**).

Word displays the Section Break dialog box.

4. Select **Continuous** under Section Break.
5. Choose **OK**.

Word inserts the section break.

6. Click in the section.
7. On the Standard toolbar, click the **Columns** button. Word displays the column choices in the sample box.
8. Drag the mouse cursor to the right to select the number of columns you want.

Word formats the section with the number of columns you choose.

Follow these steps to create a multiple-column layout using the keyboard:

1. Select the text you need to format in columns, or position the insertion point where you want to change the number of columns.
2. From the Format menu, choose **Columns** (**Alt-O, C**). Word displays the Columns dialog box.
3. Type or select the number of columns you want.
4. In the Width and Spacing box, select the size you want the columns to be.
5. Choose **OK**.

Word formats the section with the number of columns you choose.

Replacing Formatting

Sometimes you might format a document only to print it and say, "Why on Earth did I format it like THAT?" Word lets you find and replace formatting almost as easily as finding and replacing a word. For example, you might decide that the large, bold, font you chose for level-3 headings is overwhelming. Using the **Replace** command from the Edit menu, (**Alt-E, E**) you can change the formatting for all level-3 headings and redefine the style while you're at it. Follow these steps to replace formatting or formatted text:

1. From the Edit menu, choose **Replace** (**Alt-E, E**). Word displays the Replace dialog box.

2. In the Find What box, type the text you want to change.

3. Leave the insertion point in the Find What box, and choose the formats you are looking for by choosing **Font**, **Paragraph**, **Language**, or **Styles** from the Format pop-up menu. You can choose **No Formatting** if you want to remove the formats listed below the Find What box or if you want to start over.

4. In the Replace With box, follow the steps in Table 4.9.

Table 4.9   Replacement formatting suggestions

To replace	Do this
A string of specific text, leaving the formatting intact	Type the replacement characters in the Replace With box. If you see format names listed below the box, choose **No Formatting**.
A string of specific text, and its formatting	1. Type the replacement characters in the Replace With box. 2. Leave the insertion point in the Replace With box and choose **Character**, **Paragraph**, and **Styles** to select new formatting options.
Only formatting of a string of specific text	1. Delete any text in the Replace With box. 2. Leave the insertion point in the Replace With box and choose **Character**, **Paragraph**, and **Styles** to select new formatting options.

Word changes the formatted text or formatting.

5. Select any other options you need at this point.

N O T E

You can find text by typing the specific text in the Find What box, deleting any text in the Replace With box, and choosing **Find Next**.

Summary

In this chapter you learned how to make your document look like it was formatted by a professional typesetter. You learned about line spacing, tabs, indentations, paragraph alignment, applying numbers and bullets to lists, sorting lists, columns, and replacing formatting. You also learned about how you can have Word apply formatting with just the click of a few buttons.

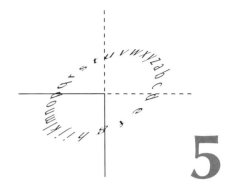

5

Formatting Tutorials

In this chapter, you can use the tutorials with the files on the disk to learn about the powerful formatting features to:

- add a header to make your letter look like you printed it on personal stationery
- align text
- move a sentence from its location to another paragraph
- format characters and words
- create a title page
- choose fonts for headings
- use paragraph formatting
- use the list feature
- add footers and page numbers
- use the spelling feature

Learning how to format text in Word for Windows and how to use its powerful desktop publishing features will help you create professional-quality documents in a short time. You might find that you save the money that you would normally pay a typesetter to make your documents look good.

Although Word for Windows comes with some preset style sheets, you need to know how to set a format that works best for your specific needs. If you use Word on the job, chances are your department has its own format and style that you will need to create or recreate in Word.

This chapter provides instructions that take you through most of Word's sophisticated formatting capabilities. Since you probably already know how to type on a word processor, we have included text files that you can copy from the disk that was packaged with this book.

- The first file is a simple letter that you can format and improve.
- The second file is a business proposal that needs work. After you load the files, follow the tutorials in this chapter to become more familiar with formatting features.

About the Tutorials

This first tutorial lets you work on a letter to become familiar with some of Word's text editing features. If you are a novice user, this is a good place to start so you can become a power user. If you have already become familiar with Word's simpler formatting capabilities, you might want to go on the next tutorial, where you will use some of the more complex features for a business-related document.

The Letter

Have you ever signed a letter only to realize that you rambled on and did not organize it the way you really wanted? Most of us have·probably done that at one time or another. In this tutorial, you can use Word's powerful formatting features.

Making the Letter Better

The first thing you need to do is copy the text file called LETTER.DOC from the disk packaged with this book to the directory of your choice and open it in Word for Windows.

Al Stevens
123 Coconut Grove
Cocoa Beach, Florida   79495

November 19, 1993

It seems like only yesterday (and not last spring) that you and I were on the phone, disagreeing about whether computer book authors should use the names of real people in their books. When I was your editor, I wanted to change them to names I knew were fictitious in case they didn't like it. And, I tried to talk you out of starting sentences with connectors like "and" and "but." But, now I'm on the other side of the fence, and look what I've just done.

The Oregon rain has set in, and we know it won't stop until July. Mike and I have decided to spend our rainy weekends sharing with the world what we know about how to make great-looking letters, forms, and documents with Word for Windows 6.0.

Figure 5.1

Follow these steps to enhance and reformat the letter.

1. Move the cursor to the date and select the whole line. Type over the date with the current date.

2. Select the fourth paragraph and release the mouse button.

3. Point anywhere in the selected paragraph, then press and hold down the left mouse button while you move the mouse pointer to the paragraph symbol at the first paragraph.

4. Release the mouse button. The fourth paragraph becomes the first paragraph. Don't you think that is a better opening for this letter?

5. Move the mouse cursor to the new fourth paragraph, "Have you performed..." and find the two book titles. Select *Teach Yourself...DOS 6.0.*

6. From the Format menu, choose **Font** (**Alt-O**, **F**). Go to the check box marked **Italic** and select it, or choose the **Italic** button from the Formatting toolbar.

7. Choose **OK**.

8. Select *Teach Yourself...Windows* and repeat steps 6 and 7.

9. From the File menu, choose **Save** to save the file.

Now keep the letter file open. There are several steps in the next part of the tutorial that you can use to make great-looking letters.

Making Letter Stationery in the Same File

You can make your letter look like you printed it on stationery by adding a name and address header to your file. This is a very inexpensive way to make business and personal letters look attractive.

Adding a Letterhead

Word does not insert any type of header into your documents automatically. You have to set the header, but it is a simple task. If you have set standard margins for letter, Word places the header you add in an area that is higher on the page than the work area where you type the body of the text. You must work in Normal view to add a header to the file.

As you create the header, you will be working in the Header window. However, when you view or print the page, you can see that the header is where it should be. Follow these steps to add a name and address header to the letter. Later, when you learn about the graphics capabilities in Word, you will see how you can create your own symbol or logo to add to your stationery header.

1. From the View menu, choose **Normal**. (Normal is the default for the default style sheet, so it should be selected already. This step is included to help you get used to the whole process.)

2. While the View menu is still open, choose **Header and Footer**. Word displays the Header And Footer dialog box.

Figure 5.2

Since this is a one-page letter, you do not need to worry about setting odd and even headers.

N O T E

3. Where the cursor is positioned, type your name and address like this:

Name

```
Street Address
City, State, ZIP
```

4. Select all three lines.

5. From the Format menu, choose **Paragraph (Alt-O, P)**. Word opens the Paragraph dialog box, with the Indents and Spacing tab displayed.

6. Click the **Down Arrow** next to the Alignment box to display the alignment options. Choose **Centered** to center the text in the header. Choose **OK** to close the box or choose the **Center Alignment** button on the Formatting toolbar. The text remains selected.

7. While the text is still selected, from the Format menu, choose **Font (Alt-O, F)**.

8. Click the **Down Arrow** next to the Font box to display the list of fonts, and choose **Modern**.

9. Click on the **Down Arrow** next to the Points box and type **10** over the default of 12. Choose **OK** to close the box.

You now have a centered name-and-address header in 10-point Modern type.

Although the header will be separated from the text with some white space, you can delineate the header a better way by adding a plain or decorative line under it. Keep the Header window open, and follow these steps to add the line.

1. Select the last line of the header.

2. From the Format menu, choose **Borders and Shading (Alt-T, B)**. Word displays the Borders tab.

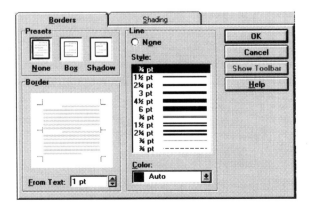

Figure 5.3

The Borders tab shows a diagram of text on a page. The pointers indicate the horizontal and vertical positions where you can place the borders. The default settings show all pointers, indicating that the entire selected area will have borders.

3. Click on the area at the bottom of the diagram so that only the bottom left and right pointers are still visible.

Figure 5.4

4. Choose **OK** to close the Borders and Shading dialog box.

The letter now has a letterhead.

If you ever have two windows open, and you want to add a header to one of the documents, you will have to enlarge the current window or close the other window. To enlarge the window, move the cursor to the bottom right corner where you see the empty square. Click the cursor on the square, hold down the mouse button, and drag down the cursor to expose more window space.

The Proposal

The proposal tutorial gives you the opportunity to make an unformatted text file into a professional-quality document.

Although Word for Windows comes with a style sheet for a proposal, there might be a time when your company or other business affiliate requires a different format and standard. The preset style includes a level-one heading, a level-two heading, and the normal style for the body of your text. That style might suffice for a simple proposal; however, if you are working with a complex hierarchy of information, you will need to use Word's more sophisticated formatting features to produce an impressive proposal.

In this tutorial, you:

- Create a proposal title page.
- Insert page breaks.
- Choose fonts for headings.
- Use paragraph formatting.
- Use the list feature to make a bulleted list of information.
- Add footers and page numbers.
- Add a header.

Additionally, the proposal you will work on contains all of the parts that a professional-quality proposal should contain. So after you print out your work, look at the structure and components of the proposal. We suggest this structure because it is easier for busy managers to get the highlights of your report without having to dig out the important information.

Making the Proposal Better

The first thing you need to do is copy the file called PROPOSAL.DOC from the disk to the directory of your choice and open it in Word for Windows as shown in Figure 5.5.

```
Proposal to Perform Customer Research
Prepared by
Bernie Kawasaki, Senior Technical Writer
Stevridge Software, Inc.

January 17, 1993
```
==============================End of Section==============================

```
[Level 1 Heading]Purpose

As you requested on December 15, 1993, I have been researching ways that we
can get to know our software users so we can provide software documentation
based on what they need most.
```

Figure 5.5

The Problems in Bernie's Proposal

When someone asks you for a proposal on the job, its appearance is often as important as the information it contains. The way you put together any business document says a lot about your organization and communication skills. Many people write in such a manner that they try to get all of the information together first, and then think about the format.

The text for the proposal in the PROPOSAL.DOC file is typical of the first draft of a document. It has the right information thrown in, but it is not easy to read because the hierarchical structure and relevance of the information is not apparent. The headings are all on the same level, the format is unattractive, and the reader must find the most important information buried in paragraphs.

In this tutorial exercise, you will gain experience using these powerful formatting features:

◆ Defining styles.

◆ Using the section break.

◆ Applying left and right running headers and footers.

◆ Defining multiple levels of headings.

◆ Indenting text.

◆ Adding a border.

◆ Using the bullets and numbering tool.

Designing the Title Page

Follow these steps to format the proposal title page.

1. Copy the file PROPOSAL.DOC from the floppy disk to the directory of your choice and open it in Word for Windows.

Notice the first five lines. This is information that you generally should place on the front cover of the proposal. In the preset proposal style sheet that comes with Word, this information is placed in the header, however, most formal proposals start with a title page that contains the name of the proposal, the author, the company name, and the date. The body of the information starts on the next page, which is page 1.

2. Select the first five lines of the file.

3. From the Format menu, choose **Paragraph (Alt-O, P)**, and select the **Indents and Spacing** tab.

4. Click the down arrow next to the Alignment box and choose **Centered**.

5. Select the options shown as follows.

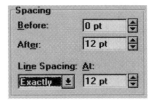

Figure 5.6

For this type of alignment, you do not need to assign spacing before *and* after. If you assigned 12 points before and 12 after, you would have double space between the lines. You will use this formatting feature later when you design a style sheet that needs more sophisticated spacing and alignment.

N O T E

6. Click **OK** to close the box. Word centers the text and places the space between the lines. The lines are still selected.

7. From the Format menu, choose **Font** (**Alt-O**, **F**) to display the Font dialog box.

8. Click on the **Down Arrow** below the Font box to display the list of fonts, and choose **Modern**.

9. In the Points box choose **14**. Choose **OK** to close the box.

This gives your title page a more typeset and professional look.

Word's Modern font is similar to the popular Helvetica font, which is often used for title pages and headers.

N O T E

Using the Section Break

Word's section break feature enables you to vary page formatting within a document. This is a powerful feature, and one of the most valuable when you are creating a document in which you need to change headers and footers from section to section. The section break is different than the page break because it allows you to set up certain formatting that the page break does not allow. Also, you can have two sections on the same page.

Once you set up a section break, all formatting for the section is stored with the section mark. You can treat the section mark the same way you treat any other character. You can cut and paste it, copy it, or delete it. However, if you delete the section mark, you will lose all section formatting.

In this exercise, you will set up a section break because the cover page of the proposal does not need a header or a footer, but the remainder of the proposal needs both.

When you create a document, such as a business document that has several sections or chapters, use the section break feature in one section instead of creating each section in a separate file. This makes it easier to work with headers, footers, and page numbering. Also, one file is usually easier to manage than several short ones if it is a manageable size.

1. Position the cursor at the end of the date line, and from the Insert menu, choose **Break (Alt-I, B)**.

2. In the Section Breaks box, choose **Odd Page**. Word inserts the section break. This causes the first page of the proposal body to be an odd page that starts with 1.

Invoking a section break does not add page numbers to your document. You use this feature in conjunction with the Header and Footer features to start the page numbering.

Adding a Running Header

A running header in a document is generally used as a reminder of the highest level topic. In this formatting exercise, you will add a running header on the even pages, showing that the information is company confidential, and one on odd pages, showing the proposal title.

Adding an Even Header

1. From the View menu, choose **Header And Footer** (**Alt-V, H**). Word displays the Header and Footer dialog box.

Figure 5.7

2. Click the **Page Setup** button. Word displays the Page Setup dialog box, with the Layout tab displayed.

3. In the Section Start box, select **Even Page**. In the Headers and Footers box, click **Different Odd and Even Pages**. This option indicates that you want to put different headers and footers on the odd and even pages. If you clear the selection, Word ignores the even header or footer, and uses the odd header or footer for all pages.

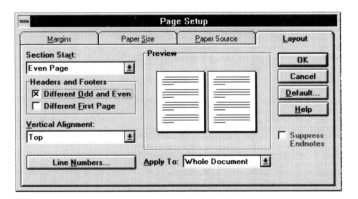

Figure 5.8

4. Choose **OK** to close the Page Setup dialog and display the Header and Footer dialog box.

5. Type this text in the heading:

   `Stevridge Software, Inc.   Company Confidential`

6. Select the words Company Confidential. From the Formatting toolbar, click the **Align right** button to right-justify that text.

7. Select the whole line, and from the Formatting toolbar, click the **Bold** button.

Most of the time, you will need to delineate the header from the text on the page. Word's Border feature lets you do this without having to type a line of hyphens, or worse, a line of equal signs. Also, remember to use

N O T E a different font in the header to further distinguish it from the body of the text.

8. From the Formatting toolbar, click the down arrow next to the Font box. Select **Modern**.

9. From the Point Size box on the Formatting toolbar, select **10**.

Figure 5.9

10. From the Format menu, choose **Borders and Shading (Alt-O, B)**. Word displays the Paragraph Borders and Shading dialog box, with the Borders tab displayed.

11. In the Border box, click the bottom horizontal border area so that the diagram shows only the bottom line pointers. In the Style box, click on the 3/4 point border and choose **OK**.

You can also choose your border options from the Borders toolbar.

N O T E

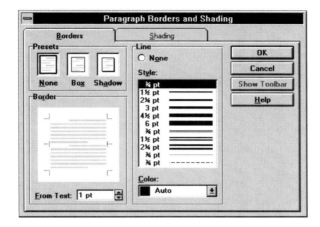

Figure 5.10

12. Click **Close** to close the Header and Footer dialog box.

You now have an even header in the proposal document.

The Preset box shows formats for borders that make boxes. By default, **None** is selected.

N O T E

If you want to see how the page looks with a header, choose **Print Preview** from the file menu.

To return to the normal working page view, select **100** in the Zoom Control. Now, save your file and keep it open (**Alt-F, L**).

Adding an Odd Header

Add an odd header that shows the name of the proposal, the author, and the date. Follow these steps:

1. From the View menu, choose **Header and Footer (Alt-V, H)**.

2. Click the **Page Setup** button to display the Page Setup dialog box.

3. This time, select **Odd Page** in the Section Start box, and choose **OK**.

4. In the header, type this text:

   `Customer Research Proposal B. Kawasaki January 17, 1993`

5. Apply the same font and border to the odd heading, and click **Close**. The proposal now has even and odd running headers.

NOTE

The Same as Previous button in the Header and footer toolbar enables you to duplicate the previous header or footer without retyping any text. If you create a header or footer and choose this option, Word asks if you want to delete the current one and link to the previous one. If you choose **Yes**, Word duplicates the header or footer. This is an excellent way to keep your running headers consistent.

Adding a Running Footer

When you are creating a business document of any kind, always show page numbers. (If someone drops your document, it can be put back together more easily if it has page numbers.) You can add the page number to the header or the footer. Follow these steps to add a running footer:

1. Make sure your document is in Normal or Page Layout view.

2. Position the insertion point at the first paragraph on the first page of the proposal body.

NOTE

Make sure the insertion point is on the first page of the proposal body— not on the title page. The title page does not need a page number.

3. From the View menu, choose **Header and Footer (Alt-V, H)**. Word displays the Header and Footer dialog box.

4. Click the **Switch Between the Header and Footer** button.

5. Click the **Page Setup** button to display the Page Setup dialog box.

6. In the Section Start box, select **Continuous**, and select **Different Odd and Even** in the Headers and Footers box.

7. Choose **OK**.

8. On the Header and Footer toolbar, click the **Page Number** button. The pound sign (#) button is for adding page numbers, the button in the middle is for adding the current date automatically, and the button on the right is for adding the current time. Since you have already put the date in your header, and the time is not important in this instance, click the pound sign to insert a page number. In a two-sided document with facing pages, the odd page number should be flush right with the margin, and the even page number flush left with the margin.

9. Format the footer with the same font you gave the header. Using the same methods for applying borders as you used in the headers, apply a border above the page number.

Your document now has a running footer that shows page numbers.

Showing Different Levels of Headings

Word's ability to use fonts and its character attributes—such as bold, italic, and underline—make it easy to distinguish headings from body text. In any document where you need to show a hierarchical structure of information, it is important to use different characteristics for each heading level. Unless all of your information is on the same level (quite unlikely in a business or academic document), never use the same font and point size for all heading levels.

In this exercise, you can select fonts and point sizes for the three levels of headings. To make the headings in the provided text easier for you to find, they are labeled as levels 1, 2, or 3. Follow these steps to format the headings. You only need to apply the options to the first of each of the level headings. In the exercise following this one, you will define those headings as styles, and apply them to the other headings the easy way.

1. Select the first level-1 heading, **Purpose**.

2. From the Formatting toolbar, click the down arrow beside the Font box to display the list of fonts, and select **Modern**. Word applies the Modern font to the heading and the heading remains selected. Do not deselect it.

3. From the Formatting toolbar, click the down arrow beside the Point size box to display the list of point sizes available for the Modern font.

4. Choose **16**. Word places the font in the 16 point size, and the heading remains selected. Do not deselect it.

5. From the Formatting toolbar, click the **Bold** option to make the heading bold. The first level-1 heading is now 16-point, bold Modern, and it stands out from the body of the text and from the other levels of headings. Ignore the other level-1 headings. You will change those when you define this proposal as a style sheet.

6. Select the first level-2 heading, **Mailing Questionnaires**, and using the same steps for the level-1 heading, apply the Modern font.

7. Change the point size to **14**, and make the heading bold, using the **Bold** button from the Formatting toolbar.

8. Select the first level-3 heading, **Questionnaire Strong Points**, and using the same steps for the level-1 heading, apply the Modern font.

9. Change the point size to **10**, and make the heading bold, using the **Bold** button from the Formatting toolbar.

Your document now has clear delineation for the different levels of headings. Don't worry about the other headings right now. The exercise in the next chapter helps you to use Word's powerful style definition feature. You will apply the styles you have just made to the other headings and build a complete style sheet that you can use any time you want to build a similar document.

Text Indentations for the Document

Most business documents are created for 8.5-by-11 inch paper. Word's default margins work just fine for this and most documents. However, you might want your body text to have different indentations than your overall document. Your documents can be easier to read if the text is indented further than the headings. This makes text more attractive and easier to read.

Word also offers multiple options from the Paragraph command for adjusting line spacing. Understanding how to use the paragraph indentations and line spacing features will help you to create more visually pleasing documents. It is also important that you understand how to adjust line spacing for use with other formatting elements such as font sizes. In the following exercise, you will change the paragraph indentations and adjust the line spacing for just the first paragraph of regular text. In the next chapter, you define that body text indentation as a style and convert the other body text very easily by applying the style.

Follow these steps to indent the text:

1. Select the first paragraph under the heading *Purpose*.

2. From the Format menu, choose **Paragraph** (**Alt-O**, **P**) to display the Paragraph dialog box. The Alignment box shows Left as the default. This is the correct alignment.

3. In the Indentation box, change the Left option to .75" and the Right option to 0.5" shown in Figure 5.11.

Word indents the text 3/4" from the left margin and 1/2" from the right margin.

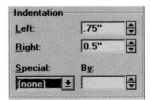

Figure 5.11

You can use the up and down arrows to display .1-inch increments. However, any other increments must be entered from the keyboard.

N O T E

4. In the Spacing box, change the After option to 12 points. This causes Word to add a line of space after each paragraph return. You will not have to press the **Enter** key twice after you finish a paragraph.

Leave the other paragraphs as they are for now. When you define this indented text as a style in the next chapter, you can apply that style to change all of the other body text.

Using Bulleted Lists

A list is the best way to show similar items in business and technical writing because the information is easier to find. Busy professionals often do not have the time to "dig" for information that is buried in paragraphs.

In this exercise, you will make some of the information into bulleted and numbered lists.

N O T E Use numbered lists to show order, for example, the steps in a task or procedure. Use bulleted lists to show items that are not dependent on each other.

Follow these steps to make a bulleted list:

1. Move the cursor to the second (one-line) paragraph under the heading Questionnaire Strong Points.

2. Select that line and the two paragraphs under it.

3. From the Formatting toolbar, choose the **Bullets** button.

Word adds bullets with hanging indents to the listed information. You can set options that change the shape and size of the bullets in the Bullets and Numbering dialog box. Choose **Bullets and Numbering** from the Format menu (**Alt-O**, **B**) to display the Bullets and Numbering dialog box.

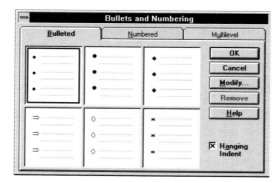

Figure 5.12

In this dialog box, you can choose any of the bullets shown as your default bullet. If you do not choose a bullet style before you make a bulleted list, Word applies the 10-point round bullet. You can change the point size of any of the bullets and you can define other bullets by choosing **Modify** and choosing a symbol. For a formal proposal or other business document, however, it is best to use a simple bullet.

Always choose a bullet style and size that does not "jump off the page" at you. Large bullets distract the reader from the information at hand. In general, a 10-point round bullet works just fine. In any case, don't use a symbol that will cause an upper-level manager to stop and ask, "What is that thing? Don't you have anything better to do than draw little pictures?" N O T E

Bulleted information looks best if you use the hanging indent. Without it, the information can be as difficult to read as if it were in a regular paragraph. Always indent the information to align with the text on the first line following the bullet. Continue this exercise, by making the short paragraphs under these headings into bulleted lists:

- ◆ Telephone Survey Strong Points
- ◆ Telephone Survey Weak Points
- ◆ Visiting Customer Site Strong Points
- ◆ Visiting Customer Site Weak Points

Using a Numbered List

As mentioned earlier, use numbered lists to show the order in which events should happen or to make a point about a number of things that need to be done. Word's Numbered List feature is powerful in that it can renumber a list automatically. This is very important because a mistake in a numbered list is very noticeable.

Follow these steps to make a numbered list:

1. Scroll to the last heading in the proposal, Breakdown of Tasks and Expenses.
2. Select the first three paragraphs, and from the Formatting toolbar choose the **Numbering** button.

Word converts the information into a numbered list. (For more detailed information about bullets and numbering, see Chapter 4.)

Tabs and Line Spacing in Lists

While Word automatically converts bullets to numbers and vice versa, it is up to you to decide whether you want to use the same text alignment for the list. You might want to indent the list, rather than have it flush left with the text. In this proposal, indent the first bullet in the first list. In the next chapter, you will define this as a style, and apply it to all other bullets. Follow these steps:

1. Scroll to the first bulleted item under Questionnaire Strong Points and select the whole line.

2. From the Format menu, select **Paragraph** (**Alt-O**, **P**) to display the Paragraph dialog box.

3. In the Left box under Indentation, click on the **Up Arrow** until you display 0.5".

4. Select the **Text Flow** tab and select **Keep Lines Together**. (This keeps Word from inserting a page break that would put part of a bulleted item on one page and part on another.)

5. Choose **OK**.

Don't worry about the other bullets or lists for now. When you define the indented bulleted list as a style in the next chapter, you can change all of them very quickly.

Checking Spelling

Always run the spelling check feature on your documents. Even if you're a great typist and an excellent speller, everyone can make mistakes, and it's best to find those mistakes before others do.

From the Tools menu, choose **Spelling** (**Alt-T**, **S**). Word stops and displays in the Spelling dialog box any words it does not recognize. You can choose to ignore the word, all instances of the word, change it, or add it to a dictionary so that Word will always recognize the term. See your documentation for details.

Summary

In this chapter you learned how to format a personal letter and a business proposal. You are well on your way to becoming a desktop publisher. Copy the two files from the disk as other file names. Experiment with them and see what you can come up with. No matter what you learn in a tutorial, you have your own tastes in what is eye-pleasing. Now, on to the next chapter, where you learn how to define styles and define a template.

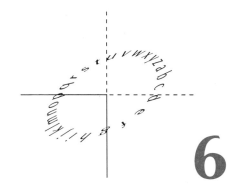

Creating Templates and Defining Styles

I n this chapter, you:

- ◆ define the styles in the proposal that you worked on in Chapter 5
- ◆ create a new template that contains all those styles

Do you ever feel like you're spinning your wheels by entering the same information to your documents over and over? Creating and using a template can help you cut down tremendously on the time you spend repeating the same actions.

By creating a template, you can store the format of a document so you can use it whenever you need to produce the same type of document. In this tutorial chapter, you actually create your template as you define styles. When you save the document as a .DOT file, you will be able to use the template again.

Creating A Template

Word for Windows is packaged with some preset templates. However, it is important that you know how to create your own templates so you can become a more independent power user. Once you master the task of creating your own formats and style sheets, you become a *desktop publisher* instead of a *word processor*.

When you save the template, you can recall it again to create a similar document. If you decide later that you want to add or delete styles, you can make the changes easily and update your template. Your templates are not set in concrete. Word enables you to change them whenever you like.

There are three ways that you can create a template in Word:

◆ Convert an existing document to a template.

◆ Modify an existing template.

◆ Choose **New** from the File menu and select the **Template** option under the dialog box.

The first exercise in this chapter helps you to master the more powerful of the three methods. You can use the text you worked on in Chapter 5 to define styles for:

◆ headers and footers

◆ all levels of headings

◆ paragraph indentations

◆ line spacing for the body text and lists

Adding A New Template To The Template List

The default template is Normal, so you need to define a new template for this proposal type. Otherwise, you would have to change or add styles to the Normal template. This is not a good idea because you might want to use the existing Normal template for another document sometime.

After you create the new template, Word adds it to the list of templates in the new dialog box.

To complete this exercise, you need to copy PROPOSAL.DOC from the floppy disk (packaged with this book) to your hard disk, and complete the exercises in Chapter 5.

Follow these steps to save PROPOSAL.DOC as a .DOT file (template):

1. From the File menu, choose **Open** (**Alt-F, O**), and in the File Name box, type **PROPOSAL.DOC** preceded by the path where you copied it.

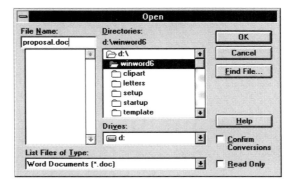

Figure 6.1

2. Choose **OK**.

3. From the File menu, choose **Save As** (**Alt-F, A**).

4. In the File Name box, type **NewProp**.

5. Select **Document Template** under the Save File As Type box, and choose **OK**.

Word displays the new template name, NewProp, along with the other preset template names in this list. Now you are ready to convert the styles in the proposal.

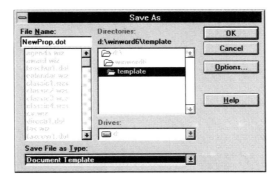

Figure 6.2

Converting Your Proposal

In this exercise, you will define your proposal's title as a *style*. By doing this, you will eliminate more than a dozen manual formatting steps.

1. Select all information on the title page.

2. From the Format menu, choose **Style (Alt-O, S)**. Word displays the Style dialog box, where you can define and modify styles.

3. Click **New**. Word displays the New Style dialog box.

4. Type **Title Page** in the Name box, and select the options shown in Figure 6.3.

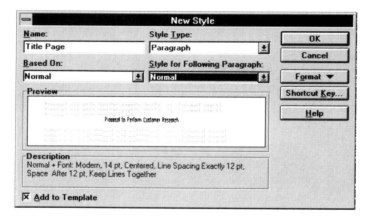

Figure 6.3

5. Select **Add to Template** and choose **OK** to close the dialog box.

6. From the Style dialog box, choose **Apply**. Word adds the Title Page style to the NewProp template.

While you're in the New Style dialog box, you can define a shortcut key that, when pressed, applies the style to selected text. You can do this for all styles that you define. However, it is important to remember that by doing this, you can accidentally overwrite another shortcut key sequence. Choose a key sequence that you know you won't need to use for anything else. Always write down the shortcut keys when you define them, since multiple shortcuts may be difficult to remember.

Defining Heading Styles

In Chapter 5 you applied some styles to one of each of the heading levels. In this exercise, you define the three levels of headings in your document as styles in your template. Again, you will save many keystrokes in future documents by performing this task.

In the Proposal document, all levels of headings are entered next to the heading, for example [Level-1 Heading]. This is added only as a reminder of what the levels should be. Delete that text for each heading.

N O T E

1. Scroll to the first heading in the document, Purpose, and select the entire line.
2. From the Format menu, choose **Style (Alt-O, S)**. Word displays the Style dialog box.
3. Choose **New**. The Preview box shows all formatting that you applied to the heading earlier.
4. Enter the name, **Head 1**, in the Name box and choose **Format**. Word expands the Format box.

Figure 6.4

The Based On box, on the New Style dialog box, is where you can base one or more new styles on another existing style. For example, if you give Head 1 a certain font and spacing, you can base other headings on Head 1, and they inherit any format changes. If you redefine the base style, then all styles based on the base style are redefined automatically as well. You don't have to define a base style, however. There may be times when you want to change some styles, but not the ones on which they are based.

Because you added the formatting to the heading earlier, you do not need to add any additional formatting. If you choose to add any other formatting, Word displays them in the Preview box.

N O T E

5. Select **Add to Template** to add the style to the template, and choose **OK**. Then choose **Apply** from the Style dialog box.

6. Scroll to the next Level 1 heading, Background and Problem, and select the whole line.

7. On the Formatting toolbar, click the down arrow beside the style box and select Head 1 to apply the style to the next level-1 heading.

8. Using the same procedure you used in steps 1 through 7, define your level-2 and level-3 headings.

Defining the Body Style

Earlier, you selected the first paragraph under Purpose, and indented it .75 inches to further separate the headings and text, and adjusted the line spacing. Now you can define that paragraph as the base style for all other body text by following these steps:

1. Select the first (indented) paragraph under Purpose.

2. From the Format menu, choose **Style** (**Alt-O**, **S**) and then **New**.

3. From the New Style dialog box, type **base text** in the Name box.

4. Click **Add to Template** and choose **OK**, and then **Apply**. You now have a style for the body text. This is the style you will use for all paragraph body text in the proposal. As you continue these exercises, you will base other styles, such as bulleted lists, on this style.

Defining Running Header and Footer Styles

Defining a style for a running header and footer is as simple as defining styles in the body of the text.

When you define a header or footer style Word does *not* automatically place the text in a header or footer. You must still open the header or footer to apply the style.

N O T E

Follow these steps to define your header and footer styles:

1. From the View menu, choose **Header and Footer** (**Alt-V**, **H**). Word opens the header, which displays the text you typed earlier.

2. Select the line of text in the footer and, from the Format menu, choose **Styles**, and then **New**.

3. Follow the same steps you used to apply styles to the Title Page and Headings.

4. Follow the same steps to define styles for the footer.

5. After you define the style, close the Header and Footer dialog box.

Basing Another Style on the Base Text Style

Consistency is one of the most important aspects of any professional document because it indicates your attention to detail in your work. Word helps you to keep your documents in a consistent style.

In this exercise, you define the bulleted items as a style and base it on the style you created in the last exercise.

Defining the Indented Bullets as a Style

Although Word defines a bullet style, you may very well want to use different spacing for the tabs, a different bullet style, such as a dingbat, or even different line spacing and indentation.

After you apply bullets to text, you can redefine them just like the other text you've been working with.

1. Select a bulleted item under the summary heading.

2. Indent the item to align with the base text (.75").

3. Define it as a style called Body Bullet, using the same steps as for the other styles.

Putting Styles To Work

In the exercises you have performed, you have been working mostly on business documents. However, Word for Windows is well-suited for an incredible number of other kinds of documents. For the remainder of this chapter, you learn about some other kinds of formatting for a variety of documents. In addition, we have included some written communication tips to help you when you use Word for Windows for personal use and for business.

Where To Start?

One could start almost anywhere when talking about defining styles and templates, but considering that many of us are hoping to recover from a recession, let's work on that all-important resume. Word's capabilities help you to construct the best possible resume, without having to pay a professional typesetter.

Styles for Your Resume

Everyone needs to keep their resumes up-to-date. You never know when that once-in-a-lifetime opportunity will occur. Even if you are happily married to your job, you should still take a couple of hours to construct your resume. If anything does happen, you've got a place to start. After you finish the resume, use the formatting you've learned about to construct a letter of interest on your own personal letterhead stationery.

Getting Started

Start at the beginning. In this exercise, you put your name, address, and phone number in the header, and define two heading styles, and a body style. Sound too simple? Well, your resume should be simple. For most professions, managers are looking for simple but complete resumes that point out your skills. However, your resume also points out certain organizational and written communication skills that are also important. Too often, resumes are tossed because the applicant either tried too hard or not hard enough to submit the right kind of resume.

Follow these steps to build a resume template.

1. From the File menu, choose **New** (**Alt-F**, **N**). Word displays the New dialog box, which shows defaults of the Normal template and document.
2. Choose **OK**. Word opens a document named Document2.
3. Save the document with a name you choose, for example, MyResume.DOC.

4. From the View menu, choose **Header and Footer** (**Alt-V**, **H**). Word opens the Header and Footer dialog box.

5. In the Header box, type your name, address, and phone number on separate lines.

6. Select all lines and, from the Formatting toolbar, apply a font and point size you like. (Modern works well, and you will apply it to other text later in this exercise.) Choose **B** for bold, and center the text.

7. Select the last line, your phone number, and from the Formatting toolbar, click the **Bottom border** button.

8. Close the Header box. Remember, you will not see the header when you work in Normal view, but you can see how it looks in Page Layout view.

9. At the insertion point, which is still on line one of the document, type **Career Summary**.

10. Select the line of text from the Format menu (**Alt-O**, **F**), choose **Font**, and select the options shown in Figure 6.5.

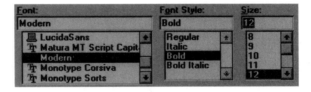

Figure 6.5.

11. Select the line again, from the Paragraph dialog box (**Alt-O**, **P**), select **Left** alignment, **1.5** Space After, and **Single** Line Spacing.

12. With the Paragraph dialog box still open, click the **Text Flow** tab, and select **Keep with Next**.

13. Define this line as a style, called **Heading 1**.

If you know that your resume will be only one page, then choosing **Keep With Next** is not important, since this feature prevents a page break between the heading and text. However, if your resume will be two pages, then select this formatting. (While many people try to keep their resumes to one page, you can break that rule, depending on how long you've been working. Some resume developers allow one page for every 10 years of service.)

N O T E

14. Using the same principles you have been applying in these exercises, choose a level-2 heading for the names of companies where you worked, your titles, and the dates you were employed.

15. Type three lines of text below Career Summary (use the summary of your own career).

16. Select the text and format it with a font and point size that you like from the Formatting toolbar.

Now continue to choose and refine formatting for your resume. Keep it simple. Never use more than two fonts and two or three character formats. No one will be impressed by your knowledge of how many styles you can apply to your resume.

When you finish, define the styles and save the file as a template. You can also modify the resume style sheet included on the disk with this book. Copy it to your hard disk, open it, and type some text in it. Even if you would like to use another format, this is a good place to start in developing your own resume style.

Chapters 5 and 6 have used hands-on exercises to let you practice formatting documents and shown you how to use your existing documents to create document templates, a powerful time-saving feature that makes you work easier. The following chapters teaches you some of the more advanced features of Word.

Summary

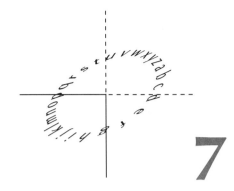

Tables of Contents and Indexes

This chapter describes how to:

- ◆ automatically generate tables of contents
- ◆ generate other types of lists, such as figure lists
- ◆ format a table of contents
- ◆ use Word to create and format an index

Tables of contents and indexes are often the most valuable tools you can give your reader. After all, to use information in any document, you have to be able to find it. Word provides the means for you to build very simple or very complex tables of contents and indexes. Even if you split your document into multiple files, you can link the files and still compile these components of your document with ease.

Tables Of Contents

There are two ways to build tables of contents and other lists:

- ♦ generating with built-in headings
- ♦ generating with styles other than built-in headings

Generating with headings is very simple. Generating with styles is relatively easy, but you need to make sure you have applied the styles consistently throughout the document. Either way, Word gives you a great alternative to the old way of compiling the Table of Contents manually, which leaves room for many errors if you change text or pagination later.

Using either method, there are two main steps that you need to follow:

1. Choose the items you want to appear in the table and apply a style or insert a Table of Contents field.
2. Generate the Table of Contents.

Generating with Headings

Generating the Table of Contents with headings is the simpler of the two methods. To generate a table of contents using headings, you must have applied a heading style to each heading type that you want to include in the document and Table of Contents. (This also applies to any subheading or caption you want to include.) Word lets you decide how many levels you want to include, and you can use this feature to generate several types of tables. For example, you can include lists such as figures, tables, or photographs in addition to the Table of Contents.

The following procedure provides the steps for generating a table of contents using headings. If you have not applied heading styles to your document, see Chapters 5 or 6 for information.

1. Make sure you have applied the correct heading styles to all headings in your document.
2. Position the insertion point where you want to include the Table of Contents in your document (generally, after your title page and before the first chapter or section).

3. From the Insert menu, choose **Index and Tables** (**Alt-I**, **X**). Word displays the Index and Tables dialog box.

4. Click the **Table of Contents** tab.

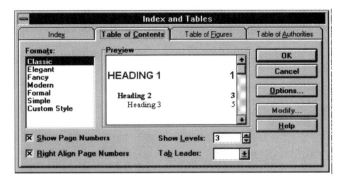

Figure 7.1

5. Select the options that you want to use.

Table 7.1   Table of Contents Options

Select	To do this
Show Page Numbers	Display page numbers in the Table of Contents. This is standard in most documents.
Right Align Page Numbers	Align the page numbers with the right margin. This is also standard in most documents.
Show Levels box	Choose the number of hierarchical levels you want in the Table of Contents.
A number in the Tab Leader box	Choose the type of leader character (the character you want to appear between the entry and the page number) you want between the Table of Contents entry and the page number.

6. Choose **OK**.

You can halt the process at any time by pressing **Esc**.

NOTE

When Word finishes compiling the Table of Contents, you can view it where you inserted it.

If you have many levels of headings in your document, you might want to include only headings 1 through 3 or 4 in your Table of Contents. If you include many levels, for example, 5 or 6, your Table of Contents might be very long and unattractive. Generally, your reader will get a clear picture of the contents with a few levels.

NOTE

Generating with Styles

Generally, you use styles to generate a table of contents when you have defined your own heading styles or if you want to create a table other than the Table of Contents. For example, you might want to include a list of graphics, such as tables, illustrations, or photographs. To generate this list, however, you must first apply the styles to the text. You can do this while you are developing your document, or afterward when you are ready to generate your table.

Follow these steps:

1. Position the insertion point where you want to insert the Table of Contents.
2. From the Insert menu, choose **Index and Tables** (**Alt-I, X**).
3. Click the **Table of Contents** tab.
4. In the Formats box, select the format you want for the Table of Contents.
5. Choose **Options**. Word displays the Table of Contents Options dialog box, shown in Figure 7.2.
6. In the Available Styles box, find the style you want to use for a specific table of contents level.
7. In the TOC Level box to the right of the style name, type a number from 1 to 9 to indicate the table of contents level you want headings formatted with that style to represent.

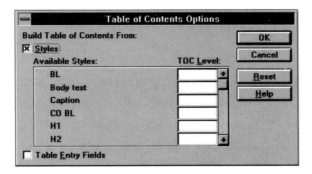

Figure 7.2

8. Repeat steps 6 and 7 for all styles you want to compile in the Table of Contents.

9. Delete any table of contents level numbers in the list that correspond to styles you do not want to include in the table.

10. Choose **OK** to close the dialog box. The Preview box shows the styles selected in the Options dialog box.

11. Choose **OK** to compile the Table of Contents.

Updating a Table of Contents

Have you ever had to go back in your document and add more information and illustrations? If you haven't, then congratulations. You are a rare find. If you have, then you probably know how frustrating it can be to renumber the items and then redo the tables and lists.

You can generate a table of contents any time you want while working in a Word document. If you add information to your document after you generate the Table of Contents, you can run it again, and Word replaces the current Table of Contents with the updated version. Even if you add some text without a new heading, update the Table of Contents again to ensure correct page numbering.

Follow these steps to update the Table of Contents:

1. Position the insertion point in the table of contents you want to update.

2. Press **F9**.

3. Perform one of the options in Table 7.2 on the next page.

Table 7.2   Table of Contents Updating Options

To update	Do this
Page numbers only	Select **Update Page Numbers Only**. Word retains any direct formatting you applied to the Table of Contents.
The entire Table of Contents	Select **Update Entire Table**.

4.   Choose **OK**.

You can generate a table of contents any time you want while working in a Word document. If you add information to your document after you generate the Table of Contents, press **F9** again, and Word replaces the current Table of Contents with the updated version. Even if you add some text without a new heading, generate the Table of Contents again to ensure correct page numbering.

Changing the Look of the Table of Contents

Word formats the Table of Contents automatically, and uses a built-in style for up to eight levels, no matter what style you apply to the text in your document.

Choosing a Formatting Style

The easiest way to change the Table of Contents formatting is to choose a format you like from the Table of Contents dialog box, because if you merely apply a new format to the Table of Contents after you generate it, Word throws out the new formatting when you compile it again. Follow these steps:

1.   From the Insert menu, choose **Index and Tables** (**Alt-I**, **X**).
2.   Click **Table of Contents**, and choose a style in the Formats box.

N O T E

Choose a style that you think will coordinate well with the text and style of your document. Otherwise, it might look out of place.

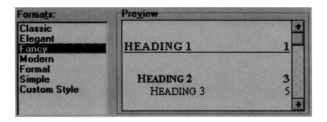

Figure 7.3

The Preview box shows how the Table of Contents will look after you generate it.

3. Choose **OK**.

After you generate a table of contents, you can also change its format the same way you format any other text. However, this is not efficient because you have to reapply it each time you replace or update the Table of Contents.

Creating Tables of Figures and Other Items

In many kinds of business, technical, and scientific documents, you need to include tables of figures and other kinds of graphics. Word enables you to do this very easily, and it saves you lots of time.

1. Insert captions in the document, and for each one, use the Caption command on the Insert menu. To do this, position the insertion point where you want the caption, press **Alt-I**, **I**, type a caption in the Caption box, and choose **OK**.
2. Position the insertion point where you want to insert the table of figures.
3. From the Insert menu, choose **Index and Tables**.
4. Select the **Table of Figures** tab.
5. In the Caption Label box, select the type of caption label you want to compile in the table of figures.

If you want, you can select the options in Table 7.3 on the next page.

Table 7.3 Table of Figures Options

Select	To do this
Show Page Numbers	Display page numbers.
Include Label and Number	Include the caption label and number in the table of figures.

Indexes

Word's indexing feature makes it easy for you to compile a simple main-entry index or a complex one with multiple levels of entries. When creating an index, you need to have a draft of your document, although it does not have to be complete. Some authors add index entries as they develop the draft. The choice is yours, but many authors prefer to have the document nearly complete before starting. That way, they don't have to remember how they listed an entry in yesterday's version.

Single-Level Entries

An index with single-level entries shows only main entries from the text, with no indented subentries. This type is the simplest index to build. For many documents, however, the single-level index will not be enough, and you will need to include a multiple-entry index.

Multiple-Level Entries

A multiple-level index is probably more useful in any long document. This type of index is a little more complicated to build in Word and requires more thought. You will need to plan what to index, and you will probably have to make some notes as you add entries.

Inserting Index Entries

Before you generate the index in Word, you need to insert the entries in the text. You have two options for inserting the entries:

- selecting text (words or phrases) in the document and marking them as index entries
- typing the entries next to the text you want to index, and marking them as index entries

You can have a maximum of 64 characters in any index entry.

If you choose to type entries to index near the text rather than select the text itself for an entry, make sure you type the entry next to the topic to index. Otherwise, the typed entry might fall on the next page, and the page numbers will not be correct in the index.

N O T E

Follow these steps to mark insert entries in the text:

1. For each index entry, select the text in the document that you want to appear as an index entry, or position the insertion point where you want to type the index entry.

2. From the Insert menu, choose **Index and Tables** (**Alt-I**, **X**), and click **Index**.

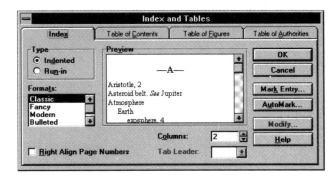

Figure 7.4

3. Choose **Mark Entry**. If you chose to make existing text an entry, the selected text appears in the Main Entry box, as in Figure 7.5 on the next page.

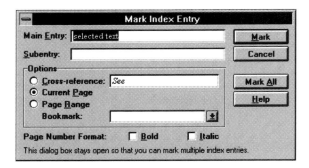

Figure 7.5

If you did not select text, the Main Entry box is clear.

4. In the Main Entry box, type an entry or edit the existing entry. If you want to include a subentry, enter it in the Subentry box.

5. If you want, you can choose to have the page number, bold, italic, or both. If you want to show a range of pages for an entry, see "Indicating a Range of Pages" following this procedure for more information.

6. Choose **OK**. Word includes the entry in the index when the index is generated. (The dialog box stays open for repeated use.).

7. Choose **Close** when you are done.

Indicating a Range of Pages

If a subject in your document is discussed over a range of pages, you can show that range in the index. For example, a topic might appear on pages 3 through 5. Follow these steps to show the range:

1. Make sure that the Main Entry box in the Mark Index Entry dialog box contains the index entry for which you want to indicate a range of pages.

2. Under Options, select the **Page Range** option. In the Bookmark box, type a bookmark name for the range of pages.

3. Choose **Mark** to create the index entry.

4. Choose **Close**.

5. In the document, select the range of text you want the index entry to refer to, and then choose **Bookmark** from the Edit menu.

6. In the Bookmark Name box, type the *same* bookmark name you typed in step 2 and choose **Add**.

Following an Entry with a Cross-Reference

Sometimes you need to cross-reference an entry with "See reference" or "See also reference" instead of a page number.

Follow these steps to add text after an entry:

1. Make sure that the Main Entry box in the Mark Index Entry dialog box contains the index entry for which you want to create the index cross-reference.

2. Under Options, select the **Cross-reference** option button, and then type the text you want to use as a cross-reference for the entry. Word displays *See* in italic before the cross-reference. You can delete the word, if you want, and add additional text.

3. If you want to apply character formatting to the cross-reference text, select the text and press formatting shortcut keys (for example **Ctrl-B** for bold text).

4. Choose **Mark**.

5. When you finish, choose **Close**.

Showing Chapter-Page Numbers in an Index

If you set up your document so that you have chapter-page numbers, then Word includes them in the index. For more information about setting up chapter-page numbers, see Chapter 2.

Generating the Index

Follow these steps to generate an index so you can include it in your document:

1. Insert all index entries.

2. Position the insertion point where you want to insert the index.

3. From the Insert menu, choose **Index and Tables** (**Alt-I**, **X**), and click **Index**.

4. Under Type, select one of the options in Table 7.3 on the next page.

Table 7.3 Generate Index Options

Select	To do this
Indented	Place subentries below the main entry.
Run-in	Place subentries on the same line as the main entry.

5. In the Formats box, select an index format.

6. Choose one or more of the options in Table 7.4.

Table 7.4 Index Format Options

To	Do this
Align page numbers with the right margin	Select **Right Align Page Numbers**.
Format the index with multiple columns	In the Columns box, type or select a number from 1 to 4. Selecting the **Auto** option retains the existing column formatting in the document.
Insert tab leader characters between index entries and page numbers	In the Tab Leader box, select the tab leader character you want to use.

7. Choose **OK**.

Word inserts the index where you positioned the insertion point.

Updating the Index

When you add or edit index entries, you press **F9** to update the index. To keep your index up-to-date, it's easiest to changes index entries in the document and then update the index. If you update the generated index only, you lose all changes each time you regenerate the index.

Summary

In this chapter, you have learned how to make your Word documents more valuable to your readers by generating and adding tables of contents, lists of figures, and indexes. In the chapters that follow, you learn how to add graphic elements, such as graphs and drawings, to your documents.

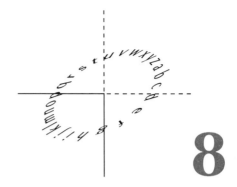

Formatting Forms and Tables

Word's table and form features can make your business or personal documents much easier to work with than if you had to create them manually. In this chapter you learn to:

- ♦ understand forms and terms
- ♦ create an online form
- ♦ create a checkbox form field
- ♦ format tables

With the forms feature, you no longer have to deal with the repetitive tasks of retyping letters, business forms, and other documents that you need to personalize for each situation. You simply write your letter or design your form in a template, and insert fields that you can update quickly and easily. For example, if you have a small business that requires you to send billing notices each month, you can create a billing form with fields that you can update for the names and addresses, date, and amount due.

With the table feature, you can create an endless variety of tables to use in business, technical, and many other kinds of documents. This time-saving feature helps you display information clearly, in tabular format, without having to insert the tabs, spaces, or lines required in manual table formatting.

In this chapter, you learn some very basic steps that will get you started with the Forms feature. The exercise saves you time in learning because the text you work with is on the disk packaged with this book, and you don't have to type the letter. The disk also contains a variety of useful forms that you can copy to your local disk and use as is, or modify to suit your needs.

Understanding Forms Terms

To get started, you need to be familiar with the term *online form*. This is a form that you create and save as a template. To update the information, you open a file in the template for the form you create, and enter the information in Word rather than printing the form and filling in the information by hand. Although Word contains several online forms you can use, you will benefit from this feature most by learning how to build and customize a form containing your own preferences.

In this chapter, you will also see the term *field* or *form field*. This is a box that you fill in with the customized information, for example, dates, check boxes, and other items.

Creating Your First Online Form

This exercise helps you learn about creating online forms. You use the Form.Dot file on the disk packaged with this book to make a simple business form letter.

1. Copy Form.Dot to your hard disk in the directory of your choice.
2. Open the file in Word.
3. Select the date in the letter, and from the Insert menu, choose **Form Field** (**Alt-I**, **M**).

Word displays the Form Field dialog box, shown in Figure 8.1.

Figure 8.1

4. Choose **Text** and then choose **Options**. Word displays the Text Form Field Options dialog box, shown below.

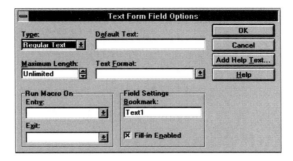

Figure 8.2

5. Under Type, select **Current Date** and under Date Format, select the **MMMM-D-YYYY** format to have Word insert today's date and highlight the field in gray.

6. Select Gaby and Gian.

7. From the Insert menu, choose **Form Field** again. This time, select **Drop-Down** and then choose **Options**. Word displays the Drop-Down Form Field Options dialog box, shown in Figure 8.3.

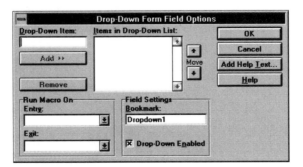

Figure 8.3

8. In the Drop-Down Item box, type the name of a friend or couple, and click **Add** or press **Enter** to add the name to the Items in Drop-Down List box. Click **OK**.

9. Add one or two other names, clicking **Add** each time. Choose **OK** when done.

10. In the first paragraph, select the word Thanksgiving, and use the same method as in steps 7 through 9 to make this a drop-down field also. Add to the Items in Drop-Down List box, Christmas, July 4th, and Easter.

11. In the second paragraph, select the words cat, Xanadu and use the same method as in steps 7 through 9 to make this a drop-down field. Add some other pet types and names, separated by a comma.

NOTE It is very important to be consistent with punctuation and capitalization and to use the same syntax for phrases when using form fields. This way, you will be sure that your letters contain grammatically correct sentences.

In the remainder of the letter, select these phrases, and make each one a form field with variable information:

- **10 percent discount** (you might change these for different seasons)
- **November 1st** (make sure this date is a week or two *before* the holiday)
- **her gentle purr** (add items that pertain to other pet habits and be sure to duplicate each item for male pets)
- **brush her** (add verbs other than brush and duplicate each item for male pets)
- **changes the cat box** (add an item for another chore).

Now you have your first online form. Experiment with it by selecting an option you've added for each field, saving the file with a new name, and printing it. Each time you need to use it, you can open it, use the Save As command from the File menu to give it a new name, and change it as you want.

Creating a Check Box Form Field

Suppose Pet Sitters, Inc. (from the previous exercise) wants to provide their customers with a list to verify chores they performed while caring for the pets. It's most efficient to have only one list, and update it as necessary for each client. For example, you might have a list that looks like Figure 8.4.

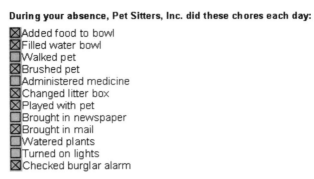

Figure 8.4

To add check box form fields:

1. Open a file.

2. Type all entries you want to use in your form.

3. Position the insertion point at the beginning of each item you want to define as a form field.

4. From the Insert menu, choose **Form Field (Alt-I, M)**.

5. In the Form Field dialog box, select **Check Box** and **Options**. Word displays the Check Box Form Field Options dialog box.

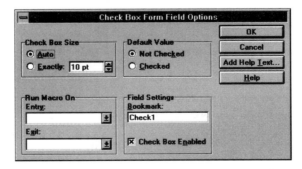

Figure 8.5

6. Select **Auto** or an exact point size, and whether you want the box checked, and choose **OK**.

7. Save the file as a template.

Now each time Pet Sitters, Inc., needs to use this form, they can open it online, click on the check box form fields, select whether to check the box, choose **OK**, **Print**, and **Save**.

Formatting Tables

If you have ever constructed a table using a typewriter or an unsophisticated word processor, you know how frustrating it can be. Setting correct tabs and spacing for each column, not to mention fitting them on the page, has made more than one author reevaluate whether to even include important information in a document.

Word's table feature is so flexible that you can use it for much more than just presenting tabular information. You can use it to construct resumes, business forms, form letters, mailing labels, and even newsletters and brochures. In fact, you can construct almost any text that you need to place in columns, using the table feature. You might even want to sit and experiment with the table feature, just playing with it, to see how much you can do.

You have two options for choosing to place information in a table: the toolbar and the Table menu. Afterward, if you decide you want to present the information in a different format, you can convert the tabular information back to a normal text format with just a couple of clicks or keystrokes.

This section of the chapter covers the basics of what you need to begin constructing and converting text and tables.

Inserting a Table Using the Toolbar

The **Table** button on the Standard toolbar is the quickest way to set up a table, but it does not give you as many options as the Table menu does. Use the toolbar for simpler table setup, for example, if you just want Word to use the default table width or if you are just beginning to type tabular information and you need two columns the full width of the page.

To insert a table from the Standard toolbar:

1. Position the insertion point where you want to insert a table.

2. Click the **Insert Table** button. Word displays a grid representing columns and rows.

Figure 8.6

3.   Drag the mouse cursor to select the number of rows and columns you need. If you need more columns and rows, you can add them, using commands from the Table menu.

4.   Release the mouse button to insert the table.

Figure 8.7

To display the table gridlines, press **Alt-A**, **L**. You can hide the gridlines the same way.

N O T E

Inserting a Table Using the Table Menu

The Table menu gives you enough options to make almost any kind of table you need. Follow these steps to insert an empty table using the Insert Table command.

1.   Position the insertion point where you want to insert a table.

2.   From the Table menu, choose **Insert Table** (**Alt-A**, **I**). Word displays the Insert Table dialog box, shown in Figure 8.8 on the next page.

3.   Type or select the number of columns and rows you want, and select the column width, or choose **OK** to accept the default settings of two columns, one row and automatic width, which you can change later.

4.   If you typed or selected settings, choose **OK**. Word inserts the empty table. You can press **Enter** to add lines of space or start new paragraphs in a cell.

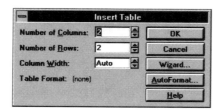

Figure 8.8

Press **Tab** to move to the cell in the next column. When you reach the last cell in a row, pressing **Tab** moves the insertion to the first cell in the next row. Pressing **Tab** in the last cell of a table creates a new row.

If you define a column that has a cell too long for your page, Word breaks the page before the row containing that cell. It will not break the page in the middle of cell.

Changing the Column Width

If you want to increase or decrease the column width, drag the mouse cursor slowly over the vertical gridline of the column you want to change. When the cursor changes to two small vertical lines with arrows pointing in both directions, you can drag the line of the table to the left or right. This action activates the Ruler, and you can see the measurements of your table column. Also, you can select an entire column (by moving the cursor over the top line of the first cell and clicking), and move the table marker on the Ruler to the left or right.

To have Word change the column width automatically:

1. Select the table (**Alt-A**, **A**), or any number of columns if you don't want them all the same width.
2. From the Table menu, choose **Cell Height and Width** and select the **Column** tab.
3. Choose **AutoFit**.

Word resizes the columns according to their content.

Converting Text to a Table

Suppose you created a table in an early version of Microsoft Word for DOS or another word processing package where you had to construct the table with tabs.

You can convert that text to a table format very easily in Word 6.0. If the table does not have tabs, insert them before you begin.

Follow these steps to convert text to a table:

1. Select the text or paragraphs you want to convert.

2. From the Table menu, choose **Convert Text to Table (Alt-A, V)**. Word either converts the text to a table with as many columns and rows as are necessary or displays the Convert Text to Table dialog box, listing different conversion options. If it displays the dialog box, you can tell it how to convert.

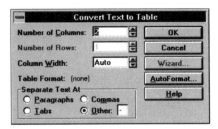

Figure 8.9

3. If necessary, in the Convert Text to Table dialog box, select the conversion options you need and choose **OK**.

If you constructed the text table with irregular tab spacing, or with a combination of tabs and spaces, you might need to cancel and use a consistent separator before converting the text to a table.

N O T E

You can undo the conversion immediately after converting by pressing **Alt-E, U**.

Converting a Table to Text

After you construct a table, you might decide later to present your information as paragraph text or in another format. You can convert the information easily, but if it is a complex table with many elements and special formatting, you will probably have to work with the text some to make it look like you want.

1. Select the rows of the table that you want to convert.

2. From the Table menu, choose **Convert Table to Text** (**Alt-A**, **V**). Word displays the Convert Table to Text dialog box with its suggested separator selected as the default.

3. Select the separator you want or choose **OK** to accept Word's suggested separator.

Word converts the table to text. Look through the text and see if you need to remove any extra formatting separators.

Inserting a Graphic in a Table

You can insert a graphic in a table cell. For example, if you need to show a table that describes the parts of an object, you can draw them in the Draw program or WordArt (or from another drawing application), and insert them in cells very easily, as Figure 8.10 shows.

Icon	Description
Shortcut	Indicates that this is an easier way to perform a step.

Figure 8.10

Follow these steps to insert a WordArt graphic in a table.

1. Create the table as described in one of the previous procedures.

2. Position the insertion point in the cell in which you want to insert a graphic.

3. From the Insert menu, choose **Object** (**Alt-I**, **O**) and then choose **Microsoft WordArt 2.0**).

4. Type your text, select a line and shape style, and close WordArt. Word inserts the graphic in the cell.

For more information about using WordArt, see Chapter 9, *Using Microsoft Draw and WordArt*.

N O T E

Changing a Table

No matter what dimensions and elements you give tables, you can change them. After you create a table you can:

- ◆ move rows, columns and cells
- ◆ insert rows, columns, and cells
- ◆ delete rows, columns and cells
- ◆ merge cells to change columns

Moving and Copying Rows, Columns, and Cells

You can move or copy a row of cells, or an individual column, or cell.

1. Select the row, column, or cells you want to move or copy.
2. Position the mouse pointer over the selection, and when the arrow points to the left choose one of the following actions in Table 8.1.

Table 8.1   Move and Copy Options

To	Do this
Move the selected row, column, or cell	Drag it to the new location.
Copy the selection	Hold down **Ctrl** while you drag the selection.

Inserting Rows, Columns, and Cells

Inserting rows, columns, and cells in a table requires a few more steps than inserting more text in a paragraph or more characters in a word. If you are working in a table, you press **Tab** to create a new row at the end of the last one in the table, but if you go back to add a cell between two others, pressing **Tab** only takes you to the next cell; it does not create a new one. Also, as you are working in a table, pressing **Enter** only adds more lines of space in a paragraph within a cell. It is still relatively simple to add more rows, columns, and cells in a table.

To insert rows:

1. Select the rows below where you want to insert a new row. Select as many rows as you want to add.

Project Task	Project Lead	Start Date	End Date
Write project plans	Jeff Haas	1/4/94	2/4/94
Assign staff	Cindy Adams	1/10/94	1/17/94
Determine documentation requirements	John Kelly	1/7/94	2/10/94

Figure 8.11

2. From the Table menu, choose Insert Rows (**Alt-A**, **I**).

Word shifts the selected rows down and adds as many empty rows as you selected.

Project Task	Project Lead	Start Date	End Date
Write project plans	Jeff Haas	1/4/94	2/4/94
Assign staff	Cindy Adams	1/10/94	1/17/94
Determine documentation requirements	John Kelly	1/7/94	2/10/94

Figure 8.12

To insert columns:

1. Select a column or group of columns to the right of where you want to insert a new column or columns.

Project Task	Project Lead	Start Date	End Date
Write project plans	Jeff Haas	1/4/94	2/4/94
Assign staff	Cindy Adams	1/10/94	1/17/94
Determine documentation requirements	John Kelly	1/7/94	2/10/94

Figure 8.13

2. From the Table menu, choose **Insert Columns (Alt-A, I)**.

Project Task	Project Lead		Start Date	End Date
Write project plans	Jeff Haas		1/4/94	2/4/94
Assign staff	Cindy Adams		1/10/94	1/17/94
Determine documentation requirements	John Kelly		1/7/94	2/10/94

Figure 8.14

If you make the table too wide for the margins, you can decrease the width of the column or reset the margins. Select the cells you need to change, choose **Cell Height and Width** from the Table menu, select the **Column** tab, and make adjustments as necessary.

To insert cells:

1. Select a cell or cells next to where you want to insert new ones.
2. From the Table menu, choose **Insert Cells (Alt-A, I)**.

You only see this command if you have a few cells selected, not a column or row.

N O T E

Word displays the Insert Cells dialog box.

3. Select how you want shift the cells, and choose **OK**.

Table 8.2   Cell Shifting Options

Select this option	To insert
Shift Cells Right	New cells to the left of the selected cells.
Shift Cells Down	New cells above the selected cells.
Insert Entire Row	A row of cells.
Insert Entire Column	A column of cells.

Deleting Rows, Columns, and Cells

Deleting rows, columns, and cells is just as easy as adding them. One thing to remember, though, is that you cannot use the Delete or Backspace keys to delete any cells in a table—only the text they contain. You have to delete cells from the Table menu.

To delete rows or columns:

1. Select the row or column you want to delete.

2. From the Table menu, choose **Delete Rows** or **Delete Columns**, depending on which you selected (**Alt-A**, **D**).

To delete cells:

1. Select the cells to delete.

2. From the Table menu, choose **Delete Cells** (**Alt-A**, **D**).

N O T E

You only see this command if you have a few cells selected, not a column or row.

Word displays the Delete Cells dialog box.

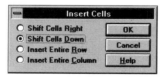

Figure 8.15

3. Select how you want shift the cells, and choose **OK**.

Table 8.3   Cell Shifting Options

Select this option	To do this
Shift Cells Left	Shift cells left after you delete the selected ones.

Shift Cells Up	Move cells up after you delete the selected ones.
Delete Entire Row	Delete the row or rows.
Delete Entire Column	Delete the column or columns.

Merging Cells

If you decide that you want to merge two or more cells to make one wider cell, select the two cells. Then, from the Table menu, choose **Merge Cells (Alt-A, M)**. Word moves all the text of the two cells into one cell. This only merges side-by-side cells.

If you change your mind and decide to split the cell, select it, and choose **Split Cell** from the Table menu (**Alt-A, P**).

Adding Borders to Tables

You can apply a border to tables, using the Borders and Shading toolbar.

1. Select the rows, columns, or cells to which you want to add a border.
2. On the Borders and Shading toolbar, select a line style, and click the **Border** button indicating where to add the border, or, from the Format menu, choose **Borders and Shading (Alt-O, B)**. Word displays the Borders and Shading dialog box.
3. Select the border and shading options you want.
4. Choose **OK**.

Word applies the border to the table.

Repeating Column Headings in Long Tables

If your table spans more than one page, you have to repeat the headers so your table will still make sense for the user.

1. Select the row or rows of text, beginning with the first row in the table, you want to use as table headings.
2. From the Table menu, choose **Headings (Alt-A, H)**.

Now, when you modify headings in a long table, Word repeats the headings on each page.

Splitting a Table

If you make a table and then decide that the information would be well-suited in two or more tables, you can split the table wherever you want.

1. Select the cells you want to split.

2. From the Table menu, choose **Split Cells**.

3. In the Split Cells dialog box, accept the number of columns Word proposes, or select a different number

4. Choose **OK**.

Summary

This chapter taught you how to save many hours of time and stress by using the Forms feature and the Table feature in Word. Now you have come a long way in learning about formatting, styles, templates, forms, and tables. Move on the next chapter, where you learn how to add professional-quality graphics to your documents.

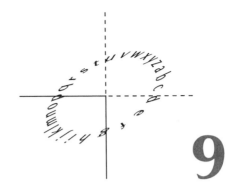

9

Using Microsoft Draw and WordArt

D raw is a graphical drawing feature that only runs inside of Word. With Draw, you can create diagrams and pictures to enhance your text documents without having to create it somewhere else and import it. This saves you a lot of time. It also saves you money because you don't have to purchase another drawing package to create simple drawings. All you have to do is decide where you want your drawing, make sure you Drawing toolbar is displayed, and start drawing.

This chapter explains how you can use Draw to:

- use the drawing tools to create objects
- import picture files created by other applications into your Word document
- edit drawing objects
- rotate, flip, or resize drawings

159

Displaying The Drawing Toolbar

You must be running Word and have a document open to use the Draw feature. Also, you can only draw in the Page Layout view.

1. Open a document.

2. From the View menu, choose **Toolbars** (**Alt-V**, **T**).

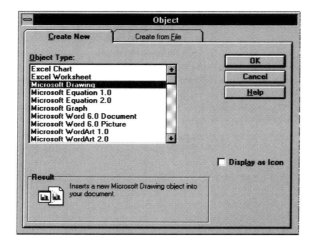

Figure 9.1

3. Select **Drawing** and choose **OK**.

Word displays the Drawing toolbar at the bottom of your work area.

You can also invoke the draw feature by double-clicking on an existing graphic.

NOTE

If you are not working in Page Layout view when you click a tool on the Drawing toolbar, Word asks if you want to enter Page Layout view. Choose **OK** and click a tool to begin drawing. Word displays the Drawing toolbar and your document in Page Layout view. If you click on an existing Draw graphic, you see the graphic in the work area.

The Drawing Toolbar

The Drawing toolbar displays all of the buttons you need to create and edit your drawing.

Position your mouse cursor on each **Drawing Toolbar** button. Word displays the name of each in the yellow pop-up box. You can check for the names of the buttons at any time while you draw.

Figure 9.2

The Basic Drawing Buttons and How to Use Them

The first five buttons are the tools you use to draw objects and insert text or callouts. Like the different brushes and tools an artist might use, each Draw tool has a unique purpose.

Line Tool

The Line tool draws a straight line in any direction.

1. From the Drawing toolbar, click the **Line tool**.
2. Hold down the mouse button and drag the pointer to where you want the line to stop. If you want to constrain the line to a straight vertical, horizontal, or 45-degree angle, hold down **Shift** while you drag.
3. Release the mouse button.

If you want to delete the line, select it (click it anywhere) and press **Del**. This action deletes only the selected line in a drawing. All unselected lines remain.

N O T E

Square and Rectangle

Use the Rectangle/Square tool to draw a square or a rectangle.

1. From the Drawing toolbar, click the **Rectangle/Square** tool.

2. To draw a rectangle:
   - ◆ Position the pointer where you want to start.
   - ◆ Hold down the mouse button and drag it in any direction.
3. To draw a square:
   - ◆ Position the pointer where you want to start.
   - ◆ Hold down **Shift** while you hold down the mouse button and drag in any direction. This causes the square to have the same height and width.

Ellipse/Circle Tool

Use the Ellipse/Circle tool to draw an ellipse or a circle.

1. Click the **Ellipse/Circle** tool.
2. To draw an ellipse:
   - ◆ Position the pointer where you want to start.
   - ◆ Hold down the mouse button and drag in any direction.
3. To draw a circle:
   - ◆ Position the pointer where you want to start.
   - ◆ Hold down **Shift** while you hold down the mouse button and drag diagonally in any direction. This causes the circle to have the same height and width.

Arc Tool

Use the Arc tool to draw an arc. All arcs are 90 degrees at first. You can edit them later to make them less than 90 degrees.

1. Click the **Arc** tool and drag to where you want to begin one end of the arc.
2. Hold down the mouse button and drag to where you want to end the arc.
3. Release the mouse button.

Freeform Tool

Use the Freeform tool to draw freehand-style objects, polygons (such as pentagons or octagons), or a combination of the two styles. Draw allows you to draw straight and "curved" lines in the same graphic. However, the curved lines are really a lot of short, straight, connected lines that appear to make a curve. Follow these steps to draw a freeform object:

1. Click the **Freeform** tool. The mouse pointer becomes a crosshair, and then a small pencil icon when you click the left mouse button.
2. Begin drawing. Click to create straight line segments, and drag to create freeform shapes.
3. Double-click to complete the object.

It's a little difficult sometimes to draw a straight line with the Freeform tool. If you don't have a very steady hand, you might want to draw your straight lines with the Line tool, and then select the Freeform tool to draw the curved lines. Also, you can hold down **Shift** while using the Freeform tool to constrict clicks to 45-degree angles, or vertical or horizontal lines.

Tools for Creating Text

Many graphics would be incomplete without some text. Much of the time, the look of the text is as important as the graphic itself. Other times, the text *is* the graphic.

Text Box Tool

Use the Text Box tool to add text to your drawing. As you type, the text box grows to accommodate the amount of text you type. The text is always in the Normal style; however, you can select the text after you type it, and apply the font of your choice.

1. Select the **Text Box** tool.
2. Drag until the box is the size you want. The mouse pointer becomes an I-beam cursor.

When you press **Enter**, you start a new line, which means that you are creating a new text object. You can move these lines independently of each other, or you can group them to move them together. See "Grouping and Ungrouping Objects" later in this chapter for more information.

Callout Tool

Sometimes a graphic is more meaningful if you add a little text to explain some of the parts. For example, if you are illustrating a machine, you can add a callout to point out the button that turns on the machine.

1. Click the **Text Box** button.
2. Position the pointer where you want to start the callout line and drag to the point where you want to place the text.
3. Type the text in the box.

Format Callout Tool

The Format Callout tool lets you add lines, a border, or both to a callout. This is helpful when you want to make it clear to your reader which piece of callout text describes which piece of your illustration.

1. Click the **Format Callout** button. Word displays the Format Callout dialog box. The diagrams in the Type box show four angle types.
2. Select an angle type for the callout line.
3. Select other options to give the callout the look you want.

Table 9.1   Callout Options

Option	Description
Gap	Lets you select the distance between the callout text and the callout line.
Angle	Lets you position the angle of the callout line.
Drop	Lets you select an amount of space between the top of the callout text and the start of the callout line segment.
Text Border	Lets you add a border around the callout text.
Auto Attach	Causes Word to move the callout to the bottom of the text when the callout text is positioned to the left of the callout line's point of origin.
Add Accent Bar	Adds a vertical line beside the callout text.

Now that you have some idea about how to use the basic drawing and text tools, follow the procedures in the rest of the chapter to create and edit drawings.

Creating a Drawing

Even if you don't consider yourself an artist, you can still create some simple graphics in Word. For example, you might need to draw an employee organization chart, which consists of mainly rectangular boxes and lines.

1. On the Standard toolbar, click the **Drawing** button to display the Drawing toolbar.
2. On the Drawing toolbar, click the drawing tool you need (described earlier in this chapter) and drag to the place where you want to begin.

Word updates your document and places the graphic where you positioned the insertion point.

Importing a Drawing

Even if you didn't use Word to create a graphic, you can still edit it in Word. You can import graphic files in many formats. For more information about these file formats, click **Help** on the Standard toolbar.

To import an entire graphics file:

1. Position the insertion point where you want to insert the graphic.
2. From the Insert menu, choose **Picture** (**Alt-I**, **P**).
3. In the File Name box, type or select the drive, directory, or folder where the file is located.
4. Choose **OK**.

To import a picture that is part of a text or other type of file:

1. Open that file.
2. Copy the graphic to the Clipboard.

3. Open your Word file and paste the graphic where you want it. Word inserts the picture at the last position of the insertion point in the Word document.

For detailed information about how to work with imported graphics, see your Word documentation.

Editing a Word Drawing

After you create a drawing, you can reshape it, add color, add text, and flip it to another angle.

To make changes to an existing Word drawing in your document, double-click a picture or object in your document. You can make changes to your graphic "onsite."

Before you begin editing, you should understand how to select objects.

Selecting Objects

Before you make any changes to an object you've drawn, you must select it.

1. From the Drawing toolbar, click the **Select Drawing Objects** (arrow-shaped) tool.

2. Do one of the following:
   - ◆ To select a drawing objects *in front of text*, position the pointer on the object.
   - ◆ To select objects *behind* text, click the **Select Drawing Objects** button on the Drawing toolbar.

3. Do one of the following:

Table 9.2 Selecting Objects

To	Do This
Select a single object	Position the pointer inside the object you want to select, and click.
Select multiple objects	Hold down **Shift** while you click each object you want to select or click the **Select Drawing Objects** button and

	drag to create a rectangle that encloses all of the drawing objects you want to select.
Select all individual line segments in a freeform shape	Click the shape to select it, and click the **Reshape** button on the Drawing toolbar.
Cancel a selection	Hold down **Shift** and click on the object.

Figure 9.3 shows three objects. The middle one is selected. Notice the selection handles, indicating that the object is selected. The anchor symbol to the left of the drawing indicates that the text is anchored, or attached, to the text where you are creating the drawing.

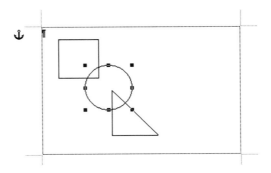

Figure 9.3

Copying Objects

If you need to have several identical objects, you don't have to draw each one individually. You just draw the first one and copy it.

To copy an object, select the object to copy, hold down **Ctrl**, and drag the object. You will see an outline of the object and when you release the mouse button, the object will be duplicated.

Resizing an Object

You can resize the graphic after you place it in the document. While you have the graphic selected, move the mouse pointer slowly over one of the corner selection handles until the handle becomes an arrow on both ends. Then, move the pointer to push in or pull out on a handle to resize it. Remember, though, that sometimes the graphic loses detail if you size it too small. Also, a graphic may need more detail if you size it too large.

To make sure you keep the original proportions, hold down **Shift** while you drag. To resize from the center, hold down **Ctrl** while you drag.

Deleting the Selected Objects

After you select an object, you can choose to delete it. Press **Del** and Draw deletes all the selected objects.

If you want to restore the object, you can choose **Undo** from the Edit menu (**Alt-E, U**). Note that Undo only reverses your most recent editing operation, so you must *not* have done any other editing operations between deleting the object and restoring it with Undo.

Placing Selected Objects in Front of or Behind All Other Objects

To create a special effect, you might want to move an object in front of or behind other objects.

In this picture, the circle is "in front" of the square (the circle obscures part of the square):

Figure 9.4

By selecting the circle and then choosing the **Send to Back** button, the square obscures a portion of the circle.

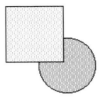

Figure 9.5

You can also move objects in front of or behind text by selecting the object and clicking the **Bring in Front of Text** and **Send Behind Text** buttons.

To place text and objects in front of or behind other objects:

1. On the Standard toolbar, click the **Drawing** button to display the Drawing toolbar.

2. Select an object.

3. Perform one of the following:

Table 9.3   Placing Objects

To do this	Click
Place the object in front of other objects	
Place the object behind other objects	
Place the object in front of text	
Place the object behind the text	

Grouping and Ungrouping Objects

When you create a drawing that contains a wide variety of objects, you might find at times that you want to do the same thing, at the same time, to a number of objects in the drawing. For example, you might want to rotate a group of objects horizontally for a special effect. *Grouping* provides a means for you to do this.

Follow these steps to group objects together:

1. Select the objects in your drawing that you want to group.

2. On the Drawing toolbar, click the **Select Drawing Objects** button.

3. Drag to select the drawing objects you want to group, or hold **Shift** and click each object.

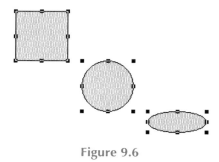

Figure 9.6

4. On the Drawing toolbar, click the **Group** button.

Figure 9.7 shows the items after grouping.

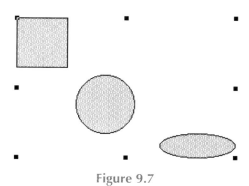

Figure 9.7

At this point, you can treat your group objects as a single object if you choose. You can also ungroup the objects.

Follow these steps to ungroup objects:

1. Select the group.

2. On the Drawing toolbar, click the **Ungroup** button.

Now, you can select each element in the group individually.

For multiple groups, you must ungroup each one separately.

N O T E

Filling an Object with Color

If you are working on a document that you plan to send out for color printing, you can choose the colors for your graphics in Microsoft Draw. (For black and white patterns, you have what you need to work with.)

1. Select the object.
2. On the Drawing toolbar, click the **Fill Color** button.

You can also choose a fill color by selecting the object, choosing **Drawing Object** from the Format menu (**Alt-O, O**), and selecting a color from the Drawing Object dialog box.

N O T E

Setting the Line Style for the Object

You can select the type of line to be drawn as a frame for the selected objects.

1. Select the object.
2. From the Drawing toolbar, click the **Line Style** button and select a line style.

If you want to select a color for the line, select the object and click the line color button.

Figure 9.8 shows an object framed with a line.

Figure 9.8

Aligning the Objects

You can choose to have Draw align objects in a graphic to give them relevant placement to each other. For example, you might draw two objects and then decide that you want to place one at the top left of the graphic, and one at the bottom right.

1. Select the object to align.

2. Click the **Align Drawing Objects** button on the Drawing toolbar. Word displays the Align dialog box.

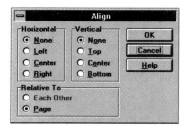

Figure 9.9

3. Choose the alignment options for the object.

You might need to experiment with the alignment a few times to get a clear idea of how align two objects relative to each other.

Rotating and Flipping an Object

Draw lets you rotate an object to the right in 90-degree increments. You cannot rotate patterns, text, or imported graphics. If a box contains graphics, the text will not move with it when you rotate. However, you can use WordArt to rotate text. (See the WordArt information later in this chapter.)

To rotate an object:

1. Select the object.

2. Click the **Rotate Right** button on the Drawing toolbar.

Figure 9.10 shows an object before and after rotation.

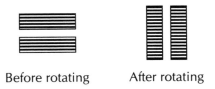

Before rotating   After rotating

Figure 9.10

You can also flip an object so that it creates a mirror image of the original object.

To flip an object:

1. Select the object.
2. Do one of the following:
   - ◆ Click the **Flip Horizontal** button on the Drawing toolbar to flip the object horizontally.
   - ◆ Click the **Flip Vertical** button on the Drawing toolbar to flip the object vertically.

Figure 9.11 shows an object before and after flipping.

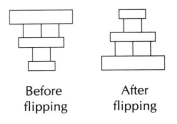

Before   After
flipping   flipping

Figure 9.11

Now you have some idea about how to draw objects and use the basic tools, using Draw. Experiment for a while to see what you can do.

WordArt

The WordArt feature is powerful, but simple and fun to use. This is another feature of Word rather than part of the Draw feature. You might consider using this feature to design a logo or add a simple graphic or icon to any type of document. Word gives you many fonts, angles or styles, and options for placement, shadowing, and stretching text.

Starting WordArt

1. Open a document.
2. From the Insert menu, choose **Object (Alt-I, O)**. Word displays the Object dialog box.
3. Under Object Type on the Create New tab, select **Microsoft WordArt 2.0**.

Word displays a text box where you enter the text.

Figure 9.12

Word also displays the WordArt toolbar.

Figure 9.13

The toolbar contains a Line and Shape drop-down box, a Font box, and Font Size box. Move your mouse pointer over the toolbar to see the name of each button.

Applying Styles to the Text

After you type your text in the text box, you can apply styles from the WordArt toolbar. The last three buttons on the toolbar display dialog boxes where you can make more choices.

1. Type the text.
2. Click buttons from the toolbar or select shapes and fonts from the Line and Shape box and the Font box.

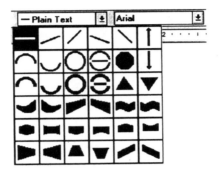

Figure 9.14

The following examples show four types of the many graphics you can create with WordArt. To create each of these, type the text, and select the style from the Line and Style drop-down list. Each time you select a style, WordArt displays the name at the top of the list box.

This is the Arch Up style:

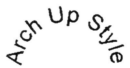

Figure 9.15

This is the Arch Down style:

Figure 9.16

This is the Slant Up (More) style:

Figure 9.17

This is the Triangle Invert style:

Figure 9.18

Experiment for a while by selecting different styles and special effects from the WordArt toolbar. For details about how to use the WordArt feature, see the Microsoft Word 6.0 for Windows documentation.

Summary

As you can see, Draw and WordArt give you many options for creating and adding drawings in your document. You don't have to be an artist or graphic designer to make your own impressive designs. If you followed the formatting tutorials in earlier chapters, go back now and open the letter you created. In the heading, you might experiment with WordArt to add a personal logo to make a letterhead. First open the document, then the heading. Play with it for a while to see what you can do.

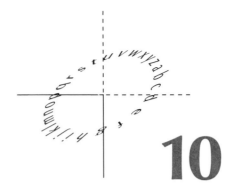

Using Microsoft Graph

T his chapter discusses the following topics:

- invoking Microsoft Graph
- the data sheet
- the chart
- trying different chart formats
- manipulating data
- the Menu bar

Microsoft Graph enables you to take numerical data, such as a line of numbers or data from a spreadsheet, and display it graphically in your Word document. With Graph, you can create bar, column, line, pie, and many other kinds of charts. Like Microsoft Draw, Graph saves charts (and data used to create the chart) as embedded objects—meaning that you can double-click a Graph chart in your document and change the characteristics of the chart, such as the font, data used to create the chart, or type of chart (from bar chart to pie chart, for example).

You can run Microsoft Graph only within Word. Since Graph stores charts and data as embedded objects in your Word document, Graph does not create a chart that you can use outside of Word.

 Although you can edit data that you import from another application, such as a Lotus 1-2-3 file, those changes are only made to the *copy* of the data Graph has stored in your document. Your original source of information—your Lotus 1-2-3 file—will not be updated.

N O T E

Overview

There are two windows in the Graph application: the *chart* window and the *datafile* window. The chart window contains the picture that Graph creates of your data. The datafile window contains the data to be charted. You use Graph by creating a datafile, then instructing Graph as to how you want the datafile to be charted. You can create this datafile manually or by importing data from another application, such as Lotus 1-2-3. Once you create the datafile, you can apply a variety of different charting formats to it and add any text you want to the chart.

When you use Graph, you will be switching back and forth between the chart and the data sheet. Graph takes data from the data sheet and uses it to generate the chart. You can control what data is used from the data sheet and you can also control how it is graphed.

When you invoke Graph from a Word application, Graph brings up a default chart and datafile windows. You may find this annoying. This chapter discusses how to change the chart and datafile to something else. However, you can't prevent Graph from displaying a chart and datafile—you can only change which chart and datafile is used by default.

Invoking Graph

You can only invoke Graph from within Word. Follow these steps to invoke Graph:

1. From Word's Insert menu (in Figure 10.1), choose **Object** (**Alt-I**, **O**).
2. Select **Microsoft Graph** from the list in the Object dialog box, shown in Figure 10.2.

Any chart you create will be inserted in your document at the insertion point.

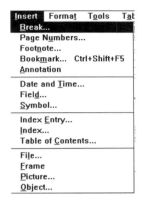

Figure 10.1

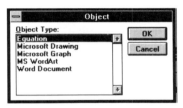

Figure 10.2

The Data Sheet

Figure 10.3 shows the default data sheet:

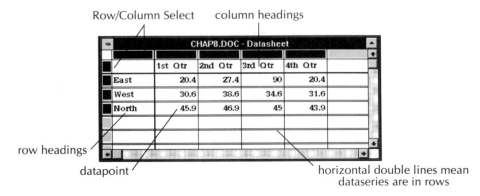

Figure 10.3

Each box in the data sheet is referred to as a *cell*. Each cell that contains data is called a *datapoint*. The datapoints are organized in groups called *dataseries*. In our example above, the dataseries are organized in rows (which you can tell by the direction of the double lines), with the dataseries named by the row headings East, West, and North. In this example, the labels at the top of the graph identify what time the datapoint occurred. Using these headings and labels, you can determine the East region had a result of 20.4 in the first quarter.

You can select a cell simply by clicking it. You can select a row or column by clicking the row or column on the left or top side of the data sheet. You can also format datapoints in the data sheet to tell Graph how you want negative numbers displayed, for example. Formatting is discussed in the "Format" section, later in this chapter, under the main heading "Microsoft Graph Commands."

The Chart

The chart consists of *data markers*, the *value axis*, the *category axis*, and the *legend*. In this case, a bar chart was generated. Graph will create a legend using the heading for the dataseries and the pattern used for the marker, so you can identify which marker is used with a particular dataseries. Graph then plots the datapoints. This chart displays the values in the default data sheet.

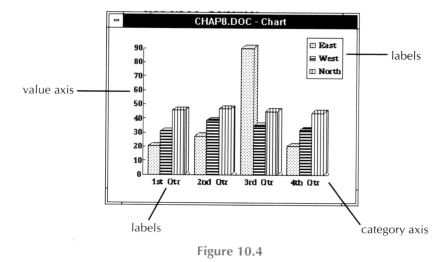

Figure 10.4

In the example data sheet, East had a value of 20.4 for the first quarter. Looking at the legend in the chart, you see that the pattern for East is small dots. Looking at the labels at the chart, you can see that the data marker for East in the first quarter is lined up with 20 on the value axis.

Graph Basics

Unlike the other Word tools and applications you've seen earlier, Graph comes with a built-in default data sheet and chart, so you do not need the program disk to use this tutorial.

Trying Different Chart Formats

As a first step, try changing the default chart to some different formats. To prepare for this exercise:

1. Have Word running, and a new, empty file open.
2. From the Insert menu, choose **Object** (**Alt-I, O**).
3. Select **Microsoft Graph** from the list in the dialog box.
4. Choose **OK**.

Graph is invoked, and your display should be similar to Figure 10.5.

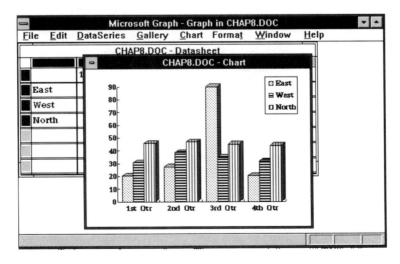

Figure 10.5

Two windows are open: one is the chart and the other is the data sheet. The first exercise shows you how to change the chart formats from one type to another.

Line Chart

The default chart type is the column chart. Another chart type is the line chart. To change to the line chart format:

1. Click the **Chart** window to make it active.
2. From the Gallery menu, choose **Line** (**Alt-G, L**).
3. Select chart number 5.
4. Choose **OK**.

You should see the Chart window change to the format in Figure 10.6.

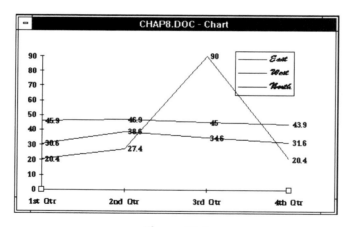

Figure 10.6

Note that this represents exactly the same data, but in a different way. The line format makes trends obvious—note how the big jump for East in the third quarter is highlighted.

Pie Chart

Next, try the pie chart format.

1. From the Gallery menu, choose **Pie** (**Alt-G, P**).

2. Choose chart number 6.

3. Choose **OK**.

You should see the chart change to the format in Figure 10.7.

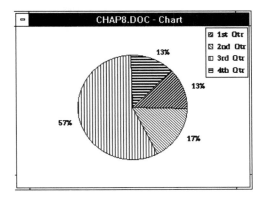

Figure 10.7

The pie chart gives you a good idea how data items in a dataseries contribute to the total. The pie chart also only uses data from one series in the data sheet—because we didn't specify one, Graph used the data from the first series. This was the data for East. If the data for East was dollars earned each quarter, the pie format would highlight that the third quarter contributed over half of the earnings.

3D Charts

Graph also has an extensive array of 3D charts. 3D charts can make the process of comparing data among many dataseries easier. In this example, you generate a 3D column chart.

1. From the Gallery menu, choose **3D column (Alt-G, O)**.

2. Choose chart number 6.

You should see the chart change to something similar to Figure 10.8 on the next page.

The 3D chart lets you see both the trends in individual dataseries and how the dataseries are related to each other. It is immediately obvious from the chart that the third quarter for East stands out from the rest of the data. The 3D format also has a more pleasing appearance than the 2D effect.

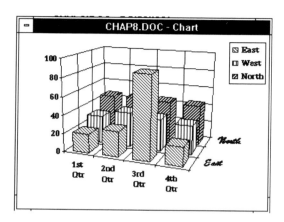

Figure 10.8

Manipulating Data in the Data Sheet

Now that you've got an introduction to using the different chart formats, turn your attention to the data sheet. You can select only certain portions of the data sheet to plot, and control how data is displayed in the data sheet.

Selecting Portions of the Data Sheet to Plot

1. Click the label **East** in the data sheet.
2. From the DataSeries menu, choose **Exclude Row/Column (Alt-D, E)**.
3. Click **Row** in the dialog box that pops up and click **OK**.
4. Click the label **North** in the data sheet.
5. From the DataSeries menu, choose **Exclude Row/Column (Alt-D, E)**.
6. Click **Row** in the dialog box that pops up, and click **OK**.

You should now have only the West row appearing in bold. Now you can create a pie chart for the data in the West dataseries:

1. Click the **Chart** window to make it active.
2. From the Gallery menu, choose **Pie (Alt-G, P)**.
3. Choose any chart type you want.

You should now see a pie chart with the data for West.

Formatting Cells in the Data Sheet

You can also choose to format the cells in the data sheet. For example, suppose the data in the default data sheet represented dollar amounts. You might want to have the data preceded with a dollar sign, but you could not simply enter a dollar sign in front of the data, as the dollar sign isn't a valid character to include in the field. You will change the formatting of the data sheet to include the dollar sign for all the cells:

1. Click the data sheet to make it active.

2. Select all the cells in the data sheet either by choosing **Select All** from the Edit Menu or by placing the cursor in the upper-left data cell (20.40), pressing the left mouse button, and holding the left mouse button down while you drag the cursor down to the bottom right-most cell that has data in it (43.90).

3. From the Format menu, choose **Number** (**Alt-T**, **N**).

4. Select the option **$#,##0.00; ($#,##0.00)** and choose **OK**.

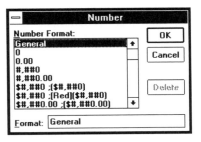

Figure 10.9

You should now see the data sheet change to have dollar signs in front of all the data cells you selected.

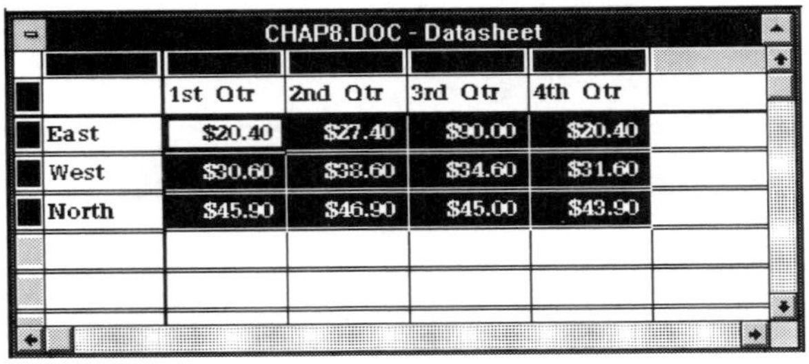

Figure 10.10

Microsoft Graph Commands

This section shows each of the menu items in the Graph menu, explains each of them, and describes when each should be applied. To help you get started, Table 10.1 tells you which section to jump ahead to.

Table 10.1 Quick Reference

If you need to	Then refer to the section for
Import data from a file or other application	File menu
See what the current version of the chart looks like in the document	File menu
Change the default data and graph file	File menu
Exit Graph	File menu
Copy, delete, or insert items in the datafile	Edit menu
Choose rows or columns of data to be graphed	DataSeries menu
Choose the type of chart (pie, line, bar, etc.)	Gallery menu
Edit the chart (add labels, arrows, legends, axes)	Chart menu
Change patterns (i.e., fill bars in the chart with dots)	Format menu
Change the font	Format menu
Change the legend	Format menu
Change the column width	Format menu
Switch between chart and overlay	Format menu
Switch between 2-D and 3-D views	Format menu
Change the color palette	Format menu
Switch between the chart and data display	Window menu
Change the size of the chart or data window	Window menu
Help	Help menu

The Menu Bar

The Menu bar is displayed along the top of the Graph window. All of the Graph commands are accessible from here.

Figure 10.11

This section discusses each of the menu commands, and the options available for each command. If the menu command has a number of different options, the options are summarized in a quick reference table.

File

Use the File menu whenever you want to import data from another application, place the chart in your Word document, or exit and return to Word.

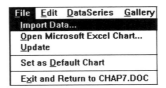

Figure 10.12

Importing Data from Another Application

Whenever you want to import data from another application, use the Import Data... command from the File menu (**Alt-F**, **I**). Graph converts data from other applications, such as Lotus 1-2-3, based on the file extension

Quattro Pro users: Note that you need to save your spreadsheets in the 1-2-3 format to import the spreadsheet into Graph.

Data is imported starting at the current cell you have selected in the data file. You can also import data from a plain ASCII text file, with the data separated by commas, or tabs, like the following:

```
1, 2, 4, 8, 16, 32, 64
```

You can also choose a certain range of cells to import if you are importing a spreadsheet.

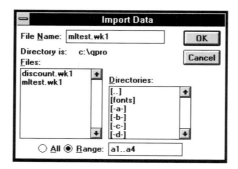

Figure 10.13

In the bottom of the Import Data dialog box, select **Range** (**Alt-R**), then type the range name of the range of cells you want to import in the box to the right.

Opening a Microsoft Excel Spreadsheet

To import data from a Microsoft Excel spreadsheet, choose **Open Microsoft Excel Chart** from the File menu (**Alt-F, O**). Graph displays a dialog box that enables you to select the Excel spreadsheet that you want to import.

Updating the Document

If you want to see how your changes will look in your document, choose **Update** from the File menu (**Alt-F, U**). This updates your chart in the document, but leaves you in Graph. Use this command when you are making changes to a chart, but are not ready to exit Graph.

When you are finished with the chart, choose **Exit** from the File menu (**Alt-F, X**). This closes Graph, then pops up a dialog box, asking if you want to update the graph in the document.

Selecting a Default Data Sheet

You may find that you want to bring up a different spreadsheet than the default sheet that Graph uses. The Set as Default sheet enables you to do this. First, you must have the chart and data in use by Graph—you cannot select a file and tell Graph to use that file as a default directly. Once you have the chart and data that you want to use as a default, choose **Set as Default** from the File menu (**Alt-F**, **D**). Graph displays this chart and data as the default from this point on, unless you go back and change the default.

Returning to the Main Document

Once you are satisfied with the document, choose **Exit and Return** to save the chart and data and return to your main document. Graph asks you if you want to update the drawing in your document before exiting.

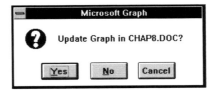

Figure 10.14

Table 10.2   Options for Returning to the Main Document

If you want to	Then choose
Update the chart in the document, and save any changes to the data file.	Yes
Exit Graph without updating the chart and losing any changes made to the data file.	No

File Quick Reference

Use Table 10.3 as a quick guide to using the File menu.

Table 10.3   File Menu Options

If you want to	Then choose	Using this quick key
Import data from a file or other application	Import Data	Alt-F, I

Import data from an Excel application	**Open Microsoft Excel Chart**	**Alt-F, O**
Update the chart in the main document without leaving Graph.	**Update**	**Alt-F, U**
Change the default for the current chart and data	**Set as Default Chart**	**Alt-F, D**
Exit Graph, save chart and data, and update document.	**Exit and Return to**	**Alt-F, X, Y,** then choose **Yes** for the Update Graph dialog box
Exit Graph, without saving chart and data and without updating dialog box	**Exit and Return to**	**ALT-F, X, N** then choose **No** for the Update Graph document.

Edit

Use the Edit menu whenever you want to edit data in your datasheet or cut or copy items in your chart. Using the Edit menu options, you can copy rows or columns of data in the datasheet, and insert and delete columns and rows.

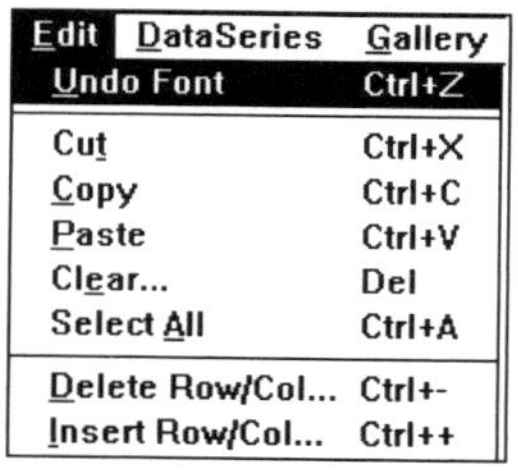

Figure 10.15

Undoing the Last Edit Operation

The Undo command reverses the last operation you performed. Note that you can undo only the previous command; you cannot undo commands that occurred earlier than the last command. For example, if you accidentally delete some data from your chart, choose **Undo** as your next step to recover the data. If you delete the data then perform another action, such as changing some text, you are able to undo only the text change. You are not able to undo again and restore the data you deleted, since that action occurred two steps back. In this case, you might simply want to exit Graph without updating the chart, so you can start over.

To undo the last action taken, choose **Undo** from the Edit menu (**Alt-E, U**). If you want to undo *all* the actions you've taken on the current chart and datasheet, you can **Exit Graph** from the File menu (**Alt-F, X**) and answer **No** to the dialog box that asks you if you want to update the document. *You will lose any changes* you made to the chart or datasheet in this session with Graph.

Cutting or Copying Objects to the Clipboard, then Inserting the Objects in a New Location

You can copy or delete items in your chart or datasheet using the commands from the Edit menu. For example, you can copy data in one or more cells to other cells in the datasheet. You can select an item in the chart, such as the legend, and delete it.

Like other Word applications, Graph divides the Cut and Paste and Copy and Paste operations into two steps—first you cut or copy the selected item from the data sheet or chart, then you paste it into the location you want in your main document.

Table 10.4   Cut and Copy Options

If you want to	Use
Move an item in a chart or datasheet from one location to another	**Cut**
Copy an item in a chart or datasheet	**Copy**

Follow these steps to cut selected items:

1. Select the objects you want to cut.
2. From the Edit menu, choose **Cut** (**Alt-E, T**).

The items are now removed from the datasheet or chart and are stored in the Clipboard. You can now use the Paste command to insert the items where you want.

Follow these steps to copy selected items:

1. Select the objects you want to copy.
2. From the Edit menu, choose **Cut** (**Alt-E, C**).

A copy of the selected items is placed in the Clipboard. You can now use the Paste command to insert the objects where you want.

Follow these steps to paste selected items:

1. Place the insertion point where you want the objects to appear. If you want to replace one or more items with the items you are about to paste, select all the items you want to replace. (Graph replaces them during the paste operation.)

2. From the Edit menu, choose **Paste** (**Alt-E**, **P**). Graph copies the object to the selected area of the datasheet or chart.

Graph uses the Clipboard to temporarily store the objects—meaning that you can actually paste the data cells into another Draw datasheet that you may have open in another window.

N O T E

Deleting the Selected Objects

As you might expect, you can simply choose to delete an object or objects, instead of using the Cut command to put the objects in the Clipboard. You can use the delete operation to remove:

◆ data from the datasheet

◆ number formatting information from the data sheet

◆ items from the chart that are *not* data points, such as legend and tables

The delete procedure is essentially the same as that for the Cut command:

1. Select the objects.

2. Delete the objects by either:

   ◆ Pressing the **Delete** key, or

   ◆ From the Edit menu, choosing **Clear**, or

   ◆ Pressing **Alt-E**, **E**

If you've selected rows or columns of data in your datasheet, Graph displays a dialog box when you choose the **Clear** command or press **Del.**

Figure 10.16

You can use the options in Table 10.5 to delete just the data, just the formatting, or both from your datasheet.

Table 10.5 Delete Options

If you want to	Then
Clear just the data, but leave the formatting information	Select **Clear Data**.
Clear just the format information, but leave the data	Select **Clear Format**.
Clear data and remove all formatting information	Select **Clear Both**.

Graph removes the objects from the display. Note that if you delete an object by mistake, choose **Undo** from the Edit menu *as your next step*. This restores the objects you deleted.

Deleting or Inserting Rows and Columns in the Data Sheet

You will often want to insert rows or columns or data into your datasheet. For example, you may have entered one column of data for each month of the year in your budget datasheet and find that you left out the data for the month of June. You can correct the error by inserting a column between the May and July columns. Graph automatically moves the July through December columns over one column.

Follow these steps to insert a row or column:

1.   Select the number of rows or columns you want to insert. If you want to insert two columns, for example, then select the two columns where you want the new data to appear.

2. From the Edit menu, choose **Insert Row/Column** (**Alt-E, I**).

For example, suppose you want to insert two columns of data between 1st Qtr and 2nd Qtr in the spreadsheet.

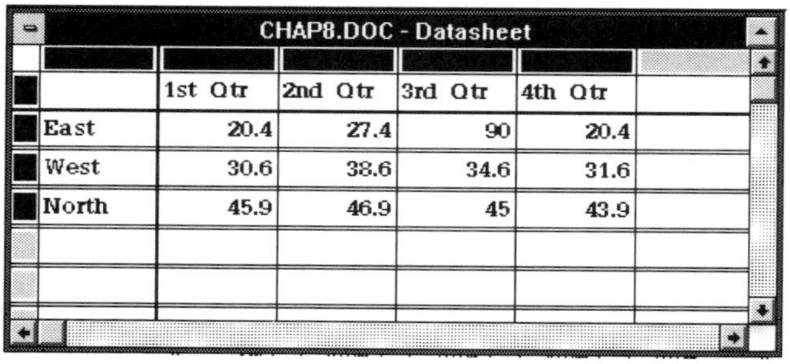

Figure 10.17

1. Select two columns before which you want the two new columns to be inserted.

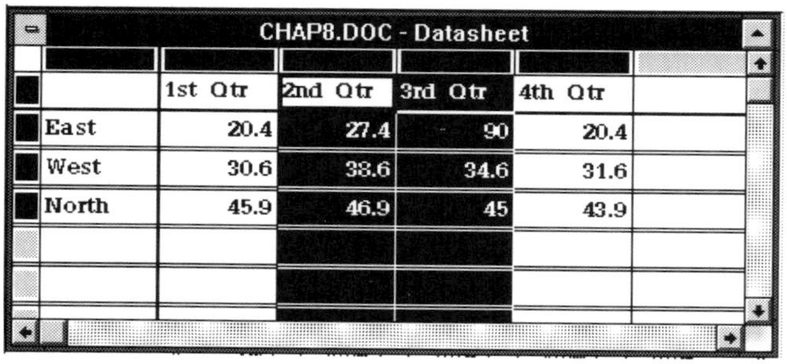

Figure 10.18

2. From the Edit menu, choose **Insert Row/Column** (**Alt E, I**).

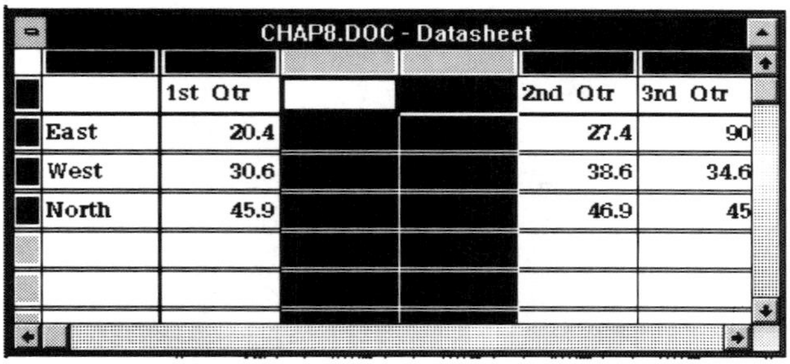

Figure 10.19

Graph inserts two empty columns.

You can delete rows or columns of data from the datasheet just as easily.
Follow these steps to delete a row or column:

1. Select the number of rows or columns you want to delete.
2. From the Edit menu, choose **Delete Row/Column (Alt-E, D)**.

Edit Quick Reference

Use Table 10.6 as a quick guide to using the edit menu.

Table 10.6   Edit Menu Options

If you want to	Then
Undo the last incorrect command	Choose **Undo**.
Move data from one location in the datasheet to another	1. Select the data. 2. Choose **Cut**. 3. Place your insertion point. 4. Choose **Paste**.
Move objects in the chart from one location to another	1. Select the objects. 2. Choose **Cut**. 3. Place your insertion point. 4. Choose **Paste**.

Copy data in the datasheet to another location	1. Select the data. 2. Choose **Copy**. 3. Place your insertion point. 4. Choose **Paste**.
Copy items in the chart to another location	1. Select the objects. 2. Choose **Cut**. 3. Place your insertion point. 4. Choose **Paste**.
Remove data or formatting from a row or column in the data sheet	1. Select the row or column. 2. Choose **Clear**.
Remove one or more columns or rows	1. Select the row or column. 2. Choose **Delete Row/Column.**
Insert one or more rows or columns	1. Select the row or column. 2. Choose **Insert Row/Column.**

DataSeries

A *dataseries* is either a row or column of data in your datasheet that produces a portion of the chart. For example, you could decide that the data in your datasheet is ordered by columns, one column of data for each month. In this case, the column of data is referred to as the dataseries. If you produce a bar chart from this datasheet, there will be one bar for each column (or dataseries).

You can also define your data to be ordered in rows instead of columns. The dataseries would then be the rows of information. Dataseries in rows is the default configuration. The DataSeries menu is shown in Figure 10.20.

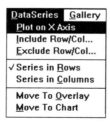

Figure 10.20

Defining Data to Use for the X Axis

You may find that you need to plot data along both the X and Y axes of your datasheet. For example, you want to plot a time-versus-distance graph that shows how various members of your track team are performing. This is referred to as an *XY (scatter) chart*, which you can choose from one of the XY chart formats in the chart gallery.

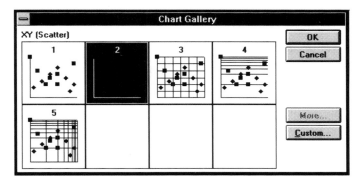

Figure 10.21

Word has a good Example Graph Help window for "Enter data for XY charts." Follow these steps to display this example:

1. From the Help menu, choose **Index (Alt-H, I)**.

2. Select **How to**.

3. Under Arrange Data for the Chart, select **Entering Data for XY charts**.

Example

The following example includes a datasheet with two series in columns, Time and Distance. In the first chart, the Time series is plotted on the x-axis. Therefore, the marker for Smith is positioned along the x-axis (horizontal axis) at 3.8 and along the y-axis (vertical axis) at 12.

In the second chart, the Distance series is plotted on the x-axis. Therefore, the marker for Smith is positioned along the x-axis at 12 and along the y-axis at 3.8.

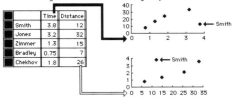

Figure 10.20

Follow these steps to create an XY chart:

1. Switch to the Chart window. You can click the **Chart window** or choose **Chart** from the Window menu (**Alt-W, C**).
2. From the Gallery menu, choose the XY graph format (**Alt-G, S**).
3. Select the XY format you want to use, then choose **OK**.
4. Switch to the Datasheet window. You can click the **Datasheet window**, or choose **Chart** from the Window menu (**Alt-W, C**).
5. Select the dataseries you want Graph to use as the X axis.
6. From the DataSeries menu, choose **Plot on X axis (Alt-D, P)**.

You will see an X at the beginning of the row or column of the dataseries.

Graph uses your selection for the X dataseries to label the X axis. Graph then plots the rest of the dataseries by plotting the first value in each dataseries lined up with the first label in the X axis, then the next value in each series lined up with the second label in the X axis, and so on.

Including/Excluding Rows or Columns of Data

You may find that you don't always need to plot every dataseries contained in your datasheet. For example, suppose you have a datasheet that has a column of data for each month of the year. You may want to graph data for only the first three months of the year.

You select columns or row of data and include or exclude them using the Exclude Row/Column or Include Row/Column menu choices.

Follow these steps to include data:

If data appears black in the data sheet (not dimmed out) then it is already included. Only data that is dimmed out needs to be selected for inclusion.

N O T E

1. Select the rows or columns you want to include.
2. From the DataSeries menu, choose **Include Row/Column (Alt-D, I)** to include the selected data.

The included data now appears in black in the datasheet.

Follow these steps to exclude data:

1. Select the rows or columns you want to exclude.
2. From the DataSeries menu, select **Exclude Row/Column (Alt-D, E)** to exclude the selected data.

The excluded data now appears black in the datasheet.

If data appears dimmed out in the data sheet (not black) then it is already excluded. Only data that is black can be selected for exclusion.

N O T E

Using Rows or Columns to Define the Data Ordering

Graph considers dataseries to be either rows or columns of information, with row ordering being the default. You can change the default by choosing **Series in Columns** from the Edit menu. To determine whether the dataseries are ordered in rows or columns, look at the datasheet. You'll see double lines between the rows of data if the dataseries are ordered in rows, and double lines between the columns of data if the dataseries are ordered in columns.

To order the dataseries in columns choose **Series in Columns (Alt-D, C)** from the DataSeries menu. Double lines appear between the columns, and a check mark is displayed next to the Series in Columns option.

To order the dataseries in rows choose **Series in Rows (Alt-D, R)** from the DataSeries menu. Double lines appear between the rows, and a check mark is displayed next to the Series in Rows command.

Moving to Overlay or Chart

You may find that you want to compare dataseries in the same chart by presenting one of the dataseries in a different format than the other. The Overlay chart does this by combining two different types of charts within a single chart.

For example, you can take the data in the default data sheet and create an overlay chart, with the first row of data plotted as a line, and the rest of the data plotted as bars, as in Figure 10.23 on the next page.

You can look at the chart and immediately see that the data for East is being compared with the data for West and North. You can also use the overlay to compare

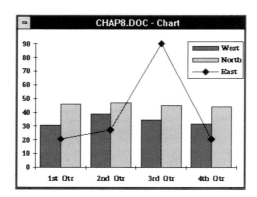

Figure 10.23

dataseries that are scaled differently. For example, suppose East had values from 100 to 1,000, but North and West had values from 1 to 10. (In the default data sheet, the values are really much closer; this is just an example.) To get the values for East to fit with North and West on the same chart, the sizes of the North and West bars would have to be so small that no meaningful trends could be observed from them. If, however, the East data was on an overlay chart, the East data could be scaled independently from North and West data, and the chart would be much more meaningful.

Follow these steps to move a dataseries to an overlay chart:

1. Make sure the current chart type is *not 3D* (a 3D chart is not compatible with the Overlay operation).
2. Click the **datasheet** to make it active.
3. Select the dataseries (rows or columns) of data you want to move to the overlay chart.
4. From the DataSeries menu, choose **Move to Overlay (Alt-D, O)**.

Graph creates an overlay chart of the default type. If you want to change the chart type, then select **Overlay** from the Format menu. (See the "Format" section later in this chapter.)

You can also move data from the overlay chart back to the main chart. Dataseries that have an "O" in front of them are assigned to the overlay chart. In the example pictured below, East is assigned to the overlay chart.

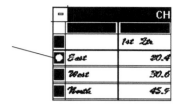

Figure 10.24

Follow these steps to move a dataseries back to the main chart:

Only dataseries that have an "O" in front of them are in the overlay and can be moved to the main chart.

N O T E

Dataseries without the "O" are already plotted in the main chart.

1. Click the datasheet to make it active.
2. Select the dataseries (rows or columns) of data you want to move to the overlay chart.
3. From the DataSeries menu, choose **Move to Chart** (**Alt-D**, **O**).

Graph moves the dataseries you selected back to the main chart.

Table 10.7 Dataseries Quick Reference

If you want to	Then
Choose the dataseries to use for the x axis in an XY plot	Choose **Plot on X Axis**.
Include rows or columns from datasheet for the chart	1. Select the rows or columns you want to include. 2. Choose Inc**lude Row/ Column**.
Exclude rows or columns from datasheet for the chart	1. Select the rows or columns you want to exclude. 2. Choose **Exclude Row/ Column**.

Order the dataseries in rows	Choose **Series in Columns**.
Order the dataseries in columns	Choose **Series in Rows**.
Move a dataseries from a 2D chart to an overlay chart	1. Select the dataseries to move to the overlay. 2. Choose **Move to Overlay**.
Move a dataseries from an Overlay chart back to the main chart	1. Select the series to move. 2. Choose **Move to Chart**.

Gallery

Use the Gallery command to select the format for the chart. There are many different types of chart formats. Use Table 10.8 as a guide to choosing the appropriate type.

Table 10.8   Gallery Options

If you want to	Then choose a chart type
Show the contribution of different dataseries to the total overtime and emphasize the amount of change	**Area, 3D area**
Compare values in a dataseries at a particular point in time	**Bar, 3D bar**
Compare values of dataseries over time	**Column, 3D column**
Show the changes of different dataseries over time and emphasize the rate of change	**Line, 3D line**
Show the ratio of an element in a dataseries to the total for all the elements in the series	**Pie, 3D pie**
See if two variables are dependent on each other	**XY (or scatter)**
Compare dataseries that are scaled much differently or highlight different dataseries	**Combination**

Area Charts

Area charts help you emphasize the total amount of change in one or more dataseries. The 2D Area menu is displayed in Figure 10.25.

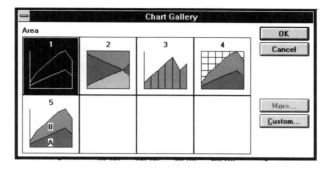

Figure 10.25

Table 10.9 Area Chart Options

If you want an area chart with	Then choose area chart type
No labels or gridlines	1
100% area (area equivalent of pie chart)	2
Vertical drop lines	3
Gridlines	4
Areas labeled	5

3D Area Chart

The 3D area chart gives you the same emphasis on the amount of change in dataseries, but makes it easier for you to compare the different dataseries. The 3D area menu is shown in Figure 10.26.

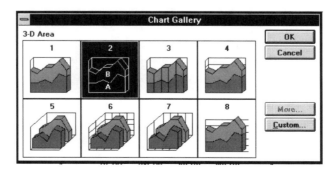

Figure 10.26

Table 10.10   3D Area Chart Options

If you want a 3D area chart with	Then choose 3D area chart type
No labels or gridlines	1
Dataseries stacked and labeled	2
Dataseries stacked with vertical drop lines	3
Dataseries stacked with gridlines	4
Dataseries separated	5
Dataseries separated with horizontal and vertical gridlines	6
Dataseries separated with horizontal and vertical gridlines	7
Dataseries stacked and horizontal gridlines	8

Bar Chart

The bar chart is useful when you want to display a set of dataseries at a particular point in time. The bar chart options follow.

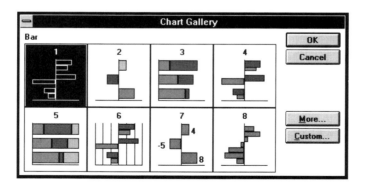

Figure 10.27

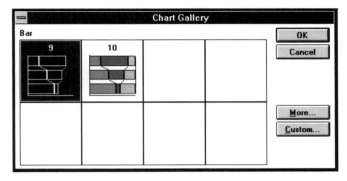

Figure 10.27

Table 10.11 Bar Chart Options

If you want a bar chart with	Then choose bar chart type
No labels or gridlines	1
Different patterns for each bar, used with a single dataseries	2
Bars for each series stacked on top of each other	3
Bars overlapping	4
Bars for each series stacked on top of each other, all bars scaled to the same length	5
Vertical gridlines	6
Value labels	7
No spaces between bars	8
Bars for each series stacked on top of each other, with lines connecting the series	9
Bars for each series stacked on top of each other, with lines connecting the series and all bars scaled to the same length.	10

3D Bar Chart

The Chart Gallery dialog box, shown in Figure 10.29, shows the 3D bar chart options.

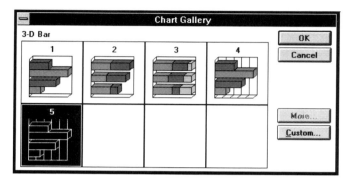

Figure 10.29

Table 10.12   3D Bar Chart Options

If you want a chart with	Then choose 3D bar type
No labels or gridlines	1
Dataseries stacked	2
Dataseries stacked, with bar lengths the same	3
Vertical gridlines in 3D	4
Vertical gridlines in 2D	5

Column Chart

Use the column format when you want to compare the values of dataseries over time. The column chart options follow.

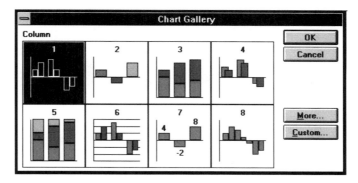

Figure 10.30

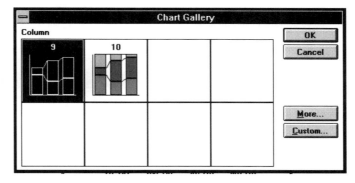

Figure 10.31

Table 10.13   Column Chart Options

If you want a chart with	Then choose column chart type
No labels or gridlines	1
Different patterns for each element in the series and just one dataseries charted	2
Dataseries stacked on top of each other	3

Dataseries overlapped	4
Dataseries stacked on top of each other, bar length remains constant	5
Horizontal gridlines	6
Value labels	7
No space between bars	8
Dataseries stacked with lines between series	9
Dataseries stacked with lines between series and column length constant	10

3D Chart

The options for the 3D chart follow.

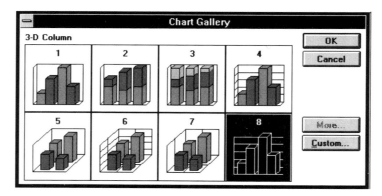

Figure 10.32

Table 10.14   3D Chart Options

If you want a chart with	Then choose chart type
No labels or gridlines	1
Dataseries stacked on top of each other	2
Dataseries stacked on top of each other, with column length constant	3

Vertical axis gridlines	4
Dataseries plotted side-by-side	5
Dataseries plotted side-by-side, with gridlines	6
Dataseries plotted side by side, with horizontal and vertical gridlines only	7
2D horizontal gridlines	8

Line Chart

Use the line chart when you want to emphasize the rate of change for dataseries. The Chart Gallery dialog box in Figure 10.33, shows the Line chart format.

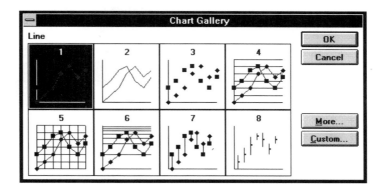

Figure 10.33

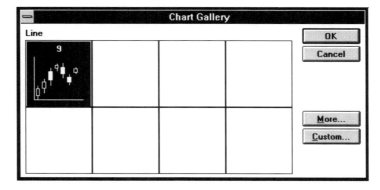

Figure 10.34

Table 10.15   Line Chart Options

If you want a line graph with	Then choose line graph type
Lines with data markers, but no labels or gridlines	1
Lines with no data markers, labels, or gridlines	2
Data markers with no lines	3
Lines with data markers and horizontal gridlines	4
Lines with data markers and horizontal and vertical gridlines	5
Lines with data markers and logarithmic scale and gridlines	6
High-low markers and lines	7
High-low-close chart	8
Open-high-low-close	9

3D Line Chart

The Chart Gallery dialog box shows options for the 3D Line chart format.

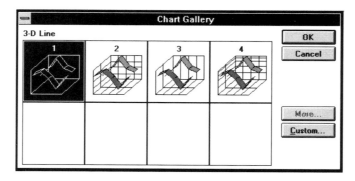

Figure 10.35

Table 10.16   3D Line Chart Options

If you want a 3D line chart with	Then choose 3D line chart type
No labels or gridlines	1
No labels with gridlines	2
No labels and horizontal and vertical gridlines	3
No labels and logarithmic gridlines	4

Pie Chart

Use the pie chart when you want to show the relationship between different elements of a dataseries to the total for all the elements of the dataseries. The pie chart shows the contribution of each element in the series to the total. The pie chart can only be used with a single dataseries. The options for the pie chart are pictured below.

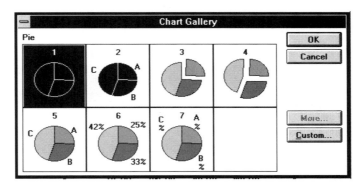

Figure 10.36

Table 10.17   Pie Chart Options

If you want a pie chart with	Then choose pie chart type
No labels, slices have different patterns, all slices together	1

Labeled, slices have different patterns, all slices together	2
No labels, one slice exploded from rest of chart	3
No labels, all slices exploded	4
Labels for each slice	5
Percentage labels for each slice	6
Series and percentage labels for each slice	7

3D Pie Chart

The Chart Gallery dialog box shows the 3D pie chart options.

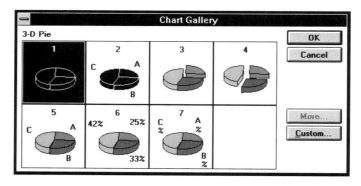

Figure 10.37

Table 10.18   3D Pie Chart Options

If you want a 3D pie chart with	Then choose 3D pie chart type
No labels, slices have different patterns, all slices together	1
Labeled, slices have different patterns, all slices together	2
No labels, one slice exploded from rest of chart	3
No labels, all slices exploded	4

Labels for each slice	5
Percentage labels for each slice	6
Percentage and data labels for each slice	7

XY (Scatter) Chart

Use the XY chart when you want to compare the relationship between two variables. The XY chart is discussed in the Dataseries section, under the heading "Defining Data to Use for the X Axis." The scatter chart options are pictured below.

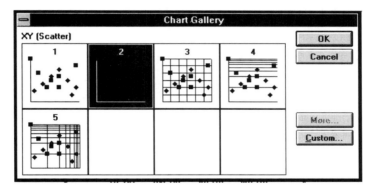

Figure 10.38

Table 10.19   Scatter Chart Options

If you want a XY chart with	Then choose XY chart type
Data markers only	1
Data markers for the same series connected by lines	2
Data markers with horizontal and vertical gridlines	3
Data markers with log scale for Y axis	4
Data markers with log scale for X and Y axis	5

Combination Chart

The combination chart is useful when you want to compare one set of dataseries against another set. The combination chart is essential for this type of comparison when one set of data has much larger or smaller values than the other set, requiring that the dataseries be scaled differently. The options for the combination chart are shown below.

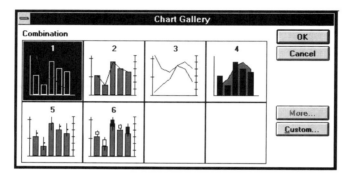

Figure 10.39

Table 10.20   Combination Chart Options

If you want a combination chart consisting of	Then choose combination chart type
A column chart overlaid with a line chart with the same scaling for the Y axis	1
A column chart overlaid with a line chart with independent scaling for the Y axis	2
A line chart overlaid with another line chart with independent scaling for the Y axis	3
An area chart overlaid by a column chart	4
A column chart overlaid by a high-low-close chart	5
A column chart overlaid by a open-high-low-close chart	6

The Chart Menu

The Chart menu allows you to:

- ◆ add titles to the chart or axes
- ◆ label data points
- ◆ add arrows to point to items of interest in your charts
- ◆ add or delete legends
- ◆ add or remove axes
- ◆ control gridlines

Figure 10.40 shows the Chart menu.

Figure 10.40

Titles

Use titles whenever you want to attach a title to the chart, or to the X or Y axis on the chart or overlay chart. Note that the example title menu shows all of the options available. You may not have all of these options available, depending on the type of chart you are editing (for example, pie charts don't have X and Y axes).

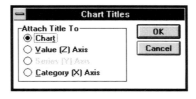

Figure 10.41

In Figure 10.42, titles have been added to the Chart and to the Z axis.

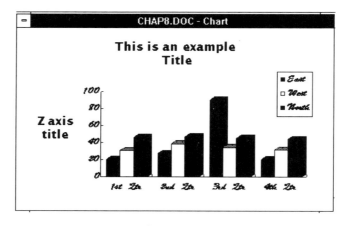

Figure 10.42

Follow these steps to add a title:

1. Make the chart the active window by clicking on it.

2. From the Chart menu, choose **Title** (**Alt-C**, **T**).

3. Select the item that you want to title (chart, X axis, Y axis) from the Attach Title dialog box and choose **OK**. Graph places a default title next to the item you selected. Edit this text by deleting it and adding the title you want.

4. Press **Esc** when you are finished.

This adds the title to your chart.

If you want to edit a title you've entered, follow these steps:

1. Position the cursor over the title you want to edit and click. Selection handles are displayed around the text.

2. Enter the new text.

3. Press **Esc** when you are finished.

Data Labels

You may want to label the data points in your chart with the values they represent. The Data Labels option allows you to attach:

◆ the values that the data point represents

◆ the percent of the total to each pie slice in a pie graph

◆ the labels from the data sheet to the data element

The following example shows the Data Labels dialog box:

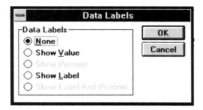

Figure 10.43

For example, suppose you have a chart and want the datapoint values displayed. You would select **Show Value** from the Data Labels menu to get a chart that looks like Figure 10.44.

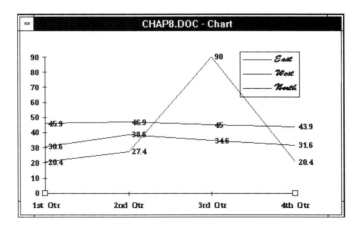

Figure 10.44

Graph isn't "smart" about how it locates label values. If you have a column chart, for example, and add labels to it, Graph may place the labels in the middle of column. Unfortunately, you can't move the labels to the top of the column, where they would be more easily visible. In this case, add text manually where you want it.

N O T E

To manually add text:

1. Ensure that no text items in the chart are selected.

2. Enter the text (don't worry about where the text is being entered, you can move it easily).

3. When you are finished entering the text, press the **Esc** key. Selection handles are displayed around the text.

4. Drag the text to the location you want.

Add Arrow

You may find that you want to highlight certain datapoints in your chart—for example, maybe sales for first quarter are exceptionally good, so you want to highlight this datapoint. You can use the Add Arrow command to do this. Figure 10.45 shows an arrow drawn to the third quarter earning, and a comment added.

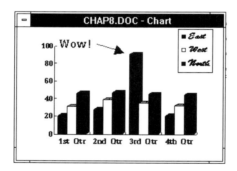

Figure 10.45

Delete Legend/Add Legend

You may decide that you do not want the legend to be displayed. In this case, select Delete Legend, and the legend is removed. If you have already deleted the legend, the menu command is replaced with Add Legend. Whenever you want to restore the legend, select **Add Legend**.

Axes

The Axes menu enables you to control the display of the X and Y axes. In the menu below, an X indicates that the corresponding axis will be displayed.

The Axes menu that you see may vary, depending on the chart type you have chosen.

N O T E

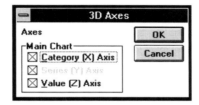

Figure 10.46

Figure 10.47 illustrates the effect of the Axes command with X axis displayed.

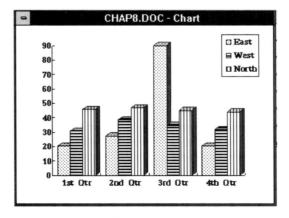

Figure 10.47

Figure 10.48 shows the effect with the X axis disabled:

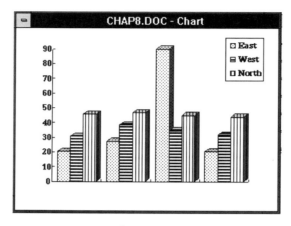

Figure 10.48

Gridlines

Gridlines are the lines along the X and Y axes that enable you to determine the values of the datapoints. You can control the display of these gridlines and also how fine the spacing is between the gridlines by enabling the Minor Gridlines option. Figure 10.49 shows an example of the gridlines menu. Note that your version may differ slightly, depending on the type of chart that is active.

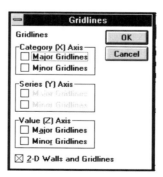

Figure 10.49

Figure 10.50 shows just the major gridlines displayed for the axes. You can determine the value that a column represents by looking along the gridlines and seeing where the top of the column is. You may find that you need more gridlines to get a more accurate estimate of the values. In this case, select the **Minor Axis** option for the axis that needs more resolution.

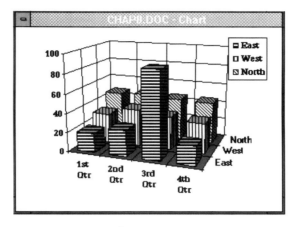

Figure 10.50

Figure 10.51 shows the Minor Gridlines enabled for the X and Z axis.

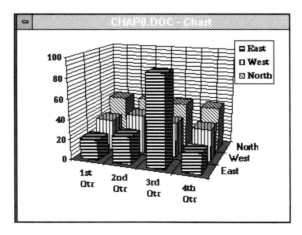

Figure 10.51

Table 10.2   Chart Quick Reference

If you want to	Then
Add a title to the chart, x axis, or y axis	1. Select the item you want to title. 2. Choose **Titles**. 3. Edit the default title inserted by Graph with the desired text.
Add value, percentage, or dataseries labels to the data points	1. Choose **Data Labels**. 2. Select the data label option you want.
Add an arrow to the chart	1. Choose the **Add Arrow** option. 2. Drag the arrow to the location you want.
Delete the legend	Choose **Delete Legend**.
Add the legend	Choose **Add Legend**.
Add or remove axes	1. Choose **Axes**. 2. Select the options you want.
Add or remove major or minor gridlines	1. Choose **Gridlines**. 2. Select the options you want.

Format

The Format menu presents the widest array of commands and deals with the widest array of items, from both the datasheet and the chart. At any one time, many of the commands may be grayed out, depending on the item you have selected. The commands that are grayed out cannot be applied to the currently selected item.

Figure 10.52

Patterns

The Patterns dialog box controls the appearance of items in the chart. With these options, you can change the border color, width, and style around almost any item, and pattern characteristics within the item. For example, you can change the pattern columns or in the background of the legend. If you're not sure if you can edit an item's pattern, simply select the item and see if the Patterns command is grayed out on the Format menu. If it is, then this item does not have an editable pattern.

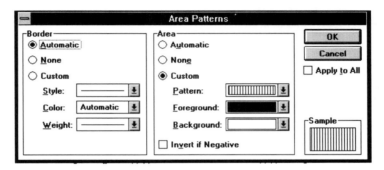

Figure 10.53

Follow these steps to change the pattern of an object in a chart:

1. Select the object within the chart.

2. From the Format menu, select **Patterns** (**Alt-T**, **P**).

3. Use Table 10.22 to determine the command to change the selected object:

Table 10.22   Changing Selected Objects

If you want to	Then select
Change the border around an object to its default	**Automatic** in the border section
Make the border invisible	**None** in the border section
Change the color, line width, or line style of the border	1. **Custom** 2. The characteristic you want to change 3. The new characteristic from the menu

Change the pattern of an object to its default	**Automatic** in the pattern section
Make the pattern invisible	None in the pattern section
Change the color, line width, or line style of the border	1. **Custom** 2. The characteristic you want to change 3. The new characteristic from the menu

Font

You can change the characteristics of text in your chart. By selecting the text you want to change and choosing the **Font** command from the Format menu, you can change such characteristics as:

◆ font

◆ color

◆ size

◆ style

◆ background

Any text you can select in the chart, such as axis text, legends, or titles, can be changed through the Font dialog box, as shown in Figure 10.54.

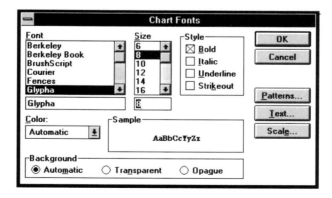

Figure 10.54

To change the text characteristics:

1. Select the text.

2. Select the appropriate option in the Fonts dialog box:

Table 10.23   Font Options

If you want to change	Then
Font	Click the font you want within the font window.
Text size	Select the font size within the size window.
Text style	Select the style (bold, italic, underline, or strikeout) from the Style window.
Color	From the color window, select **Automatic** for the default color, or select another color.
Background (this is the area surrounding the text)	Select **Automatic** for the default background, or Select **Transparent** for a transparent background, or Select **Opaque** for an opaque background.

Text

You can change the alignment of text in the chart. The default is text that flows from left to right, but you can change this to top to bottom (two choices), and bottom to top.

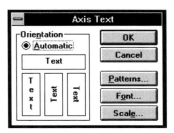

Figure 10.55

After you change the orientation of the text, you can change the characteristics of the object the text is attached to:

Table 10.24 Text Characteristics

If you want to change the	Then	For more info, refer to the Format section under
Pattern of an object to which the text is attached	1. Click **Pattern**. 2. Complete the Font dialog box.	Pattern
Font	1. Click **Font**. 2. Complete the Font dialog box.	Font
Scale, if the text is attached to an axis	1. Click **Scale**. 2. Complete the scale dialog box.	Scale

Scale

You may want to change characteristics of the scale for a particular axis, such as changing the scale from linear to logarithmic. The scale dialog boxes are shown below. The dialog boxes are different, depending on whether you have an X, Y, or Z axis selected. Figure 10.56 shows the dialog box if the Z axis is selected.

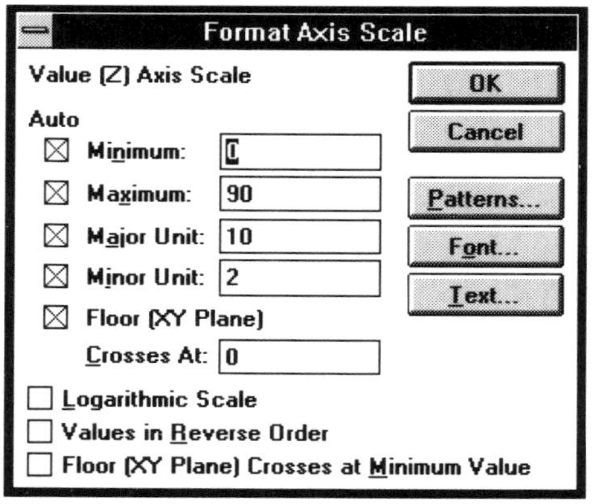

Figure 10.56

Figure 10.57 shows the dialog box with the X axis selected.

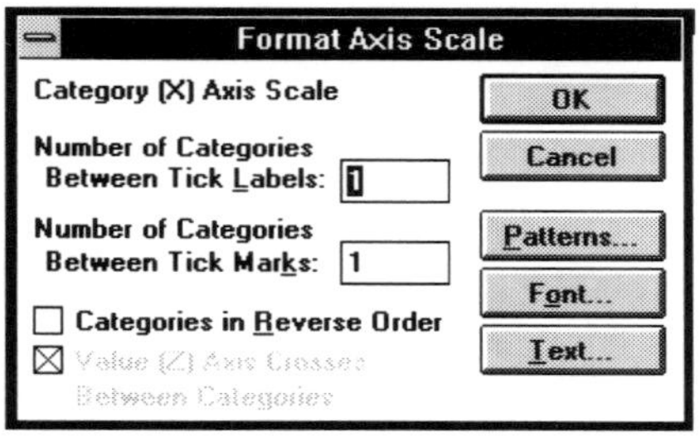

Figure 10.57

To scale an axis, click on the axis, then choose **Scale** from the format menu (**Alt-T, S**). Use Table 10.25 to help you decide the options to use when scaling axes.

Table 10.25 Axis Scaling Options

If the chart type is	And you want to	Then
Any	Change how many labels are skipped between categories (X axis)	Enter the skip value in Number of Categories between Tick Labels.
3D	Change how many labels are skipped between series (on Y axis)	Enter the skip value in Number of Series Between Tick Labels.
Any	Change how many categories (on X axis) occur between tick marks	Enter the skip value in Number of Categories between Tick Marks.
3D	Change how many series (on Y axis) occur between tick marks	Enter the skip value in Number of Series between Tick Marks.
Any	Place the categories (on X axis) in the reverse order in which they appear in the datasheet	Select **Categories in Reverse Order.**
3D	Place the series (on Y axis) in the reverse order which they appear in the datasheet	Select **Series in Reverse Order.**
Any	Control the smallest value displayed on chart (may exclude items from chart)	Enter a value in the Minimum area, or click **Auto** to choose automatically.

Any	Control the largest value displayed on chart (may exclude data items displayed on chart (may exclude data items on chart)	Enter the value in the Maximum area, or click **Auto** to choose automatically.
Any	Change the increment between major tick marks	Enter a value in the Major Unit area, or click **Auto** to choose automatically.
Any	Change the increment between minor tick marks	Enter a value in the Minor Unit area, or click **Auto** to choose automatically.
3D	Change where the floor (bottom part of 3D chart) crosses the value axis (Z axis)	Enter a value in the Floor (XY Plane) Crosses At area
2D	Change where the value axis (y axis) crosses the category axis (X axis)	Enter a value in the Value (Y) Axis Crosses At area.
2D	Change where the category axis (X axis) crosses the value axis (Y axis)	Enter a value in the Category (X) Axis Crosses At area.
Scatter (XY)	Change where the y axis crosses the X axis	Enter a value in Category (Y) axis Crosses At area.
3D	Plot the floor (XY plane) on the minimum value	Select **Floor (XY Plane) Crosses At Minimum Value.**
2D (except scatter or XY format)	Plot the Category axis(X axis) at the highest point on value (Y) axis	Select **Category (X) Axis Crosses At Maximum Value.**
Scatter (XY)	Plot the value (Y) axis at the highest point on the category (X) axis	Select **Value (Y) Axis Crosses At Maximum Category.**
3D	Plot the value (Z) axis between categories	Select **Value (Z) Axis Crosses Between Categories.**
2D	Plot the value (Y) axis between categories	Select **Value (Y) Axis Crosses Between Categories.**
2D	Plot the value (Y) axis at the last category	Select **Value (Y) Axis Crosses at Maximum Category.**
2D	Plot the value (Y) axis at a specified category	Enter value in the Value (Y) axis Crosses at Category Number area.

Legend

The *legend* is the portion of your chart that shows you what symbols identify the different categories. In Figure 10.58, the legend is showing the different colors for the East, West, and North categories.

Figure 10.58

The Legend menu, shown in Figure 10.59, allows you to place the legend at one of five different locations in the chart, to change the font for the legend, and to change the patterns used in the legend box.

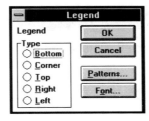

Figure 10.59

Follow these steps to move the legend:

1. Select the legend in the chart.
2. From the Format menu, choose **Legend** (**Alt-T, L**).
3. From the Type box, select the position you want for the legend.

The legend is moved to the new location.

Note that you can also move the legend with the mouse by clicking the legend and dragging it to the new location.

To change the font, click on the **Font** button (**Alt-O**). (Refer to the "Font" section earlier in this chapter for instructions on using the Font menu.)

To change the patterns in the legend, click on the **Pattern** button (**Alt-P**). (Refer to the "Patterns" section for instructions on using the Patterns menu.)

Number

There are also formatting options with the datasheet as well as the chart. You may want to control how values are displayed in the datasheet by specifying how many places are used after the decimal point, for example. Using the Number formatting option, you can specify:

◆ The number of places to add after the decimal point, including none

◆ Commas to be used every three decimal places

◆ Dollar signs to be used for numeric amounts

◆ Negative amounts to be enclosed in parentheses (and optionally displayed as red)

◆ Many other different ways of displaying data information

The number menu is displayed in Figure 10.60.

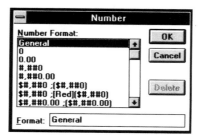

Figure 10.60

The Help system for Graph has a good explanation and examples of the different types of number formats. Follow these steps to get the Help display on number formats:

1. Open the Help menu (**Alt-H**).

2. Choose **How To...**.

3. Select **Format Data**.

4. Select **Formatting Numbers**.

This displays a help window with examples of the different types of numbering formats.

Follow these steps to format a number or group of cells in the datasheet:

1. Select the cell or cells in the datasheet.

2. From the Format menu, choose **Number**.

3. Select the format type you want to use.

4. Choose **OK**.

The formatting you specified is applied to the selected cells.

Column Width

You can change the width of columns in your datasheet by using the Column Width command. When a column in the datasheet isn't wide enough, Graph displays ### in the column, which means that there are too many characters in the data to fit in the present column width. You may also have columns where the data is only a few characters wide, and much of the space is wasted. In this case, you may want to make the column narrower. Figure 10.61 shows what your datasheet looks like when you have a column that is too narrow for the data.

	1st Qtr	2nd Qtr	3rd Qtr	4th
East	########	27.4	90	
West	30.6	38.6	34.6	
North	45.9	46.9	45	

Figure 10.61

To fix this problem, you can simply make the column wider. You can do this using the Column Width dialog box, shown in Figure 10.62.

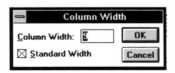

Figure 10.62

To change the column width:

1. Select the column that you want to change (or any cell in the column).

2. From the Format menu, choose **Column Width** (**Alt-T**, **W**).

3. Enter the new width of the column in the Column Width box, or select **Standard Width**, if you want to return to the default settings.

The selected column is resized to the width you specify. You can also change the column width by pointing to a line between column headers, and then dragging the line.

Chart

The Chart command on the Format menu is what you use to customize a chart's appearance. You can duplicate any chart format from the Gallery menu through use of the Format menu, or customize a chart in many different ways. Because using the Gallery command is a much easier way to format the chart, you should use the Chart command only when you can't get the appearance you want by using the predefined formats in the Gallery.

With the Chart command, you can:

◆ Choose a different display type (for example, switch from bar to column).

◆ Choose a display format (for example, stacked bars versus side-by-side).

◆ Control various characteristics of the chart (for example, bar depth and width).

The Chart menu is shown in Figure 10.63. Note that this menu may vary, depending on the type of chart, such as bar or column, that you have selected.

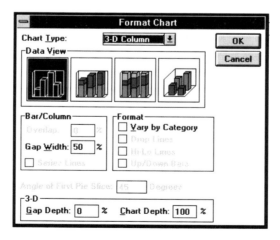

Figure 10.63

To get more information about the various options, use the Help menu.

1. From the Help menu, choose **Commands and Menus**.

2. Select **Format Chart**.

This displays a help window that explains the different chart format options.

Overlay

The Overlay menu allows you to customize the overlay graph, in the same way the Chart command allows you to customize the charts. You can duplicate any overlay format from the Gallery menu or customize a chart in many different ways by using this command. Since using the Gallery command is a much easier way to format the chart, use the Overlay command only when you want a format that is unavailable using the Gallery command.

With the Overlay command, you can:

◆ Choose a different overlay type (for example, switch from line to bar).

◆ Choose an overlay format (for example, stacked bars versus side-by-side).

◆ Control various characteristics of the overlay (for example, bar depth and width).

The Format Overlay dialog box is shown in Figure 10.64. Note that this menu varies, depending on the type of overlay such as bar, column, or line, that you have chosen.

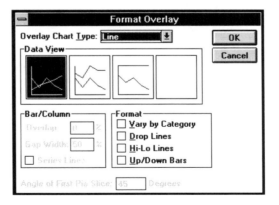

Figure 10.64

3-D View

You can customize the 3D display of any chart by using the Format 3D View menu. With this menu, you can rotate the chart around the vertical and horizontal axes, change perspective, and more. The menu is shown in Figure 10.65.

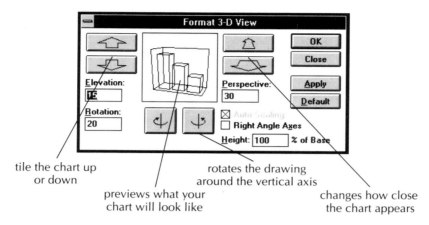

tile the chart up
or down

rotates the drawing
around the vertical axis

previews what your
chart will look like

changes how close
the chart appears

Figure 10.65

In the center of the dialog box, you can see a preview of how your chart will look after you apply a command. Table 10.26 has a brief summary of how to use the menu.

Table 10.26   Format 3D View Menu Options

If you want to	Then
Rotate the chart around the vertical axis	Use the rotation controls in the bottom center of the dialog box.
Tilt the chart up or down	Use the tilt controls in upper-left of the dialog box.
Change the perspective of the chart	1. Make sure the Right Angle Axes box is not checked. 2. Use the arrows in the top right of the dialog box.

For a detailed explanation of what each of the commands means, refer to the Help menu for the 3D chart:

1. From the Help menu, choose **Commands and Menus**.
2. Select **Format Chart**.

Table 10.27 Format Quick Reference

If you want to	Then
Edit the pattern within or bordering an item in the chart	1. Select the item. 2. Select the **Pattern** option. 3. Select the configuration you want.
Change characteristics of the font, such as the font, size, color, bold, italic, underlined, or background	1. Select the text. 2. Select the **Font** option. 3. Select the font characteristics you want.
Change the alignment of text (vertical or horizontal)	1. Select the text. 2. Select the **Text** option. 3. Select the text orientation you want.
Change the scale of one or more axes (from linear to logarithmic, for example)	1. Select the axis to change. 2. Select **Scale**. 3. Select the scale you want.
Change the position of the legend	1. Select the legend. 2. Select the **Legend** option. 3. Select the new position from one of the standard positions, or 1. Select the legend. 2. Drag the legend to the new position.
Change the format of numbers in the datasheet (adding dollar signs, for example)	1. Select the cells to be formatted. 2. Select the **Format** option. 3. Select the format you want.
Change the width of a column in the datasheet	1. Select the columns to be changed. 2. Select **Column width**. 3. Enter the new value for the width.
Customize the chart	1. Select the **Chart** option. 2. Select the new characteristics.
Customize the overlay	1. Select the **Overlay** option. 2. Select the new characteristics.
Change characteristics of a 3D chart, such as how it is rotated	1. Select **3D View**. 2. Select the new characteristics.

Summary

Now you have the skills necessary to prepare sophisticated graphs and incorporate them into your final document. Word provides you with an advanced graphing tool that can be used while preparing text documents. You can take a set of data and prepare attractive 2D and 3D charts to greatly enhance any document that needs to present a large amount of numerical information.

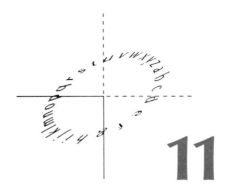

The Equation Editor

The Equation Editor enables you to create equations, from simple to extremely complex, and import them into your Word document. The Equation Editor has a built-in range of styles for different types of mathematical constructs, which allows you to enter a wide range of functions and symbols and have them appear correctly formatted in your final equation. Although the default formatting provided by the Equation Editor will probably be adequate, you can always adjust the appearance of the final equation by using the custom formatting options.

This chapter includes the following Equation Editor topics:

- an overview of how to use the Equation Editor
- the key features
- the Equation Editor Window
- the symbol and template palettes
- instructions for creating basic mathematical building blocks

Using the Equation Editor to Create an Equation

To create an equation using the Equation Editor, you will generally use the following process:

1. Invoke the Equation Editor from within your Word document.
2. Begin the process of building your Equation:
   - ◆ Select a template.
   - ◆ Enter symbols or text.
3. Adjust formatting, if required.
4. Exit the Equation Editor, and import the equations into your Word document.

Invoking the Equation Editor

Invoking the Equation Editor follows the standard Word procedures:

1. From the Insert menu, choose **Object (Alt-I, O)**.
2. Choose **Microsoft Equation 2.0** from the Object dialog box, shown in Figure 11.1.

The Equation Editor window is displayed on top of your Word document window. At this point, you are in the Equation Editor and can begin entering equations.

Table 11.1 shows the main features of the Equation Editor Window:

Table 11.1   Equation Editor Main Features

Feature	Description
Menu bar	The place where you choose menu options.
Slot	The location for text that is logically grouped together (an index, for example, or the integrand of an equation).
Insertion point	Identifies which slot you are in, and where text you type will appear.
Symbol palette	The choices for mathematical symbols.

Template palette	The choices for mathematical expressions.
Status bar	Shows the formatting currently in effect.

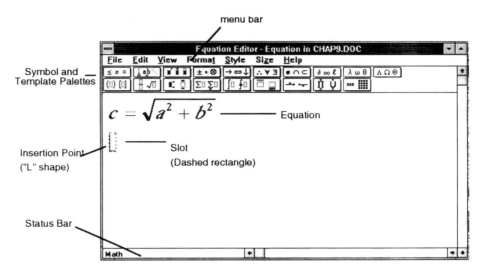

Figure 11.1

Key Features

This section gives you a brief overview of the Equation Editor's key features.

Embedded Object

Equations created with the Equation Editor are stored as *embedded objects*. This means that you can double-click an equation stored in your Word document to invoke the Equation Editor with the equation entered and ready for editing.

The Slot

The *slot* is the "building block" for the equation editor. All equations are made up of slots, which are filled with text, symbols, or even other slots. These slots contain related blocks of information that have the same formatting characteristics, such as font size. When you first invoke the Equation editor, you see a single dashed box. The dashed box represents the empty slot. When you type text, select a symbol or a template, the results of your action will be placed within the slot.

An equation may consist of many different slots. These slots can be nested, one slot inside of another slot, which is inside of another slot, and so on, enabling you to make extremely complex equations. An example of a complex equation that nests slots is shown in Figure 11.2, with the slots enclosed in rectangles:

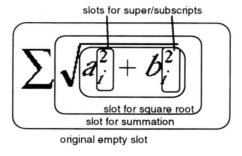

Figure 11.2

Templates consist of one or more slots, depending on the different formatting requirements. For example, there is an integral template that has both upper and lower limits. The upper and lower limit each have their own slots, since the limits require smaller characters than the contents of the integral.

Note that you can insert new templates into the slots of existing templates. For example, look at the definite integral shown in Figure 11.3, with the limits of integration left as empty slots:

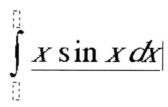

Figure 11.3

You can insert new templates into these empty slots. For example, Figure 11.4 has summation templates inserted into the empty slots of the definite integral template:

$$\int_{\Sigma y}^{\Sigma z} x \sin x \, dx$$

Figure 11.4

The Insertion Point

The insertion point indicates which slot you are in. Examples of the insertion point are shown below.

$$\sum \sum |x_i y_j$$

Next character will be inserted before the x

$$\sum \sum x_i | y_j$$

Next character will be inserted before the y

$$\sum \sum x_i y_j|$$

Next character will be inserted after the y

The horizontal bar runs the length of the slot you are currently in. The vertical bar runs from the top to the bottom of the slot, and indicates where the next item you insert will appear.

Moving the Insertion Point

Use Table 11.2 as a guide to moving the insertion point.

Table 11.2   Moving the Insertion Point

If you want to move	Then press
To the end of the slot	**Tab**
To the end of the next slot or if already there	**Enter** (Press **Tab** repeatedly to cycle through all the choices)
To the end of the previous slot	**Shift+Tab**
Right one character	**Right Arrow**
Left one character	**Left Arrow**
Up one line	**Up Arrow**
Next line	**Down Arrow**
Beginning of slot	**Home**
End of slot	**End**
Previous screen	**Page Up**
Next screen	**Page Down**

Selecting an Item

Before you can copy or delete an item, you must select it.

Table 11.3   Selecting an Item

To select	Do this
Part of an equation or matrix	Double-click the part of the equation, or, position the cursor at the start of the equation, hold down the mouse button down, and drag to the end of the item you want to select.

| A symbol | Hold **Ctrl**. When the cursor changes, click the symbol. |
| Everything in a slot | Position the cursor in the slot, and double-click. |

Deleting Selected Items

Use the options in Table 11.4 to delete selected items.

Table 11.4   Deleting Selected Items

To delete	Do this
The character to the left of the insertion point	Press **Backspace**.
The character to the right of the insertion point	Press **Del**.
The slot	1. Delete its contents. 2. Press **Backspace**. **Note:** Some slots (such as the integrand in the integral template) can't be deleted.
The selected items	From the Edit menu, choose **Clear**, or **Enter the New Text.**

Remember: You can always restore a deleted item by selecting **Undo** from the Edit menu (**Alt-E, U**), or **Ctrl-Z**.

Nudging Text

You may want to "fine tune" spacing (called *nudging*), by moving a selection one pixel at a time. You use nudging to:

- ◆ Move embellishments to better alignment with other embellishments.
- ◆ Form overstrikes or other special characters.
- ◆ Adjust kerning.

First, select the item(s) you want to move. Then perform an action from Table 11.5.

Table 11.5 Nudging Options

If you want to move one pixel	Then press
Left	**Ctrl+Left Arrow**
Up	**Ctrl+Up Arrow**
Down	**Ctrl+Down Arrow**
Right	**Ctrl+Right Arrow**

Vertically Aligning Equations (Piles)

You may want to enter a series of equations in successive line, and have the equations aligned vertically. Enter a carriage return after each equation, then choose the aligment method from Table 11.6.

Table 11.6 Vertical Alignment Options

To align the equations	Do this	Example
With left alignment	From the Format menu, choose **Align Left**, or **Ctrl- Shift L**.	$a = \sin x$ $b = \cos x + y \sin z$
With right alignment	From the Format menu, choose **Align Right**, or **Ctrl-Shift R**.	$a = \sin x$ $b = \cos x + y \sin z$
With center alignment	From the Format menu, choose **Align Center**.	$a = \sin x$ $b = \cos x + y \sin z$
With the equals sign (=)	From the Format menu, choose **Align At =**.	$a + b = \sin x$ $b = \cos x + y \sin z$

With the decimal point (.)	From the Format menu, choose **Align At ..**	$a + b = 15.75$ $b + c = 172.1$

With a different point in each equation

From the Space/Ellipses palette, choose the alignment symbol, and insert in each equation where you want the alignment point to be. (In the example, we choose to align with the 'b' variable).

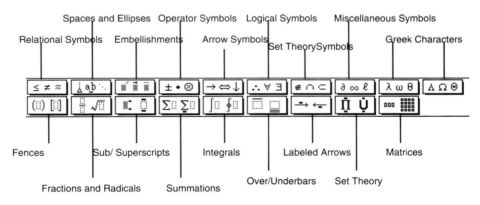

$a + b_{\triangle} = 15.75$
$b_{\triangle} + c = 172.1$

Symbol and Template Palettes

Spaces and Ellipses Operator Symbols Logical Symbols Miscellaneous Symbols

Relational Symbols Embellishments Arrow Symbols Greek Characters

Set TheorySymbols

Fences Sub/ Superscripts Integrals Labeled Arrows Matrices

Fractions and Radicals Summations Over/Underbars Set Theory

Figure 11.5

Relational Symbols

Description: Contains symbols to express relationships between two quantities, such as greater than, less than, or equal to.

Comments: The less than (<) and greater than (>) symbols are avaible on the keyboard, and are not included in this palette.

Spaces and Ellipses

Description: Contains the alignment symbol,

the spacing symbols,

and the ellipses symbol.

Comments: Use the alignment symbol when you to align equations vertically (see section on aligning equations). The spacing symbol is used to overide the Equation Editor default spacing. Use the ellipses when you want to indicate items that have been omitted (see section for matrices).

Embellishments

Description: Add embellishments, such as prime symbols, hats, dots, and so on, to a symbol.

Comments:

- ♦ You can put a slash through any symbol by using the slash embellishment at the end of the first row

- ♦ If you want to remove embelishments from a symbol, choose the first embellishment in the first row

- ♦ Change the height of all embellishments by using the Spacing command from the Format menu.

- ♦ Change the height of a single embellishment by using the Nudge commands (see the section on Nudging).

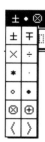

Operator Symbols

Description: Used to denote mathematical operators.

Comments: The angle brackets

are fixed size (one symbol in height). If you need angle brackets that expand to fit the expression, choose **Brackets** from the Fences template.

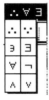

Arrow Symbols

Description: The arrow symbols are used to indicate convergence or implications.

Comments: Use the last symbol to indicate a carriage return. ↵

Logical Symbols

Description: Contains shorthand symbols for logic expressions such as "not", "and", "such that", and so on.

Set Theory Symbols

Description: Contains symbols for set union, intersection, membership, containment, and elements.

Comments: Note that the second and third rows contain the same symbols, with the third row being a heavier font. The heavier style looks better with summation signs.

Miscellaneous Symbols

Description: Contains symbols that don't fit into other categories.

Greek Characters

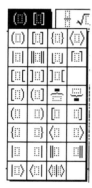

Description: Two palettes are included, one for upper case Greek letters, another for lower case.

Comments: You can also enter Greek characters by using the keyboard. To enter a Greek letter via the keyboard, Press **Ctrl-G**, then enter the corresponding English character. Enter the uppercase English character for the uppercase Greek letter, lowercase for the lowercase Greek letter.

Fences

Description: Used to enclose expressions.

Comments:

◆ Fences expand to accomadate equations that span several lines.

◆ If you want to increase overhang for all fences(the amount of the fence that extends above and below the expression) use the **Spacing** option from the Format menu. If you just want to change the overhang for the selected fence, use the Size menu.

Fractions and Radicals

Description: Contains templates for fractions and radicals.

Comments:

◆ Templates with slots that are dotted boxes will be normal size. Templates with solid black boxes for the slots will have the slots smaller size (suitable for super/subscripts).

◆ You can nest radicals; the radical sign will be resized to fit correctly:

$$\sqrt{x + \sqrt{y + \sqrt{z}}}$$

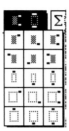

Sub/Superscripts

Description: Provides templates for subscripts and superscripts.

Comments:

- ◆ The small black dots indicate the location of the superscripts and subscripts.
- ◆ To attach a superscript or subscript to an existing expression, use the solid blocks (first two rows). Use the dotted blocks to bring up a slot with a superscript slot attached to it. For example, the solid block: gives you

$$a \sin x^{[]}$$

where the dotted block gives you

$$a \sin x \,[\,]^{[]}$$

- ◆ To change the spacing between the radical and the expression choose **Spacing** from the Format menu.

Summations

Description: Contains a variety of different summation sign formats. The dotted boxes are the slots for the summation expressions, the small solid boxes are the slots for the limits.

Comments:

- ◆ To create a repeated sum such as

$$\sum_x \sum_y \sum_z a_{xyz}$$

insert the summation in the slot of the previous summation, as many times as needed.

- ◆ To create a two line limit, such as

$$\sum_{\substack{0<j<10 \\ 0<i<100}} a\, ij$$

simply enter a carriage return after entering the first line of the limit.

◆ To change the default spacing of all summations, use the **Define** option from the Size menu. To change the spacing of the current summation, use the **Spacing** option from the Format menu.

◆ The size of the summation sign does not change with the size of the summand. To change the size of the summation sign, press **Ctrl**, and select the expression, then use the Size menu to choose the desired size.

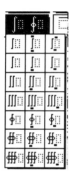

Integrals

Description: Includes a variety of different integral formats.

Comments:

◆ To create repeated integrals

$$\int \int_{x\ y} z\, dz$$

insert the new integral in the slot of the previous integral, as many times as needed.

◆ If you want the integral sign to expand to meet the height of the expression, hold down **Shift** when selecting the integral template.

Over/Underbars

Description: Insert single or double bars above or below expressions.

Labeled Arrows

Description: Labeled arrows indicate convergence to a limit, or properties of a function.

Comments: The small black box indicates the position of the label with respect to the arrow. For example, ⬚→

will let you generate a labeled arrow like: ████████

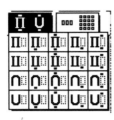

Set Theory

Description: Symbols for relationships between sets (unions and intersections), products, and coproducts.

Comments: The small black box indicates where indices are, the dotted box indicates the primary slot. For example,

will allow you to generate a symbol such as

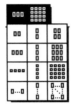

Matrices

Description: Create vectors and matrices.

Comments: The first row has templates for vectors and matrices of width two. The second row has templates for vectors and matrices of width three. The third row has templates for vectors and matrices of width four. The fourth row has templates for vectors and matrices of arbitrary size. When you select a template from this row, a dialog box will appear (see discussion below). Insert the matrix inside of a Fences bracket or template to enclose the matrix using conventional notation:

The Matrix Dialog Box

Whenever you select a template from the last row, the program displays the Matrix dialog box:

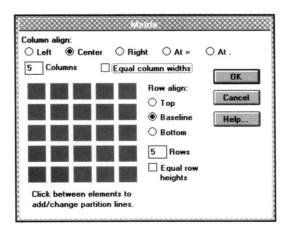

Figure 11.6

This dialog box allows you to:

- Choose the number of rows or columns in your matrix or vector.
- Control the alignment of the columns and rows.
- Create tables or boxes around the equations.

Aligning Column Entries

You can control how equations are aligned horizontally in the columns, as seen in Table 11.7.

Table 11.7 Aligning Column Entries

If you want the column entries to be	Click
Left aligned	**Left**
Center aligned	**Center**
Right aligned	**Right**
Aligned with the equal (=) sign	**At=**
Aligned with the decimal point (.)	**At (.)**

Controlling Column Width

If you want all the columns to be the same width, click the **Equal Column Widths** box. The Equation editor takes the width of the widest column, and changes all other columns to this width. If this box is left blank, the Equation editor adjusts the space of each column to fit the widest equation in the column.

Aligning Equations Along the Rows

You can choose whether rows are aligned with the tops of the equations, bottoms, or baselines (bottom) of text in the equations, as seen in Table 11.8.

Table 11.8   Aligning Equations Along the Rows

If you want rows to be aligned with	Then choose the Row Align option
The top of the equation	**Top**
The bottom of the text	**Baseline**
The bottom of the equation	**Bottom**

Cutting and Pasting Templates

You may often find that you need to put an equation you've created *inside* of another template. For example, suppose you're calculating the length of a line using the quadratic formula for some set of points:

$$\sqrt{\left(x_{i+1} - x_i\right)^2 + \left(y_{i+1} - y_i\right)^2}$$

Figure 11.7

After you create this equation, you realize that you need to put it inside of a summation sign, to indicate that you're going to sum the lengths of the lines over the index "i." You cannot simply select the summation sign and have it inserted in front of the expression, since you want this expression inside of the summation sign's slot, instead of ouside the summation sign slot.

To insert the expression inside of the summation sign, select the expression (from the Edit menu choose **Select All**, or drag the cursor over the entire expression with the mouse button pressed). The expression will appear in reverse video, indicating it is selected:

$$\sqrt{\left(x_{i+1} - x_i\right)^2 + \left(y_{i+1} - y_i\right)^2}$$

Figire 11.8

From the Edit menu, choose **Cut**. This places the expression in the Clipboard, and removes it from the Equation Editor window. Next, choose the summation sign template:

$$\sum_i \begin{bmatrix} \end{bmatrix}$$

Figure 11.9

Place the insertion point inside of the insertion slot (the dotted box) for the summation sign, and from the Edit menu select **Paste**. The expression is now pasted inside of the summation sign slot.

$$\sum_i \sqrt{\left(x_{i+1} - x_i\right)^2 + \left(y_{i+1} - y_i\right)^2}$$

Figure 11.10

Summary

This completes the section on the use of the Equation Editor. Now you have acquired the necessary skills to enter simple to complex mathematical expressions in the Equation Editor. You can accept the default formatting provided by the Equation Editor or you can alter the formatting as desired. The Equation Editor has a different look and feel to it than the other options in Word. The best way to gain familiarity with the Equation Editor is to use it. Once you get comfortable with the user interface, you'll find that the Equation Editor is an indispensible tool when you need to express mathematical equations.

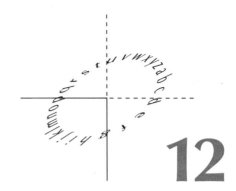

Saving Time with Macros

This chapter discusses one of the most powerful features in Word for Windows—the ability to automate a complex series of operations into a single operation called a macro. It covers:

- what are macros?
- why use macros?
- how to create macros
- how to save macros
- how to invoke a macro
- how to record a macro
- how to run a macro
- how to test a macro
- macro tutorial

What Are Macros?

Macros are programs for Word. They contain a sequence of steps that you need to perform repeatedly. They can be as simple as a series of keystrokes, or as complex as a several-hundred-line WordBasic program.

Why Use Macros?

Instead of forcing you to repeat the same steps at the keyboard, macros allow you to save time and only enter a single command to perform these actions.

The following example shows the power of macros. Suppose you find yourself changing the order of columns in a table, switching the first column, for example, with the last. This can be a time consuming process to perform manually. A macro called RotateTableColumn (included in the NEWMACROS.DOC file in your Word package) can automate this process for you.

This is the example table:

a	b	c
d	e	f
g	h	i
j	k	l

Figure 12.1

Suppose you want to swap the first column (a, d, g, j) with the last (c, f, i, l). If you install RotateTableColumn as a macro in the Table menu, you can perform this operation easily. You can select the macro from the Table menu.

After selecting this macro, Word rotates the columns of the table automatically:

b	c	a
e	f	d
h	i	g
k	l	j

Figure 12.2

When you select the table menu, you most likely won't see RotateTableColumn as one of the options. That's because we installed RotateTableColumn as a menu option on our version of Word. Customizing Word menus is just one of the many ways you can configure Word to your exact liking.

Macros are not limited to just operations on tables. As you gain more experience with Word macro capability, you may find yourself creating more and more sophisticated macro applications.

How To Create Macros

There are several different ways to create macros. You can:

- ◆ Capture a series of keystrokes.
- ◆ Create a WordBasic program.
- ◆ Edit an existing macro.

You capture a series of keystrokes by using the Macro command from the Tools menu, or by double-clicking the **REC** button on the Status bar (for details, see the section "How to Record a Macro" later in this chapter). This feature of Word lets you type a series of keystrokes that you find yourself performing repeatedly, save them as a macro, then have Word repeat the same sequence of keystrokes whenever you choose to run the macro.

How To Save Macros

There are two basic types of macros—macros that are available only for a particular template (*template macros*), and macros that are available for every document (*global macros*). At first, you might think that every macro should be saved as a global macro, since you could then access it from any document. If you're going to create only a few macros, this approach may be acceptable. But once you start adding a lot of macros to your global library, you'll find that giving all of them unique names can become confusing. Also, you may find that one type of template requires a slightly different version of a macro than another template. By associating a macro with a particular template, you can avoid this confusion, and customize each macro to the template you need.

Table 12.1   Template versus Global Macros

If you plan to use the macro that is	Then select
Unique to a particular template	**Template**
Used by many different templates	**Global**

Assigning the Macro to a Template

By default, Word puts new macros in the Normal template. The normal template is the default template, and any macros in the normal template are available globally, meaning that the macros are accessible from any template. However, you may find that not all macros are needed by every template, or that you want to have two or macros with the same name in different templates. In this case, you will want to move the macro out of the normal template into the template you want to associate it with. To do this, you would use the Organizer, by selecting **Macro** from the Tools menu, then clicking the **Organizer** button in the Macro dialog box.

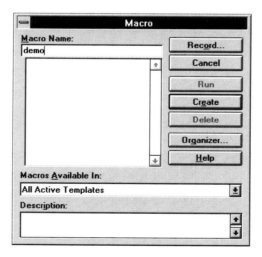

Figure 12.3

After you double click the **Organizer** button, the Organizer dialog box is displayed, allowing you to copy, delete, or rename a macro.

Figure 12.4

How To Invoke A Macro

Word allows you to pick the best way to select and run your macro. You can:

- ◆ Select the macro from the list of macros in the Tools/Macros command.
- ◆ Select a special key combination to run your macro automatically.
- ◆ Assign the macro to one of the pull-down menus.
- ◆ Place an entry for the macro in the toolbar.

In general, using the list of macros from the Tools/Macro command gives you the greatest flexibility, with nearly unlimited choices for the macro name. You can select any macro using this method, as any macro saved for the current template and all global macros are visible. Key combinations, while providing faster access, provide a more limited set of possible macros, as there is a more limited set of unique key combinations available. You can also insert a macro in one of the pull-down menus as an option. The quickest way to find and invoke your macro is by using the Toolbar option, which allows you to associate an icon on the toolbar with the macro. There are, however, only a very limited number of spaces for new icons, and you may be forced to remove existing icons to accommodate your macro-naming scheme.

This gives you some idea of how to proceed—use the Toolbar option only for the very few macros that you expect to use very often, key combinations for macros that will see a fair amount of use, and simply use the default method of selecting through the Tools/Macro macro list for macros that you will use infrequently.

Table 12.2   Frequency of Macro Use

If you expect to use the macro	Then
Very frequently	Assign it as a toolbar icon.
Frequently	Assign it as a keystroke combination.
Somewhat often	Assign it as a menu option.
Occasionally	Use the macro list from the Tools/Macro command (that is the default; no action on your part is required).

Assigning the Macro as a Toolbar Icon, Menu Item, or Shortcut Key

You can always run a macro by name, by entering the Macro name in the Macro dialog box and clicking the **Run** button. But if you expect to use the macro frequently, you may wish to assign it to either a toolbar icon, menu item, or shortcut key. To do this, simply click either the **Toolbar**, **Menu**, or **Keyboard** icon in the Record Macro dialog box, shown in Figure 12.5. To get to the Record macro dialog box, simply double click the **REC** button on the Status bar.

Figure 12.5

If your macro will expect text to be selected prior to the macro being invoked (for example, if the macro changes the font of the selected text), select the text *prior* to recording.

N O T E

How To Record A Macro

Now that you understand the different ways that you can name your macros, you can go through the procedure for recording a macro. This is a process where Word starts recording every keystroke you enter, until you indicate that you want it to stop recording. You may find that you often want to make your macro more flexible—you will learn about both ways to do that later. First, you will learn about the basics of recording a macro.

Starting Macro Recording

The first step in recording a macro is to double-click the **REC** button on the Status bar or select the **Record** button in the Macro dialog box. Note that Word automatically assigns a name for the macro in the Macro Name box. If you don't like the macro name assigned, you can type another one over it.

You can also assign a shortcut key combination to start recording a macro. You'll see that the default is for a key combination that simultaneously requires the Ctrl key, the Shift key, and any other alphabetic key (a, b, c) combination. If you don't want the Ctrl key or the Shift key, simply click on the corresponding box to remove the X.

Be careful when selecting a key combination that does not require you to press the **Ctrl** key, and only uses the Shift key plus some alphabetic key. Suppose you choose **Shift-A** to be the name of your macro. From this point on, whenever you press **Shift-A**, even when you're just capitalizing the first letter of word beginning with A, the macro will be executed. This probably isn't what you intended.

WARNING

Word tells you when you are in macro record mode. Look at the bottom line in your Word window, the Status bar. You will see:

- ◆ a tape icon added to the cursor when the macro recorder is on
- ◆ a macro icon displayed in the document window

◆ the REC button on the Status bar will be highlighted

Figure 12.6

The macro icon allows you to either stop macro recording (by clicking the left button), or temporarily pause recording (by clicking the right button). If you've paused the recording by pressing the right button, you can restart the recorder again by clicking the right button again. The right button simply toggles the recording on and off. When you're finished recording, click the left button.

Recording Your Keystrokes

After you've started the macro recording feature, all keystrokes that you enter will be recorded into the macro until you stop recording. Note that you cannot use the mouse to select text or move the cursor because the macro recorder cannot record mouse movements. This really isn't a disadvantage, when you stop to think about it. Since macros will probably be used in a variety of different documents, the location of the affected text will change as well. You can, however, use the mouse to select menu items, as you normally do.

If You Make Mistakes While Recording Keystrokes

If you're recording a fairly short macro, then it is a simple matter to stop the recording and restart again under the same name. If you're recording a long macro, chances are that you will make at least one mistake, and it is impractical to go back and re-record your macro each time. Depending on the nature of the mistake, you can simply use the Undo command (click the **Undo** button in the toolbar), or press **Alt-E**, **U**, or **Ctrl-Z** to remove your last entry. After you choose the **Undo** command and see that the mistake is corrected, enter the correct keystrokes.

Note that the macro recorder is simply recording all of these actions, the incorrect keystrokes, followed by the Undo, followed by the correct keystrokes. This means that you have not removed the incorrect action from the macro. When your macro runs, the incorrect keystrokes will be executed, followed by the Undo command, which will reverse their actions, followed by the correct keystrokes.

You may find that you've made mistakes that you can't undo easily, or there are other changes you'd like to make to your macro once you're finished. Word has a macro editor that allows you to edit an existing macro or create a new macro. You can use this to remove commands or add new ones. You can edit a macro that has incorrect keystrokes followed by Undo commands, and remove the incorrect statements and Undo command to make your macro run more efficiently. You use the macro editor after you finish recording your macro, since you cannot correct your mistakes with the editor while recording. The macro editor is discussed in more detail in a later section of this chapter.

Running Your Macro

There are four ways that you can run a macro:

◆ with a macro name
◆ with a keystroke combinations
◆ from a pull-down menu
◆ with a button on the toolbar

Table 12.3 shows how:

Table 12.3   Four Ways to Run a Macro

If your naming method is	Then run your macro by
A name	Choosing **Macro** from the Tool menu, then selecting the name (**Alt-T**, **M**, name).
Keystroke	Typing the keystroke combination you assigned to the macro.
Menu	Choosing the macro name from the pull-down menu.
Toolbar button	Clicking the button on the toolbar.

If You Forget How You Named Your Macro

It is easy to forget the name you've used for your macro. By use of Word's display options, finding your macro is an easy task.

Table 12.4   Finding a Macro Name

If you're trying to find a macro by	Then
Name	1. From the Tools menu, choose **Macro (Alt-O, M)**.
	2. Select **Where To Search** for the macro in the macros available in the pull-down list.
	3. Check the list of macros to find the one you need.
Keystroke	1. From the Tools menu, choose **Customize (Alt-T, C)**.
	2. Select **Keyboard.**
	3. Select **Macros** in the Categories section (see Figure 12.7 below).
	4. Check the list of macros to find the one you need.
Menu	1. Choose a menu from the categories section of the Tools/Customize dialog box.
	2. Check the list of menu options.
	3. Continue steps 1 and 2 until you find the one you need.
Toolbar	1. From the Tools menu, choose **Customize (Alt-T,C)**.
	2. Select **Toolbar.**
	3. Select **Macro** from the Category section.
	4. Check the list of macros to find the one you need.

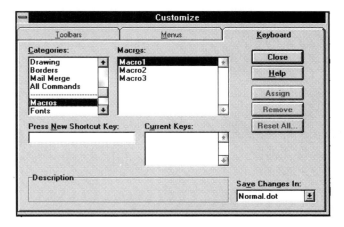

Figure 12.7

How To Test A Macro

Once you've created your macro, the next step is to verify that it works correctly on the documents in which you want to use it. The basic testing procedure is as follows:

1. Create a copy of the document on which you want to test the macro.
2. Run the macro on the document.
3. Verify that the changes are correct.
4. If the macro isn't performing as you expected, then use the **Step** option in the toolbar through the Macro Edit dialog box to run your macro, one line at a time, until you see where the problem is occurring.
5. Edit and correct the macro.

The following sections explain each of these steps in more detail.

Creating a Copy of Your Document

Creating a copy of the document you want to test your macro on is an important first step. After all, you're testing your macro for the first time, and you really don't know if the macro will do what you intended, or if it's going to damage the document.

Copying your document is an easy process in Word.

1. From the File menu, choose **Save As (Alt-F, A**). Word displays the Save As dialog box.

2. Enter a new name for the document in the File Name box, and choose **OK.** Now the new document is the one you're currently editing, and the macro will be run on this copy. Remember to go back to your original document when you are finished testing.

Running the Macro

After you've made a copy of your document, the next step is to actually run the macro on your new copy and verify that the macro performed as you intended.

Table 12.5   Running a Macro

If you're trying to run a macro by	Then
Name	1. From the Tools menu, select, **Macro (Alt-T, M**).
	2. Check the list of macros to find the one you need.
	3. Select the macro name you want to run.
Keystroke	1. Enter the keystroke combination for your macro.
Menu	1. Choose the menu that contains the macro.
	2. Select the macro name or use the access key (the underlined character).
Toolbar	1. Select the **Toolbar** icon for your macro.

Verifying the Changes

After your macro finishes running, examine your document. Did the macro make the changes you intended? If not, then you'll need to enter the next phase of macro design—the debugging phase. In this next step, you will see how to run a macro one instruction at a time, to see exactly where the error is in the macro.

Using Macro Edit to Step Through Your Macro

To single-step through a macro, use the **Macro Editing** option within the Tools window:

1. From the Tools menu, select **Macro (Alt-T, M)**.
2. Select the macro name you want to step through.
3. Click on the **Edit** button.

Word displays the macro editing window. You will see several icons across the top of the macro edit window.

Figure 12.8

The leftmost portion of the toolbar displays the name of the macro you are currently editing. The icons to the right of the macro name are described in Table 12.6.

Table 12.6 Macro Icons

Turns macro recording on or off.

Records the next executed command.

Starts the current macro.

Highlights each statement as it is executed.

Continues running the macro from the currently active statement.

Stops recording or running the macro.

Single-steps the macro, either by stepping over subroutines (left icon) or into it (right icon). If you know that a subroutine is working correctly, for example, you wouldn't need to step through it. In this case, you would use the left icon.

Lists the active variables in the macro.

 Adds or removes a REM to each selected line. Use this to comment out sections of code while debugging, and remove the comments when through.

 Runs, creates, deletes, or revises a macro.

 Runs the macro dialog editor.

Notice that we've introduced some new concepts. A macro may call other macros to avoid making you duplicate instructions that have already been saved as a macro. Your macro, for example, may call other macros that you created earlier. If you already debugged these other macros and know that they are functioning properly, then there is no need to waste time debugging them. This is the reason for the Step and the Step Sub options. Use Step Sub when you want to simply execute the instructions in a called macro without tracing through them, and Step when you want to trace through every macro called.

One thing you'll want to do while debugging your macro is to have both the macro and your test file visible. This way you can actually see the changes your macro is making to the document as you step through the macro, one line at a time.

To split the screen into two windows, one for the macro, and the other for the test file, follow this procedure:

1. Bring up your macro in the macro edit window:

   ◆ Press **Alt-T**, **M** to display the list of macros.

   ◆ Select the macro in the macro list.

   ◆ Select **Edit.**

2. Choose the **Arrange All** option from the Window menu (**Alt-W, A**). You'll see something similar to Figure 12.9.

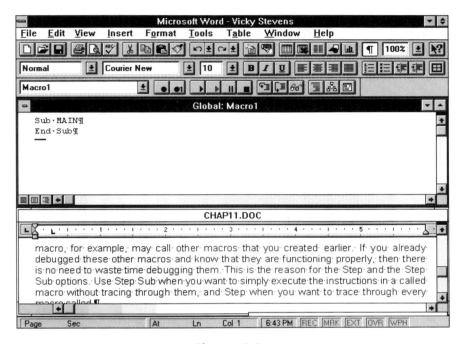

Figure 12.9

To start stepping through your macro, click the document window to make it active, then select the **Step** or **Step Subs** option, and watch the changes to your original text file as your macro runs.

Editing Your Macro with the Macro Editor

As you might have suspected, you can also use the macro editor to edit existing macros, and create new macros. You'll find the editing process quite similar to normal document editing, with a few exceptions. Formatting rules don't apply to macros, since you're not creating a document to be printed.

If you want to learn about the WordBasic macro language as you modify existing macros, place the insertion point at the beginning of any statement in your macro that you want to understand, then press **F1**. You'll get a help window explaining the function.

Macro Tutorial

Now that you've learned the basics of creating, invoking, editing, and debugging macros, you can go through the actual process of creating a macro. The tutorial draws on information you learned in the previous sections, so if at any point you need more information than is contained in this tutorial, refer to the information presented earlier.

Often when you create tables, you perform two steps: the first step is the creation of the table, the next step is drawing a border around the table. As you repeat these operations frequently, it would make sense to put both of them in the form of a single macro. You've also seen that you need to perform these operations in a variety of different templates, which gives you a hint to use later on when deciding the best way to store and invoke your macro.

There are two basic ways to proceed in creating the macro—you can record the macro as a series of keystrokes or you can create it "from scratch" in WordBasic. Since you may not be an expert in WordBasic at this point, this section discusses the keystroke recording method.

First, follow these instructions for stepping through the process of creating a table and drawing a border around it. Then you can start recording the keystrokes as a macro. Gaining a little familiarity with the mechanics of how to create a table with borders will help you avoid entering errors into our macro as you record. Since the macro recorder cannot record mouse movements, you need to use the pull-down menus to create the table, not the Table button on the toolbar. (The toolbar icon requires use of the mouse to define the size of the table.)

1. From the Table menu, choose **Insert (Alt-A, I)** to create a table. For now, assume a fixed table size of two columns by three rows. You will fill in those values in the Insert Table dialog box, which requests table size information.

2. Choose **OK.** Word inserts an empty table, two columns by three rows, at the current insertion point.

3. From the Table menu, choose **Select Table (Alt-A, A)** to select the entire table. Remember that the macro recorder cannot record mouse movements, so you cannot use the mouse to select the table.

4. From the Format menu, choose **Border (Alt-T, B)**. Word draws a border around the table.

5. Select the **Grid** option **(Alt-G)**, and click on **OK.** Word draws a border around the table, and lines between each of the cells.

Now that you understand the mechanics of the table creation process, you can go about the process of recording the keystrokes into a macro.

Follow these steps to make this process easy:

1. Open a new file. The Normal template is attached to it by default, and all macros created will be global.

2. From the Tools menu, choose **Macro**. In dialog, type the name first, then choose **Record.** You can also double-click **REC** in the status bar.

3. In the Record Macro Name box change the name to TableWithBorder.

4. In the Description box, assign a meaningful description to the macro, so when you choose the macro name later on, you can look at the description and remember what it is supposed to do. Move to the description window, and enter a description, such as **Create a table with borders.**

5. Select **OK** to start macro recording.

Now repeat the process you used earlier to create a table with borders: create the table, select the table, then draw the border around the table. After you finish, and the table with borders is created, choose **Stop Recorder** from the Tools menu, or click the **Stop** button in the Macro. Recording dialog box is displayed in the upper left of your document window. The keystrokes you used to record the macro are now saved under the name TableWithBorder. Also note that the REC button is no longer highlighted.

Now verify the operation of your macro. Before you assign the macro to a menu, try it out. Follow these steps to see how to use the various macro debugging features.

1. From the Tools menu, choose **Macro (Alt-T, M)**.

2. Select your macro **(TableWithBorder)**.

3. Select **Run.**

You should see a table with a border created at the position of insertion point.

Now suppose that your macro didn't work as intended. To debug the macro, you create two windows, one which contains the macro, and another that has the file you're working on. Follow these steps:

1. From the Tools menu, choose **Macro** to create the macro debugging window (**Alt-T, M**). Word displays the Macro dialog box.

2. From Word's main Menu bar, choose **Window**, then **Arrange All**. You'll see the macro in one window, and the document in another.

3. Position the insertion point on the **Step** option in the macro window, and click.

4. Click this option repeatedly, noticing the line of the macro that is highlighted, and the action the macro performs on the document.

The highlighted line shows you the *next* line to be executed when you choose the **Step** option. This debugging process is valuable when you are trying to determine why a macro isn't working properly.

If you're satisfied that the macro is working properly, decide how to invoke it. Because you want to use this macro in a variety of different templates, this should be a *global macro*. Otherwise, you would need to recreate the macro for every template in which you might use it. This is something you are doing frequently— but not so often you need to insert it as a button on the toolbar. Instead, you'll add the macro to the Table menu, so you can access it easily.

Follow these steps to add the macro to the Table menu:

1. From the Tools menu, select **Customize** (**Alt-T**, **C**).

2. Select the **Menus** tab.

3. In the Categories window, select **Macros**.

4. In the Macros window, select **TableWithBorders**.

5. Choose **Table** for the Change What Menu, and **TableWithBorders** for Name on Menu.

6. Select **Close** to exit this option or you can select **Add** if doing multiple additions.

Now you can invoke this macro from the Table menu. Open the Table menu, and TableWithBorders will be displayed as one of the last menu choices. Now you can invoke your macro just like any of the Word menu choices.

Summary

Now you can create and edit Word macros and customize the toolbar and menus with functions you design just for your applications.

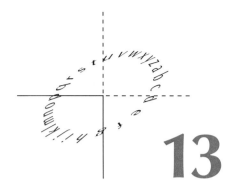

Using Mail Merge

T his chapter discusses the basics of mail merge. You learn how to:

- ◆ create form letters and documents
- ◆ create and edit the data file and header files
- ◆ import data files from other applications

If you've ever found yourself printing several versions of the same letter that differs in only a few areas, building documents from "boilerplate" text, or if you need to create mailing labels, then Word for Windows can help eliminate a lot of drudgery. By allowing you to create a "master" copy of a document, along with a "data file" that contains the frequently changing information, Word can automate the tedious process of creating form letters and documents.

What Are Form Letters And Documents?

The term *form letter* refers to a letter that has a few sections that change often, but the bulk of which stays constant. One example would be a letter that is part of a mass mailing. The copy you get has your name and address on it, but the rest of the text stays the same for everyone who gets the letter.

Form letters are not restricted to simply having a customized name and address, however. Word allows you to embed decision-making fields in your form letters to make them even more personalized. For example, suppose that you were marketing a product for both men and women, but wanted to stress different aspects of the product, depending on whether the recipient of the letter was male or female. Word would allow you to create a form letter that used different paragraphs, depending on the gender of the recipient.

Form documents use exactly the same concept. Suppose there is a basic contract that you send out to clients, but some of the specific sections in the document change, depending on the type of service the client is being provided. Word allows you to insert other documents into these sections, on the basis of some decision-making fields that are included. For example, if a client is a Medicare patient, you could code instructions into your document to insert another document that deals with Medicare patients. If the client is privately insured, then you could code instructions to insert another document directed privately insured patients.

The Basics Behind Mail Merge

Now that you've gotten an idea of how mail merge can be useful, look at the process in more detail. There are two files used in the mail merge process: the *data file* and the *main document.* The data file contains all of the variable information in your document, and the main document contains the text that remains constant as well as instructions (referred to as *fields*) about how to fill in the variable information. You can also can select only portions of the data file to be used at mail merge time, by using the Mail Merge/Merge/Record Selection menu commands. For example, suppose you just want to send the documents to customers who live in Oregon. You could tell Word to pull only the records from the data file that have Oregon in the state field.

The Data File

The data file can be either a Word document you create yourself, or a Microsoft Excel, dBase, Lotus 1-2-3, or WordPerfect file.

If you create the data file in Word, the file contains two basic sections: a header section and a record section. Both the header and record sections are made up of fields. If the concept of records and fields is new to you, the next paragraph will help. Most of time, you will not need to understand how the data file is structured. Word has macros to help you create and edit the data file when the data file is created at the same time as the main document.

Think of a file as consisting of lines of information, with each line containing all of the information on a particular item. Each distinct piece of information on the line is considered a field. For example, suppose your data file was a list of all of the employees in the company, one employee per line, and each line consisting of information like the employee name, home address, social security number, phone number, and emergency contact. The line of information associated with the individual employee is called a *record*. The individual items within the record, such as the phone number and social security number, are the *fields*.

The first record, or line, in the data file is the *header record*. Each field in the header record is the name of the corresponding information below it. Using our previous example, the header record would consist of employee name, home address, social security number, phone, and emergency contact. The header record has the names for the columns of information underneath it. These names are what you use in the main document fields to extract information from the data file.

The header section is only the first line of the data file. The second through last records in the data file are the actual data. In the following example, this might be information like "John Smith," "13079 SW Pickleberry Way," "508-83-4171," "555-2025," "Mrs. Adolphus Smith," and so on, one line for each employee.

The data file would then look something like Table 13.1.

Table 13.1   A Sample Data File

name	address	ssnumber	phone	contact
John Smith	13079 SW Pickleberry Way	508-83-4171	555-2025	Mrs. Aldophus Smith

Again, don't be too concerned about how the data file is structured. You can use Word's built-in macros to guide you through the creation and editing process. The following chapters describe in detail how to use these macros.

You can leave out the header record information if you create a separate header file. (See "The Header File" in this chapter for more information.) However, this is really only needed for data files that come from other applications. If you are creating a data file from Word, it would probably be most convenient for you to have the header and data information in the same data file.

The Header File

You may want to use a data file created by another application, and this data file may not have a header record at the beginning of it. You then have two choices: either edit the data file and add a header record manually, or create a separate header file that contains all of the field name information. If the data file you're getting from another application may be changing frequently, then you won't want to edit the file continually and add a header record with each revision. In this case, it is much simpler to create a separate file, called a *header file*, where the field name information is entered once, and doesn't need to be updated with each new version of the data file. Use of the header file is explained in the following sections.

The Main Document

The main document contains all of the text that you want to appear in all documents, plus one or more of the following type of fields:

- merge
- if
- ask, prompt, fillin, quote
- mergerec
- next
- skipif, nextif

Merge fields are what you use in place of variable text in your main document. In the case of a form letter, a merge field might be the recipient's name and address. *If fields* allow you to make decisions based on values of text, such as using a record only if the state in the address is Oregon. *Ask, prompt, fillin,* and *quote fields* insert information that is not available in the data file, either as information that the user enters for each version of the main document or as constant information that appears the same way in every version of the document. *Mergerec fields* print the record number being used in the current version of the document (you can use this to see where information is coming from in the data file). The next field pulls information from the next record in the data file, without starting another version of the document. This is useful in situations where you might want to generate a list of names in the document, for example, all of the employees who live in Washington. The *skip if field* skips a record that does not meet your requirements, such as skipping any employee records that have a blank entry in the emergency contact field. The *next if field* merges the next record like the next field, but it allows you to specify conditions for its use.

A Simple Form Letter Example

Suppose you're trying to find a job, and you want to send out dozens of cover letters, but you need to customize the letter in some areas, such as the name of the company and the contact person. First, you would develop a general cover letter and think about what information might change:

```
                              13079 SW Easy Street
                                Tigard, OR 97224
                                (503) 555-2000
                                January 29, 1992

Mr. Elmer Fudd
Fudd's Factory
12 Fuddy Duddy Rd.
Marmot, OR 97666

Dear Mr. Elmer Fudd:

I read in the Marmot News about an opportunity for a NitPick. I feel that
I am well-qualified for a position as a NitPick, and would like to submit
my resume for your consideration.

I have a great deal of experience in NitPicking, having done almost
exactly this kind of work for the past several years. Additionally, I
am a wonderful and entertaining employee. My coworkers are constantly
entertained by my incessant joking and my prying into their private
lives.

Sincerely,


Mr. Wonderful
```

Figure 13.1

Looking at our (facetious) cover letter, you can see a few things that will change from letter to letter, for example:

◆ The data under the address

◆ The person and company to whom the letter is directed

◆ Where you read about the position

◆ The nature of the position advertised

The date can be inserted as a date field, which has nothing to do with mail merge. (Simply place the cursor where you want the data, then press **Alt I, T** and select the appropriate date option.) For the rest of the information, you would replace the text in the letter with the names for the fields in the data file. Because you can name the fields in the data file anything you want, you can make the names meaningful. Here's how the example letter looks after the field codes are inserted:

```
                        13079 SW Easy Street
                         Tigard, OR 97224
                          (503) 555-2000
                     {date \@ "MMMM d, yyyy" }
{mergefield towhom}
{mergefield compname}
{mergefield compaddr}
{mergefield compcsz}

Dear {mergefield towhom}:

I read in the {mergefield wherefound} about an opportunity for a
{mergefield jobdesc}. I feel that I am well-qualified for a position as
a {mergefield jobdesc}, and would like to submit my resume for your
consideration.

I have a great deal of experience in {mergefield jobdesc}ing, having done
almost  exactly  this  kind  of  work  for  the  past  several  years.
Additionally, I am a wonderful and entertaining employee. My coworkers
are constantly entertained by my incessant joking and my prying into
their private lives.

Sincerely,


Mr. Wonderful
```

Figure 13.2

For this type of letter, you need to create a data file with a column for each of these items. An example follows.

Table 13.2 Sample Data File

towhom	compname	compaddr	compcsz	wherefound	jobdesc
Mr. Smithers	IRS	1099 Taxfield Lane	King City OR 55555	Oregon Fishwrapper	Gopher
Gomer Pyle	Gomer's Service Station	01 Brambleberry Lane	Mayberry, NC 66655	Mayberry Scream 'n Tattler	Pump Jockey

When you perform the mail merge, Word reads from the data file and inserts the information into a copy of your master document. Your letters will look something like Figure 13.3.

```
                              13079 SW Easy Street
                               Tigard, OR 97224
                               (503) 555-2000
                               January 31, 1992
    Mr. Smithers
    IRS
    1099 Taxfield Lane
    King City, OR 55555

    Dear Mr. Smithers:

    I read in the Oregon Fishwrapper about an opportunity for a Gopher. I
    feel that I am well-qualified for a position as a Gopher, and would like
    to submit my resume for your consideration.

    I have a great deal of experience in Gophering, having done almost exactly
    this kind of work for the past several years. Additionally, I am a
    wonderful and entertaining employee. My coworkers are constantly
    entertained by my incessant joking and my prying into their private
    lives.

    Sincerely,


    Mr. Wonderful
```

Figure 13.3

```
                            13079 SW Easy Street
                             Tigard, OR 97224
                             (503) 555-2000
                             January 31, 1992
        Gomer Pyle
        Gomer's Service Station
        01 Brambleberry Lane
        Mayberry, NC 66655

        Dear Gomer Pyle:

        I read in the Mayberry Scream n' Tattler about an opportunity for a Pump
        Jockey. I feel that I am well-qualified for a position as a Pump Jockey,
        and would like to submit my resume for your consideration.

        I have a great deal of experience in Pump Jockeying, having done almost
        exactly this kind of work for the past several years. Additionally, I
        am a wonderful and entertaining employee. My coworkers are constantly
        entertained by my incessant joking and my prying into their private
        lives.

        Sincerely,

        Mr. Wonderful
```

Figure 13.4

This is an easy, but practical, example of what you can do with mail merge (remember the last time you sent out dozens of cover letters?). No complicated decision-making fields were used, just simple mail merge fields, which are probably adequate for most purposes.

An Overview of the Mail Merge Process

The mail merge process begins with selecting **Mail Merge** from the Tools menu (**Alt-T, R**), which brings up a menu like Figure 13.5.

Figure 13.5

After selecting **Mail Merge**, Word brings up the Mail Merge Helper. The Helper guides you through the mail merge process. There are three steps to the process:

1. Creating the main document.
2. Selecting a data source.
3. Merging the data source with the main document.

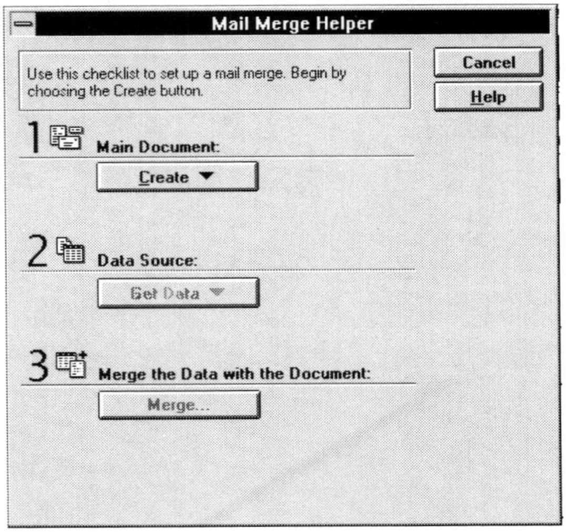

Figure 13.6

In step 1, creating the Main Document, you can decide to create one of the following mail merge options:

- ◆ form letters
- ◆ mailing labels
- ◆ envelopes
- ◆ catalog

For any of these options, you can either choose the document that is currently open in the active document window, or choose a new main document, for the main text of your Mail merge application. You will see a dialog box like the one in Figure 13.7. Choose the button that corresponds to the source of your main document.

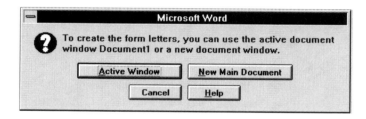

Figure 13.7

Selecting the Data Source

After choosing a format for the main document, the next step is to choose the source of the data. This is the information that will be placed into your form letters, mailing labels, envelopes, or catalog. Choose the **Get Data** button in the Mail Merge Helper dialog box to start the process.

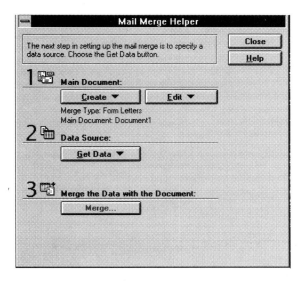

Figure 13.8

After selecting the Get Data option, you will be asked whether you want to:

- ◆ Open an existing data source,
- ◆ Create a new data source, or
- ◆ Create or edit a header file.

Use the Table 13.3 below to determine the option you should choose:

Table 13.3   Get Data Options

If you are	Then choose
Using a data file created earlier	**Open Existing Data File**
Creating a new data file	**Create Data File**
Using an existing datafile that doesn't have any header information	**Header File Options**

Creating a Data Source

When you create a data file, you are defining the information that will be used in the Mail Merge application. We discussed the data file in detail earlier in this chapter, but the main concept to keep in mind is that the data file consists of just the information to be used in the mail merge process with one line per record.

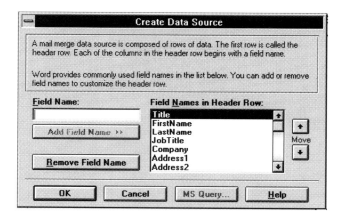

Figure 13.9

Opening an Existing Data Source

When you choose the Existing Data Source option, Word opens a dialog box that lists possible file names to use as the source for the data. Click the file name that you want to use for the data source.

NOTE You can tell Word to only display files of interest by selecting an extension in the List Files of Type option in the bottom of the dialog box. In Figure 13.10 all files are displayed, since the extension is the wildcard "*".

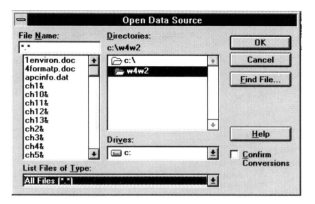

Figure 13.10

Choosing Different Types of Merge Documents

There are several different types of main documents, in addition to the typical form letter application mentioned earlier. These are discussed in the following sections.

Mailing Labels

Choose the Mailing Labels option when you wish to print mailing labels from a datafile. The concept is quite similar to that of creating form letters; the mailing labels are simply less complex.

Follow these steps to create mailing labels:

1. Choose **Mail Merge** from the Tools menu.
2. Click the **Create** button from the Main Document dialog, and choose **Mailing Labels.**
3. Click the **Active Window** button.
4. Click the **Get Data** button.

5. Choose **Open Data Source**, then choose **Open Data Source** if the data source already exists, or **Create Data Source** if this is a new data file.

6. In the Label Options dialog box, choose the type of label you are using, then click **OK** to cancel.

7. In the Create Labels dialog box, put the insertion point in the Sample Labels box, click the **Insert Merge** button, then add whatever merge fields you want to include. If you want to insert a POSTNET bar code, click the **Insert Postal Code** button. Click the **OK** button to close the dialog box.

8. Click the **Merge** button under Merge The Data With the Document.

9. In the Create Label dialog box, insert merge fields into the sample label. Word duplicates the information onto each mailing label.

Envelopes

If you are using Mail Merge to send letters to a wide variety of people, you may also want to print envelopes for those letters using the same datafile. The envelopes can be printed using this option and the same selection criteria used to create the form letters.

Follow these steps to use the Mail Merge option with envelopes:

1. Choose **Mail Merge** from the Tools menu.

2. Click the **Create** button, and choose **Envelopes**.

3. Click the **Active Window** button.

4. Click the **Get Data** button from the Data Source section of the MailMerge Helper.

5. Choose **Create Data Source**, verify that all of the field names you want to use are displayed, and click **OK**. Save the Data Source file when the Save File dialog box appears.

6. Choose **Edit Data Source**, and fill in address information in the Data Form dialog box.

7. Click the **Mail Merge Helper** button on the Mail Merge toolbar, then click **Setup** in the Main Document form.

8. Select an envelope size on the Envelope Options, changing the font and formatting if desired.

9. Select the printer options, verifying the options are correct for your printer.

10. Click **OK** to close the dialog box.

11. When the Envelope Address dialog box is displayed, position the insertion point, and click the **Insert Merge Field** button. Choose the fields you want to appear in the address, adding any punctuation or spacing between fields as required.

12. If you want to insert a POSTNET bar code, click the **Insert Postal Code** button, then select the address and zip code fields.

13. Choose **OK** to close the Envelope Address dialog box.

14. Click the **Edit** button, and Word displays the envelope in page layout view. Verify that the envelope appears correct, and delete the return address if you are using envelopes with preprinted return addresses.

You can use the Merge dialog box to specify a range of records to print, so you do not print more envelopes than are in your envelope cassette in the printer.

N O T E

Catalog

Specify catalog when you want to print information from the datafile in a single merge document. An example would be when you want to create a telephone directory from a datafile. Instead of printing a separate page for each entry in the datafile, like a form letter, the catalog option lets you specify how to format a single record of the datafile in the print merge document. Word then fills the print merge document with the datafile records, using the format you specified.

Using More Complex Fields for Additional Control

In the previous examples, the mergefield was the only type of field used. That is sufficient for most applications, as Word allows you to choose a portion of the data file if you want to pull only certain records from the data file.

However, there may be times when this is not sufficient. You may need to get additional information from the user at the time you perform the print, to get special comments to insert in the document, or to test to see if records meet conditions that are difficult or impractical to specify in the merge menu. You may want to combine several records from the data file into one document.

Getting Data from the User at Merge Time

The ask and fillin fields allow you to get information from the person who is performing the print merge. There may be information that needs to be in your print merge documents that simply won't be available in the data file. For example, suppose you have a data file of customers, and each month you want to send them mail indicating what items you have "on special" for that month. The information for what you have "on special" changes, but it is not the sort of thing you would want to have in the data file. (If you had a field called onspecial, then you would have to copy the same information into the onspecial field for each customer record.) Another possibility is that you could have a paragraph in the main document about specials, and simply edit it.

The ask and film fields allow you to avoid editing the main document. By inserting one of these field types, you can print a message to whoever is running the print merge to enter the required information. Word displays a dialog box when it encounters a field type like {ask special "Enter the special sale items"}.

The user would enter the appropriate response, like "shoes at 15% off," and your response would be stored in the label special. Now, wherever you want this information to appear in your document, you would simply insert a field with the label "special" in it:

```
Our special for today is {special}
```

If there were only one place in your document where you wanted to insert this information, then you could simply use the fillin field instead. The fillin field displays a dialog box, just as the ask field does. The difference is that the fillin field does not store your response in a label. Instead, it inserts your response in its location in your document:

```
The special for this month is {FILLIN "Enter the special for
this month"}
```

Whatever you type in response to the question "Enter the special for this month" is displayed at the location of the fillin field in your main document. If you typed "shoes at 15% off," you would see this in your print merged documents:

```
The special for this month is shoes at 15% off.
```

Using More than One Record at a Time from the Data File

There may be occasions when you want several records from your data file to be printed in your print merge document. Suppose you are creating a directory of all of your customers and how to contact them. You certainly don't want to print a separate document for each customer, but if you use the mergefield commands by themselves, that's exactly what you'll wind up with. That's where the next, nextif, and skipif commands come into play.

The next command tells Word to get the next record in the data file and use that record for whatever field statements follow. Suppose you want to create a document that has five records from the data file, using the name and address field of each record. You would enter something like:

```
"Directory Listing" {MERGEFIELD name} {MERGEFIELD address}
{NEXT}{MERGEFIELD name} {MERGEFIELD address}
{NEXT}{MERGEFIELD name} {MERGEFIELD address}
{NEXT}{MERGEFIELD name} {MERGEFIELD address}
{NEXT}{MERGEFIELD name} {MERGEFIELD address}
```

This is a somewhat tedious way to proceed, since a directory listing of 100 customers would require 99 {NEXT}{MERGEFIELD..} statements. Still, it gives you an idea of what the next command can do.

If you need to generate a directory listing with a large number of entries, you're much better off specifying "catalog" when the Mail Merge helper prompts you for the type of merge document you are creating.

N O T E

Now, suppose you just want to print five entries from your data file, but these entries are for customers with sales greater than $500. Assume you've got a field in your data file called "total," where you store the total sales information for each customer. You could use the nextif field to select only the customer records that meet your criteria:

```
"Directory Listing" {MERGEFIELD name} {MERGEFIELD address}
{NEXTIF {MERGEFIELD total} > 500}{MERGEFIELD name} {MERGEFIELD
address}
```

```
{NEXTIF {MERGEFIELD total} > 500}{MERGEFIELD name} {MERGEFIELD
address}
{NEXTIF {MERGEFIELD total} > 500}{MERGEFIELD name} {MERGEFIELD
address}
{NEXTIF {MERGEFIELD total} > 500}{MERGEFIELD name} {MERGEFIELD
address}
```

Suppose you want to send a letter to all your good customers, those who have bought more than $500. Another way of looking at the problem is to say that you want to skip creating a document for any customers who have less than $500 in purchases. You could use the skipif field to do this:

```
{SKIPIF {MERGEFIELD total} < 500}

Dear {MERGEFIELD name}

Thanks for your orders this year! We have really enjoyed
spending the money you gave us.

Sincerely

Mr. Widget, Inc.
```

More and More Decisions

The decision-making examples you've seen so far deal with using or excluding certain records from the print merge process. Often, though, you may want to make decisions based on the value of a field and use the results of that decision to determine text to include or exclude from your document. For example, suppose you want to modify the example letter shown above to praise customers who purchased more than $500, and criticize those who didn't (indicating you're not very good with customer relations). You could modify the main document to the following:

```
Dear {MERGEFIELD name}

{IF {MERGEFIELD total} > 500} "Thanks for your orders this
year! We have really enjoyed spending the money you gave us."
"Orders from you were pathetic! Maybe next year will be
better..."}

Sincerely

Mr. Widget, Inc.
```

This is an example of an if field—if the total is greater than 500, then print the first message, else print the second.

Comparing Fields with Text Values

You've seen examples of how you can use the if field to see if a line is blank and not print it if it is. You've also learned how to compare against numeric values—if a field is greater than some value, then print the record.

You can also use if fields with text fields—if a field is equal to "Oregon," then print the record. You can also use *wild cards*, which make the selection more flexible. For example, you may want to print all employee records whose last names begin with "L." The wild card character * allows you to do this—the statement `{IF{MERGEFIELD name} = "L*" "{MERGEFIELD name}"}` prints all employee names who have an L as the first character of their last names.

Including Other Documents

You can include other documents in your print merge applications and use tests to determine whether to insert the document or not. To *always* include another document, use the include field and the document name, like this:

```
{INCLUDE c:\\mydir\\mydoc.doc}
```

Note that Word requires you to use double slashes (\\) instead of the single slash that you commonly use when accessing a DOS file. This example inserts the document mydoc.doc from the mydir directory in the field location. You can insert the include field by using the **Field** command from the Insert menu (**Alt-I, D**).

You may find, though, that you need to choose between two or more documents. This is possible by use of the if field. For example, suppose you want to insert a document for patients that are using Medicare, and you have a field in your data file called "insurance" that tells you whether the patient is using Medicare or some other form of insurance. You would insert an include field like this:

```
{IF {MERGEFIELD insurance} = "Medicare" "{INCLUDE
c:\\dir\\medcare.doc} " }
```

Refer to Table 13.4 on the next page for information about defining and using fields.

Table 13.4   Defining and Using Fields

If you want to	Then use the field type	Example	Result
1) Specify certain conditions for data to be merged.	IF	{IF {mergefield amount} > 100 "As your total is more than $100, you are automatically entered in our preferred customer program."}	If the field amount is greater then 100, the text is inserted at the field marker.
2) Prevent blank fields from being printed.		{IF{address}<>"" "{If your application does not have a header record, then you must create one and attach it as a separate header file when you perform the print merge. Header files are discussed in address)"	If the address field is not equal to a blank, then print it at the field marker.
Get information from the user, assign it a label, and use it later in the document in one or more places.	ASK	{ASK name "Enter the recipient's name"}	Get the recipient's name from user and assign it to the label "name". No text is the printed at the field marker, the response is stored in the label.
Get information from the user and use it in one place.	FILLIN	{FILLIN "Enter the recipient's name}	Take the user's response and enter it at the current field location.
Define a label as being equal to some string of text, and use it one or more places in the document.	SET	{SET tax "={cost}*4%}"}	Evaluate the expression, and assign the result to the label "tax."No text is printed at the field marker, the results are stored in the label.
Insert a string into the document, performing any calculations needed.	QUOTE	QUOTE {={cost*4%}"}	Evaluate the expression and print it in the current field location.

Insert the record number of the record being merged.	MERGEREC	{MERGEREC}	Inserts the current record number of the data file at the field location. If the current record is 10. the number "10" is printed.
Get the next record in the data file without starting a new document.	NEXT	{MERGEFIELD name} {NEXT} {MERGEFIELD name}	Print the name field of the current record, go to the next record in the data file, and print the name from that record.
Skip a record in the data file based on certain.	SKIPIF	{SKIPIF {MERGEFIELD total<100}	Skip this record entirely if the total field is less than 100, and get the next record from the data file.
Get the next record if certain conditions are met.	NEXTIF	{MERGEFIELD name} {NEXTIF {MERGEFIELD total}<100} {MERGEFIELD name}	Print the name field of the current record, then, if the total field in the next record is less than 100, get the next record and print the name field.

Editing the Data Source

You can edit the data source file by selecting the **Edit** option from the dialog box. This brings up a form of all of the fields you currently have defined. You will be able to scroll up and down through the data file to select a record of interest, then edit the information in that record. Or, if you want to add new information to the data file, you can add the information by clicking the **Add New** button. This clears all of the fields in the dialog box, and allows you to enter the new information.

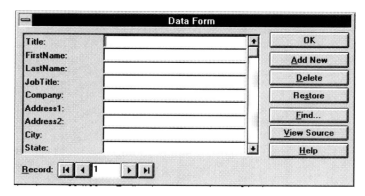

Figure 13.12

Editing the Main Document

Once you've configured the document for Mail Merge you can begin editing your main document. Note that there is now a Mail Merge toolbar at the top of the document.

Figure 13.13

At this point, you can begin entering field codes for the document. Click the **Insert Merge Field** button. Word then brings up a list of the valid fields from the data document that you can use.

Figure 13.14

Table 13.5   The Mail Merge Toolbar

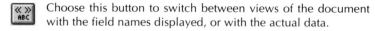 Click the name of the field you want to use, and Word inserts it in the main document. When you perform the mail merge later on, Word reads this field from the data file, and inserts it in this place in the main document.

Choose this button to switch between views of the document with the field names displayed, or with the actual data.

These buttons move you to either the beginning of the data file or to the previous record in the data file.

These buttons move you to either the end of the datafile or the next record in the datafile.

This button invokes the Mail Merge Helper dialog box. Use this when you want to begin the merge process again.

Use this button to check the mail merge main document against the datafile. If there are field names in the main document that do not appear in the datafile, this identifies them.

These buttons control the mail merge process and are used to perform a mail merge, send a mail merge document to a printer or to a file instead.

These buttons allow you to find a particular field in the datafile, or open a datafile for editing.

Performing the Merge

When you start the merge process, Word displays a Merge dialog box that enables you to:

- ◆ select where the merge results will be sent.
- ◆ check for errors, where field codes in the main document don't match up with field names in the data file.
- ◆ select all records or a range of records to merge.
- ◆ select query options, where fields of records must match certain constraints to be included in the merge output.

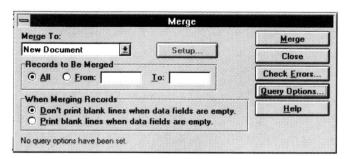

Figure 13.15

Selecting Records for Mail Merge

If you want to select certain records for merging, like only residents of a particular state, click the **Query** button, and fill out the Query Options dialog box.

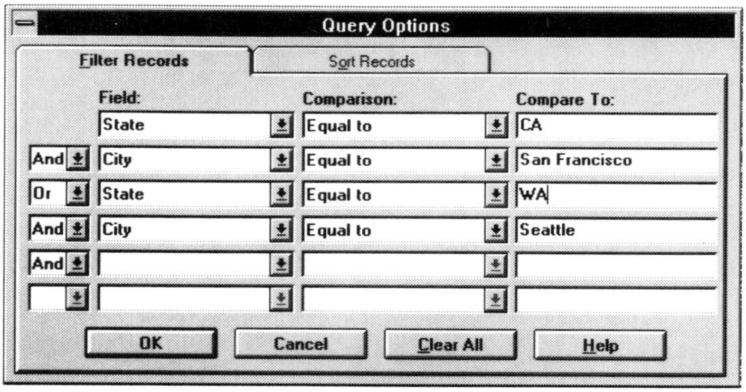

Figure 13.16

There may be many times when you do not want to use every entry in your data file. Suppose you want to send an overdue billing notice to customers whose account balance is greater than $500. The record selection feature for print merge allows you to use only those records from the data file that meet this account balance criterion. This feature of print merge is not limited to just a simple comparison. You can combine many conditions with ANDs and ORs of rules. For example, if you want to use only records from the data file that have San Francisco, CA and Seattle, WA as the city and state, you can specify a rule like:

```
State equal to CA AND City equal to San Francisco OR State equal
to Washington AND City equal to Seattle.
```

Summary

You can now automate the tedious task of creating form letters and documents by using the Word for Windows Mail Merge features explained in this chapter.

Index

Z

Zoom button, 21

Understanding
Adobe Photoshop CS6

THE ESSENTIAL TECHNIQUES FOR IMAGING PROFESSIONALS

Richard Harrington

Understanding Adobe Photoshop CS6:
The Essential Techniques for Imaging Professionals

Richard Harrington

Peachpit Press
1249 Eighth Street
Berkeley, CA 94710
510/524-2178

Find us on the Web at: www.peachpit.com
To report errors, please send a note to errata@peachpit.com

Peachpit Press is a division of Pearson Education

Project Editor: Nancy Peterson
Production Editor: Myrna Vladic
Development/Copy Editor: Anne Marie Walker, Robyn G. Thomas
Technical Editor: Wayne Palmer
Compositor: Kim Scott, Bumpy Design
Interior Design: Danielle Foster
Proofreader: Liz Welch
Cover Design: Mimi Heft
Indexer: Jack Lewis
Media Producer: Eric Geoffroy

ISBN-13: 978-0-321-83462-1

ISBN-10:   0-321-83462-3

9 8 7 6 5 4 3 2 1

Printed and bound in the United States of America

Dedication

To my wife Meghan, your patience and support fill my life with meaning. Thank you for your love and all that you do.

To my children Michael and Colleen, your curiosity and love inspire me. As you grow, you teach me what it means to be a better man.

To my family, thanks for your support and teaching me so much.

Acknowledgments

Several people have played an important role in this book coming to life:

- Ron Hansen and Michael Davidson, who gave me my first job teaching Adobe Photoshop at the Art Institute of Washington.

- Ben Kozuch, who believed in me enough to let me teach Photoshop to a room full of media professionals.

- Scott Kelby and the other instructors and staff of the National Association of Photoshop Professionals for their inspiration and support.

- Susan Rimerman and Nancy Peterson for challenging me to write the best book possible. Anne Marie Walker and Wayne Palmer for guiding me through the process and fixing my flaws.

- To James Ball, Jim Tierney, and Abba Shapiro, thank you for your generous gift of photos.

- To my many students through the years, thanks for the challenges and the motivation.

- To the staff of RHED Pixel for helping to bring the podcasts to life.

Richard Harrington, PMP

Richard has surrounded himself with media for his entire professional career. He's held such diverse jobs as directing television newscasts and publishing a music magazine to managing video production departments and consulting to nonprofit agencies. Currently, Richard is a founder of RHED Pixel (www.RHEDPixel.com), a visual communications company in the Washington, D.C. area.

RHED Pixel is a successful consultancy that provides technical and design services to clients such as the Community Health Charities, National Foundation of Credit Counseling, the Smithsonian Institution, Data Robotics, and the Children's National Medical Center. RHED Pixel creates everything from broadcast commercials to live events to interactive projects for a diverse clientele.

The Project Management Institute certifies Richard Harrington as a Project Management Professional. He holds a master's degree in project management as well. Additionally, Richard is an Adobe Certified Instructor and Apple Certified Trainer. He is a member of the National Association of Photoshop Professionals Instructor Dream Team.

His personal philosophy is communicate, motivate, create. Richard is a firm believer that media can have powerful results. You can follow his evolving interests in all things digital at www.RichardHarringtonBlog.com.

Contents

DVD Bonus Material

Chapter 3 Scanner Operation

Chapter 5 Quick Mask Mode

Chapter 6 Creating Spot Color Channels

Chapter 14 The Guide to Standard Filters

Introduction

The Role of Photoshop in Education

Learning Adobe Photoshop is essential to success in digital media industries. Photoshop is a gateway into several related technologies. From digital image acquisition and processing to typography and compositing, Photoshop is often your first introduction. If you can master this program, you can go on to success with several other technologies. With this in mind, it is important to learn Photoshop with one eye on the present and the other on the future.

The Role of Photoshop in Professional Industries

It's been said that if you know Photoshop, there's always work to be had. Photoshop is used by everyone from photographers to Web developers, video professionals to graphic designers. In fact, Photoshop is used in more places than you'd expect—including the medical, architectural, and legal fields. Adobe Photoshop is a portal to Adobe's other software applications, but it is also much more. Mastering the tools in Photoshop will teach you more about creative technology tools than any other program. With a solid knowledge of Photoshop, you'll be well on your way to being comfortable with an entire digital toolbox.

Purpose of This Book

When I decided to write this book, it was to fill a need. I have worked with Photoshop students of all levels, from the college classroom to working professionals across all industries. What I've heard time and time again is that people wanted an objective book that gave them everything they needed to truly understand Adobe Photoshop. Readers have grown tired of books that talk down to them or waste time promoting only the latest features.

It's not that there's a shortage of good books for the professional; I've read many of them and know several of their authors. But what has happened over the years, as Photoshop has become such an established program, is that we are left with two types of books: those for complete beginners and those for pros looking to dig deep on specific areas of the program. What was missing? A book that addresses the need of the learner who wants to understand the important features of Adobe Photoshop, as well as the core technology behind it, to build a solid foundation for future learning as well as immediate success.

This book is for learners who learn best by not just reading but by doing. Every chapter contains extensive hands-on exercises and all the files you need to practice. With the purchase of this book you also have immediate access to more than 100 videos that show you advanced skills and special techniques. In addition, interactive quizzes help you check your progress to ensure that the knowledge is "sticking." The accompanying DVD or digital download has everything you need. And you'll want to be sure to visit www.richardharringtonblog.com for updates and bonus downloads.

If you are learning Photoshop in a classroom, this book should combine with your instructor's knowledge to give you a rich, interactive learning experience. For those working professionals looking to fill in their understanding of Photoshop, this book answers and reinforces the essential information that you'll need. For both audiences, this book teaches you what you need to succeed in the professional workplace. As a teacher and a working pro, it's my goal to prepare you for professional success.

Suggestions on Learning

Photoshop is a very comprehensive program; don't try to learn it overnight. In fact, rushing to learn is often what causes problems. In an effort to learn quickly, skills don't have time to be absorbed. To combat this problem, I have eliminated nonessential topics from this book. I've also included a hands-on example or activity for every skill.

The truth is you'll learn best by doing. Don't skip the hands-on activities in a rush to make it through the book. I strongly encourage you to try each one. After completing the book's activities, you should repeat the techniques with your own photos. Nothing makes a topic as clear as you experiencing it interactively and achieving success. With practice—regular and thorough—you can understand and master Photoshop.

Understanding Adobe Photoshop DVD or Downloads

To help you get the most from Adobe Photoshop CS6, I've included several hands-on and interactive exercises.

Lesson Files

You'll find more than 250 images as well as Photoshop actions on the DVD or in the download to bring the lessons to life. The hands-on exercises are meant to be fun and informative, so be sure to use the lesson files as part of your learning process.

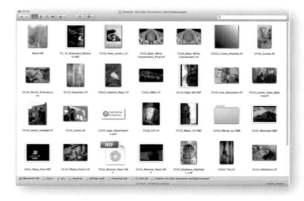

Interactive Quizzes

To help measure your progress, you'll find a Quizzes folder. Open the file Launch Quizes. html with a Web browser and take a short quiz for each chapter. Just answer ten questions and see if you've learned the key concepts from each chapter. The quizzes use Adobe Flash Player 9 or later, so be sure that is loaded on your system.

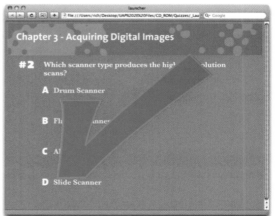

Video Training

Throughout the book you'll see Video Training icons that call out more than 100 additional modules you can watch. But what fun is just watching? You'll also find extra images in each lesson's folder to use with the videos.

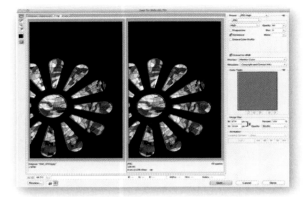

Bonus Exercises

We've included ten additional Photoshop exercises to hone your skills. These projects include all the images you'll need, along with an outline on how to approach the project. These self-paced exercises help you refine your skills and gain important practice.

Resource Blog

The author maintains a resource blog at www.richardharringtonblog.com. Here you'll find news about graphics technology, tutorials, bonus videos, and great resources like free images. You can subscribe to the blog for free with an RSS reader or by email for notification of all posts.

Bonus Exercises

For additional hands-on practice, try these ten bonus exercises. You will find these exercises well suited for exploring the many features of Photoshop. Each exercise provides source images and general instructions to guide you in approaching the project. The exercises should be undertaken after you have completed the book's chapters.

Exercise #1: Digital Painting

A popular technique is to turn a photo into a painting-like image. There isn't a one-click answer, but a little experimentation can go a long way.

Exercise #2: Creating a Collage

You can combine multiple images into a new composite image. This can be for experimental or artistic purposes as well as to create an advertisement or cover image.

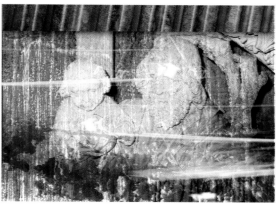

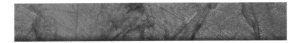

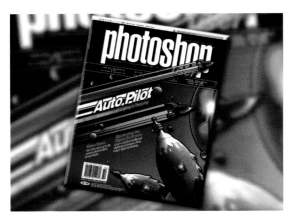

- **Photoshop is an essential program**
- **Can be used to create content for use with other programs**
- **Use of Layers and Styles can enhance appearance**
- **Never have more than seven bullets per page**

Exercise #3:
Designing Speaker Support

Creating a custom background or series of backgrounds is important when designing a custom electronic portfolio. It allows a designer to create a custom look for a client to use with Microsoft PowerPoint or Apple Keynote.

Exercise #4:
Designing a Magazine Cover

Designing a magazine cover is an excellent exercise for practicing with type and layout. Precise positioning of elements as well as creative use of color and design are important to capture the audience's attention.

Exercise #5:
Preparing Images for the Internet

Properly sizing and compressing images for the Internet is an essential skill. Finding the right balance of compression and image size is important to ensure that the end user can quickly download the images, yet still have them look good.

Exercise #6:
Designing a CD/DVD Label

Whether you're creating a music CD for a band or a DVD for a client, a professional-looking label is important. Use of text and effects are important to create a readable yet compelling design.

Exercise #7:
Creating a DVD Menu

Designing a DVD menu is an important task. More and more projects are being distributed on DVD, and it is the most quickly adopted format in consumer technology history. There are a lot of design options for a DVD menu (and it will depend on the DVD-authoring software used). But a lot of design work can happen in Photoshop, which allows you to fully explore design options.

Exercise #8: Artistic
Reinterpretations of a Photo

Working with a single image and processing in several ways is an excellent way to explore the power of filters. By creating unique looks through filter combinations, blending modes, and image adjustments, you have great design options.

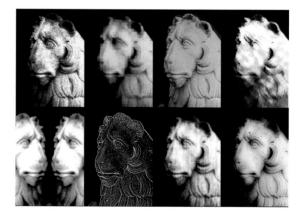

Exercise #9: CD/DVD Package

In this project, you'll create a label for a DVD or CD using an Amaray-style case. A template for printing is provided from a DVD replicator (each replication facility usually uses a custom template). The design will include text and photos—a completed sample image is provided for reference.

Exercise #10: Preparing Images for CMYK Printing

Preparing images for CMYK printing requires special processing. Certain bright, saturated colors cannot be printed using the CMYK process. These out-of-gamut colors need to be reduced and brought into range.

Digital Imaging Essentials

1

Before you open your first image in Adobe Photoshop, it's very important that you understand how a digital image is built. Knowing how computers represent your digital image data is essential to your career. Being a "technical" person will not make you more creative, but it will make you faster and more confident. Let's take a quick look at what a working professional must understand.

VIDEO 1:
Pixels in Depth

Pixels: Digital Building Blocks

When it comes to digital cameras, most photographers (and salespeople) seem obsessed with megapixels—because "everybody knows" that having more pixels means better images (it doesn't by the way). What's lacking in all this hoopla is a clear understanding of what pixels are and just how many of them you need. The more pixels you have, the more RAM you'll need to open the images and the more hard drive space to store them all. So it's in your best interest to understand some of the technology behind the images you want to capture, manipulate, output, and store.

ISTOCKPHOTO/LORAN NICOLAS

In the Beginning...

Essentially, computers, cameras, and video devices use pixels to express image information. Each pixel is a small square of captured light. The pixel is the smallest portion of an image that a computer is capable of displaying or printing. Too few pixels and an image will appear "blocky" because there is not enough detail to work with. Too many pixels and the computer or output device slows down because it has to process more information.

ISTOCKPHOTO/ALAN GOULE

A close-up of TV picture elements, or pixels.

The red circle shows an enlargement of the image. Notice how you can see actual pixels when you increase the magnification of an image. These squares of light are the building blocks of all digital photos.

IMAGE COURTESY SANDISK CORPORATION

Digital cameras use card-based storage, like this Secure Digital card, to hold the captured pixels.

But where did the term *pixel* come from? Pixel is an abbreviation for *picture element*. The word was coined to describe the photographic elements of a television image. In 1969, writers for *Variety* magazine took pix (a 1932 abbreviation of *pictures*) and combined it with *element* to describe how TV signals came together. There are even earlier reports of Fred C. Billingsley coining the word at NASA's Jet Propulsion Laboratory in 1965. Although the exact origins of the word may be disputed, its meaning is not. The word *pixel* quickly caught on, first in the scientific communities in the 1970s and then in the computer-art industry in the mid 1980s.

So What Are Megapixels?

When you shop for a digital camera, you are bombarded with talk of megapixels. Consumers are often misled about what megapixels are and how many are needed. A *megapixel* is simply a unit of storage, whether internal or on a removable card. A megapixel is one million pixels and is a term commonly used to describe how much data a digital camera can capture. As with your car, just because your tank can hold more gallons of gas doesn't mean it's more fuel efficient or better than your friend's car.

For example, if a camera can capture pictures at 3000 × 2400 pixels, it is referred to as having 7.2 megapixels (3000 × 2400 = 7,200,000). If you were to print that picture on paper at 300 ppi (pixels per inch), it would roughly be a 10" × 8" print. Professional photographers may need more pixels than this, but a consumer may not. It all depends on how the pixels are meant to be displayed or printed.

The more pixels you capture, the larger the image is (both in disk space and potential print size). Consumer usage (such as email or inkjet prints) is less demanding than professional usage (such as art books or magazines). Professionals need more megapixels than consumers; hence, high-end cameras cost more because they are targeted at people who make money by taking photos.

Understanding Resolution

OK, prepare to be temporarily confused (but not for long). A lot of terms are used to describe image resolution. The problem is that many people (and companies) use the wrong terms, which (understandably) leads to a great deal of confusion. Let's take a quick look at the most common terms and their accurate meanings. Knowing how to describe the resolution of images and output devices will help you make the right decisions when purchasing or choosing gear to use.

Dots per Inch (dpi)

The most common term used to describe image resolution is *dots per inch (dpi)*. Although you'll hear it used for digital cameras and scanners, it is really only appropriate for printers. As a measurement of output resolution, dpi is fairly straightforward.

To determine dpi, it is necessary to count the number of dots that can fit in a 1" × 1" area. A higher dpi can mean smoother photographs or line art; for example, newspapers tend to use around 150 dpi, whereas magazines can use up to 600 dpi. Consumer printers easily print at 600 dpi or even higher, which can produce extremely good results (when using the right paper). An increase in dpi can produce even better-looking images. You'll see (and hear about) dpi used a lot, but it solely refers to print and physical output.

TIP

Don't Believe the Megapixel Myth

More megapixels do not guarantee a better picture. Instead of picking a camera solely on how many pixels it will capture, investigate cameras with better lenses or options that are important to you. If you are shooting for large-format output, you'll need a larger megapixel-count camera, but if you're shooting for personal use, consider how you output most of your pictures.

TIP

A Fix for Those with Less Than Perfect Eyesight

Are you working with a high-resolution monitor and having a hard time seeing your menus in Photoshop? You can change the size of the display text. Press Command+K (Ctrl+K) to open the Preferences window and select Interface. From the UI Font Size menu, choose Medium or Large to give your eyes a break.

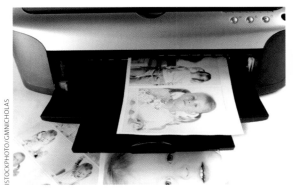

It's only in evaluating printers that the term dots per inch (dpi) makes sense. DPI is a function of the printer and can operate independently of the PPI settings of the file you send it.

In a commercial printing environment, very high-resolution images are required.

Detect Displays

Color LCD
✓ 1680 × 1050
1440 × 852
1280 × 1024 (stretched)
1280 × 1024
1280 × 800
1152 × 720
1024 × 768 (stretched)
1024 × 768
1024 × 640
800 × 600 (stretched)

Number of Recent Items   ▶
Open Displays Preferences…

Modern computer monitors support various screen resolutions. Changing the monitor resolution results in a different amount of pixels per inch displayed on your monitor. Do not run Photoshop at a screen resolution of less than 1024 x 768, or it will cause user interface problems (1280 x 800 or higher is recommended).

Pixels per Inch (ppi)

When you view your images on a computer monitor, you are seeing pixels displayed on your screen. Computer monitors use the concept of logical inches. Originally, the Mac OS most commonly used 72 *pixels per inch (ppi)* to match the concept of the printing idea of 72 points per real inch of paper. The Windows OS has traditionally used 96 ppi.

As computer monitors and portable devices have evolved, they've advanced to support variable resolution settings. As such, the actual ppi for a screen can vary greatly depending on the physical size of the screen and the resolution being used by the computer's graphics card. For example, modern laptops often use resolutions between 100 ppi and 140 ppi, and devices like an iPhone can jump all the way up to 326 ppi to make images crisper on the small screen.

Worry less about the ratio of pixels per inch on your screen and simply accept that the standard measurement of resolution in Photoshop (and most computer programs) is ppi. When talking about displayed graphics, its ppi, not dpi.

Samples per Inch (spi)

Although scanners are less common than they used to be, many professionals still use them to load sketches, photos, and original negatives. Manufacturers often tout the dpi capabilities of their scanner. This is inaccurate. Scanners don't use dots, they use samples. A *sample* is when a scanner captures part of an image. *Samples per inch (spi)* is a measurement of how many samples are captured in the space of one inch. In general, an increase in sampling leads to a file that is truer to its analog original. However, there is a threshold: Once a certain amount of information is surpassed, human senses (and electronic output devices) cannot tell the difference.

Consumer-level scanners can capture optical resolution ranging between 300 spi and 4800 spi. Professional devices can capture significantly higher optical resolution. If you're working with a large image, a lower number of samples is fine. If you're enlarging a very small image, a large number of samples is crucial. More samples per inch translates into more information available as pixels, which can then be harnessed in output when they

are converted to dots in the printer. So if your scanner's software specifies dpi, it really means spi, but you can see how the two are closely related.

Lines per Inch (lpi)

In professional printing environments, you'll often hear the term *lines per inch (lpi)*. This is from the traditional process where images with gradiated tones (such as photographs) are screened for printing to create a *halftone*. This was originally performed by laying film with dots printed on it over the film before exposure. In the digital age, this process and these terms are used less often, but it is still good for you to have a basic understanding.

These days, the work of converting an image to lines is performed by an imagesetter. The dots are arranged in lines, and the lpi measurement refers to the number of lines per inch. An increase in lpi results in smoother images. **Table 1.1** shows the most common lpi settings for different output formats.

Table 1.1 Common lpi Measurements

Output Method	Typical lpi
Screen printing	35–65
Laser printer (matte paper)	50–90
Laser printer (coated paper)	75–110
Newsprint	60–85
Offset printing (uncoated paper)	85–133
Offset printing (coated paper)	120–150+
High-quality offset printing	150–300

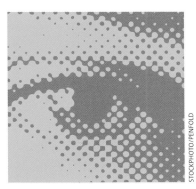

STOCKPHOTO/PENFOLD

This image has been converted to a halftone, as is evident by the visible dot pattern.

Image Mode

Within Photoshop, you need to choose from one of eight image modes when working with a document. The mode you pick will depend on what you need to do with the image and how you intend to output it. For example, the mode used for web graphics will differ from those used for professional printing. The three most common modes used are RGB, Grayscale, and CMYK, but it's worth taking a quick look at all eight.

VIDEO 2:
Converting Image Modes

RGB Color

The most common mode for graphics in Photoshop is RGB. The RGB Color mode uses additive color theory to represent color (a 100% value of red, green, and blue light creates white light). Different intensity values of red (R), green (G), and blue (B) combine to form accurate colors. By mixing intensity values, virtually every color can be accurately represented.

When working in Photoshop, most designers choose RGB Color mode for its wider range of available color (also known as *gamut*) and extensive support for filters and adjustments. Additionally, computer monitors use RGB mode to display color, and this is the native color space for onscreen display. Because you'll most often be processing images on a computer, it is easiest to work in the same color space as your monitor.

CMYK Color

Professional printing uses a four-color process to simulate color. The four inks are cyan (C), magenta (M), yellow (Y), and black (K, for *key*). The CMYK Color mode uses the subtractive color model to re-create color. Subtractive color explains the theory of how ink or dye absorbs specific wavelengths of light and reflects others. The object's color is based on which part of the light spectrum is not absorbed. Although print designers use CMYK Color mode for professional printing, they will work in RGB mode throughout the design stage. CMYK Color mode has a smaller color gamut, so CMYK conversion is saved until the last stage of image preparation.

Grayscale

A grayscale image uses different shades of gray to represent image details. For example, an 8-bit image is represented by 256 levels of gray (see "Bit Depth" later in this chapter). Likewise, a 16-bit image would show 65,536 levels of gray (a substantial improvement, but it requires an output device that can utilize the data). When creating grayscale images, it is important to perform test prints with the output device and paper to see how contrast is maintained.

Duotone

A duotone image can actually be monotone, duotone, tritone, or quadtone. Grayscale images that use a single-colored ink are called *monotones*. *Duotones*, *tritones*, or *quadtones* are grayscale images printed with two, three, or four inks, respectively. Using both black and gray ink to represent the tonal values, duotones create better-quality printed grayscales. This mode should be used when you know the printer is set up specifically to handle the job. If you just want the look of a duotone, you can create that look by working in RGB mode and using the Black and White adjustment layer.

The most popular form of duotone is a sepia-tone image (often seen in historical prints). In modern times, a designer may use a duotone for style purposes or to save money by using fewer inks.

Duotone Options

Preset: Custom

Type: Tritone

Ink 1: PANTONE Black 3 C

Ink 2: PANTONE 186 C

Ink 3: PANTONE 7409 C

Ink 4:

OK
Cancel
☑ Preview

Overprint Colors...

Bitmap

A bitmap image uses only one of two color values—black or white (no gray)—to represent the pixel data. These 1-bit images have a very small file size. To create a bitmap, you first must convert the image to an 8-bit grayscale formula, and then convert to the Bitmap image mode. Do not confuse Bitmap mode with a bitmap image, which is another name for *raster* (or pixel-based) images. Additionally, avoid confusion with the BMP file format, which is a standard Windows file format that dates back to the earliest version of Windows. An image in the Bitmap mode simply uses only black and white to represent image data.

Indexed Color

Indexed Color mode severely limits the number of colors used to represent an image. In Indexed Color mode, up to 256 colors are available. To reduce file sizes (and download times), some web designers use fewer colors in their graphics. They will turn to specialized formats like GIF and PNG-8. Although this mode reduces file size, it also visibly lowers the quality of the image. Indexed Color mode works well for illustrations or logos but not so well for photos on the Internet. Instead of converting your original image to Indexed Color mode via the Image menu, use the Save For Web command (File > Save For Web). This will convert the file to a GIF or PNG-8 (both use the Indexed Color mode), but leave the original image in its original mode.

Lab Color

L*a*b* Color is the most complete color mode used to describe the colors visible to the human eye. The three parameters of color are L for luminance of the color, a for the color's position between red and green, and b for its position between yellow and blue.

The Lab Color mode was created to serve as a device-independent, absolute model to be used for a reference. Lab attempts to simulate the full gamut of color; however, it is a three-dimensional model and can't be represented properly within Photoshop. Therefore, the * after the L, a, and b is used to signify that it is a derivative model. Lab images can only be printed on PostScript Level 2 and Level 3 printers; for all other professional printers, Lab images must first be converted to CMYK mode. The Lab Color mode is generally only used by imaging professionals seeking the truest color fidelity because it supports all the colors in both the RGB and CMYK Color modes.

Multichannel

Multichannel mode is a highly specialized mode used for complex separations for professional printing. You may never need to use it. Photoshop automatically converts to Multichannel mode when you delete a channel from an RGB or CMYK image. The color onscreen is no longer accurate because Photoshop cannot describe it. This is sometimes done for an effect or as part of the image repair process if one channel did not capture properly (such as from a malfunctioning digital camera). Most likely, you'll *never* want to work in Multichannel mode.

Bitmap
Grayscale
Duotone
Indexed Color...
✓ **RGB Color**
  CMYK Color
  Lab Color
  Multichannel

✓ **8 Bits/Channel**
  16 Bits/Channel
  32 Bits/Channel

Color Table...

Bit Depth

Besides resolution (the number of pixels) and color mode (the way colors are processed), one other variable affects image quality. Bit depth measures how much color is available for display or printing of each pixel. A greater bit depth means each pixel contains more information for describing the color. A pixel with a bit depth of 1 can display the pixel as either black or white. The most common bit depth is 8-bit mode, which has a possible value of 256 intensity levels per color channel. However, depending on the version of Photoshop you are working with as well as the file type and image mode, you can access 8, 16, or 32 bits per channel. It's important to note that larger bit depth can limit image adjustment commands.

Time to Move On

There's a lot more ground to cover, but you'll explore the topics discussed here and others in greater depth in each chapter. You'll feel a bit more comfortable with the language used to describe images and color as you read on. With the knowledge you've gained so far, you can jump into using Photoshop and start to navigate its interface.

TIP

Shooting Raw

One of the major benefits of shooting images in a camera raw format is that you can often choose to work in 16 bits per channel in Photoshop. This offers superior options for manipulating color and exposure.

NOTE

32 bits per channel

You won't encounter 32 bits per channel images very often. They come into play when working with generated imagery (such as those from 3D modeling applications). They can also be created by merging multiple photos together into a high dynamic range (HDR) image. You'll learn about the HDR process later in the book.

Photoshop's Interface

2

Adobe Photoshop's interface can be pretty intimidating. Among all those panels, tools, and menu commands it's easy to get lost. However, it's worth it to master these components. Photoshop is by far the most-used image editing application on the planet, and knowing how to properly use it unlocks a world of design opportunities. Working professionals use it for a variety of tasks, from enhancing magazine photos to designing web animations and from creating television graphics to performing medical imaging.

Most important is to learn the essential features you need right away and then gradually learn the rest as needed. I frequently tell students of all levels that often there are three or more ways to perform the same task in Photoshop. Adobe's software engineers have tried their best to make the program intuitive (and everyone certainly doesn't think the same way). Additionally, new features are often unveiled with product updates, yet the old features frequently remain for those who resist change or prefer the older method.

Learning Photoshop is a very doable task, especially if you take a balanced and measured approach by matching learning new features with practical application. I've seen older professionals as well as young students become proficient Photoshop users. Just remember that a Photoshop expert is usually just someone who's mastered the skills to put three or four basic skills together in the right order to solve the task at hand.

VIDEO 3:
Setting Preferences
in CS6

Understanding the Interface

So let's start with a quick tour of the Photoshop interface. Adobe offers two versions of the application: Photoshop and Photoshop Extended. The standard version of Photoshop is suited for all users, whereas Photoshop Extended offers specialized features for medical researchers, 3D artists, architects, and engineers. This book shows the Photoshop Extended interface, because many users have access to that version of the software. But the book covers in depth only those features that are common to both versions of the application. Throughout this book you'll encounter a few bonus movies to help you understand Photoshop Extended's capabilities.

If you haven't done so already, launch Photoshop. Because many of Photoshop's panels will be new to you, we'll tackle them in the order in which you'll likely encounter them. The goal here is to get the "lay of the land" and just figure out what each panel is used for. Throughout the rest of the book you'll dig much deeper into how (and when) to use these specific panels and tools. As you learn Photoshop, you'll often need to use features before you've had a chance to learn about them in depth, so a basic knowledge right away is very important.

TIP

A Great Frame-up

Photoshop CS6 keeps all your documents and panels in an Application Frame to keep the interface clean. If you're using the Mac OS, you can toggle the frame off or on by choosing Window > Application Frame. Experiment to see which look you prefer.

1. Open the file Ch02_Eagle.psd from the Chapter 2 folder in the book's Lessons folder to explore Photoshop's interface. Many of the panels in Photoshop require an image to be open before they display any detail.

2. Choose Window > Workspace > Essentials (Default) to ensure that the application is in its default state.

3. Choose Window > Workspace > Reset Essentials to ensure that all the panels are in their default position.

VIDEO 4:
Switching Tools

Tools

All the hands-on tools are contained in the Photoshop Tools panel (typically displayed on the left edge of the screen). Photoshop groups similar tools together. You can access these hidden tools by clicking and holding on a particular tool. Whenever you see a triangle in Photoshop, click it to open additional nested options.

The first keyboard shortcuts you should master are those for the Tools panel because you'll use these the most. Frequently, the first letter of the tool is the keyboard shortcut. If you can't remember the shortcut, click the tool while holding down the Option (Alt) key to cycle through the available tools.

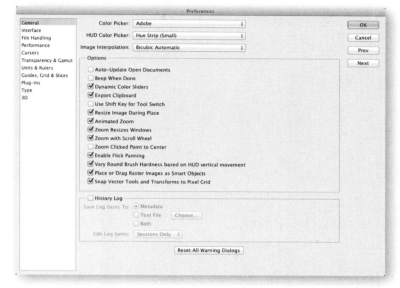

An alternative method to cycle through the tools is to press the keyboard shortcut multiple times while holding the Shift key (for example, Shift+M cycles between the Rectangular and Elliptical Marquee tools).

If you'd like to simplify the shortcuts even more, press Command+K (Ctrl+K) to call up the Preferences dialog box.

In the General category:

- Deselect the Use Shift Key for Tool Switch option. You can then press a shortcut key (such as G for the Gradient tool) and cycle through the tools contained in that tool's drawer. This speeds up your ability to switch tools.

- Select the Zoom with Scroll Wheel option if you have a three-button mouse. This makes it easier to zoom in or out of your working document.

In the Interface category:

- Make sure the Show Tool Tips feature is selected to assist you in learning common keyboard shortcuts. Tool tips teach you the proper name and the keyboard shortcut for each tool. Just hover over a user interface element to learn more about it.

- Set the UI Font Size to Medium or Large if you'd like to increase the size of screen elements so they are easier to read on high-resolution monitors.

Many tools are available, and each tool has multiple purposes (as well as strengths and weaknesses). Throughout this book you'll learn how to effectively use these tools. With patience, you'll get the most from Photoshop's powerful feature set.

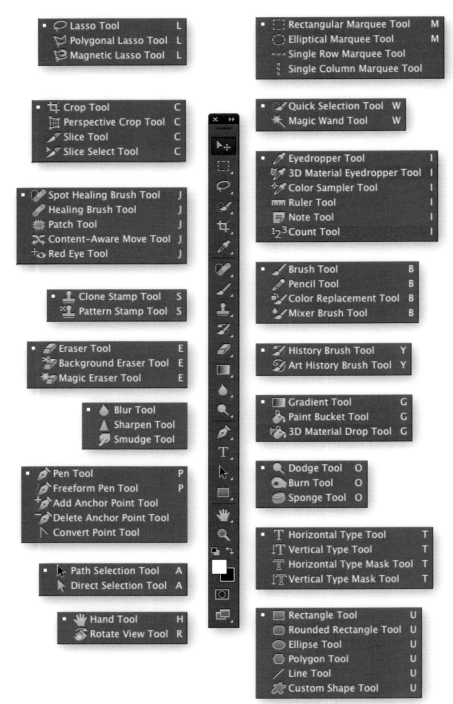

Tools shaded in blue are only available in Photoshop CS6 Extended.

Options

The Options bar is essential because it contains the majority of controls for the currently active tool. It consolidates the most used (and useful) options for the active tool and moves them to the forefront for easy access. The Options bar is visible by default. It runs the length of your monitor across the top of the frame.

In the right corner you'll also find the Workspace switcher, which lets you switch between different arrangements of windows designed for specific tasks like Photography, Typography, Motion, and Painting. For the remainder of this chapter, you'll be using the Essentials workspace.

NOTE

The Options Bar Is Essential

Be sure to keep the Options bar open because you'll always need it. If you accidentally close it, bring it back by choosing Window > Options.

VIDEO 5:
Managing Workspaces

A CUSTOM WORKSPACE

You'll find that the more you work with Photoshop, the more you'll want to use different tools for different situations. For example, you'll want Layer Styles and the Color Picker handy for text work, but you'll turn to the Histogram and Adjustment panels when doing image restoration.

You can save any combination and arrangement of panels that you want to reuse. Then you can access it in one click with Workspaces. Effectively, using Workspaces enables you to switch between different production tasks (such as image touchup and type work) with ease. Plus, it is a way to customize the application and make it feel more welcoming to your way of working. Try it out.

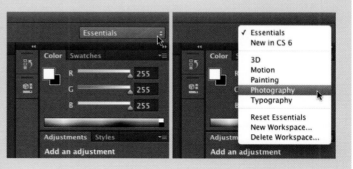

1. Open the windows you need and arrange them into the desired positions.

2. To save the current workspace layout, click the Workspace switcher menu (in the upper-right corner of the screen) and choose New Workspace.

3. Enter a unique name for the workspace and click OK.

To activate a workspace, choose it from the Workspace switcher in the Application bar. To update a workspace, resave it with the same name. To delete a workspace, click the Workspace switcher and choose Delete Workspace.

Layers

In Photoshop, a layer can contain artwork and transparency information. This allows you to combine (or composite) multiple images into a new piece (such as a postcard or advertisement). Originally, Photoshop did not have layers. You could open a picture to process it, but that was about it. However, over time the demands placed on Photoshop by its users led to its evolution. As Photoshop moved beyond being a mere touchup tool, the flexibility of layers emerged to meet the demand. Photoshop now has several special layer types including adjustment layers, shape layers, and fill layers. By isolating discrete elements to their own layers, designers can make several changes and freely experiment with their design.

Without sounding like a zealot, layers in Photoshop mean everything to a designer. You will spend much of this book (and your early career using Photoshop) getting comfortable with layers. With that said, *always* leave your Layers panel open while you work (press F7 to open it); this is where most of the action takes place. The Layers panel is like the steering wheel of a car. You'll dig much deeper into layers in Chapter 7, "Layer Masking," and Chapter 8, "Compositing with Layers."

VIDEO 6:
Understanding Layers

Channels

The previous chapter explained different image modes that a computer graphic could occupy. In the Channels panel you can view the individual components of color. The brighter the area in the individual channel, the more presence there is for that color. Let's look at a simple example of an RGB graphic.

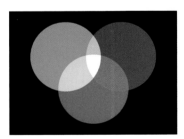

1. Choose File > Open and navigate to the Chapter 2 folder in the book's Lessons folder.

2. Open the image file Ch02_RGB_Overlap.psd. You should see red, green, and blue circles overlapping one another. The overlap has also created new colors: red + green = yellow; blue + green = cyan; red + blue = magenta; and red + green + blue = white.

3. Activate the Channels panel. By default it is docked with the Layers panel (just click on its name and the panel will switch to display Channels). If you don't see it, choose Window > Channels.

4. Look at the individual channels; you'll see a definitive area for each color. Channels look like grayscale images when viewed independently. Notice how the full circles are visible (and white) where there is 100% value of each channel.

5. Close the document by choosing File > Close.

VIDEO 7:
Understanding Channels

Fully understanding Channels unlocks a wealth of image-processing power. Harnessing a color's individual components is difficult at first but well worth the effort. You'll delve much deeper into Channels in Chapter 10, "Color Correction and Enhancement."

Paths

Although Photoshop is known as a raster-editing tool (because of its several pixel-based functions), it does contain several vector tools as well. Vectors use lines that are defined by math equations; as such, they can be scaled indefinitely and always remain crisp. Several of Photoshop's vector tools can create paths, which are useful for complex selections. You can create a path with the Pen tool. By clicking around an image, anchor points are created, and then Photoshop connects the dots with vector lines. Paths can also be created using the vector Shape tools. Use the Paths panel to select the path you want to update. For more on complex selections, see Chapter 5, "Selection Tools and Techniques."

Adjustments

One of the most common tasks in Photoshop is making adjustments to images to fix tone and color. Photoshop offers an Adjustments panel to provide easy access to the most common, nondestructive adjustment commands. The adjustments are grouped into three categories:

- **Tonal controls.** Use these controls to adjust Brightness/Contrast, Levels, Curves, and Exposure in a nondestructive fashion.

- **Color controls.** Use these controls to adjust Vibrance, Hue/Saturation, Color Balance, Black & White conversion, Photo Filter, Channel Mixer, and Color Lookup properties.

- **Creative/Advanced controls.** These controls are special-purpose adjustments and include Invert, Posterize, Threshold, Gradient Map, and Selective Color.

NOTE

Future Learning Opportunity
You'll explore these adjustments more in later chapters.

Properties

If you're using an adjustment layer, you'll need to control how it affects your image. Additionally, adjustment layers (and optionally all layers) can have a mask applied to control the visibility of the layer. Photoshop uses masks to obscure parts of an associated item; transparency is defined by the use of white, black, and gray. In fact, you can apply a mask to a layer, a vector, or even a smart filter.

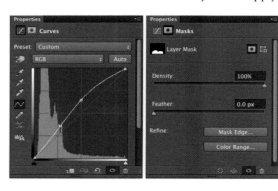

Photoshop CS6 offers precise control over masks, including the ability to adjust their density and edges. Masks are a useful way to erase parts of a layer nondestructively, which allows for future changes. They can also be used to isolate an adjustment to only parts of an image.

Both masks and adjustment layers are controlled using the Properties panel. To view the panel, just select an adjustment layer in an open image. Here you'll find buttons across the top to switch between the two. You'll see multiple masks in use in the sample document (Ch02_Eagle.psd) to isolate the effects of color correction. You'll explore masks in depth in Chapter 7.

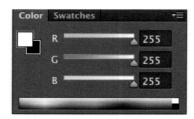

Color

Don't confuse the Color panel with the color mode of the document. The Color panel allows you to modify and select colors using six different color models. You can choose colors using RGB sliders or the more intuitive Hue, Saturation, and Brightness (HSB) model. To adjust color, move the sliders for the corresponding value. Sliding the Red slider to the right increases the amount of red in the new color. Choosing colors is independent of image mode in that you can use a CMYK model for an RGB image. However, picking a color to use in a grayscale document will not introduce color into that image.

Spend some time exploring the Color panel and find a method that works best for you. Clicking on a color swatch opens the powerful Color Picker, which unlocks a larger visual interface for exploring color and enhances the use of the Eyedropper tool to sample color from a source image. You'll use color in several of the chapters in this book, and the Color panel and Color Picker are fairly easy to understand.

Swatches

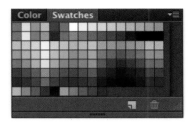

The Swatches panel is like a painter's palette in that it holds several colors ready to use. Many colors are loaded by default, which are useful when painting or using filters that utilize those colors. If you click the panel's submenu, you'll discover many more swatch books to load for specialty purposes like web browser colors, spot color printing, or thematic color swatches (such as a blue saturated range). You can also store any custom colors you create for easy access by clicking on an empty space to store the swatch.

TEMPORARY BANISHMENT OF PANELS

If you want to hide your panels, you can quickly toggle them off and on:

- **Press the Tab key to hide all the panels.**
- **Press the Tab key again and they return.**
- **Press Shift+Tab to hide everything except the Options bar and Tools panel.**
- **To focus on only your image, press the F key once to go to Full Screen Mode With Menu Bar. Press the F key again to go to Full Screen and hide all the user interface elements. Press the F key once more to cycle to Standard Screen Mode. You'll also find the Screen Mode Switcher located at the bottom of the Tools panel.**

TIP

Docking Panels

To save space, any floating panel can be collapsed to an icon. Simply drag a panel to any new panel's edge or the edge of the screen, and a blue line will appear (which indicates where the panel will dock). The most common place to dock panels is on the right edge of the screen, but they can be docked on the left or bottom edges as well.

Styles

The Styles panel is where you can visually access Layer Styles, which are the combination of layer effects (they can also be applied singularly to create effects such as beveled edges, drop shadows, or glows). Effects are most useful in combination, and advanced photorealistic effects can be achieved. Photoshop ships with several built-in styles, and many more are available for download from Adobe's website (www.adobe.com/exchange) as well as many other Photoshop sites. Layer Styles are frequently used for text and image effects but can also be used for web rollover effects for buttons. For more on Layer Styles, be sure to read Chapter 13, "Layer Styles."

VIDEO 8:
Using the Navigator

Navigator

While working with photos, you'll often need to zoom in to touch up an image. It may sound cliché, but it's easy to lose your perspective when working in Photoshop. When you zoom in to a pixel level for image touchup, you often won't be able to see the entire image onscreen. This is where the Navigator comes in handy.

1. Open the photo Ch02_Bike.psd from the Chapter 2 folder.

2. Select the Zoom tool from the Tools panel or press Z (the tool looks like a magnifying glass). Make sure the Scrubby Zoom option is selected in the Options bar.

3. Click and drag near the bike tire head to zoom in.

4. Call up the Navigator panel by choosing Window > Navigator. Drag the corner of the Navigator panel to make it larger and easier to see.

5. You can now navigate within your photo:

   • Drag the red view box around the thumbnail to pan within the image.

   • Resize the Navigator panel for a larger image preview.

   • Move the Zoom slider to zoom in or out on the image.

   • Click the Zoom Out or Zoom In buttons to jump to a uniform magnification.

6. Close the document by choosing File > Close.

Histogram

When you are color correcting or adjusting exposure, the histogram can be a great help. This graph illustrates how the pixels in the image are distributed across brightness levels. To read a histogram, start at the left edge, which shows the shadow regions. The middle shows the midtones (where most adjustments to an image are made), and to the right are the highlights. Image touchup and enhancement are covered in Chapter 10. You may want to leave the Histogram panel open as you work, because it is an easy way to learn to read the graphical details of a digital image.

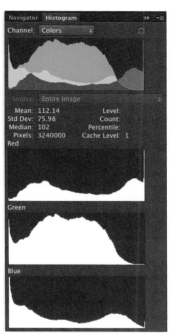

The Histogram panel has been set to Show All Channels view (click the triangle in the upper-right corner and choose All Channels view). The top histogram is a composite histogram for the Red, Green, and Blue channels combined; the next three show them individually.

Info

The Info panel is a useful place to find a plethora of image information, even when you're using the default options. You can get information about color values as well as precise details about the active tool. However, by customizing the panel you can make it truly useful.

1. Select the Info panel by choosing Window > Info or by pressing F8.

2. From the Info panel submenu (the triangle in the upper-right corner) choose Panel Options.

3. The resulting dialog box has several options; I recommend the following choices for a new user:

   - Leave Mode set to Actual Color.

   - Set Second Color Readout to CMYK if you're doing print work, or set it to RGB color if you are preparing images to use on the Internet or in video exclusively.

   - Set Mouse Coordinates to Pixels.

   - Enable the following choices under Status Information: Document Sizes, Document Profile, and Document Dimensions.

   - The last option, Show Tool Hints, provides a detailed explanation for each tool you select from the Tools panel.

4. Click OK.

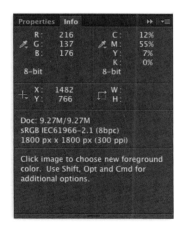

History

The History panel will quickly become your best friend. It's here that Photoshop keeps a list of what you have done to the image since you opened it. By default Photoshop keeps track of the last 20 steps performed on an image, but you can modify this number. A higher number means more levels to undo.

1. Press Command+K (Ctrl+K) to call up the Photoshop Preferences dialog box.

2. In the Performance section, change History States to a higher number, such as 100. Note that more levels of undo require more RAM, so you may need to balance this number if your system is underequipped.

3. Click OK.

Actions

Actions are among the least-used features of Photoshop but offer huge time savings. Actions allow for visual scripting, which means you can record commands or adjustments that you need on one image and play them back on other images. For example, you could record an action that adjusts the size of an image, runs an adjustment to lighten the image, and then converts it to a TIFF for commercial printing. You could then play that series of commands back on another image or even batch process an entire folder of images (which can eliminate boring, repetitive work). Actions can be very useful for both design and production tasks.

You'll explore actions fully in Chapter 15, "Actions and Automation."

VIDEO 9:
Editing Video in
Photoshop CS6

NOTE

Tools Meet Actions

Starting in Photoshop CS6, you can record the use of tools in an action. This means that you can record items like brush strokes to draw your signature and sign a photo. To enable the recording of tools not normally actionable, simply click the menu in the upper-right corner of the Actions panel and choose Allow Tool Recording.

Timeline

Photoshop CS6 adds an improved Timeline that allows for the editing of video files directly in Photoshop. A new video playback engine and essential trimming tools make it possible to perform basic video-editing tasks right in Photoshop CS6.

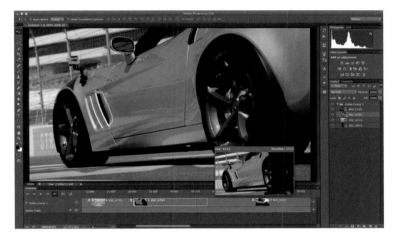

How Much RAM Do You Need?

With Photoshop CS6, Adobe has made the move to a 64-bit application (which requires a 64-bit operating system as well). A major advantage is the ability to address more memory. Although Photoshop needs a minimum of 1 GB to run, a better approach is to have 2–3 GB of memory per processor core in your computer. Memory has become much cheaper in recent years. Although you can run in a 32-bit mode under Windows, you should really upgrade for the best performance.

Character

Although Photoshop began its life as an image editor (essentially a digital darkroom), it has greatly evolved over the years to also include an extensive text tool. Many people start and finish their entire designs within Photoshop. These designs include advertisements, posters, packaging, and DVD menus. A close look at the Character panel reveals complex control over the size, style, and positioning of individual characters within a word. The Type tool is explained in depth in Chapter 12, "Using the Type Tool."

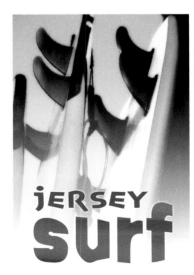

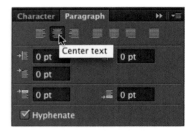

Paragraph

The Paragraph panel contains controls that impact paragraph text. When using the Type tool, you can click and type, which creates point type. Or, for more control, you can click and drag to create a text block and then access paragraph type. This causes the text to have boundaries and wrap when it hits a margin. Within a text block, you have a significant level of control over how your type is aligned and justified. For much more on text, see Chapter 12.

VIDEO 10:
Browsing in Mini Bridge

Mini Bridge

Mini Bridge is a useful panel in Photoshop that helps with tasks related to browsing and opening files. It lets you visually browse your files and makes it easy to manage files by ranking, sorting, and renaming them. Mini Bridge attempts to bring the core features of Adobe Bridge (a companion application) right into Photoshop. Choose File > Browse in Mini Bridge to open the panel. For you to use this panel, Adobe Bridge needs to be running in the background.

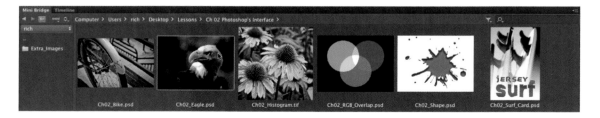

Acquiring Digital Images

3

Some of the core tasks of processing digital images involve sizing, manipulation, and processing. Even though their contents may vary, all digital images are essentially the same: They are composed of pixels that contain color and luminance information. Adobe Photoshop's powerful features allow you to adjust those pixels to better match your needs and desires.

And although the destination may be the same, the path your digital images take to get inside Photoshop will vary. Some may start out as digital images acquired with a still camera, whereas others may be archival images loaded via a scanner. You might also search online websites to find specialized images. Let's take a look at the many ways to acquire image files that can be loaded into Photoshop and manipulated.

Pixels in detail: When you zoom into an image at 1600% magnification, the pixels are very easy to see. You can open the photo CH03_Owl.tif from the Chapter 3 folder and use the Zoom tool (Z) to magnify the image. In fact, you can zoom up to 3200%, which makes pixel viewing quite easy. To toggle the visible grid at high magnifications, choose View > Show > Pixel Grid.

Digital Cameras

This book will not teach you how to use your digital camera. Many excellent books on that subject as well as classes are offered. What this book will address is how the pixels are converted, what file format you should choose to shoot your images, and how to transfer them to your computer.

IMAGE COURTESY NIKON INC.

Sensors in a digital camera acquire an image by converting light into pixel data.

Digital Camera Technology

Shooting a photo digitally produces a less accurate image than scanning a photo shot on film with a flatbed scanner using a high samples per inch setting. This is because digital cameras capture data using photosensitive electronic sensors. These sensors record brightness levels on a per-pixel basis. However, the sensors are usually covered with a patterned color filter that has red, green, and blue areas. Although the filter attempts to capture all detail that the lens sees, it is unable to completely do so due to its design.

A CMOS sensor (left), such as this one from Nikon, is the standard imaging device on a digital camera. The Bayer filter arrangement (right) uses red, green, and blue pixels, and is very common in digital cameras.

The filter used is typically the Bayer filter arrangement, which contains a repeating pattern of two green pixels, one red pixel, and one blue pixel. The Bayer filter uses more green because the human eye has an increased sensitivity to green. This filter allows the image to record the brightness of a single primary color (red, green, or blue) because digital cameras work in the RGB color space. The RGB values combine using the additive color theory (which was briefly discussed in Chapter 1, "Digital Imaging Fundamentals") and form an image when viewed from a suitable distance.

Not all the properties of film can be fully imitated by the computer sensors in a digital camera, so the camera must interpolate the color information of neighboring pixels. This averaging produces an anti-aliased image, which can show visible softening. When anti-aliasing is present, hard edges are blended into one another. Sometimes this can be desirable (with low-resolution Internet graphics where you reduce file size by limiting color). Other times, anti-aliasing can produce an undesirable softness when you print an image. Depending on the colors in the original image, a digital camera might only capture as little as one-fourth of the color detail. For example, if you had a desert scene with lots of red detail and little green or blue, the sensor would rely on the red areas of the filter (which only cover a fourth of the sensor face).

TIP

Camera-specific Training

I highly recommend the *Snapshots to Great Shots* series from Peachpit Press to learn more about specific cameras. Several popular cameras are covered in depth in dedicated books to help you get the most from your camera.

Does this mean you should shoot film only? Of course not; it's getting awfully difficult to even buy film these days. Ultimately, film captures a high-quality image that can be optically enlarged using the negative. However, digital capture can be more convenient and affordable because you eliminate the time-consuming processes and costs associated with developing the film. Huge strides have made in the improvement of image quality in digital cameras, and the ability to experiment and shoot multiple exposures with real-time feedback makes them a much better learning tool.

It is important to shoot at a high pixel count (which can be accomplished by setting the camera to shoot in a high- or best-quality mode or choosing to shoot raw). You can always crop or shrink the image for output or display, but you should avoid enlarging the image if you don't have to. When a digital image is enlarged, it can create unwanted image softness or pixelization (a visible blockiness). Capture as much pixel data as possible to minimize digital upsampling (increasing the resolution of the image).

Shooting JPEG vs. Raw

When digital cameras became commercially available, the memory cards used to store pictures were very expensive. Many photographers couldn't afford multiple or high-capacity cards, so they wanted more images to fit on a single, smaller card. Many users also emailed their pictures to friends and family. Small file sizes enabled consumers who lacked an understanding of digital imaging to attach photos to emails with minimum technical headaches. With these two scenarios in mind, manufacturers turned to an Internet-friendly format, JPEG (Joint Photographic Experts Group). It was a proven technology and one that was familiar to many users.

IMAGE COURTESY NIKON INC.

The JPEG format is extremely common because most hardware and software manufacturers have built support for it into their products. The JPEG format is also extremely efficient at compressing images, and it is a good format for continuous tone images, such as photos. A JPEG file looks for areas where pixel detail is repeated, such as the color blue in a photo of the sky. The file then discards repeated information and tells the computer to repeat certain color values or data to re-create the image.

IMAGE COURTESY LEXAR.

The JPEG Options dialog box is available when you modify or first save a JPEG file with Photoshop. When saving, you can adjust the Quality slider to reduce file size. It is best to leave Quality set to maximum if you will be making future edits to the image: This applies the least compression that could damage the image's appearance.

Although JPEG is a good format for distributing images (due to their compatibility and small file size), it is not great for image acquisition or production. A JPEG file is lossy, meaning that every time you modify it in Photoshop and resave as a JPEG, additional compression is applied to the image. Over subsequent compressions, the image quality can noticeably deteriorate. This is similar to the act of making a photocopy of another photocopy: Additional image deterioration occurs with each processing step. The visible loss in image detail or accuracy is referred to as *compression artifacts.*

So, if JPEG is inferior, why do so many people use it? Money and resistance to change are the simple answers. It's cheaper to shoot JPEG images because you don't need to buy as many memory cards (however, the price of memory cards nowadays is so low that this is almost a moot argument). Certain scenarios like sports and photojournalism often rely on the speed associated with smaller files as well (but camera manufacturers are adding larger buffers

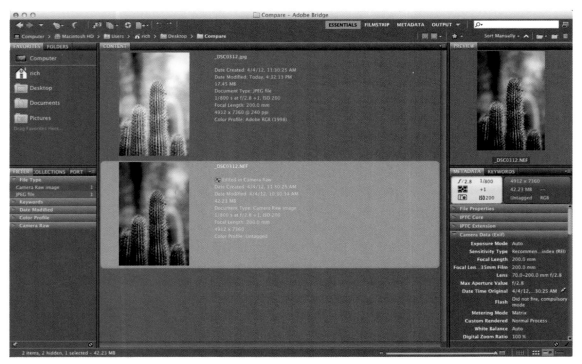

This image was captured as both a raw and a JPEG file when it was shot. The picture was taken with a Nikon D800, which can simultaneously write both files to the memory card when shooting. The raw file offers significantly greater latitude for post-processing and can recover more detail than the JPEG version.

in cameras to allow for high-speed raw shooting). Additionally, even many pros have been slow to abandon JPEGs due to fear of change. Learning how to use new technology requires time, something that many people are short of these days.

Newer digital cameras, generally the pro models, offer the ability to shoot raw (or native). The images are captured at a higher bit rate, which means that the pixels contain more information about the color values in the image. Most raw files have a bit depth of 10, 12, or even 16 bits per channel instead of the 8 used by JPEG. Raw formats also have a greater tonal range; hence, there is a better exposure for shadows and highlights. This extra information makes your work in Photoshop easier because it adds greater flexibility and control in image adjustments. You should have less work to do in Photoshop as well, because the image captured has more color information than a JPEG version.

Raw files can be four to ten times larger than JPEG files. This extra data is used to hold more image detail, which can reduce, or even eliminate, compression artifacts found in JPEG files. However, that extra data can increase the time it takes for the files to write to the memory card. As such, a memory card with a faster speed rating is a good investment and will help your camera keep up with the action you are shooting.

The raw file captures the unprocessed data from the camera's image sensor. Although your camera may contain settings for sharpness, exposure, or lighting conditions, the raw file stores that setting as modifiable information and captures the original (unmodified) data that came through your camera's sensors. This is very useful because it lets you easily adjust white balance within Photoshop. Each manufacturer treats the format differently, using a proprietary format. Fortunately, Photoshop frequently updates its raw technology to support the newest cameras on the market. To find out if you can access a particular camera format from within Photoshop, visit Adobe's website at www.adobe.com/products/photoshop/cameraraw.html.

Because the raw data is unprocessed, you must essentially "develop" the image data inside Photoshop. You'll be presented with several choices when opening a raw image. You can choose to adjust several options related to the image, as well as the lens and lighting conditions. All the adjustments made in the Camera Raw dialog box are nondestructive, meaning the original image is

TIP

Workaround for Unsupported Cameras

If Photoshop does not support a particular raw format used by your camera, use the software that shipped with the camera. The image can be converted into a 16-bit TIFF image (a high-quality file with no compression), which Photoshop can open.

TIP

Camera Raw for TIFF and JPEG?

Although the Camera Raw interface can be used for JPEG and TIFF files, those images have already had the camera's processing permanently applied to the image. Shooting raw has many benefits and should be fully explored by reading the documentation that accompanies your camera.

VIDEO 11:
Camera Raw Interface

VIDEO 12:
Localized Adjustments in Camera Raw

The Adobe Camera Raw dialog box is a versatile environment for "developing" your pictures. The image Cho3_Overhang.RAW is included on the DVD. Choose File > Open and navigate to the file in the Chapter 3 folder. In Photoshop CS6, you can even make localized adjustments by painting an area to select it and then use sliders to modify it.

preserved in pristine condition. You can "tweak" the image after shooting it, including being able to easily save those changes and apply them to similar exposures.

The Camera Raw dialog box has continued to evolve since it was first introduced as a purchased add-on to Photoshop 7. Subsequent versions of Photoshop have updated the user interface. Be sure to watch the detailed video tutorials to learn more about this powerful developing tool. Fortunately, the Camera Raw dialog box is fairly intuitive, especially once you understand the concepts of adjusting images. After you have completed Chapter 10, "Color Correction and Enhancement," you should feel much more confident using the options in the Camera Raw dialog box.

NOTE

Other Applications

Digital photographers who have large collections of digital images to manage will often use a library management application. Two of the most popular are Adobe Lightroom and Apple Aperture. Both have excellent integration with Adobe Photoshop.

IS DNG THE NEW RAW?

In 2004 Adobe released the **Digital Negative Specification (DNG) file format. The code and specifications were made publicly available so manufacturers could build support for the format into their products.**

The goal was to replace several proprietary raw file formats with a universal format. Despite initial optimism, camera manufacturers have been slow to adopt it (some even refusing). At this point, DNG files are a useful way to archive raw files and attach additional metadata. You can find out more about DNG by visiting Adobe's website at www.adobe.com/products/dng/main.html.

Acquiring Images from a Digital Camera

There are two major ways of downloading images from a digital camera. Which connection type you choose will depend on your work environment and budget for additional hardware.

The first method involves plugging the camera directly into the computer. Many cameras ship with a connecting cable (generally USB). The advantage of this approach is that it doesn't require an extra hardware purchase. The primary disadvantages of this method are that it ties up the camera, and it is hard on delicate ports built into the camera. If you break the USB port by constantly plugging in and unplugging a camera, it can lead to an expensive service bill. The data port is interconnected with several other systems on the camera; a break at one end can result in problems in other areas. Additionally, if the camera's battery were to be depleted during image transfer, the memory card and its contents can become corrupt.

A better option for downloading images from a digital camera is to purchase a stand-alone memory card reader. There are many options available, so consider these questions and choose wisely:

- Do you need only one card format, or do you need to read multiple formats?

- How fast do you want your files to transfer? Be wary of card readers that are USB 1, which can take a long time to transfer files. Look for USB 2, USB 3, FireWire, or eSATA for faster data rates. Laptop users with a card slot can purchase an effective card adapter for fast file transfers without tying up ports. Some laptops and desktops even ship with built-in card readers that tend to be reasonably fast.

- Do you want to transfer multiple cards at once? Some readers allow for two or even four cards to be mounted at one time so you can initiate a large transfer and walk away.

Transferring Files

The actual transfer of photos is not handled by Photoshop. Rather, you can use Adobe Bridge CS6, which includes a Photo Downloader (File > Get Photos from Camera). If you are not using Adobe Bridge, the files are handled natively by your computer's operating system. Just manually copy them to a folder on your computer.

TIP

Make Backup Copies

You may want to work with a copy of your transferred image, especially if you are just getting started in Photoshop. Many users will duplicate a folder of images and work with those. Others will burn a copy of the original images to a CD or DVD for backup. Preserving an original digital file is a good idea for future use.

But if you're shooting raw, there is no need to duplicate the raw file. The modifications to the image are stored in a separate sidecar file in the folder with your images. However, it is still a good idea to make sure your images are backed up to a second location in case your hard drive fails. For more on backup and image-management workflow, see www.dpbestflow.org.

VIDEO 13:
Importing Images
with Adobe Bridge

Need a Scanner?

Many all-in-one printers combine a printer and scanner, essentially creating a fax machine and photocopier in the process. Be sure to check if your printer offers scanning software to load your traditional photos. You can also rent scanners at many local photocopy shops.

VIDEO 14:
Crop and Straighten Command

Scanners

Many purists swear that shooting film adds richness in detail and color, as well as introduces subtle nuances like film grain, which cannot be replicated with a digital camera. Additionally, many pictures that you'll need to work with may only exist on traditional media (such as prints) or as a negative. You'll need to use a scanner to turn these optical formats into digital formats.

Choosing a Scanner

If you work in a computer lab or other work environment, your choice in scanners may have already been made for you. However, it is still important to understand the different types of scanners that are available to consumers.

Flatbed scanners

The most common scanner type is a flatbed scanner on which photos are loaded face down on a piece of glass. The scanner then moves a charge-coupled device (CCD) across the image to capture/digitize the image. High-quality scans can greatly increase the amount of data that is captured. So, be sure to look at high-speed scanner-to-computer connection options. For a modern computer, FireWire or USB 2 or 3 are the best options.

Be sure to pay close attention to the optical resolution of the scanner: This is the maximum size of the image before using software interpolation to enlarge it. Most users doing intermediate-level work or desktop publishing find a scanner capable of 600 to 1200 spi to be adequate. Remember, samples per inch can translate fairly well into pixels per inch. It is a good idea to have more pixels to start with, and then reduce the size of the image for delivery.

Film/slide scanners

Specialized scanners load in slides or film negatives. These scanners use a tray to hold the material, and then a motor pulls the tray slowly across an optical sensor. This process is relatively slow due to the resolution needed. The scanner must capture a lot of data from a very small surface area to produce a usable image. These scanners are slightly more expensive than flatbed scanners but are essential if you frequently work with slides or negatives.

Drum scanners

When top image quality is a must, pros turn to drum scanners. These units are expensive (starting at $5,000 and increase significantly). This is the oldest scanning technology. It calls for the image to be mounted on a drum. The drum is then rotated in front of a photomultiplier tube. The tube is much more sensitive than the CCDs used in flatbed scanners. Drum scanners' primary advantage is resolution, and they should be used when you need to significantly enlarge a scanned image (such as museum archival pieces or for magazine output). Because the machines are expensive and very complex (as well as potentially destructive), users will often send images to a service bureau for drum scanning.

A drum scanner is a highly specialized piece of equipment. These machines are expensive and are usually found only in high-end, service bureau facilities. ©iStockphoto

What Size to Scan? Think in Pixels

People often get confused when determining which settings to scan with. Too little informa-tion and the picture goes soft. Too much informa-tion and the scanner slows to a crawl. The answer is to know your intended output resolution as well as your device.

COMMON PPI REQUIREMENTS FOR FINAL FILES

Output Method	Typical ppi
Onscreen (web/slides)	72–96
Laser printing	150–250
Newsprint	120–170
Offset printing	250–300
High-quality offset printing	300–600

For example, if you need to create a 20-inch-wide poster that will be printed on a high-quality press requiring 300 ppi, use this calculation:

20 (inches) × 300 (ppi) × 1.25 (pad for flexibility) = 7500 pixels

Do not adjust your scanner's dpi (or ppi) settings. Rather, crop the image after running a preview scan. You can then adjust the scan-ner's resolution by looking at the output size of the scanned file. As you adjust the output file size, the scanning software will automati-cally determine the appropriate settings for samples per inch. All scanners tell you just how many samples you are about to capture. Looking at these numbers gives you a truer sense of the end result. Total pixel count is much more important than dpi, especially when scanning images of various original sizes.

More Advice on Scanning

On the DVD you'll find a bonus PDF called Scanner_Operation.pdf in the Chapter 3 folder.

Importing from CD/DVD/Blu-ray Disc

For many users, the practice of backing up images to optical discs has become very common. Additionally, many educational books (like this one) include media on their discs as well. This is a great way to distribute images because they are cheap to manufacture, are large-capacity discs, and are cross-platform compatible. You'll want to copy the images to your hard drive before you bring them into Photoshop. This will significantly increase the speed at which you can work on the images (hard drives transfer data faster than optical media drives). Additionally, you will be able to save your work in progress to your hard drive; you can't update a file once it's been burned to a disc.

NOTE

Royalty-free Does Not Equal Free

Don't confuse royalty-free and free. A royalty-free image must still be purchased. This is how the photographer and distributor make money. Royalty-free images can be a big savings because you can eliminate model releases, talent charges, location fees, travel, and many other costs associated with a photo shoot. However, keep in mind that someone had to pay those charges in the first place, and selling their pictures is their livelihood. Remember to pay for what you use. It's the professionally responsible way, as well as the law.

Stock Photo Services

Professionals find it is often necessary to purchase images to complete their projects. Whether it's a shot of a sports car for a magazine layout, a photo of a handshake for a Microsoft PowerPoint presentation, or the Chicago skyline for the cover of a DVD, stock photo services can help. But finding the right stock photo service is a balancing act. You must consider several factors when making a choice:

- **Cost.** There is a lot of competition out there, and photos are priced accordingly. Some services offer annual subscriptions; others charge per image.

- **Resolution.** Sites charge more for high-resolution images. Be sure to know how you'll use the image. Website designers will pay less for an image than someone designing an annual report. A website uses low-resolution images, whereas the report will be professionally printed and require high-resolution photos.

- **Exclusivity.** Does the image need to be yours and yours alone? Or is it OK if the photo is also used in someone else's project? Images that have their usage rights managed cost significantly more. A rights-managed image has restrictions placed on who can use the image for a certain time period. In contrast, a royalty-free image is purchased once and can be used as many times as the designer desires.

Public Domain Images

I'd say, "The best things in life are free," but that wouldn't be accurate here. More appropriately, "Why pay twice?" The United States has several federal agencies that document their work and make it available to the public. This work was paid for with tax dollars, and the people of the United States own the work. Fortunately, through the Internet, the U.S. government is willing to share it with most of the world.

I've created a portal page on my blog that points to the best government sites. These pages offer print-resolution images that you can use. Nearly every image is either copyright free or cleared for use, but you may be required to cite the source. Be sure to look at the terms of use posted on the site. Take the time to fully explore each site; you'll be surprised by the wealth (and diversity) of available images.

Visit www.richardharringtonblog.com/resources/freeimages.

STOCK PHOTOS ONLINE

Several stock photo sites are available to choose from. Here are some that offer high-quality images. Be sure to compare prices and usage rights to ensure they work for your project:

- **iStockphoto** (pay per image and subscription). www.istockphoto.com
- **Fotolia** (pay per image and subscription). www.fotolia.com
- **Photos.com** (subscription). www.photos.com
- **Thinkstock** (subscription). www.thinkstockphotos.com

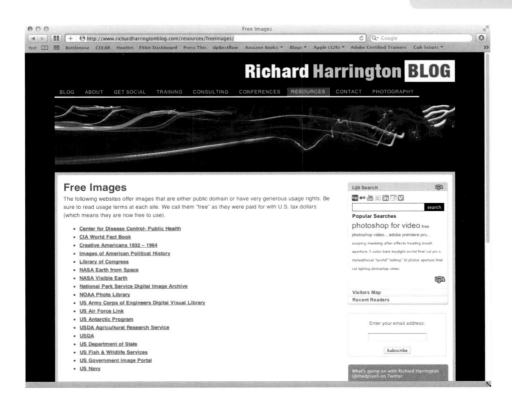

THE FAIR-USE MYTH

A popular myth in academic cultures is *fair use*. The doctrine provides situations where copyrighted works can be used without paying. It places restrictions on:

1. The purpose and character of the use, including whether such use is of a commercial nature or is for nonprofit educational purposes

2. The nature of the copyrighted work

3. The amount and substantiality of the portion used in relation to the copyrighted work as a whole

4. The effect of the use on the potential market for or value of the copyrighted work

Students and teachers alike get caught up in exemption number one. It is true that in a classroom situation you can use virtually any image you want for practice or class exercises. However, here is the problem: As soon as a student wants to start looking for a job and builds a portfolio, those images are being used for financial gain. If you are a student, you need to build work samples that help you get a job. Use images that you have the rights to (or that you have photographed).

The other clause that is often seen as a loophole is number four. People often think that because their project was small or personal that damage cannot be claimed. It is relatively easy for a copyright holder to claim damages or lost revenue. Even though they may not go after you, why take the chance? As a content creator, you should respect the law and the welfare of your fellow designers and photographers. For more on copyright and fair-use doctrine, visit www.copyright.gov and www.asmp.org/content/registration-counts.

Sizing Digital Images

4

Once you've acquired your digital images, you'll need to size them for your project (as well as ultimate output). For many Photoshop users, such as photographers, this may be as straightforward as cropping and sizing. This chapter explores several techniques for sizing your images. You'll learn about the concept of resampling, which addresses how the computer adds or subtracts information from a digital image while trying to retain detail and clarity.

Resolution Revisited

Chapter 3 looked closely at the process of acquiring digital images. If you skipped ahead or just skimmed that chapter, go back—a solid understanding of those concepts is required to move forward. Quite simply, you must know the capabilities of your digital camera or scanner to process information.

This photo was scanned at two different resolutions. The image on the left was scanned at 300 spi, and the image on the right was scanned at 72 spi. Examine the detailed enlargements to see the impact of different scanner settings.

Previous chapters also briefly discussed resolution requirements for different output formats. The second part of the image-sizing puzzle is a clear understanding of these output requirements. What resolution does your printer need? Are you sending the image to a service provider such as a commercial printer? You'll need to make lots of choices, but they should be based on where the image needs to end up. Know the destination of your image so you'll know which path to take.

TIP

**Start Out Right:
Digital Cameras**

If you're acquiring a digital image, be sure to capture enough pixels. If you want an 8 x 10 inch print and need 300 dpi, do the math before shooting. Multiply the inch size by the print resolution. In this example: 8 x 300 = 2400 and 10 x 300 = 3000—therefore, 2400 x 3000 = 7,200,000, which is about 7.2 megapixels. To allow for cropping, you'll want to shoot at an even higher resolution.

Resampling

The process of resampling allows you to change the pixel dimensions of your image. This will affect the display and print size of your image. This part of the resizing process is important for several reasons:

- Images will print faster when they are sized properly for your output device.

- Images will print clearer when you size them to a target size and then run a sharpening filter to enhance the edge detail.

- Images appear crisper when they are displayed at 100 percent on a computer screen (such as for a PowerPoint presentation or website).

The process of resampling is often identified based on whether you are scaling the image smaller (downsampling) or larger (upsampling):

- **Downsampling.** If you decrease the number of pixels in an image, you are downsampling the image, which permanently discards data. You can specify an interpolation method (discussed in the next section) to determine how pixels are deleted.

- **Upsampling.** When upsampling, you create new pixels to expand the image. Again, you can specify an interpolation method to determine how pixels are added. When upsampling, you add information that did not previously exist, which generally just makes a larger image that may appear less sharp than the original.

Choose an Interpolation Method

When you resample an image, Photoshop creates new pixels. Those new pixels are created based on the neighboring pixels. How those new pixels are formed is determined by the interpolation method you specify. Photoshop offers up to six methods to resample your image.

Choose one of the following methods:

- **Nearest Neighbor.** This method is fast but not precise. It's useful for resizing illustrations but it can produce jagged edges.

- **Bilinear.** This approach uses pixel averaging. It is a balance of speed and quality, and produces medium-quality results.

- **Bicubic.** This method is slower but more precise than the first two (and more desirable). Photoshop spends more time examining surrounding pixels before interpolating new ones. The math at work is very complex, so this method will produce smoother results than Nearest Neighbor or Bilinear.

- **Bicubic Smoother.** This method is a refinement of Bicubic. It is specifically designed for upsampling (enlarging images).

- **Bicubic Sharper.** This is also a refinement of Bicubic. It's useful for downsampling (shrinking images). It does a better job of maintaining sharpness (when reducing) than other methods.

- **Bicubic Automatic.** Photoshop CS6 offers a new choice that automatically switches among the three bicubic methods based on the task at hand. For most, this is the best option.

Setting the Default Method

Photoshop allows you to choose a default interpolation method. This will be used when you invoke a sizing command, such as the Free Transform or Image Size command (more on both in the pages ahead). Choose the method that best matches your workflow.

1. Choose Edit > Preferences or press Command+K (Ctrl+K) to call up the Preferences dialog box.

2. From the Image Interpolation menu, choose your default method (Bicubic Automatic is the most flexible method and is highly recommended).

3. Click OK to store the setting.

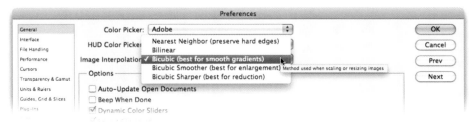

VIDEO 15:
Changing Image Size

Resizing an Image

Most of your images will not be sized to the exact dimensions you need. You have several options at your disposal. To change the size of an image, you can use the Image Size or Canvas Size command. You can also use the Crop tool or Free Transform command to make an adjustment. You can use these choices individually or in combination to achieve the desired results.

Image Size

The Image Size command lets you permanently reassign the total pixel count, as well as resolution, for a particular image. You can also use this command to upsample or downsample an image. This is an easy way to size an image to a specific height or width. Let's put the command into action:

1. Open the file Ch04_Resize.tif from the Chapter 4 folder.

2. Choose Image > Image Size or press Command+Option+I (Ctrl+Alt+I).

   The Image Size dialog box offers several choices. You can choose to manipulate the pixel dimensions of the image (measured in pixels or percent). You can also modify the print size, which is the size of the image when printed. You can modify the print size based on percent, inches, centimeters, millimeters, points, picas, or columns. The most common choices are percent, inches, or centimeters, because most users easily understand these units of measure.

3. Set the Document Size to measure in inches. Specify a new height of **6** inches.

4. Be sure to select the Resample Image option if you want to change the pixel dimensions. Choose the method to Resample Image that is most appropriate for your image. Bicubic Automatic is the most common method, but you may have special circumstances. See "Choose an Interpolation Method" earlier in this chapter.

TIP

Return of Focus

You can avoid the need for upsampling by scanning or shooting the image at a sufficiently high resolution. If you want to preview the effects of changing pixel dimensions onscreen or to print proofs at different resolutions, resample a duplicate of your image.

5. Leave the Constrain Proportions check box selected, or you will introduce distortion. You generally want to keep the width and height constrained to the same ratio so the image resembles its original appearance.

6. Enter a resolution of **300** pixels per inch for professional printing.

7. Click OK.

Canvas Size

The canvas size is your work area. When you create a new document, you can specify the size of your canvas. When you scan a photo or import a digital image, the canvas size is automatically set to the edge of the image. You may need to change the canvas size to crop or extend the canvas of your image to work on specific areas of the image. Let's try it out:

VIDEO 16:
Changing Canvas Size

1. Open the file Ch04_Canvas.tif from the Chapter 4 folder.

2. Choose Image > Canvas Size or press Command+Option+C (Ctrl+Alt+C).

In the Canvas Size dialog box you'll see the dimensions of your current canvas. You can specify a new canvas size using a variety of measurements. Pixels is a useful measurement if you're creating screen graphics, whereas inches or centimeters is easier to understand for print work. Using percentage is also good for incremental amounts.

Let's place a uniform border around the image.

3. Select the Relative check box. This disregards the numerical values of the current canvas size and allows you to specify a new amount to be added to the existing image.

4. Ensure that the anchor point for the image is set to centered. This will expand the border in all directions around the center of the current image.

5. Add a half-inch border on all sides. Type **.5** inches into the Width and Height fields.

6. Specify a Canvas extension color. This is the color that Photoshop places around the image when you change the canvas size. You can choose to use the foreground or background colors that are loaded in the toolbox. You can also use white, black, gray, or other, which can be any color you specify. In this case, choose white.

7. Click OK.

TIP

Use Overlays

Photoshop CS6 offers six different composition overlays when cropping. You can press the O key after you start a crop to cycle through the different guides. These overlays offer different theories for the placement of key subjects within a photo.

Crop Tool

With the Crop tool you can change a viewer's perception of an image. You can choose to tighten the area of interest of an image, which allows you to de-emphasize (or even eliminate) parts of a photo and improve the image by better framing the subject.

You can invoke cropping in two ways. The first method involves making a selection with the Rectangular Marquee tool and then choosing Image > Crop. Although this works fine, it does not offer as much control as using the second method, the Crop tool. Let's put method two into action:

1. Open the image Ch04_Crop.tif from the Chapter 4 folder.

2. Select the Crop tool from the Tools panel or press C.

   Handles for the Crop tool automatically appear at the edges of the canvas. Let's crop to a specific ratio.

3. Click the Aspect Ratio menu and choose 1 x 1 (Square).

   This automatically changes the shape of the crop to a 1:1 aspect ratio.

4. You can refine the crop selection after it is made.

   Mouse over a corner of the crop until the pointer changes to a double-headed arrow, and then click and drag on the crop selection border to pull the crop tighter or to expand it.

5. Examine the crop to determine if you like the composition.

   If desired, you can click and drag inside the crop boundary to reposition the image within the crop box.

NOTE

Back in Time

If you don't like the new cropping mode, you can restore most of the previous functionality of cropping in Photoshop CS5. With the Crop tool active, just click the gear icon in the Options bar and choose the Use Classic Mode option.

TIP

Leave a Note

You can use Photoshop's Note tool to leave a comment that the image was cropped nondestructively to help you remember in the future.

6. In the Options bar, make sure the Delete Cropped Pixels option is deselected. This will simply hide the cropped pixels instead of deleting them.

7. When satisfied with the crop, press Return (Enter) or click the Commit button (check mark) in the Options bar. The shielded (darkened) areas will be cropped. To cancel, press the Esc key.

8. After applying the crop, you can still grab the crop handles at the edge the image and recompose the shot. You can also drag the image within the frame for a better composition.

Power crop

It is possible to crop and resize an image at the same time. I refer to this technique as a *power crop*, and it is a huge time-saver. Before cropping, you can choose the desired size of your final image in the Options bar. When you drag to crop the image, your box will constrain to the proper aspect ratio. Cropping will change the aspect ratio and the resolution setting, allowing you to resize and crop in one step.

Let's crop an image to a 5-inch by 7-inch shape at 300 ppi:

1. Open the file Ch04_Power Crop.tif from the Chapter 4 folder.

2. In the Options bar, click the Aspect Ratio menu and choose Size & Resolution.

3. Enter a width of **5** inches, a height of **7** inches, and a resolution of **300** ppi.

4. Click OK to apply the initial crop.

The aspect ratio has likely been transposed with the image set to 7 × 5 inches.

VIDEO 17:
Power Cropping

NOTE

Cropping Freely

If you want to crop to a custom aspect ratio, just use the default Unconstrained option.

TIP

Straighten and Crop

In the Options bar for the Crop tool is a Straighten button. Clicking this button switches to a measuring tool. Just find a straight line in the image (or choose your own reference), and then drag to rotate the image into a better orientation and remove any unwanted rotation.

5. Drag a corner to reset the orientation of the crop to portrait, and set the crop to a better composition for the elephant on the left. Use the figure as a guide.

6. Click the Commit button or press Return (Enter). When you're finished cropping, you may want to click Clear to reset the tool's default settings.

7. Press the V key to switch to the Move tool. You can drag the image within the canvas freely to reposition the crop as needed (as long as you didn't delete cropped pixels earlier).

Reduce Motion

In the Additional Options controls for the Crop tool (click the gear icon) you can toggle Auto Center Preview off. This disables the "image moving while resizing" behavior that attempts to keep the crop box centered.

Pixel Restoration

Because the cropped pixels were hidden (instead of deleted), details were preserved outside the cropped area. This allows for the image to be restored. You can choose Image > Reveal All to restore all hidden pixels after a crop (provided you left the Delete Cropped Pixels option deselected).

VIDEO 18:
Nondestructive Cropping

VIDEO 19:
Perspective Cropping

Perspective cropping

Some images will have visible distortion, which is often caused by the camera not being square with the subject. If the photographer was higher (or lower) than the image or if the photo was taken at an angle, you will see distortion. In some cases, this distortion is part of the shot composition and is desirable. In others, the distortion can be distracting. Let's square off an image:

1. Open the file Ch04_ Perspective.tif from the Chapter 4 folder.

2. Select the Perspective Crop tool by clicking the Crop tool in the Tools panel and choosing the second tool in the well.

3. Crop around the window in the photo as tight as you can to frame it.

Use the pixel grid to help position the initial crop. If it is not visible, select the option Show Grid in the Options bar.

TOOL PRESETS SAVE TIME

If you have a specific image size that you use often, harness the power of Photoshop's Preset Manager. You can create tool presets that already have the values for a tool loaded.

1. In the Options bar, click the Aspect Ratio menu and choose Size & Resolution.

2. Enter a desired size and resolution into the dialog box.

3. Select the Save as Crop Preset check box at the bottom of the dialog box and click OK.

4. When the Crop tool is selected, you'll see its icon in the upper-left corner of the Options bar. Click the triangle to access the menu.

5. You'll see several preset sizes that are stored in Photoshop. Select the Current Tool Only check box to narrow the presets. Photoshop stores the preset crop size in a temporary preferences file.

6. To permanently save cropping sizes, click the submenu icon in the menu (the small gear in the right corner of the panel) and choose Save Tool Presets to save them in a desired location.

4. Drag the upper-right and upper-left corners in toward the center to line up the crop borders parallel to the edge of the window.

   The crop selection will no longer look rectangular.

5. Click the Commit button or press Return (Enter). The result should appear as if the angle was squared and the camera was level.

   Depending on how you cropped the image, it may look slightly distorted. You can use the Image Size command with the Constrain Proportions option deselected or the Free Transform command to reshape the photo.

Rotate Canvas Command

Sometimes your image will need to be rotated or flipped. Loading your image upside down on the scanner, loading a slide backwards into a slide scanner, or turning the camera on its side when taking a portrait may cause inverted or reversed images. You may also want to make a change to your image for compositional purposes.

The Rotate Canvas command offers several choices: rotate the image 180° (half a rotation), 90° clockwise or counterclockwise, or an arbitrary amount (the user types in a number of degrees). Additionally, the entire canvas can be flipped (creating a mirrored image). You can flip the canvas horizontally or vertically:

1. Open the image Ch04_Rotate.tif from the Chapter 4 folder.

2. Choose Image > Rotate Canvas 90° CCW (counterclockwise). The image is now properly oriented.

VIDEO 20:
Adaptive Wide Angle
Correction and
Content-Aware Fill

VIDEO 21:
Free Transform Command

Free Transform Command

The Free Transform command is another useful way to rotate and size an image. It works best when you have an object located on its own floating layer (not a *Background*) or if you have an active selection. You'll explore selections and layers in much greater detail in future chapters. For now, let's work with a simple layered image that has already been prepped:

1. Open the file Ch04_Free_Transform_ Basic.psd from the Chapter 4 folder.

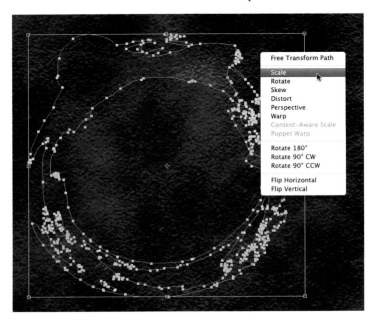

This image has two layers: a background, which is a pattern, and a vector shape layer. A vector layer is a special layer in Photoshop. It can be resized and transformed repeatedly with no degradation in quality. Vector layers use math to describe curved lines and can be freely manipulated.

2. If it's not visible, call up the Layers panel by choosing Windows > Layers.

3. Select the Vector Shape layer so it is active.

4. Choose Edit > Free Transform or press Command+T (Ctrl+T).

You can access several controls for the Free Transform command by Control-clicking/right-clicking. Try the following transformations on the Vector Shape layer. You can press the Esc key to cancel the transformation or Return (Enter) to apply it:

- **Scale.** You can scale by dragging a handle. Hold down the Shift key as you drag a corner handle to scale proportionately. Hold down the Option (Alt) key to scale in both directions simultaneously. To scale numerically, enter a value in the Options bar.

- **Rotate.** You can rotate a preset amount by selecting Rotate 180°, Rotate 90° CW, or Rotate 90° CCW. To rotate freely by dragging, move your mouse outside the Free Transform box. It will become a curved, two-headed arrow. Hold down the Shift key while rotating to constrain the rotation to 15° increments. Additionally, you can rotate numerically by entering degrees in the rotation box in the Options bar.

- **Skew.** Skewing an image creates a sense of distortion, as if the image were leaning. To skew the image, hold down Command+Shift (Ctrl+Shift) and drag a side handle (not a corner handle). The cursor will change to a white arrowhead with a small double arrow.

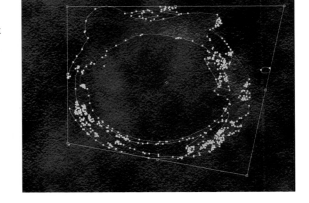

- **Distort.** If you want to distort an image freely, choose Distort. This allows you to move the corners of the image freely (a process also known as corner-pinning). You can also access this command by pressing Command (Ctrl) while dragging a corner point.

- **Perspective.** Transforming perspective creates the illusion that the image is being viewed from above or from the side. You can access this command by pressing Command+Option+Shift (Ctrl+Alt+Shift) or from the context menu. This is a useful command to fix perspective problems or to add perspective effects.

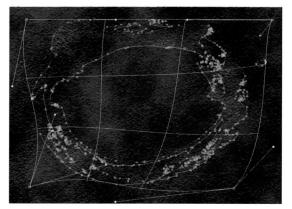

- **Warp.** The Warp command was first introduced in Photoshop CS2. It allows you to distort an image into a number of predefined shapes available in the Options bar (such as Arch, Flag, or Twist). When you choose Custom, several points can be freely dragged to distort the image as desired.

- **Flip Horizontal and Flip Vertical.** These simple commands let you flip an individual layer without flipping the entire canvas.

The Free Transform command has one major benefit over choosing individual transform commands from the Image menu: Free Transform lets you apply transformations in one continuous operation, which reduces quality loss in raster images.

Open the file Ch04_Free_Transform_Additional.psd. Using the Free Transform command, you can rotate, size, and flip the images to create a better layout.

Content-Aware Scaling

The Content-Aware scaling feature is a way to intelligently scale an image that allows for certain details to be preserved while others are distorted. It can be used to recompose an image. When used correctly, the image will automatically adapt to preserve vital areas during the scale.

VIDEO 22:
Advanced
Content-Aware Scale

1. From the Chapter 4 folder, open the image Ch04_Content_Aware_Scale.psd.

2. Select the layer called Headshot. The photo is not big enough to fill the entire canvas and needs to be resized.

3. Choose Edit > Content-Aware Scale.

4. In the Options bar, make sure the Protect Skin Tones button is pressed to tell Photoshop to attempt to preserve regions that contain skin tones.

5. Drag a resize handle on the bounding box to scale the image. Hold down the Shift key to scale proportionately. You can also hold down the Option (Alt) key to scale from the center of the image.

6. Size the image so it fits the width of the canvas. Notice that the face shows little to no distortion, but the background has been changed significantly.

7. Click the Commit button or press the Return (Enter) key to apply the change.

Puppet Warp

The Puppet Warp command is similar to the Free Transform command in that it allows for selective warping of a layer. The technology works by creating a geometric mesh that lets you dramatically warp specific regions of an image. The command takes a little getting used to in order to create natural results, but it can be quite useful because the image will automatically adapt so vital areas are preserved during scaling.

VIDEO 23:
Puppet Warp

1. From the Chapter 4 folder, open the image Ch04_Puppet.psd.

   This image has already been masked to isolate the elephant to its own layer; you'll learn more about masking in Chapter 7, "Layer Masking." The background has also been filled in using the Content-Aware fill command, which you'll learn about in Chapter 11, "Repairing and Improving Photos."

2. Select the layer named Elephant.

3. Choose Edit > Puppet Warp. Photoshop draws a polygonal mesh to allow the object to be distorted.

4. In the Options bar, adjust the mesh settings to create a refined mesh:

   Mode. Photoshop offers three levels of elasticity for the mesh. Normal is fine for this image.

   Density. Choose More Points to increase the precision of the warp (it will take more computer processing time).

   Expansion. If needed, you can contract or expand the mesh. The default value is usually best.

   Show Mesh. At times you may want to deselect this to see the image without the visible mesh applied.

5. Click on the image to add control pins. Add pins to areas you want to transform as well as points you want to anchor in place.

   Use the figure for guidance. Add pins to the trunk and in a few places on the elephant's body. Add additional points as needed as you manipulate the figure.

6. Experiment with dragging pins to warp the elephant. Try to curve her trunk and reposition her legs:

- Drag pins to warp the mesh.

- Try adding pins to keep nearby areas intact.

- If an area doesn't overlap properly, you can click the Pin Depth buttons in the Options bar. These can be used to control how much something overlaps.

- To remove a pin, right-click on it and choose Delete Pin.

- If unwanted warping occurs with a pin, select it, and then hold down the Option (Alt) key and drag.

7. When you're satisfied with your transformation, press Return (Enter) or click the Commit button in the Options bar.

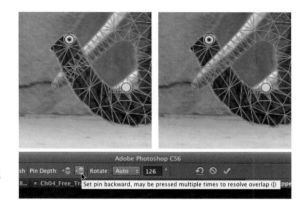

Using Smart Objects Before Transforming

VIDEO 24:
Transforming
Smart Objects

Smart Objects are a bit of "under the hood" Photoshop magic. Essentially, this powerful command allows you to embed raster or vector data into a layer. The layer can then be transformed indefinitely because the embedded data remains editable and scalable. You can convert one or more layers into a new Smart Object or choose to add new content as a Smart Object.

A Smart Object is simply one file embedded inside another. This can be very useful because Smart Objects allow greater flexibility than simply applying the Free Transform command to a regular layer. With a Smart Object, you can perform multiple nondestructive transforms with no loss in quality (as long as you don't exceed the pixel dimensions of the original raster object).

TIP

Another Path to a Smart Object

Besides using the Place command to create a Smart Object, you can select one or more objects in the Layers panel and choose Layer > Smart Objects > Group into New Smart Object.

TIP

Smarter Smart Objects

In Photoshop, you can apply perspective transformations to Smart Objects as well. Simply follow the instructions in the "Free Transform Command" section earlier in this chapter.

1. Open the file Ch04_Smart_Object_BG.psd from the Chapter 4 folder. A background design for a multimedia presentation opens. Let's add a photo layer.

2. Choose File > Place to add a new document as a layer. Select the file Ch04_Smart_Object.tif from the Chapter 4 folder and click Place.

3. Size the image using the control handles. The controls are identical to those you used with the Free Transform command. Scale down the image to a very small size. Apply the transformation by clicking the Commit button.

4. Now, let's try scaling the image larger. Invoke the Free Transform command for the selected layer by pressing Command+T (Ctrl+T). Scale up the image to its original size. Apply the transformation. Notice that the image remains sharp. This is because the Smart Object contains a full resolution copy of the image embedded inside the layer.

Selection Tools and Techniques

5

If you really want to get things done in Photoshop, you have to be good at making selections. You might want to extract a subject from a photo or maybe change the sky to another shade of blue. Or, maybe the sweater in your advertisement needs to be orange instead of red, or you'd like to duplicate some of the background crowd so your photo doesn't look so empty. In each case, you'll need an accurate selection.

Why? You may be able to look at a digital image and clearly recognize that it's a shot of a rock outcropping in the desert. The scene has many similar colors for the red rock, as well as contrasting color in the sky. Unfortunately, your computer just sees a bunch of pixels. A little human intervention is necessary to distinguish which part of the image you want to manipulate or process. In Photoshop, this is called making a selection.

By selecting the rock outcropping, I applied a Curves and Vibrance adjustment to boost the contrast and color in the specified area.

Although this means extra effort, it also means that most digital imaging tasks require a human brain (which means jobs for designers and artists). Accurate selections are important, and there are several techniques you can employ to get them just right. Some are easier than others, and some are more accurate. You may in fact need to combine multiple techniques to get the job done. Knowing several different methods lets you make an accurate selection no matter what your source image looks like.

Basic Selection Tools

Photoshop's Tools panel contains three categories of tools that you can use to create a basic selection: Marquee tools, Lasso tools, and Wand tools. Although these three are very useful, many users forget that they are only starting points.

Marquee Tools

The Marquee tools (M) allow you to click and drag to define a selection. To toggle between the Rectangular and Elliptical Marquee tool, press Shift+M. Descriptions of the Marquee tools follow:

- **Rectangular Marquee tool.** Use this tool to make a rectangular selection. Press the Shift key to draw a square.

- **Elliptical Marquee tool.** Use this tool to make an elliptical selection. Press the Shift key to draw a circle.

- **Single Row or Single Column Marquee tool.** Creates a selection that is 1 pixel wide in the shape of a row or column. These two tools are not used often, which is why Adobe didn't assign the keyboard shortcut M to trigger them.

A FASTER TOOLS PANEL

There are a few ways to access tools from the Tools panel:

- You can click the tool icon.

- To access nested tools (those that share the same well), click and hold the mouse button on the tool icon.

- You can also hold down the Option (Alt) key and click an individual tool in the Tools panel to cycle tools.

- You can press the letter shortcut key. Hovering over a tool's icon will teach you the shortcut keys when the tool tip pops up.

- To switch to a nested tool, hold down the Shift key and press the tool's shortcut key.

- If the Shift key is an extra step you'd rather not use, modify your user preferences. Press Command+K (Ctrl+K) to call up your General Preferences screen. Deselect the check box next to Use Shift Key for Tool Switch.

Putting the Marquees into action

Let's give the Rectangular and Elliptical Marquee tools a try and make some selections.

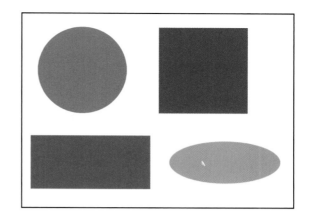

1. Open the file Ch05_Marquee_Practice.tif from the Chapter 5 folder.

2. Practice selecting each of the four objects using both the Elliptical and Rectangular Marquee tools. Remember to use the Shift key to constrain proportions for the square and circle shapes. Don't worry about perfection; you'll learn lots of ways to tweak selections in the coming pages.

Selection options for Marquee tools

When using the Marquee tools, you have several options available in the Options bar. These modifiers can improve or alter your selection.

The first four icons specify the kind of selection:

A **New selection.** Creates a new selection.

B **Add to selection.** After you create one selection, you can click this button so subsequent selections are combined with the existing selection. You can also hold down the Shift key to add to a selection.

C **Subtract from selection.** After you create one selection, you can click this button so subsequent selections are subtracted from the existing selection. You can also hold down the Option (Alt) key to subtract from a selection.

D **Intersect with selection.** Requires you to make a first selection. When you draw a second selection, Photoshop creates a new selection where the two selections overlap.

VIDEO 25:
Selection Basics

The following options modify the selection tool and must be chosen *before* making a selection:

E **Feather.** A normal selection has a crisp edge. Feathering a selection creates a gradual blend at the selection's edges. Think of it as the difference between a line drawn with a pencil and one drawn with a felt-tip marker. Feathered selections are useful when you want to extract objects.

F **Anti-alias.** When working with the Elliptical Marquee tool, you can select Anti-alias to create a smoother edge for curved lines (especially if your image is at a low resolution).

G **Style.** For the Rectangular Marquee tool and Elliptical Marquee tool, you can choose from three styles in the Options bar:

- **Normal.** This is the default option. Click to draw your marquee freehand.

- **Fixed Ratio.** You can set a width-to-height ratio. For example, to draw a marquee three times as wide as it is high, enter **3** for the width and **1** for the height.

- **Fixed Size.** You can specify an exact size for the marquee's height and width. You can enter the value in pixels (px), inches (in), or centimeters (cm).

H **Refine Edge.** This button refines any selection based on several criteria. You'll explore this functionality later in this chapter.

Moving a selection

There are a few ways to reposition a selection:

- While drawing a selection (with the mouse button still depressed) you can hold down the spacebar and move the selection.

- With an active selection, move the tool's cursor inside the selection border (marching ants). The icon changes to a triangle with a marquee border. You can then click inside and drag the selection to move it.

- To modify a selection using controls similar to the Free Transform command, choose Select > Transform Selection. All the options available to the Free Transform command can be applied to the selection border. For more on Free Transform, see Chapter 4, "Sizing Digital Images."

Selection Lassos

The Lasso tools allow you to draw freeform segments with your mouse to create a selection border. The Lasso tools are most often used to create a rough selection (which can then be refined using techniques such as Quick Mask mode (see the bonus article in the Chapter 5 folder). The keyboard shortcut for selecting the Lasso tool is the letter L. To select the next Lasso tool, press Shift+L. The following list describes each of the Lasso tools:

- **Lasso tool.** Use this tool to make a freehand selection. You must return to your starting point to close the selection loop. If you don't return to start and simply double-click, Photoshop will draw a straight line and close the selection point for you.

- **Polygonal Lasso tool.** Use this tool to draw straight-edged segments for a selection border. With every click, a part of the segment is drawn. Continue clicking to set endpoints for additional segments. Click your starting point to close the loop and create an active selection. To constrain the tool to 45-degree angles, hold down the Shift key while drawing.

- **Magnetic Lasso tool.** When you use the Magnetic Lasso tool, Photoshop attempts to snap the border to the edges of the image. If the anchor point doesn't snap accurately, click once to manually add a point.

Putting the Lasso tools into action

Let's give these tools a try.

1. Open the file Ch05_Channels.tif.

2. Try using both the Polygonal and Magnetic Lasso tools to select the boat. Make multiple attempts at practicing the selection.

In the middle of making a selection with the Polygonal or Magnetic Lassos, you can press the Delete key to remove segments. Press and hold once, and then release and press subsequent times to remove segments (one per click). If you need to stop a selection, press the Esc key. If you need to deselect and start over, just press Command+D (Ctrl+D).

Selection options for Lasso tools

When using the Lasso tools, you have several options available in the Options bar to improve or alter your selection. These modifiers are very similar to those for the Marquee tools, so I'll just briefly mention them.

The first four icons specify the kind of selection:

A **New selection**

B **Add to selection**

C **Subtract from selection**

D **Intersect with selection**

The next three options create a smoother selection:

E **Feather.** This option creates a softer edge on your selection.

F **Anti-alias.** This creates a smoother edge for curved lines.

G **Refine Edge.** This button brings up a window with several sliders to adjust an active selection with intuitive controls.

Magnetic Lasso options

The Magnetic Lasso has a few additional options that mainly deal with its snapping behavior. You can change the following properties in the Options bar:

- **Width.** The width specifies how wide an area the Magnetic Lasso looks at when trying to detect edges. To see the width visually, activate the Caps Lock key before making a selection.

- **Edge Contrast.** This value determines the lasso's sensitivity to edges in the image. Higher values detect high-contrast edges, whereas lower values detect lower-contrast edges. On an image with well-defined edges, you should use a higher width and edge contrast setting.

- **Frequency.** The rate at which Photoshop adds anchor points is based on the Frequency setting. An anchor point is where the lasso attaches, so you can move the selection border in another direction. You can enter a value between 0 and 100. Higher values add more anchor points to your selection border.

- **Stylus Pressure.** Click the Stylus Pressure icon if you have a tablet connected. This lets you to use the pressure of the pen to affect edge width.

VIDEO 26:
Quick Selection Tool

Wand Tools

The Quick Selection and Magic Wand tools (W) allow you to click an area of color to create a selection based on adjacent pixels and your Tolerance setting. The Magic Wand is a much older tool that works reasonably well on photos with large areas of similar color. The Quick Selection tool is a significant improvement over the Magic Wand tool, however, and has quickly become a favorite tool of Photoshop pros.

Quick Selection tool

The Quick Selection tool allows you to create a selection that quickly forms based on color and contrast.

1. Open the file Ch05_Quick_Selection.tif from the Chapter 5 folder.

2. Select the Quick Selection tool by pressing W.

3. Choose the Auto-Enhance option in the Options bar.

4. Press the right bracket key (]) to make the selection brush larger; press the left bracket key ([) to make it smaller.

5. Click and drag in the flower to make an initial selection.

6. To add to the selection, click and drag again. If too much of a selection is made, hold down the Option (Alt) key to subtract from the selection.

TIP

Get Better Results Automatically

The Auto-Enhance option in the Options bar can quickly improve any selection made with the Quick Selection tool. You'll need to choose this option before you click. It automatically smooths out the edges of the generated selection.

A Better Wand

The Magic Wand tool works best if you turn on the pixel-averaging option. In the Options bar, use the Sample Size menu to change the Sample Size to a 5 by 5 Average (or 11 by 11 Average). The Magic Wand tool will then become less sensitive to erroneous clicks.

VIDEO 27:
Magic Wand Tool

Selection options for the Magic Wand tool

When using the Magic Wand tool, you have several options available in the Options bar that can improve or alter your selection. These modifiers are very similar to those for the Marquee and Lasso tools, so I'll cover them briefly.

The first four icons specify the kind of selection:

A **New selection**

B **Add to selection**

C **Subtract from selection**

D **Intersect with selection**

The remaining settings allow you to refine your selection parameters:

E **Sample Size.** This determines how additional pixels are selected. The targeted color value can be based on just the color you click on or an average of neighboring pixels.

F **Tolerance.** This setting determines how similar the pixels must be to your initial click in order to be selected. You can enter a value in pixels, ranging from 0 to 255. A higher value selects a broader range of colors.

G **Anti-alias.** This creates a smoother edge when you click.

H **Contiguous.** When Contiguous is selected, only adjacent areas with the same colors are selected. If deselected, all pixels in the entire image that use the same colors will be selected.

I **Sample All Layers.** If you have a multilayered document and want to select colors on all layers, select this check box.

J **Refine Edge.** This button brings up a window with several sliders to adjust an active selection with intuitive controls.

A B C D	E	F	G	H	I	J

Sample Size: Point Sample | Tolerance: 32 | ☑ Anti-alias ☑ Contiguous ☐ Sample All Layers | Refine Edge...

Subtract from selection

Putting the Magic Wand into action

Although the Magic Wand can be a little coarse at first, it is possible to get an accurate selection. Let's try out the Magic Wand tool.

1. Open the file Ch05_Magic_Wand.tif from the Chapter 5 folder.

2. Select the Magic Wand tool by pressing Shift+W for *wand.* You can press the keys multiple times to toggle between the Quick Selection and Magic Wand tools.

3. Set the Tolerance to **20** and select the Anti-alias check box.

4. Change the Sample Size menu to a 5 × 5 sample to average out the blue in the sky.

5. Click the sky in the upper-left corner to make an initial selection.

6. Part of the sky will be selected. Hold down the Shift key and click another area of the sky to add to the selection. Repeat as needed until the entire sky is selected.

Additional Selection Commands

A few more Selection commands are found on the Select menu or by choosing Select > Modify. For a sense of completion, let's take a quick look:

- **All.** The All command selects everything on the active layer or in your flattened document within the edges of the canvas. The keyboard shortcut is Command+A (Ctrl+A) when the canvas window is selected.

- **Deselect.** The Deselect command removes the active selection. You may need to do this when you're finished altering your selection to avoid accidentally modifying your image. The keyboard shortcut is Command+D (Ctrl+D) when the canvas window is selected.

- **Reselect.** The Reselect command is truly useful because it allows you to reactivate the last selection in your document. It only works with selections made since you've last opened the document. The keyboard shortcut is Shift+Command+D (Shift+Ctrl+D) when the canvas window is selected.

TIP

Actionable Detection

You'll learn about Photoshop actions later in this book. These macros let you record several steps for playback on an image (which can really save time for repetitive tasks). The Skin Tones and Face Detection options can be recorded into a custom action, which can really save you time when you're cleaning up several portraits.

- **Inverse.** The concept of inverse is very important. It is often far easier to select what you don't want, and then inverse the selection to get what you do want. The keyboard shortcut is Shift+Command+I (Shift+Ctrl+I) when the canvas window is selected.

- **Grow.** The Grow command selects adjacent pixels that fall within a certain tolerance range. To modify the range, adjust the Tolerance settings of the Magic Wand tool.

- **Similar.** The Similar command also selects pixels based on the Tolerance settings of the Magic Wand tool. However, the pixels do not need to be adjacent.

- **Transform Selection.** The Transform Selection command allows you to modify an existing selection. Invoking it gives you controls similar to the Free Transform command (see Chapter 4 for more on the Free Transform command).

The following commands appear on the Modify submenu:

- **Border.** If you have an existing selection, you can use the Border command. You can enter a value between 1 and 200 pixels. A new selection that frames the existing selection will be created.

- **Smooth.** The Smooth command simplifies the selection by adding more pixels to the selection to make it less jagged.

- **Expand.** The Expand command allows you to add pixels in an outward fashion to the selection. The border will get wider based on the number of pixels you add.

- **Contract.** The Contract command works the opposite of the Expand command. Specify the number of pixels that you want the selection to decrease.

- **Feather.** The Feather command blurs the edge of the selection. Although this creates a loss of detail at the edges, it can be very useful to create a blending transition (such as when extracting an object with a soft edge, like fabric or hair). The feather becomes apparent when you move, copy, or fill the selection. If you feather the edges too much, you might lose the selection border (marching ants), which is only visible above a 50% threshold. The keyboard shortcut is Shift+F6 when you have an active selection.

Let's try out the concept of Inverse, as well as some of the other commands.

1. Open the file Ch05_Inverse.tif from the Chapter 5 folder.

2. Select the Magic Wand tool.

3. Set the Tolerance to **32** and select the Anti-alias and Contiguous check boxes.

4. Click the sky to make an initial selection.

5. When most of the sky is active, choose Select > Grow. If needed, repeat the command.

6. Choose Select > Inverse to capture the castle.

Intermediate Selection Techniques

Simply put, don't stop now! Most Photoshop users develop an overdependence on the Magic Wand tool. Although the basic selection techniques are important, they are not necessarily the best solution.

Color Range Command

If you liked the Magic Wand tool, then prepare to love the Color Range command. The Color Range command allows you to select a specified color within the document. You can then easily add to the selection to refine it. All of its speed and power is complemented by a very intuitive user interface.

VIDEO 28:
Color Range Command

Let's experiment with the Color Range command.

1. Open the file Ch05_Color_Range.tif from the Chapter 5 folder.

2. Choose Select > Color Range. Set the Fuzziness to **25** to start and deselect Localized Color Clusters.

3. With the eyedropper, click a pink flower. You'll see an initial selection created in the dialog box. A black and white matte is shown to preview the selection. The white areas indicate the selection you are creating.

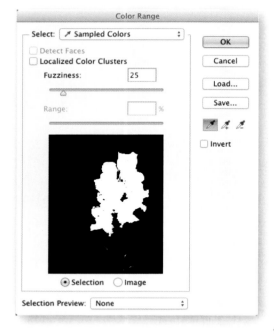

4. Hold down the Shift key and click more of the flower to build a larger selection.

5. Adjust the Fuzziness slider to your preference.

6. If too much of the image is selected, you can hold down the Option (Alt) key to subtract from the selection. You can also select the Localized Color Clusters option to require similar pixels to be closer together.

7. When you're satisfied, click OK.

8. Soften the selection further by choosing Select > Feather and entering a value of **5** pixels.

9. Let's use the selection to make an isolated image adjustment. One way to do this nondestructively is with an adjustment layer. Choose Layer > New Adjustment Layer > Hue/Saturation and Click OK.

10. Adjust the Hue slider to change the colors of the flowers (try a value of **−25** to make the flower more purple) and adjust the saturation to your preference.

Adjustment layers are covered in greater detail throughout the rest of the book.

Adjusting Skin Tones

The Color Range command has been expanded in Photoshop CS6 so it can intelligently recognize skin tones and human faces. These options make it easy to localize an adjustment to just the subject of a portrait and can be used to subtly improve the color and exposure of your subject.

VIDEO 29:
Adjusting Skin Tones

1. Open the file Ch05_Skintones.tif from the Chapter 5 folder.

2. Choose Select > Color Range.

3. From the Select menu choose Skin Tones.

4. Select the Detect Faces check box to further refine the skin tone selection using face detection.

NOTE

Custom Choice for Skin Tones

You can still use the custom Sample Colors option to select the initial skin tone. Simply enable the Detect Faces option and adjust the Fuzziness slider to taste to refine the adjustment.

NOTE

No 32-bit Support for Skin Tones

The Skin Tones and Detect Faces options will work with both 8-bit and 16-bit RGB images. For those of you working with 32-bit or HDR images, you'll need to first convert the image.

5. Adjust the Fuzziness slider to refine what is selected in the image.

   This slider lets you adjust the fuzziness based on the face detection point. The white areas are fully selected, and gray areas are partially selected.

6. When you're satisfied, click OK.

   Let's make a small adjustment to the face to boost the flesh tones.

7. Click the Vibrance button in the Adjustments panel to affect the skin tones with a color correction adjustment. You'll explore this adjustment and more in greater detail in later chapters.

VIDEO 30:
Quick Mask Mode

Saving and Reloading Selections

If you'd like to save your selection for later use, you need to create a channel. With an active selection made, choose Select > Save Selection. Name the selection and click OK to save the selection as an alpha channel. Alpha channels are simply saved selections that can be reloaded at a later time. They are also stored with your document when you close the file (unlike a quick mask, which is discarded when you exit the selection). Channels are covered in greater depth in Chapter 7, "Layer Masking."

Creating a Path with the Pen Tool

You can use the Pen tool to create paths (vector-based lines that you freely draw). Many users swear by the Pen tool, but be warned: It's not the easiest tool to use. The Pen tool allows you to click around the image, adding anchor points. Photoshop then connects those points with vector lines, which can be adjusted or resized. Those users coming to Photoshop from Adobe Illustrator generally find the Pen tool relatively easy to use. Reading about the Pen tool is very difficult; be sure to watch the video to see the tool in operation.

Let's give the Pen tool a try.

VIDEO 31:
Pen Tool

1. Open the file Ch05_Paths.tif from the Chapter 5 folder.

2. Choose the Pen tool from the Tools panel or press the keyboard shortcut P.

3. Choose the following options from the Options bar:

   - Choose Shape Layer from the Tool Mode menu to put a solid color over your image and make it easier to see if you are accurately tracing the object. You can click the color well and choose the color you want to use.

   - Change the shape stroke width slider to **0.00** pt to remove any stroke.

   - Select Auto Add/Delete so anchor points will automatically be added when you click a line segment. Likewise, Photoshop will automatically delete a previous anchor point if you click directly on the anchor point with the Pen tool.

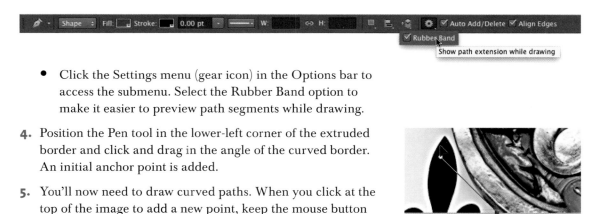

   - Click the Settings menu (gear icon) in the Options bar to access the submenu. Select the Rubber Band option to make it easier to preview path segments while drawing.

4. Position the Pen tool in the lower-left corner of the extruded border and click and drag in the angle of the curved border. An initial anchor point is added.

5. You'll now need to draw curved paths. When you click at the top of the image to add a new point, keep the mouse button pressed. You can drag to create the curve: Remember that clicking adds a point and a straight line, whereas clicking and dragging produces a point with a curved line:

   - Drag away from the curve for the first point.

   - Try to minimize the number of anchor points added. Move forward along the object and pull to form the curve. You don't need a perfect shape yet.

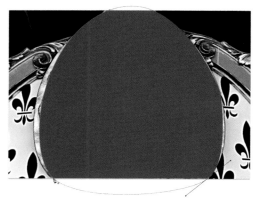

6. When you reach the end of your path, click to close the shape. As with the Polygonal Lasso tool, you must click your starting point to close the path. The path for this photo can be created with only four points.

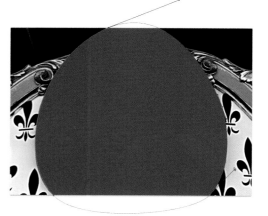

7. You can adjust the path by using the Direct Selection tool (A). This allows you to click an anchor point, or handle, and adjust the position or shape.

8. The Convert Point tool can be used to add a Curves handle to any path point that doesn't have one and allows you to curve any straight lines (just click and drag on a point).

9. When you're satisfied, Command-click (Ctrl-click) on the path's thumbnail in the Layers panel. You will see the marching ants, which indicate an active selection has been made.

And that is how paths work. Either you found that enjoyable (and if so, keep practicing—it gets easier) or you disliked it. Like many features in Photoshop, paths are optional and don't have to be part of your Photoshop workflow. They are worth learning, though, because they make it easier to select curved objects.

Refine Edge Command

Even though the Select menu offers several options, there is always room for improvement. Photoshop provides a powerful option for refining an existing selection—the Refine Edge command, which can be accessed in two ways. It is available in the Options bar for all selection tools. You can also access it by choosing Select > Refine Edge. This command is very intuitive, and its sliders provide quick feedback as you refine a selection. Let's try it out.

VIDEO 32:
Refine Edge Command

1. Open the file Ch05_Refine Edge.tif from the Chapter 5 folder.

2. Make an initial selection using a tool of your choice (the Quick Selection tool works well).

3. Click the Refine Edge button in the Options bar. A new dialog box opens with additional controls.

4. Click the View button to change the viewing mode for how the selection is displayed (or use the corresponding keyboard shortcut). Try the different modes to see the results:

- **Marching Ants (M).** Shows the selection with the started dashed line.

- **Overlay (V).** Behaves similarly to the Quick Mask mode.

- **On Black (B).** Previews the layer over black, which is good for light edges.

- **On White (W).** Shows the selected region over a white background.

- **Black & White (K).** Simulates a channel view where the selection displays as a black (transparent) and white (opaque) layer (with gray indicating partial transparency).

- **On Layers (L).** Composites the image over any other layers (or transparency if single-layer image). For this exercise, choose the On Layers option.

- **Reveal Layer (R).** Shows the entire, original layer contents.

TIP

Change Your Refined View

To cycle through the different viewing modes in the Refine Edge dialog box, just press the F key repeatedly. If you'd like to temporarily disable the view, press the X key.

TIP

Smarter Refinements

You can select the Show Radius or Show Original check box to make it easier to see the changes created with the Edge Detection options.

5. Next you can use Edge Detection to clean up the edges further. These controls work best for areas of partial transparency. For this image, try to clean up some of the dark fringe and any of the edges of the hair that should be partially see-through:

- **Radius.** Drag to refine the selection edge. Try a value of **8** for this image.

- **Smart Radius.** This option automatically evaluates contrast in the edges and attempts to correct for better transitions. If your object lacks uniform hardness and softness, use this option. Select this option for this image (and in most cases).

- **Refine Radius tool.** Use this brush-style tool to paint over any edges that need additional refinement. You can also hold the Option (Alt) key to switch to an erase mode to undo any unwanted refinements. Paint over the left edge of the skull.

6. The next group of sliders allows you to adjust the edge globally. Experiment with the following sliders:

- **Smooth.** Removes any jagged edges.

- **Feather.** Softens the edge of the selection.

- **Contrast.** Increases the contrast of a selection's edge. You'll get better results in most cases with the Smart Radius and refinement tools.

- **Shift Edge.** Grows or shrinks a selection. This is a quick way to tighten a rough selection and remove color spill.

7. The last category, Output, determines how the processed selection is treated.

Decontaminate Colors applies color correction to remove any color spill from the background onto the selected object. For this image, select this option.

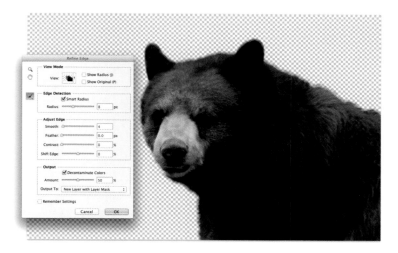

8. Finally, you'll need to determine what Photoshop does with the new selection. The choices are many (and useful):

- **Selection.** Creates an active selection.

- **Layer Mask.** Creates a nondestructive mask that produces transparency in the highlighted layer.

- **New Layer.** Creates a new layer with only the selected area.

- **New Layer with Layer Mask.** Creates a new layer with only the selected area masked. This is the most flexible option. Choose this option for this document.

- **New Document.** Creates a new document with only the selected area.

- **New Document with Layer Mask.** Creates a new document with the selected area masked.

9. Click OK to create the selection and masked image.

The original image exists in the background with a new masked copy on top.

Advanced Selection Techniques

Two additional selection techniques–channels and Calculations–are advanced (in that they utilize channels). Remember, channels represent the components of color. The brighter the area in the individual channel, the more coverage there is for that color. By harnessing the black and white details of one (or more) channel you can create a mask. These two techniques won't be appropriate to use every time (they are image dependent), but they are pretty easy to use and should be part of your skill set.

VIDEO 33:
Selecting with a Channel

Using a Channel

In many images, there is often high contrast between the different elements. For example, a person framed by a bright blue sky may clearly stand out, since there are a lot of red values in skin and a lot of blue in the sky. You can make a quick decision whether the channel selection technique will work by looking at the Channels panel. Look for a single channel that is high contrast. It doesn't need to be perfect; you can use the Paintbrush tool to touch up the channel to make a more accurate selection.

Let's use the channel selection techniques to select and modify a logo on the side of a building. By isolating the logo, you can make a targeted selection to improve its appearance.

1. Open the image Ch05_Hotel.tif from the Chapter 5 folder.

2. Open the Channels panel. Click the Channels panel submenu (the triangle in the upper-right corner). Choose Palette Options and set the thumbnail to the largest size.

3. In the Channels panel, click the word *Red* to view just the red channel. Examine the channel for contrast detail. Repeat for the green and blue channels. Look for the channel with the cleanest separation of the motel's name. The blue channel should appear the cleanest.

4. Control-click/right-click on the blue channel and choose Duplicate Channel. Name it **Selection** and click OK to create a new (alpha) channel.

5. The new channel should automatically be selected; click its visibility icon (the small empty box next to its name). Turn off the visibility of the blue channel (click the eye icon next to its name).

6. Press Command+L (Ctrl+L) to invoke a Levels adjustment. This will allow you to adjust contrast on the mask. Make sure the Preview check box is selected.

7. Move the Black Input Levels slider to the right to increase contrast in the black areas.

8. Move the White Input Levels slider to the left to increase contrast in the white areas.

9. Move the middle (gray) input slider to the right to touch up the spotty areas.

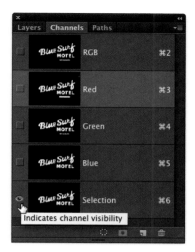

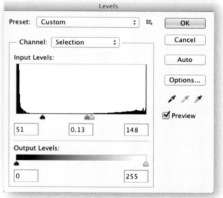

10. Click OK to apply the adjustment to the channel.

11. To soften the edges of the channel, choose Filter > Blur > Gaussian Blur. Apply the filter with a value of **2** or **3** pixels to soften the edge.

12. To load the selection, Command-click (Ctrl-click) the Selection channel to create an active selection. By selecting the logo, you can make a controlled adjustment.

You now have a great selection that's ready to use for image adjustments or layer masking. Both topics will be covered in depth in the coming chapters.

Calculations Command

You can use the Calculations command to create a new selection based on the details in an image's channels. This technique is hit or miss, because it won't work with every image. But when it succeeds, it's a big success. The Calculations command works well when there is high contrast between the subject and the background. You should look at each channel independently until you find those with the highest contrast. Depending on the source photo, the selection you can generate will be anything from a great start to perfect.

Let's put the Calculations command into action to create an active selection and a saved alpha channel. You will first create a new channel based on the existing channels.

1. Open the file Ch05_Calculations.tif from the Chapter 5 folder.

2. Bring up the Channels panel (Windows > Channels) and look for the highest contrasting channels. Because you want to remove the background, look for the contrast between the foreground and background. The blue channel should stand out the most.

3. Choose Image > Calculations and make sure the Preview check box is selected. You'll now combine two of the color channels to create a new alpha channel. An alpha channel is simply a saved selection. You can Command-click (Ctrl-click) it to turn it into an active selection.

4. In the Source 1 area, set the Channel to Blue.

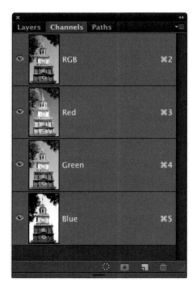

VIDEO 34:
Calculations Command

5. In the Source 2 area, you'll experiment to find the right combination. The red channel is a good place to start, because it looks very different than the blue channel. It's also a good idea to experiment by clicking the Invert button to reverse the channel. Calculations is all about trial and error, but since it works so well, taking a little time to experiment is worth it.

6. Combine the red and blue channels by using Blending. From the Blending menu, try different blending modes. Blending modes control how two different images or channels blend together based on their color and luminance values (for more on blending modes see Chapter 9, "Using Blending Modes"). Different source images will need different modes. Experiment by clicking through each mode on the list. You may also want to try deselecting the Invert check box when working with other images. In the Independence Hall image, the blue and red (inverted) channels combine most effectively using the Vivid Light blending mode. This will create a new channel that has a clean separation between the building and sky.

7. Click OK to create a new channel. The channel, called Alpha 1, should be selected in the Channels panel. Photoshop turned off the RGB channels for now.

8. Choose the Brush tool and set the foreground color to white.

9. Paint over the trees so the sky becomes pure white.

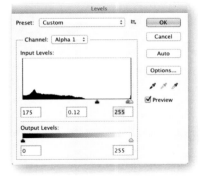

10. Run a Levels adjustment on the channel to adjust the contrast between black and white. Choose Image > Adjust > Levels or press Command+L (Ctrl+L). Move the Black Input Levels slider to the right to darken the gray areas to black. Move the White Input Levels slider to the left to brighten the whites in the image. Move the gray (gamma) input slider to the right to close up gray areas.

11. Click the OK button to apply the Levels adjustment.

12. Zoom in to 100% magnification to look for gaps in the alpha channel. You should see a few in the tower. With your Paintbrush set to black, paint out the spotting. You can also run a 1 pixel Gaussian Blur on the channel with the Filter command.

13. Command-click (Ctrl-click) on the alpha channel thumbnail to load the selection. You will need to choose Select > Inverse to choose Independence Hall.

14. Click the visibility icon next to the RGB composite channel to enable it.

15. Click the visibility icon next to the alpha channel to disable it.

Look closely at the selection; it should be pretty impressive. At this point, you could use the selection, copy the image, and add it to a different composite image, or you could run a filter or image-processing command on the building. With a little experimentation, you can generate a perfect alpha channel and turn it into a layer mask (you'll try this in Chapter 7). Calculations won't work every time, but it's a great solution that's worth a try when you have high-contrast channels.

Advice on Selections

No single technique is ideal for making the perfect selections. Every image is unique and will require you to analyze it. Knowing multiple techniques is very important, because it expands your options. Get comfortable with all the techniques in this chapter and be sure to practice. Practice really does make perfect.

Painting and Drawing Tools

6

Photoshop has a very rich set of painting and drawing tools. These tools have been in Photoshop since its first release, yet they have evolved greatly over time. The painting and drawing tools have many uses. To name a few:

- Fine artists can paint entire works into Photoshop with its realistic painting system. Using software can be an affordable alternative to traditional methods, which require more space and supplies.

- Comic book colorists can use Photoshop to paint the color into the inked drawings.

- FX designers can create background paintings for movie special effects work. In fact, the co-creator of Photoshop, John Knoll, is a lead visual effects supervisor at Industrial Light and Magic, the group behind the *Star Wars* franchise and many other well-known films.

- Commercial photographers can touch up and enhance photos using digital tools instead of a traditional airbrush. Nearly every photo you see in a fashion or entertainment magazine has undergone some digital touch-up in Photoshop to paint out imperfections.

These tools appear simple at first, and in fact they are. After all, the technology behind a paintbrush is pretty straightforward. It's the skill of the user holding the tool that determines results. A thorough understanding of the painting and drawing tools can come in handy while working in many areas of Photoshop. Whether you use Photoshop for image touch-up or to create original images from scratch, be sure to master these tools by practicing the exercises in this chapter.

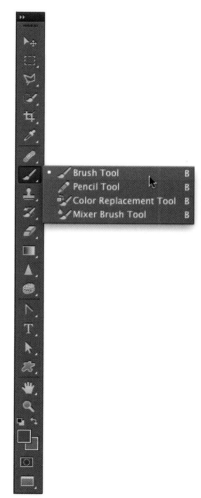

Working with Color

Working with painting and drawing tools requires you to use color. Photoshop offers several flexible ways to choose colors. You can sample a color from an open image, choose a color from a library, or mix a new color by entering numerical values. Which method you use depends on a mixture of personal choice and the job at hand. Let's explore the different options.

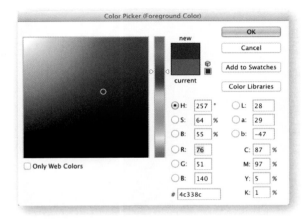

Adobe Color Picker

The Adobe Color Picker is a consistent way to choose colors while using any Adobe software program. Both Macintosh and Windows systems have their own color pickers, but it's best to stick with the standardized Adobe Color Picker because it is a more full-featured and cross-platform tool.

You can choose a color from a spectrum or numerically. Use the Adobe Color Picker to set the Foreground color, Background color, and text color. Additionally, you can use the colors for gradients, filters, or layer styles.

Click the Foreground or Background color swatch in the Tools panel to open the Color Picker. In the Adobe Color Picker, you can select colors based on:

- Hue, Saturation, Brightness (HSB) color values
- Red, Green, Blue (RGB) color values
- Lab color values
- Cyan, Magenta, Yellow, Key (or Black) (CMYK) color values
- Hexadecimal color value
- Web-safe colors

Color Libraries

In some cases, designers need to access specific colors—those that come from a particular hue and brand of ink. This is most often to match colors used by a specific company. For example,

McDonald's always uses the same red on all its printed materials (PMS 485). This helps create a specific look or identity by branding based on color.

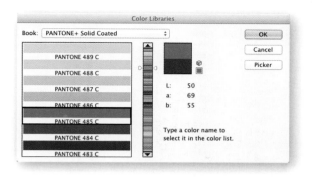

A designer can keep color consistent by specifying Pantone colors. The Pantone Matching System (PMS) is the most widely accepted color standard in the printing industry (www.pantone.com). Each color is assigned a PMS number, which corresponds to a specific ink or mixing standard, thus ensuring that a client will get consistent printing results. Accessing Pantone colors within Photoshop is easy:

1. Activate the Adobe Color Picker by clicking either the Foreground or Background color swatch.

2. Click the Color Libraries button to open the Color Libraries window.

3. From the Book menu you must choose among several options. Always ask your clients for specific color information. You can quickly jump to a specific color by typing in its number.

4. When you have a color selected, click OK.

5. Photoshop loads the closest equivalent color into your color picker. Essentially, the Pantone color will be simulated as accurately as possible by an RGB or CMYK equivalent.

6. If you need to have the exact color for printing, you will need to make a spot color channel (see the article "Creating Spot Color Channels" in the Chapter 6 folder or watch the video).

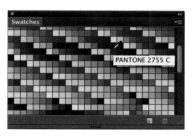

Color Libraries can also be loaded as color swatches. Just click the submenu (triangle) in the upper-right corner of the Swatches panel. Choose the library you need from the menu.

VIDEO 35:
Spot Color Channels

Kuler

Another tool that offers intuitive controls is Adobe Kuler. Originally an online-only tool, it lets you quickly create new color themes. Kuler began its life as a web-hosted application for experimenting with color variations and also allows for the sharing of color themes through an online community. To view the Kuler panel, choose Window > Extensions > Kuler.

TIP

Spot Color Channels

Are you doing professional printing? Learn how to assign specific colors to an area of an image. You'll find an exercise on creating spot color channels in this chapter's folder.

VIDEO 36:
Designing with Kuler

The Kuler panel is divided into three tabs:

- **About.** Introduces you to Kuler and links to the online community. You can create a free account to store themes as well as participate in Kuler forums and rate other users' themes.

- **Browse.** Allows you to browse thousands of color themes created by the Kuler community. Be sure to check back often because you can view by criteria such as the newest, highest rated, and most popular themes. You can also search for themes by tag word, title, creator, or hex color value.

- **Create.** Allows for the use of multiple color rules that are rooted in traditional design and is one of Kuler's best aspects. Kuler supports the following color rules: Analogous, Monochromatic, Triad, Complementary, Compound, and Shades—all are based on color theory.

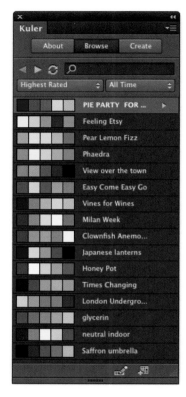

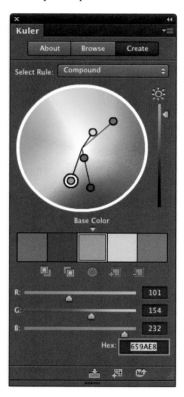

To use a color you create, simply double-click its swatch to load it as the Foreground color in Photoshop. Across the bottom of the Kuler panel are additional options to save a theme, store it in the Photoshop Swatches panel, or upload it to the Kuler community.

TIP

Access Kuler Almost Anywhere

If you have web access, you've got Kuler. Just visit kuler.adobe.com to access the interactive design environment for color. You can even log in and sync your creations.

Eyedropper Tool

The Eyedropper tool lets you sample colors from any open document. This can be a useful way to choose colors that work well with an image. Let's try out the tool:

1. Open the file Ch06_Sampler.tif from the Chapter 6 folder.

2. Select the Eyedropper tool from the Tools panel or press the keyboard shortcut I.

3. Adjust the Sample Size in the Options bar:

- **Point Sample.** This method reads the value of a single pixel. It is very sensitive to clicking because you can have slight variations in color at the pixel level. For example, if you clicked on a blue sky, adjacent pixels could vary from each other.

- **3 by 3 Average.** This method reads the average value of a 3×3 pixel area. This is a more accurate method for selecting a color using the Eyedropper tool.

- **5 by 5 Average.** This method reads the average value of a 5×5 pixel area. It creates a more representative color sample.

  The remaining options simply use a larger sample area to produce an averaged color. The larger sample areas should be used on higher resolution images.

- 11 by 11 Average

- 31 by 31 Average

- 51 by 51 Average

- 101 by 101 Average

4. Click the reddish-brown feathers to set the foreground color.

5. Make sure the Show Sampling Ring option is selected in the Options bar. Click again to sample a new color. The ring shows you both the new color and the original for comparison.

6. Option-click (Alt-click) the grassy area to set the background color.

VIDEO 37:
Eyedropper Tool

More Precise Eyedropper

Be sure to open Photoshop's preferences by pressing Command+K (Ctrl+K), and then choose the Cursors category. Set the Other cursors option to Precise to see a useful sampler target.

A Better Eyedropper

Adobe added a few useful features to the Eyedropper tool in Photoshop CS6. The Sample menu lets you choose from many new options, including the ability to ignore adjustment layers and to select layers current and below.

Using the Eyedropper tool, you can sample the color of the rooster's feathers. This can be useful for painting as well as color correction. For example, you can check the color details on two different shots of a rooster and then adjust color to make the images match more closely. For more on adjusting color, see Chapter 10, "Color Correction and Enhancement."

Color Panel

The Color panel is another way to access color without having to load the Adobe Color Picker. The Color panel shows you the values for the Foreground and Background colors. You can quickly mix or pick new colors from within the panel:

- You can adjust the sliders to mix a new color. To change color models, click the panel's submenu.

- You can click the spectrum across the bottom of the panel to pick a new color.

The Color panel might display two alerts when you select a color:

- An exclamation point inside a triangle means the color cannot be printed using CMYK printing.

- A cube means the color is not web-safe for color graphics viewed on a monitor set to 256 colors.

Swatches Panel

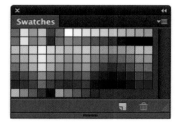

The Swatches panel holds color presets. You can quickly access frequently used colors by clicking their thumbnails. You can load preset swatches by clicking the Swatches panel submenu (top-right arrow). Additionally, **Table 6.1** shows several important shortcuts when working with the Swatches panel.

Table 6.1 Keyboard Shortcuts for the Swatches Panel

Result	Macintosh	Windows
Create new swatch from Foreground color	Click empty area of panel	Click empty area of panel
Select Foreground color	Click swatch	Click swatch
Select Background color	Command-click swatch	Ctrl-click swatch
Delete color swatch	Option-click swatch	Alt-click swatch

Painting Tools

Several tools are available in Photoshop for painting. Although these tools have subtle differences, they have one important component in common—the use of Photoshop's dynamic brush engine. Before exploring the unique tools, let's look at how to control your brushes.

Brushes Panel

The Brushes panel contains several options. Most of these will be well beyond what you'll need to get started. I'll briefly cover the options, but be sure to return to this panel as you increase your skills and confidence.

Brush presets

Photoshop has several brush presets to get you started right away. You access these presets from a panel that is docked with the Brushes panel; several are loaded and more are in the Photoshop Presets folder. Let's check them out.

1. Create a new document. Because this exercise is just for practice and you won't be printing the file, choose the 800 × 600 preset from the New Document dialog box.

2. Press D to load the default colors of black and white.

3. Select the standard Brush tool by pressing B.

4. Choose Window > Workspace > Painting to arrange the Photoshop interface so the most commonly used panels for painting tasks are visible.

5. Click the Brushes panel tab.

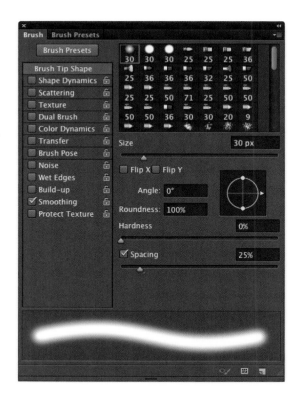

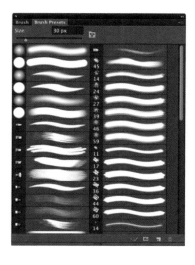

6. Click the button labeled Brush Presets. Photoshop displays a list and thumbnails of several brush styles in a new panel (it should be docked above the Layers panel).

7. Scroll through the list and choose a style.

8. Draw a stroke in your blank document to see the brush preset in action.

9. Repeat using different presets and create strokes to become familiar with your options.

10. Click the Brushes panel submenu (the triangle in the upper-right corner) and load a new Brush library.

11. Experiment with these brushes.

12. Load additional presets and continue to become familiar with your many options.

13. When done, you can restore the default set of brushes. Click the panel's submenu and choose Reset Brushes.

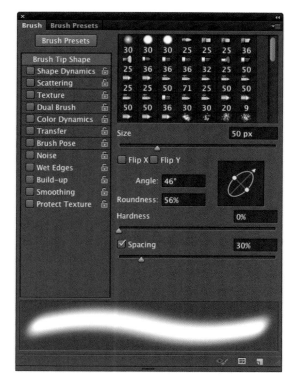

Brush Tip Shape

Although the brush presets are readily available and very diverse, they won't cover all your needs. Fortunately, Photoshop offers a flexible interface for customizing existing brushes as well as creating new ones.

1. Make sure you have the Brush tool selected.

2. Bring the Brushes panel to the forefront and make it active.

3. Choose a brush preset (from the thumbnail icons) that you'd like to modify. You can see the changes in the preview area or click your test canvas to try out the brush.

TIP

Dynamic Previews

Some brushes provide animated previews to show you how they interact with the canvas. Be sure to play with the Shape menu on the Brush Tip Shape tab to see the many different options.

You can modify the following brush tip shape options in the Brushes panel by clicking the words Brush Tip Shape:

VIDEO 38:
Creating Custom Brushes

- **Size.** Controls the size of the selected brush. You can enter a value in pixels (px) or drag the slider to a new size.

- **Use Sample Size.** Resets the brush to its original diameter. This is only visible if the brush was created by sampling pixels (such as part of a photo or a scanned brush stroke painted on paper or canvas).

- **Flip X.** Changes the direction of a brush by flipping it on its X-axis (essentially making a mirrored image). This is useful if the brush is asymmetrical.

- **Flip Y.** Flips the brush on its Y-axis.

- **Angle.** Specifies the angle of a brush. This works well for sampled or elliptical brushes. You can type in a number of degrees or visually change the angle of the brush by dragging the arrow in the brush preview interface. You can use angled brushes to create a chiseled stroke.

- **Roundness.** Specifies the ratio between the short and long axes. A value of 100% results in a rounder brush, whereas 0% creates a linear brush. Elliptical shapes can be used to create natural-looking strokes.

NOTE

How Big Can Brushes Be?

In Photoshop CS6, brush size diameter can go up to 5000 px. That's a lot bigger than you'll likely need, so be sure to pay attention to your brush size.

NOTE

Where Did My Brush Go?

Can't see a brush preview? Check if you've pressed the Caps Lock key.

CREATING CUSTOM SAMPLED BRUSHES

You can use an image to create a custom brush. This image can be a scan that you input or a stroke that you draw using other brushes. Let's give it a try:

1. Open the file Ch06_Brushes_to_Sample.tif from the Chapter 6 folder.

2. Select the first brush shape using the Rectangular Marquee tool. You can sample an image in size up to 2500 pixels x 2500 pixels.

3. Choose Edit > Define Brush Preset. A new box opens for naming the brush.

4. Name the brush and click OK. The brush is added to the set you currently have loaded in the Brushes panel.

5. Activate the new brush and paint in a new document to experiment with it. You might want to adjust the Spacing option to your preference.

6. Repeat for the other three brush shapes.

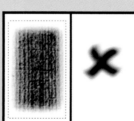

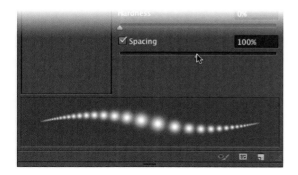

NOTE

Brushes Can Be Recorded

If you want to create a complex series of brush strokes and reuse them, you can now record them as an action. For more, see Chapter 15, "Actions and Automation."

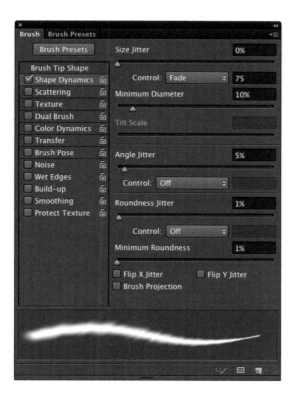

- **Hardness.** Creates brushes with soft edges. This can be useful to create more natural-looking strokes. You can adjust hardness between 0% (very soft) and 100% (no feathering). You cannot adjust hardness for sampled brushes.

- **Spacing.** Controls the distance between brush marks when you create a stroke. You can adjust spacing using the slider or type in a number. If you deselect the check box, the speed of your cursor will determine spacing.

Shape Dynamics

To create a more natural brush, you should adjust the Shape Dynamics of the brush. This can create natural variances that make the brush more realistic. The Shape Dynamics option adjusts the currently selected brush; therefore, be sure to choose a brush from the Brush Presets or Brush Tip Shape area.

- **Size Jitter and Control.** Specify how much variety Photoshop places in the size of the brush (trying to simulate the natural variation a real brush would produce). You can specify a total jitter size in percentage. Additionally, you can specify how to control the jitter from the Control menu:

  - **Off.** Select Off if you do not want to limit control over the size variance of brush marks. The jitter is random.

  - **Fade.** Allows the brush to taper off (like it ran out of ink or paint). The brush will get smaller based on a specified number of steps. Each step is one mark of the brush tip. If you specify 15, the brush will fade out in 15 steps.

- **Pen Pressure, Pen Tilt, Stylus Wheel, or Rotation.** Let you tie jitter to different features of a pen or stylus. Some Photoshop users unlock more features by connecting a stylus and graphics tablet. The most popular tablet manufacturer is Wacom (www.wacom.com).

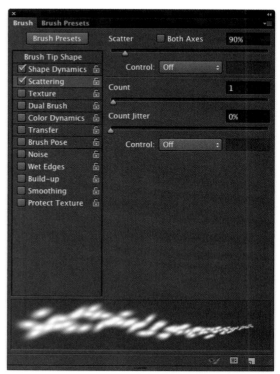

- **Minimum Diameter.** Sets a limit on how much variation in scale can be introduced in the brush. A 0% value lets the brush shrink to a diameter of 0, whereas 25% allows the brush to range from full size to a quarter of its starting width.

- **Tilt Scale.** Ties the amount of scale to the tilt of the pen (or stylus). You must have a graphics tablet attached to utilize this feature.

- **Angle Jitter and Control.** Specify how much variety in the angle of the brush can occur. A larger number creates more variety. The control area ties the jitter to your pen.

- **Roundness Jitter and Control.** Introduce jitter into the roundness of the brush. Additionally, you can control the jitter with a pen.

- **Minimum Roundness.** Limits the amount of jitter.

Scattering

Enabling Scattering can add variation to the placement of strokes. This can simulate splattering or wilder strokes. There are a few options to work with:

- **Scatter and Control.** Distribute brush strokes from the center of the click. The Both Axes option distributes strokes radially. When the option is deselected, the strokes are distributed perpendicular to the stroke path.

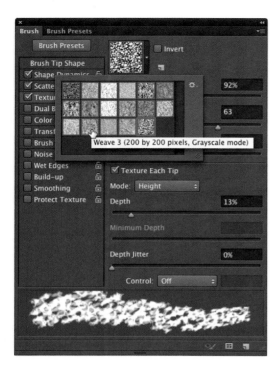

- **Count.** Specifies the quantity of brush marks applied at each spacing interval. This option works in conjunction with the Spacing option from Brush Tip Shape.

- **Count Jitter and Control.** Specify how much variety there is in the number of brush marks for each spacing interval. A high value will put more brush marks into the stroke. These properties are controlled in the same way as Shape jitter.

Texture

You can enable the Texture option to introduce a pattern into your strokes. This can help simulate canvas in your texture. Click the pattern sample to choose from one of the loaded patterns. Click the triangle menu to open the pattern picker to choose from the loaded textures. If you'd like to load additional textures, click the submenu in the pattern picker to load a built-in texture library. You can adjust several other options in the window and examine their effects in the preview area.

Dual Brush

What's better than one brush? Two, of course. By using a dual brush, you can use two brush tips to create a more dynamic brush. When selected, you'll have the option of choosing from a thumbnail list of presets for the second brush. You'll also see several options to modify the brush tip. You can modify the diameter of the second brush as well as specify spacing and scatter amounts.

Color Dynamics

By now you might be thinking, those brushes are pretty dynamic, what else can Photoshop change? Well, color, of course. When you select Color Dynamics, you can enable several options that will produce subtle (or dynamic) variations in color:

- **Foreground/Background Jitter and Control.** Allow the brush to utilize both the Foreground and Background colors that you have loaded. This can create a nice variation in color by loading lighter and darker shades of one color as your Foreground and Background color swatches.

- **Hue Jitter.** Allows you to specify how much variety of color can be introduced. Low values create a small change in color and higher values create greater variety.

- **Saturation Jitter.** Introduces variation in the intensity of the selected color.

- **Brightness Jitter.** Adds variety in brightness. A low value creates very little change in the brightness of the color. A higher value creates greater variations.

Transfer

The Transfer section offers additional styles of jitter that can be added:

- **Opacity Jitter and Control.** Add variety to the brush so the opacity varies throughout the stroke. You can tie the opacity variation to a pen and tablet for greater control.

- **Flow Jitter and Control.** Affect how paint flows through the brush. A larger number means more paint flows through. The default value is 100%, which creates even strokes. A lower value causes less ink to be applied with each stroke.

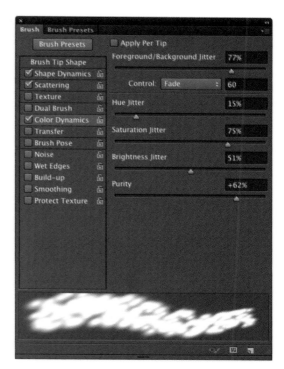

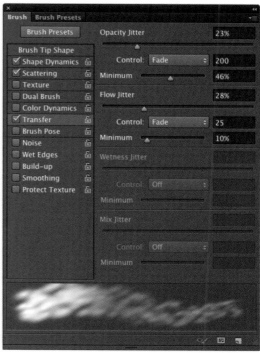

Other brush options

A few other options can affect your active brush. These are either enabled (selected) or disabled (deselected); they have no modifiable properties:

- **Brush Pose.** Lets you specify a default tilt, rotation, and pressure for a brush. You can combine these with the dynamic settings of a stylus or choose the Override options to maintain a static pose.

- **Wet Edges.** Causes the paint to appear darker at the edge of the stroke. It simulates the effect of painting with watercolors.

- **Build Up.** Allows you to simulate a traditional airbrush (a device that uses pressurized air to spray paint out of a nozzle). Like an airbrush, this option applies gradual tones and allows the paint to build up. You can also access this option by clicking the Airbrush Build Up (Airbrush) option in the Options bar.

- **Smoothing.** Produces better curves in your brush strokes when painting.

- **Protect Texture.** Is a good option to enable if you are using Texture in your brush strokes. It keeps the pattern and scale consistent when switching between textured brushes. This will make your strokes more consistent.

Table 6.2 shows the frequently used Brushes panel keyboard shortcuts.

Table 6.2   Shortcut Keys for Using the Brushes Panel

Desired Result	Macintosh	Windows
Decrease/increase brush size	[or]	[or]
Decrease/increase brush softness/hardness in 25% increments	Shift + [or Shift +]	Shift + [or Shift +]
Select previous/next brush size	, (comma) or . (period)	, (comma) or . (period)
Display precise crosshair for brushes	Caps Lock	Caps Lock
Delete brush	Option-click brush	Alt-click brush
Rename brush	Double-click brush	Double-click brush
Toggle Airbrush option	Shift+Option+P	Shift+Alt+P

Brush Tool

After all this talk of brushes, there are still a few notable things to say about the Brush tool. Be sure to look in the Options bar for important brush controls. From left to right, these options are the most useful brush controls:

- **Tool Presets.** Stores frequently used brush configurations for convenient access.

- **Brush Preset Picker.** Displays a greatly reduced Brushes panel. You can access thumbnails of the loaded brushes as well as adjust diameter and hardness.

- **Mode.** Lets you change the blending mode of your painted strokes. Blending modes attempt to simulate real-world interactions between two elements. For example, Multiply allows the strokes to build up, much like a magic marker. You'll find much more on blending modes in Chapter 9, "Using Blending Modes."

- **Opacity.** Affects the opacity of your strokes.

- **Flow.** Reduces the amount of paint flowing to the brush.

- **Airbrush button.** Enables the Airbrush.

- **Brushes panel button.** Toggles visibility of the Brushes panel. Click it to open the Brushes panel, which gives you greater control over the brush shape and dynamics.

TIP

New Bristle Tips

Be sure to check out the Bristle Tips options. These offer lifelike brush strokes. There are several customizable characteristics including Shape, Bristle density, Length, Thickness, and Stiffness. If you have a supported graphics card, you even get an interactive preview of the brush.

NOTE

The #2 Pencil

The Pencil tool is similar to the Brush tool. It shares many of the same options and controls. The fundamental difference is that it can only be used to create hard-edged strokes. Although there is a Hardness setting available for some brushes, it does little to change the stroke. The Pencil tool is fairly useless compared to the Brush tool and its many options.

NOTE

Color Replacement Tool

The Color Replacement tool can replace a selected color with a new, user-specified color. This tool was originally positioned as a way to remove "red eye" from photos. Photoshop CS2 added a new Red Eye tool specifically for that purpose.

VIDEO 39:
Using the Color
Replacement Tool

Mixer Brush Tool

The Mixer Brush tool was a new addition to Photoshop CS5 and goes a long way toward simulating realistic paint strokes. It mimics real-life brushes by allowing colors to mix on the canvas and simulating properties like stroke wetness.

1. Open the file Ch06_Color_Mixer.tif from the Chapter 6 folder.

2. Select the Mixer Brush tool (click and hold the Brush tool in the Tools panel to reveal the Mixer Brush).

VIDEO 40:
Using the Mixer Brush

3. Choose a soft brush and make sure it is a large size (25 px or greater). Set the Spacing to 5% for tighter strokes.

4. Click the Preset list in the Options bar to try different presets. For this image, use the Very Wet, Heavy Mix option.

   The Wet Controls affect how much paint the brush picks up from the canvas. A higher setting produces longer paint streaks.

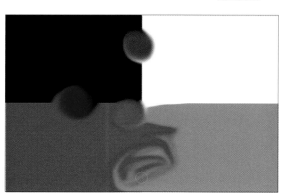

5. Select the layer called Swatches in the Layers panel and try painting brush strokes near the intersection of different-colored squares to see the colors mix. Try painting circular stokes as well to see the color values mix.

6. Try changing the blending mode or opacity for the layer containing brush strokes to blend it with the original photo layer below.

Now that you see how the strokes can mix, let's explore a more realistic use for the tool. The Mixer Brush can be used effectively on a photograph to create paint strokes based on the colored image. This can produce an attractive effect, creating a painterly like image.

1. Turn off the visibility icon for the Swatches layer and select the layer Glass.

2. Choose the Moist, Heavy Mix preset. In the Options bar select the Sample All Layers check box.

3. Create a new, empty layer.

4. Select a brush preset. Option-click (Alt-click) on the image to sample a color, and then paint in the canvas.

Clean Strokes

Be sure to experiment with the automatic Load or Clean options for the Mixer Brush. These make it easy to keep the brush clean and mix the color details in a picture.

5. Experiment with different brush strokes and Mixer Brush presets or settings to see the full depth of the tool. The bristle brushes work very well, especially if you trace some of the details in the underlying image.

History Brush Tool

The History Brush is easy to use but a little hard to understand at first. Essentially, it allows you to paint backward in time. This can be very useful because it enables you to combine the current state of an image with an earlier state. For example, you can process an image with a stylizing filter, and then restore part of the image to its original state.

The History Brush is directly tied to your History panel. This helpful panel shows you each action you have taken on an image. You can then move backward through your undos by clicking them. By default you have 20 levels of undo, but you can change this setting by increasing the number of History States in your general preferences.

Let's put the History panel and History Brush into action:

1. Choose Window > History to activate the History panel.

2. Open the file Ch06_History_Brush.tif from the Chapter 6 folder.

3. Press D to load the default colors of black and white.

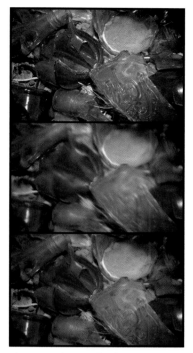

The original image (top); the painted layer (center); Opacity of painted layer set to 80% and the Darken blending mode (bottom).

VIDEO 41:
History Brush

4. You'll now run a Brush Stroke filter to stylize part of the image. You can use Filters to create special effects in an image. (For more on filters, see Chapter 14, "Maximizing Filters.") Choose Filter > Filter Gallery.

5. In the Brush Strokes category choose the Sumi-e filter. Adjust the sliders to your preference. Click OK to apply the filter.

6. Clean up any areas in the dark background with the Brush or Mixer Brush tool.

7. Open the History panel and drag its resize handle to see more states (and snapshots). The History panel shows you all the actions you have performed on the open image.

   The image looks more like a painting at this point, but some key areas (like the text on the pump) are too heavily stylized.

8. Look at the top of the History panel to see a snapshot of the document. It was automatically created when the document was first opened. The brush icon next to it indicates that it has been set as the source for the History Brush.

9. Choose the History Brush from the Tools panel or press Y. Be sure to not choose the Art History Brush.

10. Select a soft-edged brush sized at approximately 70 pixels, and set the Opacity to 70% to restore 70% of the original details while preserving 30% of the new state.

11. Paint in the text to restore the original details.

NOTE

What About the Art History Brush?

Officially, you can use the Art History Brush tool to create stylized paintings. Unofficially, it doesn't work very well. A better option is to use the Color Mixer Brush tool or the new Oil Paint filter.

CONTROLLING SNAPSHOTS

Snapshots can also be used as "digital breadcrumbs" so you can find your way back to earlier versions of the image. You can add more snapshots so you can quickly jump back to specific points in time by:

- Clicking the **Create new snapshot** button (camera icon) at the bottom of the History panel.

- Changing the preferences for the History panel. Click the submenu icon for the History panel and choose **History Options**. You can choose to **Automatically Create New Snapshot When Saving**.

Remember, History States and snapshots are temporary. When you close the open document, they are discarded.

The original image (left); the filtered image (center); details restored with the History Brush (right).

12. Try lowering the Opacity to 25% and paint in additional details of the original image. You can combine multiple strokes as needed to build up an area.

The History Brush can be valuable when either filtering an image or performing color-correction tasks. It allows you to selectively paint back in time to restore lost or important details.

Working with Gradients

VIDEO 42:
Designing Custom Gradients

A gradient is a gradual blend between two or more colors. You can use gradients to create a photorealistic backdrop or to draw in areas like a blown-out sky. The Gradient tool is extremely flexible and offers the versatile Gradient Editor for creating custom gradients. Before you utilize the Gradient tool, let's explore how gradients are formed.

Gradient Editor

All gradients are edited using the Gradient Editor (which becomes available when you activate the Gradient tool). To access it, click the thumbnail of the gradient in the Options bar:

- **Presets.** You have several preset gradients to choose from, and you can browse them by thumbnail. Additionally, you can load other gradients by clicking the panel's submenu.

- **Name.** Naming each gradient can make gradients easier to sort through.

- **Gradient Type.** The two major categories of gradients are Solid and Noise. Solid gradients use color and opacity stops with gradual blends in between. Noise gradients contain randomly distributed colors within a user-specified range. Each has a unique interface.

Solid Editor

Solid gradients blend from one color to another, providing a traditional gradient type.

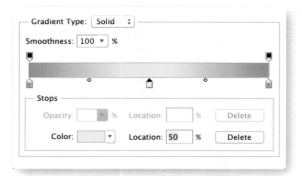

- **Smoothness.** This option controls the rate at which the colors blend. You can set it to be gradual or steep. The larger the number, the more Photoshop optimizes the appearance of the blend.

- **Opacity stops.** A gradient can contain blends between opacity values. To add a stop, click in an empty area on the top of the gradient spectrum. To adjust a stop, click it, and then modify the Opacity field.

- **Color stops.** A simple gradient contains only two colors. However, you might want to use a more complex gradient in your project. You can click below the gradient to add another color stop. Double-click a stop to edit its color with the Adobe Color Picker.

- **Stop Editor.** Selected gradient stops can be adjusted numerically. You can edit the opacity, color, and location (0–100%, read left to right.)

- **Midpoint.** Between stops are midpoints. By default the midpoint is halfway between two stops. You can adjust the midpoint to shift the balance of the gradient.

Noise Editor

Noise gradients use a specified range of color to create noise. These gradients do not blend smoothly between colors; rather, they create a new gradient each time you click the Randomize button:

- **Roughness.** Noise gradients use a roughness setting to determine how many different colors are used to create noise.

- **Color Model.** You can choose between three models: Red-Green-Blue, Hue-Saturation-Brightness, or Lab.

- **Color Range sliders.** Adjust the range of colors available to the gradient. Bring the black and white sliders closer together to limit the amount of color present in the noise gradient.

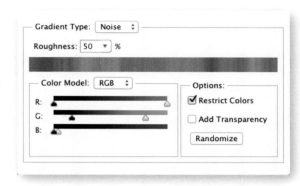

- **Options.** You can choose to further restrict colors as well as introduce random transparency. To create a new gradient, click the Randomize button. Every time you click, a new gradient is generated.

- **New button.** To add a gradient to the Presets window, type a name into the Name field, and then click the New button. This new gradient is not yet permanently saved but is stored temporarily in the Preferences file. You must click the Save button and navigate to your Presets folder (inside the Photoshop application folder) to save it. Be sure to append the filename with .grd to inform Photoshop that it is a gradient set.

Gradient Tool

You can use the Gradient tool to manually draw a gradient on a layer. To access the Gradient tool, select it from the Tools panel or press G. The Paint Bucket shares the same well as the Gradient tool, so if you don't find the Gradient tool, press Shift+G to cycle through your tools.

The Gradient tool can use any gradient you create in the Gradient Editor or from the Presets menu. To select a gradient, you can choose from those available in the Options bar. You can also load preset libraries or manually load gradients by accessing the panel's submenu.

You must choose one of these five methods to build your gradient:

- **Linear Gradient** (**A**). Blends from the starting point to the ending point in a straight line.

- **Radial Gradient** (**B**). Blends from the starting point to the ending point in a circular pattern.

- **Angle Gradient** (**C**). Blends in a counterclockwise sweep from the starting point.

- **Reflected Gradient** (**D**). Blends symmetrically on both sides of the starting point.

- **Diamond Gradient** (**E**). Blends in a diamond-shaped pattern outward from the starting point.

You have a few available options to further modify the gradient:

- You can specify a blending mode to affect how the gradient is applied to the layer. (For more on blending modes, see Chapter 9.)

- To reverse the direction of colors in the gradient, select the Reverse check box.

- To create a visually smoother blend by adding noise, select the Dither check box.

- To use a gradient's built-in transparency, select the Transparency check box.

Let's use the Gradient tool to fix a common problem, a washed-out sky:

1. Open the file Ch06_Grad_Sky.tif from the Chapter 6 folder.

2. Choose Select > Color Range to create an active selection in the sky area. Adjust Fuzziness to get a gentle selection.

3. Load a dark blue as your Foreground color and a lighter blue as your Background color. You can try to select colors from the existing sky to make your gradient believable.

4. Choose the Gradient tool and select a Linear Gradient. Set the mode to Multiply and set Opacity to 40%.

5. Select the Foreground to Background gradient from your preset list (it's the first one).

6. Click at the top of the sky and drag down toward the buildings.

The first click is where the foreground color will start; where you release the mouse is where the second color will be placed. Photoshop will blend the colors in between using the settings in the Gradient Editor.

The sky should look more natural now with greater variation in colors. If your sky has a lot of texture in it, try setting the Gradient tool to Color mode before drawing.

Eraser Tools

Photoshop offers three kinds of Eraser tools to complement your drawing tools. These tools can be useful for cleaning up a brush stroke, but that's about it. They often produce crude edges in the erased area that lower the quality of your project.

The three tool options include:

- **Eraser tool.** This tool deletes pixels as you drag over them. On a layer they are replaced with transparency. On a Background, the pixels are replaced with your Background color. To use, just drag through the area you want to erase.

NOTE

Mask, Don't Erase

From years of personal experience, I strongly suggest avoiding the Eraser tools. These three tools are relatively primitive in their approach to selecting pixels for deletion. Additionally, the erasers are permanent—the discarded pixels are gone for good. It bears repeating: If you have anything beyond a basic image that you need to extract from its background, the answer is layer masking, which is covered in depth in Chapter 7.

VIDEO 43:
Gradient Maps

- **Background Eraser tool.** This tool is designed to help erase the background from an image. The difference between foreground and background in the image must be very clear and high contrast. This tool is significantly less flexible than the technique of layer masking, which is covered in Chapter 7, "Layer Masking."

- **Magic Eraser tool.** This tool is most similar to the Paint Bucket tool in that it attempts to select and modify similar pixels under your click point. Instead of filling those pixels with a color, however, the Magic Eraser tool deletes them.

GRADIENT MAPS OFFER UNIQUE COLOR

Gradient Maps are another way to harness the power of gradients to enhance an image. The Gradient Map can be applied as an adjustment layer or image adjustment command (stick with the adjustment layer for greater flexibility). You can create a new Gradient Map by choosing Layer > New Adjustment Layer > Gradient Map.

The Gradient Map will map a new gradient to the grayscale range of an image. A two-color gradient produces a nice duotone effect. Shadows map to one of the color stops of the gradient fill; highlights map to the other. The midtones map to the gradations in between. A multicolored gradient or noise gradient can add interesting colors to an image. This is an effective technique for colorizing textures or photos.

Open the file Cho6_Gradient_Map_Demo1.psd and Cho6_Gradient_Map_Demo2 to see Gradient Maps in action. Turn on each map one at a time to see the effect. By using blending modes in conjunction with the Gradient Map, you can get a more pleasant effect.

PHOTO BY ABBA SHAPIRO

You'll find a great new set of Gradient Maps included with Photoshop CS6. In the Gradient Map dialog box just click the gear icon to access its settings. Load the Photographic Toning set to experience a wealth of toning options, including sepia and duotones. These can also be combined with blending modes to produce all new results.

Vector Drawing Tools

Even though Photoshop is best known as a pixel-based (or raster) program, it does have a respectable set of vector drawing tools. Vector graphics are made up of mathematically defined lines and curves. Vector graphics are resolution-independent, because they can be scaled and repositioned with no loss of quality. Vector graphics are a good choice for creating shapes (such as rectangles, circles, or polygons) within your Photoshop document. The added benefit to using the drawing tools is that you can then scale the shapes and modify the design while still maintaining a crisp image. With Photoshop CS6, vectors have become more robust and include the ability to assign custom fills and strokes (much like Adobe Illustrator).

VIDEO 44:
Vector Drawing Tools

Choosing the Right Drawing Tool

Photoshop offers six Shape tools. They can be used to create vector shapes, vector paths (which can be used to make a selection), or raster shapes. The following list explains how to change how the Shape tools work:

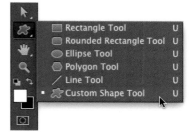

- **Rectangle tool.** The Rectangle tool draws rectangles; if you hold down the Shift key, it draws squares.

- **Rounded Rectangle tool.** The Rounded Rectangle tool is well suited for drawing buttons for websites. Adjust the Radius setting to modify the amount of curvature.

- **Ellipse tool.** The Ellipse tool draws ellipses; if you hold down the Shift key, it draws circles.

- **Polygon tool.** The Polygon tool creates polygons. The fewest number of sides a polygon can have is three (which is a triangle). The most complex polygon you can create is a hectagon (a 100-sided figure). Enter the number of sides in the Options bar. Additionally, the Polygon tool can be used to create stars by clicking the Geometry Options button in the Options bar.

- **Line tool.** The Line tool draws lines. Specify a thickness in the Options bar. The line can be between 1 and 1000 pixels in width. You can also choose to add arrowheads by clicking the Geometry Options button in the Options bar.

You can create custom shapes and save them for future use:

1. **Create a shape with the Pen tool or paste one into Photoshop from Adobe Illustrator.**

2. **Select the Paths panel, and then select a path. It can be a vector mask from a shape layer, a work path, or a saved path.**

3. **Choose Edit > Define Custom Shape.**

4. **Enter a descriptive name for the new custom shape in the Shape Name dialog box. The new shape now appears in the Shape pop-up panel, which can be quickly accessed from the Options bar.**

5. **If you'd like to permanently save the shape by adding it to a library, choose Save Shapes from the submenu in the Custom Shape Picker.**

- **Custom Shape tool.** The Custom Shape tool is *very* versatile. There are several shapes built into Photoshop. These can be extremely useful during the design process. To view your loaded shapes, click the Custom Shape pop-up panel in the Options bar. Additional shapes can be loaded by clicking the submenu in the Custom Shape panel. Choose from the built-in libraries or load more.

Loading Custom Shapes

Thousands of free shapes are available to download for Photoshop. An Internet search using the keywords "Photoshop," "Free," and "Custom Shapes" returns plenty of great results. You can choose to load these custom shapes temporarily or add them to your preset list.

For a temporary load of shapes:

1. From the Custom Shape pop-up panel in the Options bar, click the submenu.

2. Choose Load Shapes.

3. Navigate to the desired shape library (it should end in the extension .csh).

4. Select the shape and click OK.

5. You can choose to Replace the current shapes or Append the new shapes to the end of the old list.

To permanently store shapes, load them into Presets:

1. Navigate to your Photoshop application folder.

2. Open the Presets folder.

3. Open the Custom Shapes folder.

4. Copy the custom shapes files into the Custom Shapes folder. Be sure the shapes are not compressed (such as a .sit or .zip file).

5. Restart Photoshop; the presets will be loaded into the submenu in the Custom Shape Picker.

Drawing Shapes

Using the Shape tools is very similar to using the Marquee tools. In fact, the same shortcut keys apply: Holding down the Option (Alt) key after you start drawing causes the shape to draw from the center of the initial click, whereas holding down the Shift key constrains the width and height to preserve a constant ratio.

Let's try using the Shape tools.

1. Create a new RGB document sized at 1024 × 768 pixels. Set the Background Contents to Transparent. Name the document **Playing Card**.

2. Select the Rounded Rectangular Shape tool. Set the Radius to 10 pixels.

3. In the Options bar, make sure the tool mode is set to Shape to create a Shape Layer and set the fill to White.

4. Click and draw a rectangle in the vector shape of a playing card.

5. With the vector shape layer selected, click the stroke width menu and change it to 10 pixels.

6. Click the well next to the Stroke type and choose a textured stroke.

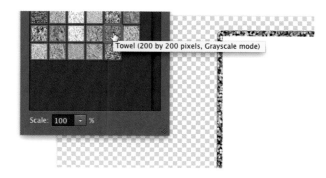

7. Choose the Custom Shape tool. Open the Custom Shape Picker and select the Heart shape. If it is not visible, choose Reset Shapes to load the default set.

8. In the Options bar, set the fill color to a custom red gradient. Go from a darker red to a brighter red.

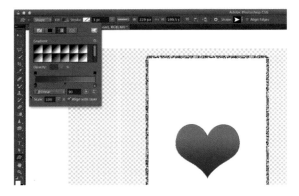

THREE KINDS OF SHAPES

You can use the Shape tools to create shapes in three different ways:

- **SHAPE LAYERS.** Creates a shape on a separate layer. A shape layer has a fill layer that defines the color and a linked vector mask that defines the shape.

- **PATHS.** Draws a work path on the current layer. This path can then be used to make a selection. It can also be used to create a vector mask, or it can be filled or stroked. Paths appear in the Paths panel.

- **FILL PIXELS.** Paints directly on the active layer. It makes the Shape tools perform like Paint tools. In this mode you create raster, not vector, graphics.

9. Draw a large heart in the center of the card (hold down the Shift key to constrain its proportions).

10. Use the Alignment tools to center the heart in the middle of the card. Select both layers in the Layers panel. Activate the Move tool and choose the Horizontal and Vertical Alignment buttons in the Options bar.

11. Draw a heart icon near the upper-left corner of the card. Leave room for a letter A (for *Ace*).

12. Press Command+J (Ctrl+J) to duplicate the current heart layer. Move it to the lower-right corner. Invoke the Free Transform command and rotate the heart 180°.

13. Press T to select the Type tool. In the Options bar choose a font such as New York or Palatino. Set the style to Bold, the size to 100 pt, and the color to Red.

14. Click in the upper-left corner and add the letter A.

15. Press Command+J (Ctrl+J) to duplicate the current "A" layer. Move it to the lower-right corner. Invoke the Free Transform command and rotate the A 180°.

If you'd like to look at the completed project, open the file Ch06_Playing_Card.psd and check it out.

Layer Masking

7

When you're working in Photoshop, you'll often need to combine multiple images together into a new composite image. Those original images, however, may have backgrounds or objects that you no longer want. This is where Layer Masks come in. Far superior to erasing pixels, Layer Masks allow you to hide (or mask) part of a layer using powerful painting and selection tools. The more you work on combining multiple images, the more you'll use masks.

In this chapter, you'll revisit several techniques that you learned in Chapter 5, "Selection Tools and Techniques," but here you'll convert them into Layer Masks.

Layer Mask Essentials

Masks generally start as a selection, which is then attached to a layer. The mask can be refined by adding to it with black or subtracting from it with white. Learning to create and modify masks is an important skill that becomes significantly easier with a little practice.

The mask is the black-and-white area attached to the layer thumbnail. It contains all the transparency information that the layer needs to isolate the bird from the background.

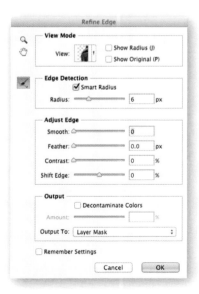

Adding Layer Masks

The best way to learn about Layer Masks is to jump right in and create one. You'll start with an easy image, but one that will help illustrate the important concepts. Let's get started.

1. Open the file Ch07_Mask_Start.tif from the Chapter 7 folder.

2. To mask the image, you'll need to convert the *Background* layer into a floating layer. Double-click the layer name in the Layers panel. Name the layer **Tower**.

3. Select the Quick Selection tool from the Tools panel.

4. Make a selection of the blue sky.

5. Reverse the selection by choosing Select > Inverse. The building is now selected.

6. Click the Refine Edge button in the Options bar.

   The Refine Edge dialog box opens. Here you can adjust the selection as well as create a mask.

7. Select the Smart Radius check box and adjust the Radius slider to refine the edge of the selection.

8. From the Output To menu, choose Layer Mask and click OK.

   A new mask is added to the layer.

9. To make it easier to see the edges of the border, place a solid color layer behind the Tower layer. Choose Layer > New Fill Layer > Solid Color and click OK. Choose a color that is not in the image, such as green.

10. Drag the fill layer below the Tower layer in the Layers panel.

11. Depending on the accuracy of your initial selection, your mask may be usable as is. If needed, you can quickly touch it up using the Brush tool.

12. In the Layers panel, click the Layer Mask thumbnail to select it.

13. Activate the Brush tool by pressing B or by choosing it from the Tools panel. Press D to load the default colors of black and white.

14. Zoom in to better see your edges. You can use the Zoom tool or the Navigator panel to get a better look at your edges.

15. Paint with a soft-edged brush to refine the mask. Paint with black to add to the mask (to add transparency) or white to make an area opaque.

If you add too much to the mask, press X to toggle the mask colors and paint with the opposite color you were just using.

16. Delete the solid color fill layer.

Disabling Layer Masks

The primary benefit of masks is their flexibility. In the previous section you explored that flexibility by adding and subtracting to a mask. This flexibility can also be used to temporarily disable a mask, which can be useful if you want to check your progress or if you need to restore the original image to use on another project.

1. Work with the Tower image from the previous exercise or open the file Ch07_Mask_End.tif from the Chapter 7 folder.

2. Select the Layers panel so it is active.

3. Shift-click the Layer Mask thumbnail to disable it. Alternately, you can Ctrl-click (right-click) the mask's thumbnail to access more options, such as deleting it and permanently applying it.

4. To reenable the mask, Shift-click its thumbnail again.

Shift-clicking a Layer Mask's thumbnail will temporarily disable the mask.

VIDEO 45:
Layer Masking

Deleting Layer Masks

After going through the effort of creating a mask, you are unlikely to want to permanently discard it. But if you change your mind and are certain you want to delete it, doing so is easy.

1. Work with the Tower image from the previous exercise or open the file Ch07_Mask_End.tif from the Chapter 7 folder.

2. Select the Layers panel so it is active.

3. Click the Layer Mask thumbnail. Drag it to the trash icon in the Layers panel.

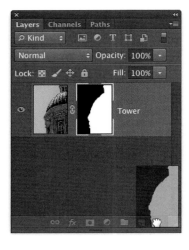

4. A dialog window appears asking you to decide what to do with the mask:

   - **Delete.** Discards the mask and restores the image to its pre-masked state.

   - **Cancel.** Allows you to cancel the command and return the image to its masked state.

   - **Apply.** Permanently applies the mask and deletes the pixels that were originally masked.

5. Click Apply to permanently apply the mask. The mask is used to permanently discard portions of the masked layer in a destructive edit.

VIDEO 46:
Alpha Channels

Mask Creation Strategies

There are many different approaches to creating Layer Masks. The approach you should take will vary based on your source image. Let's try using four different images and techniques to perfect your Layer Masking ability.

Using a Gradient as a Mask

When you're designing, you may need to gradually blend the edges of an image. This can be easily accomplished by combining a Layer Mask and a gradient. Let's give it a try.

1. Open the file Ch07_Gradient_Mask.tif from the Chapter 7 folder.

2. Duplicate the *Background* layer by pressing Command+J (Ctrl+J).

3. Select the top layer and choose Image > Adjustments > Desaturate.

4. With the topmost layer active, click the Add layer mask button at the bottom of the Layers panel (it looks like a rectangle with a circle inside). A new, empty Layer Mask is added to the layer.

5. Press G to select the Gradient tool.

6. Press D to load the default colors of black and white.

7. From the Options bar, choose the black-to-white gradient. If it's not available, choose Reset Gradients from the Gradient Picker's submenu.

8. With the Layer Mask selected, click and drag to create a new linear gradient going from top to bottom in the document window.

9. The new Layer Mask creates a gradual blend from the grayscale version to the colored version.

This technique of adding a mask can also be used on one layer to create a gradual fade to transparency or to a different layer stacked beneath.

The gradient mask allows the image to blend between the grayscale and color image.

Using a Channel

Often, a channel will get you very close to a perfect Layer Mask. This technique works particularly well when the subject is against a high-contrast background (such as a sky or a wall), and it works very well with fine details like hair. The image can be masked so it is ready for integration into a composite image. For example, a masked image could be used to add a palm tree to another photo. Let's give it a try.

1. Open the file Ch07_Channel_Mask.tif from the Chapter 7 folder.

VIDEO 47:
Refine Edge Command
for Fine Edges

2. Switch to the Channels panel and examine the Red, Green, and Blue channels.

   Look for one with high contrast from the background. Although all three channels are fairly high contrast, the Blue channel stands out the most.

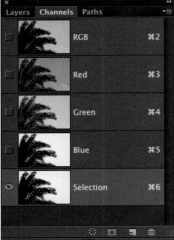

3. Duplicate the Blue channel by dragging it onto the New Channel icon at the bottom of the Channels panel (it looks like a pad of paper).

4. Rename the new channel **Selection** by double-clicking its name.

5. With the Selection channel selected, press Command+L (Ctrl+L) to invoke a Levels adjustment. Levels is a powerful command that allows you to adjust the gamma (gray) point as well as the black and white points.

6. Move the black slider to the right, setting the Input Level to around **60**. The black in the channel should get crisper.

7. Move the white slider to the left, setting the Input Level to around **190**. The gray areas in the channel should switch to pure white.

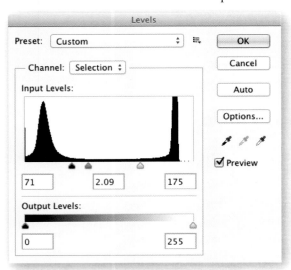

8. Move the middle (gray) slider to refine any gray spots in the channel. A value of **1.5** should be approximately correct.

9. Click OK to apply the Levels adjustment.

10. Command-click (Ctrl-click) on the Selection channel's thumbnail to load the selection (you'll see the marching ants).

11. Choose Select > Inverse to reverse the selected area from the sky to the palm tree.

12. Turn on the visibility for the RGB channels by clicking the RGB composite channel's visibility icon. Turn off visibility for the Selection channel.

13. Switch to the Layers panel.

VIDEO 48:
Color Range Command
and Masking

14. Click the Add layer mask button at the bottom of the Layers panel to turn the palm tree into a layer with a mask added.

Using Calculations

You explored the Calculations command to create an advanced selection in Chapter 5. This command uses channel data to create a new alpha channel. You can then refine the channel to create an accurate selection. You can also take this one step further to make a high-quality Layer Mask. Let's give it a try.

VIDEO 49:
Calculations for Masking

1. Open the file Ch07_Calculations.tif from the Chapter 7 folder.

2. Turn the *Background* layer into a floating layer by double-clicking its name in the Layers panel. Name the layer **Banana Tree**.

3. Call up the Channels panel and closely examine the channels for a high contrast between the tree and the background. Although all three channels have contrast between the sky and the tree, the Blue channel has the best.

4. Invoke the Calculations command by choosing Image > Calculations.

5. Set Source 1 to the Blue channel, set Source 2 to the Red channel, and select the Invert check box. The Red channel differs most from the Blue channel in this image, so it will create a good matte.

6. Experiment with different blending modes so you get a clearer separation between the tree and the sky. In this case, the Vivid Light mode works best to create a new channel. Click OK.

7. The new channel will need a little touch-up. You can get the channel near perfect with a Levels adjustment. Press Command+L (Ctrl+L) to invoke the Levels dialog box.

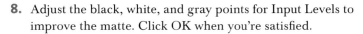

8. Adjust the black, white, and gray points for Input Levels to improve the matte. Click OK when you're satisfied.

9. You then need to reverse the channel so the area you want to discard is black. Press Command+I (Ctrl+I) to invert the channel.

10. Soften the selection by blurring it. Choose Filter > Blur > Gaussian Blur, set it to a value of **1** pixel, and click OK.

11. Load the channel as a selection by Command-clicking (Ctrl-clicking) the channel's thumbnail.

12. Turn on the visibility icon for the RGB channels and turn it off for the alpha channel.

13. Switch to the Layers panel and select the Banana Tree layer.

14. Click the Add layer mask button to apply a mask to the selected layer.

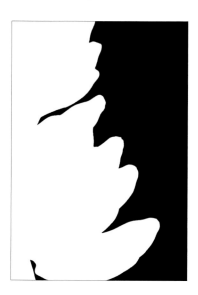

TIP

The Masks Panel Is Essential

The Masks panel offers several other useful commands. You can load a mask as a selection, apply a mask, disable its visibility, or discard it. Additionally, you can use the Color Range or Invert command to further refine the selection. The Masks panel consolidates all the masking commands into a single location, which can save you valuable time.

Refining Masks

By now you should be feeling more comfortable making Layer Masks. However, there's always room for improvement (at least where masks are concerned). Let's take a look at three ways to refine or adjust a mask.

Using the Properties Panel

If you need to refine an existing mask, one of the easiest ways is to use the options in the Properties panel. The panel combines several tools and commands into one location and makes it very easy to adjust a mask (even after first adding it). In fact, the Mask Edge and Color Range options are identical to the selection commands you've previously explored.

1. Open the file Ch07_Masks_Panel.psd from the Chapter 7 folder.

2. Select the Panda layer's mask.

3. In the Properties panel, experiment with the Density and Feather sliders to see their effects (if the panel is not visible, choose Window > Properties):

   • **Density.** Reduces the overall impact of the mask by essentially lowering the opacity of the Layer Mask.

   • **Feather.** Creates a gentle edge to the mask.

4. Set Density to **100%** and Feather to **0** px.

5. Click the Mask Edge button to open the Refine Mask dialog box. The controls are identical to the Refine Edge dialog box except here they are used to modify the Layer Mask.

6. Adjust the Mask Edge properties to remove fringe from around the image. Use the same techniques you learned in the previous chapter for the Refine Edge command.

   Setting the View option to On Layer makes it easier to see the fine edge details over the solid color layer.

7. Experiment with the Smart Radius option and the Refine Radius tool to enhance the edge and get a better processing for the fur.

8. Click OK to apply the change to the Layer Mask.

Using Smudge and Blur

Sometimes a mask is close to being ready to apply but needs a little touch-up. What better way to do this than to paint? By using the Blur and Smudge tools you can polish problem edges:

- **Blur.** Choose the Blur tool to soften a hard edge that looks unnatural. Just be sure the mask is selected before blurring.

- **Smudge (Lighten).** Choose the Smudge tool and set its mode to Lighten in the Options bar. This is useful for gently expanding the matte. Leave the Strength set to a low value to make subtle changes.

- **Smudge (Darken).** Choose the Smudge tool and set its mode to Darken in the Options bar. This is useful for gently contracting the matte. Leave the Strength set to a low value to make subtle changes.

Open the file Ch07_Bird_Mask.psd to experiment with the Smudge and Blur tools.

Adjusting Content Within a Mask

By default, Layer Masks are linked to their respective layers. Applying a transformation (such as a Free Transform command) affects a layer and its Layer Mask. However, there are times when you won't want this default behavior to occur. Sometimes it is useful to adjust the contents of a masked layer without repositioning the mask. Let's give it a try.

VIDEO 50:
Adjusting Content Within a Mask

1. Open the file Ch07_Mask_Content.psd from the Chapter 7 folder. Even though the Layer Mask is accurate, too much of the layer's content is obscured.

NEWSPAPER IMAGE ISTOCKPHOTO

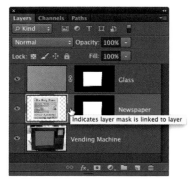

2. Click the chain icon between the layer thumbnail and Layer Mask icons for the Newspaper layer. You can now manipulate the layer content or its mask independently.

3. Select the Newspaper layer's thumbnail to modify the visible pixels of the layer.

4. Press Command+T (Ctrl+T) to invoke the Free Transform command. Scale the Newspaper layer smaller and move it slightly to better fit the opening in the newspaper stand. Click the Commit button to apply the transformation.

Advice on Masks

Layer masking and advanced selections go hand in hand. The more you practice one, the easier both will get. New users often lapse into bad habits and are drawn back to features like the Eraser tools or Copy and Paste commands. Although these may seem easier, in the long run they are not. Learn to work like a professional, and you'll achieve professional results.

Compositing with Layers

8

When Photoshop debuted, it did not have layers. Its original purpose was to touch up frames of motion picture and photography film. It was, as its name implied, a photo shop that provided a digital darkroom where photos could be enhanced, color corrected, and repaired. Over time, people wanted to do more with Photoshop, such as create print advertisements and television graphics. As people expected Photoshop to do more, Adobe responded with the introduction of layers. In this chapter you'll learn how to combine multiple layers together to create complex image composites.

What Are Layers?

In traditional cel animation, artists would paint their animations onto clear sheets of acetate. These clear sheets would often contain a single character or element. They could then be laid together with sheets containing other characters and backgrounds to create a composited scene.

Layers work the same way. Each layer can contain discrete elements of your design. You then combine them to create the finished product. Layers can contain photos, text, logos, shapes, and even textures. There are lots of ways to create and manage layers, but it all comes back to having an organized design. Every layer should have a clear, descriptive name to make your design workflow easier.

Why You Need Layers

If you plan to create complex designs in Photoshop, layers are a must for a few reasons:

- **Easy modification.** Layers make it simple to modify your design. Separate elements can be easily accessed and edited.

- **Easy manipulation.** If you are using Photoshop to create web or video animation as well as multimedia elements like slides or DVD menus, individual elements can be animated, high-lighted, or revealed.

- **Interface with other programs.** Many other software programs rely on Photoshop layers as a content creation tool because these other programs lack Photoshop's drawing and painting tools. By supporting the layered Photoshop format, these software programs cleanly interface with the best-selling, image-editing tool.

Dissecting a Composite Image

Let's examine a practical example of how layers work by analyzing a menu from a DVD. Open the file Ch08_Layered_DVD.psd from the Chapter 8 folder. This nine-layer document is a good example of using the general features of the Layers panel. To start, all layers are turned off; don't be surprised to see an empty screen or checkerboard pattern. (The checkerboard is Photoshop's default way of showing transparency.)

1. Begin turning layers on from the bottom up, starting with Texture.

   The bottommost layer is a simple pattern that adds a sense of depth to the piece. This pattern was made by painting a physical canvas with traditional media. A digital photo was taken and tinted using Photoshop.

2. Turn on the next layer, Water, and click its name to select the layer.

At the top of the Layers panel, you should notice that the layer is set to 60% opacity. Opacity is the opposite of transparency. A layer or image that is 60% opaque is 40% transparent.

There's a great shortcut for changing opacity of a layer, but you must have a tool selected that does not have its own transparency settings (such as the Move or Marquee tools). To change the opacity of a layer, type the corresponding number on the numeric keypad. For example, press the 2 key for 20%, the 5 key for 50%, and so on. If you want to be even more specific, you can quickly type a number such as 23 for 23%, and Photoshop will adjust the layer accordingly.

3. Turn on and select the third layer, Skyline. This layer introduces another layer feature: blending modes. This layer is set to the Overlay blending mode.

In this case a grayscale image is used to add a silhouette of a building. Blending modes combine the contents of one layer with another based on the luminosity or colors of the layer.

4. Turn on and select the fourth layer, Vignette, and you'll see a similar technique employed to add an area of focus to the image.

A good technique is to try changing the blending mode before you make an opacity change. This subtle change to your working style will give you dramatic results.

5. Turn on and select the fifth layer, which looks different than the rest. It is an adjustment layer.

   A Levels adjustment (used to control balance and contrast) is being applied to multiple layers simultaneously. A Levels adjustment affects the overall balance of lights and darks in an image. The key benefit of the adjustment layer is that it is non-destructive; the effect is "live" in that you can alter or disable it at any time.

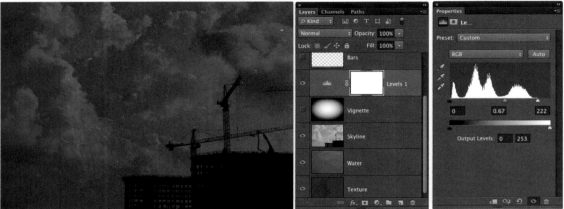

6. Locate or open the Properties panel. Try adjusting the middle slider and note the resulting changes.

   You will likely make a Levels adjustment on every image; it is the key to maintaining proper image contrast.

7. Turn on the next layer, Bars.

   These borders will be used to create an edge effect. The empty area between the bars is transparent and allows other layers to show through.

8. Turn on and select the Logo layer (which is vector based).

   This logo is a Smart Object as indicated by its special icon on the layer thumbnail. Smart Objects can add flexibility to the design process because they allow for the ability to scale and transform a vector object repeatedly without losing quality. This layer also has layer effects applied to create a slight beveled edge with a drop shadow.

9. Turn on the final layer, Text.

Photoshop has a robust text engine that is useful for creating screen-ready text (such as for television or Internet use). You will fully explore the robust text capabilities of Photoshop in Chapter 12, "Using the Type Tool."

By employing proper use of layers, you've generated a professional-looking DVD menu that you can use as is or import the layers into another application to animate. Proper naming makes it easy to find each layer. To name a layer, double-click on the name in the Layers panel.

Creating Layers

You can create a new layer easily in several ways. You can click the Create new layer icon (looks like a notepad) at the bottom of the Layers panel. If menus are your thing, choose Layer > New > Layer or press Shift+Command+N (Shift+Ctrl+N).

Additionally, you can drag layers up or down the layer stack or from one document to another, if you are so inclined. You can move layers or reorder them with keyboard shortcuts to change your image. **Table 8.1** shows a few keyboard shortcuts for just this purpose.

Table 8.1 Layer Mobility

Layer Movement	Mac	Windows
Move current layer down one position	Command+[	Ctrl+[
Move current layer up one position	Command+]	Ctrl+]
Move current layer to bottom of Layers panel	Shift+Command+[	Shift+Ctrl+[
Move current layer to top of Layers panel	Shift+Command+]	Shift+Ctrl+]

Jump It Up

Press Command+J (Ctrl+J) to duplicate (or "jump") the current layer to a copy above. With a selection made, it will "jump" only the selection and create a copy above. Adding the Shift key to the Jump command will cut the selection and place it on its own layer above its previous position.

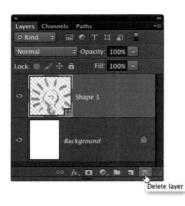

Duplicating Layers

When you need to duplicate a layer, you have a few choices. You can choose Layer > Duplicate Layer or right-click (Ctrl-click) the layer's name in the Layers panel and choose Duplicate Layer. Another method is to drag one layer onto the Create new layer icon at the bottom of the Layers panel. My favorite method is to press Command+J (Ctrl+J)—think *jump*—to create a copy of a layer immediately above itself.

Deleting Layers

If you decide you don't need a layer, you can throw it away. This reduces the size of your file, which means it'll take up less disk space and require less memory to work with. To throw away layers, drag them into the trash icon at the bottom of the Layers panel. You can also right-click (Ctrl-click) a layer's name and choose Delete Layer to throw it away or choose Layer > Delete > Layer. If you are in a hurry, you don't have to throw away layers one at a time. Just Command-click (Ctrl-click) on multiple layers, and then delete the layers using one of the previously mentioned methods.

NOTE

Delete Can Delete

In Photoshop CS6, you can select a layer in the Layers panel and press the Delete key to remove it. Be careful because this can easily happen by accident.

Adjustment Layers

While clicking through your Layers menu, you likely noticed Adjustment Layers (like Levels or Hue/Saturation). These important layers are for image enhancement and color correction. They offer a nondestructive way to fix image problems. These special layers can contain one of 15 image manipulations. Unlike normal image adjustments, these can be enabled or disabled as well as modified with no loss in image quality. For now, be patient—you'll tackle these in depth in Chapter 10, "Color Correction and Enhancement."

Fill Layers

Photoshop allows you to create specialty Fill Layers, which let you quickly create graphical content for your designs. Choose Layer > New Fill Layer, and then choose Solid Color, Gradient, or Pattern (alternatively, click the black and white circle icon on the bottom of the Layers panel). Create a new document (sized 1024 × 768) and try out these new layers:

VIDEO 51:
Using Random Fills

- **Solid Color.** Choose Layer > New Fill Layer > Solid Color. Pick from any color using the Color Picker or Color Libraries. To edit the color layer, just double-click its thumbnail in the Layers panel.

- **Gradient.** Choose Layer > New Fill Layer > Gradient. A *gradient* is a gradual blend between two or more colors. You can use gradients as backgrounds or blend them over an image to perform the same function as a camera filter. Photoshop supports five types of gradients: Linear, Radial, Angle, Reflected, and Diamond. You can double-click the gradient in the Gradient Fill window to launch the Gradient Editor. Within the editor you can modify the gradient or click the submenu to load addition gradient presets. For more on gradients, be sure to read Chapter 6, "Painting and Drawing Tools."

- **Pattern.** Choose Layer > New Fill Layer > Pattern. Photoshop comes with a variety of built-in seamless patterns, which you can access from the Pattern Fill window. To choose a different pattern, click the drop-down menu to see the active patterns. To load even more patterns, click the triangular submenu on the right edge of the drop-down panel.

TIP

New Layer Behaviors in CS6

If you've selected multiple layers, you can make several changes at once. For example, you can now change the label or blending mode for more than one layer at a time.

Working with Multiple Layers

As Photoshop has continued to evolve, so has its ability to offer powerful layer management. When creating complex designs, such as website mock-ups or print advertisements, it is important to maintain control over your design. This includes naming all your layers, as well as creating relationships or linking between them. Depending on which version of Photoshop you are using, you may find slight differences in layer behavior.

To get some practice, open Ch08_Layer_Organization.psd from the Chapter 8 folder. This file contains several color-coded layers that you will manipulate (the color coding identifies layers that will interact with each other). You might want to change the color of layers in your own documents to better organize them. To change the label color of a layer, right-click it and choose the new color. You can also choose from a list of default colors to label the layer.

Selecting Multiple Layers

One of the first skills to learn is how to select multiple layers. In the Ch08_Layer _Organization.psd file, select the Right Foot and Left Foot layers (which are color-coded red). Hold down the Shift key and click to select multiple contiguous layers or hold down the Command (Ctrl) key to select noncontiguous layers.

Linking Layers

Linking layers creates a family relationship. When one of the family moves, the others move along with it (the same goes for scale and rotation). You link two layers together to create a relationship of particular elements that need to react to one another. For example, if you had a logo and text that you wanted to scale at the same time, you'd link them together.

1. Link the Right Foot to its companion Left Foot. You can click multiple layers to select them using the techniques mentioned in the preceding section.

2. With both layers selected, they are temporarily linked; simply use the Move tool to reposition both layers.

3. To make the connection persist when you deselect the layers, click the link (chain) icon at the bottom of the Layers panel.

Aligning Layers

A design can look sloppy if the designer relies solely on his or her eyes for a precise layout. Alignment is the process of positioning multiple objects on a straight line. This line is usually determined by one of the edges of the selected objects. This is useful to create a professional-looking design where the objects appear precise and organized. Align the two layers you are working with.

1. Make sure the Right Foot and Left Foot layers are selected or linked.

2. Press V to activate the Move tool.

3. In the Options bar you will see the alignment options. Hover your pointer over each to become familiar with their names.

4. Select the object that you want to use as a reference point for the alignment. In this case let's use Left Foot.

5. Click the Align bottom edges button. Notice that the feet shapes are aligned along their bottom edge.

Distributing Layers

Distribution places an identical amount of space between multiple objects. This can be an important step in creating a professional-looking design. Distribution is similar to alignment in how it is accessed. However, the intent is slightly different. You will need three or more objects to distribute them. Let's distribute a few layers.

1. Turn off the visibility icons for all layers except *Background*, Spring, Summer, Fall, and Winter. Click the eye icon to make a layer invisible.

2. Select the Spring, Summer, Fall, and Winter layers.

3. Choose the Move tool by pressing V.

VIDEO 52:
Layer Organization

4. In the Options bar you will see distribution options (to the right of the alignment options). Roll over each to become familiar with their names.

5. Click the Distribute horizontal centers button to spread the images apart evenly.

6. Click the Align bottom edges button. Your image will now be evenly aligned and distributed.

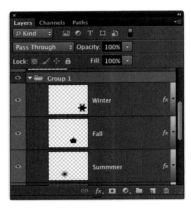

Grouping Layers

Sometimes you'll want to take several layers and treat them as if they were one layer. This is useful for aligning a design composed of multiple images or just general cleanup for organizational purposes. The process of nondestructively joining layers is called grouping. A permanent technique is called *merging* (see "Merging Layers" later in this chapter), but that is pretty decisive. Let's group some layers together so they still retain their individual identity, yet behave as a group.

1. Select the Spring, Summer, Fall, and Winter layers using the Command-click (Ctrl-click) technique.

2. Press Command+G (Ctrl+G) or choose Layer > Group to place these layers into a new group (which looks like a folder). If you'd like to name the group, double-click the folder's name in the Layers panel.

3. You can now move these elements together. For example, select both the *Background* and Group 1, and then use the horizontal center and vertical center alignment commands to center these images on the page.

TIP

Multiple Locks

If you've selected multiple layers, clicking a lock button will apply that state to all of the selected layers.

Locking Layers

Sometimes you need to protect yourself from your own worst enemy (you). Photoshop gives you the option of locking properties of a layer to prevent accidental modification. Just click the icons next to the word Lock in the Layers panel. You can lock three separate properties (or a combination of the three):

- **Lock transparent pixels.** The grid icon locks all transparent areas of an image, but you can still modify any data that was on the layer prior to locking.

- **Lock image pixels.** The paintbrush icon locks all image pixels in the layer.

- **Lock position.** The arrow icon prevents you from accidentally moving a layer out of alignment or changing its position.

- **Lock all.** The padlock icon locks all three properties in one click.

Let's try locking a layer.

1. Turn off the visibility icons for all layers except *Background* and Key.

2. Select the Key layer.

3. In the upper-left corner of the Layers panel, click the Lock transparent pixels and Lock position icons.

4. Press B to select the Brush tool.

5. Click the foreground swatch and load a color of your choice.

6. Paint on the Key layer. Notice that the paint stays "inside the lines."

7. Choose the Move tool (V) and try to move the layer. (A dialog box should pop up indicating that Photoshop "Could not complete your request because the layer is locked.")

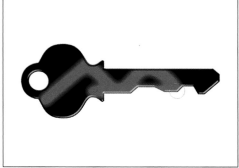

Clipping Mask

Sometimes you'll want to place the contents of one layer inside those of another. Designers often use this technique to fill text with a pattern or to constrain a photo to fit inside a shape. The concept is called a Clipping Mask (earlier versions of Photoshop called it Group with Previous), and it's fairly easy and flexible. All you need to do is place the content layer above the container layer (the one you want to "fill") and choose Layer > Create Clipping Mask.

1. Turn off the visibility icons for all layers except *Background*, Ribbon, and Texture.

2. Select the Texture layer.

Quick Clip

You can create a clipping group quickly by Option-clicking (Alt-clicking) between two layers in the Layers panel.

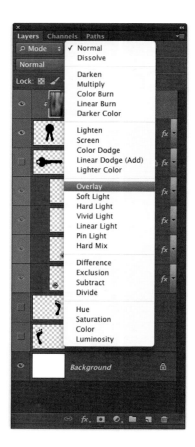

3. Choose Layer > Create Clipping Mask or press Command+Option+G (Ctrl+Alt+G). In the Layers panel, you'll see that the layer indents and fills the opaque areas in the Ribbon layer below. Notice that the layer style applied to the layer is still visible.

4. Choose Layer > Release Clipping Mask or press Command+Option+G (Ctrl+Alt+G) to toggle the mask on and off.

Filtering the View of Layers

As you build a complex layered graphic, the Layers panel can get pretty cluttered. Photoshop CS6 introduces the ability to filter which layers appear in the list based on user-specified criteria. To change which type of filter is used, click the Filter Type menu. These criteria make it easier to find a specific layer or layer type based on the following filter types:

- **Kind.** You can choose to see one or more category of layers by clicking on the associated icon type.

- **Name.** You can enter text into the field to search by a layer's name.

- **Effect.** Once the Effect filter is chosen, a second pop-up menu lets you choose a specific type of layer effect.

- **Mode.** This method lets you choose from any one of Photoshop's blending modes.

Filtering Your View

When you filter the visibility of layers, it only impacts what appears in the Layers panel list. The visibility of a layer in the canvas is determined by the layer visibility switch (eye icon) next to each layer's name.

- **Attribute.** Filtering by attribute type lets you find very specific types of layers. For example, you can choose to look for Empty layers to discard them or to find all locked layers at once.

- **Color.** If you've used colored labels to organize your layers, this filter will show you a specific color, which makes it easier to find layers you've marked for review.

Merging Layers

Sometimes you'll want to permanently merge layers together to commit to a design. This can be useful to reduce file size or to improve compatibility when importing a layered Photoshop document (PSD) file into another application (such as Apple Final Cut Pro, Adobe Premiere Pro, or Adobe After Effects). This process is destructive (in that it permanently joins the layers, which limits future changes).

To merge layers, follow these steps.

1. Select two or more layers by Command-clicking (Ctrl-clicking) on their names in the Layers panel. For practice, select the Texture and Ribbon layers.

2. Choose Layer > Merge Layers or press Command+E (Ctrl+E).

Flattening an Image

If you want to merge all your visible layers and discard all the layers with visibility disabled, choose Layer > Flatten Image. However, flattening an image is a permanent change. You work hard for those layers—*keep them!* Here are some alternatives to flattening that will preserve future flexibility:

- Save a copy of your image in a flattened format. By choosing File > Save As (with the As a Copy check box selected) or File > Save for Web, you can save another version of your image.

- If you need a flattened copy to paste into another document (or within your current document), use the Copy Merged command. Select an active, visible layer, and then choose Select > All. You can copy all visible items to your clipboard as a single layer by then choosing Edit > Copy Merged or by pressing Shift+Command+C (Shift+Ctrl+C).

NOTE

One Type of Filter at a Time

You can only use one category of filters at a time. When you switch categories, the filtering of the list will switch to unfiltered.

NOTE

Not a Permanent Filter

The filter state that you've applied to a layer is not saved with the document when you close it. When you open the document again, the filtered view is reset.

NOTE

Flattening Images

Remember that flattening is permanent. Be 100 percent positive before you discard your layers permanently. If you need a flattened image, choose to save a flattened copy (File > Save As and select the As a Copy check box). You can also group multiple layers into a Smart Object by selecting the layers and then choosing Layer > Smart Object > Convert to Smart Object. You can always edit the Smart Object and extract the layered file.

VIDEO 53:
Create a Panorama

Creating a Panorama

By using layers, you can take several photos from one location and merge them together to create a large panoramic photo. Many people take an assortment of photos of a subject while holding the camera, but it's best to use a tripod. It's important to ensure that you have some overlap between each frame; that is to say, the adjacent photos share some common subject matter—about 25 percent overlap is usually enough.

Let's try piecing together some photos using the Automation command called Photomerge.

1. Choose File > Automate > Photomerge. Photomerge is a specialized "mini-application" within Photoshop that assists in combining multiple images into a single photo.

2. Click the Browse button and navigate to the Chapter 8 folder.

TIP

Professional Panoramic Photography

Pros know that it's best to use a tripod and slightly move the camera to create overlap. There are even specialized tripod heads that you can purchase from companies like Kaidan (www.kaidan.com), Manfrotto (www.manfrotto.com), and Really Right Stuff (www. reallyrightstuff.com) that make leveling and rotation more precise.

TIP

Want to Know More About Panos?

Be sure to check out a website I contribute to called Triple Exposure (www.3exposure.com). It covers panoramic, time-lapse, and HDR photography.

3. Select the folder Ch08_Pano, and then select all the files within the folder (hold down the Shift key to select a range of images). Once selected, click Open.

4. Several Layout options are available that attempt to fix problems (such as distortion) caused by panoramic photography. A good place to start is Auto, which attempts to align the images but will bend them as needed.

5. Select the check boxes next to Blend Images Together and Vignette Removal. These two options attempt to blend the edges of the photos together and can hide subtle differences in exposure.

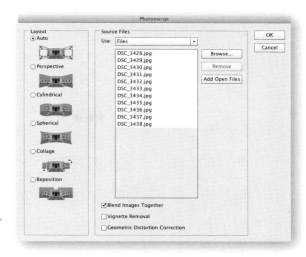

Photoshop attempts to straighten the image. Although this photo was shot with a tripod, the wall was not level. Photoshop attempts to compensate and corrects the image using the horizon automatically.

6. Click OK to build the panoramic image. Photoshop attempts to assemble the panorama based on your choices in the dialog box. Because layers are preserved, however, you can still tweak the position of individual layers.

VIDEO 54:
Repairing Panoramic Images with the Adaptive Wide Angle Command

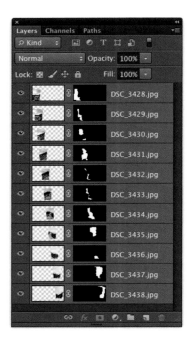

7. Although unlikely, you can nudge any layers with the Move tool if your alignment is off. You may need to adjust the Layer Masks.

8. The Layer Masks help to blend the photos together. They can be modified as needed using the techniques you learned in the previous chapter.

9. Choose Layer > Flatten Image.

10. Crop the image to a clean rectangular shape using the Crop tool (C). You may need to fill in some additional areas of the image if there are holes in the panorama. If so, you could use the Clone Stamp and Content-Aware Fill options, which you'll learn about in Chapter 11, "Repairing and Improving Photos."

Be sure to check out the file Ch08_Pano_Complete.psd to see how the image was further enhanced with adjustment layers.

Auto-Aligning Layers

VIDEO 55:
Auto-Align Command

The technology that powers the Photomerge command can also be harnessed to stitch together nonpanoramic shots or scans that take multiple images to capture a larger print. The Auto-Align Layers command is a useful way to stitch together multiple shots or scans of a large object or a group photo. The command is very easy to use and produces impressive results.

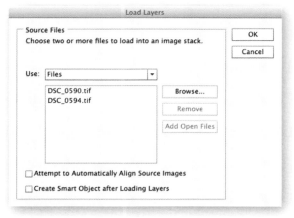

1. Choose File > Scripts > Load Files into Stack to combine two or more files into one document.

2. In the Load Layers dialog box, click the Browse button to navigate to the files you need.

3. Open the folder Ch08_Cyborg, select both images inside, and click Open.

4. In the Load Layers dialog box, select the check box next to Attempt to Automatically Align Source Images.

5. Click OK. Photoshop opens both images and aligns them, and does a good job (especially since the top layer was taken at such an angle). This alignment can be refined even further.

6. Make sure both layers are selected in the Layers panel.

7. Choose Edit > Auto-Align Layers.

8. Select the Auto option to enable both Vignette Removal and Geometric Distortion options for Lens Correction.

9. Click OK. Photoshop removes some of the distortion in the glass case, giving it a more rectangular shape.

   The layers can be seamlessly blended together using the Auto-Blend Layers command. This applies Layer Masks as needed to each layer to mask out exposure issues and create a seamless composite.

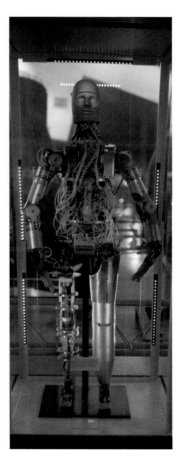

10. Choose Edit > Auto-Blend Layers, specify the Panorama method, and click OK (be sure the Seamless Tones and Colors check box is also selected).

11. Crop the image as needed, adjust Levels, and flatten.

LAYER COMPS

Photoshop CS introduced Layer Comps, which allows Photoshop to memorize combinations of layer visibility, opacity, and position. This can be useful for storing multiple designs inside one document. When experimenting with layouts, you'll often use several options in one document. You might set the headline in three different typefaces and try the main photo in two different positions. Using Layer Comps allows you to set up different options within one document (instead of having to save and keep track of several).

VIDEO 56:
Layer Comps

1. Open the file Cho8_Layer_Comps.psd. If you get any font warnings, dismiss them.

2. Make sure the Layer Comps window is visible. If not, choose Windows > Layer Comps.

3. Click the forward triangle to Apply Next Selected Layer Comp. Click through and examine the different layer comps.

4. For Layer Comp 1, move the words around onscreen to a new position.

5. Click the Update layer comp icon at the bottom of the Layer Comps panel (it looks like two arrows in a circle).

6. Switch to Layer Comp 2. On the layer called This is, click the visibility icon next to the Layer Style Outer Glow. A black glow should be added.

7. Click the Create new layer comp icon (it looks like a pad of paper) on the bottom edge of the Layer Comps window. Name it Comp 2 Alternate.

8. Save a copy of each layer comp to send to a client. Choose File > Scripts > Layer Comps to PDF. Photoshop creates a new PDF with all four layer comps in one document. This is a convenient way to email a project to a client for review.

Layer Comps are a bit confusing at first, but as you master what layers can do, you'll turn to Layer Comps for flexibility. Be sure to check out the Adobe Help Center for more on Layer Comps.

Using Blending Modes

9

Blending modes are both a mystery and a source of great design power. Each blending mode controls how one layer's pixels are affected by those in another layer (or by a tool from the Tools panel). Most users give up on blending modes because the technical definitions of each mode get very tricky. The secret is to not worry too much about the technical issues and to learn how to experiment. Although you'll explore the technology and the creativity behind blending modes in this chapter, there are only a few basics that you must know to make blending modes part of your design toolbox.

About Blending Modes

There are 27 different blending options available from the Layers panel and a few additional blending options that work with specific tools. How do they work? The simple answer is, it depends. Your response is likely, depends on what? Simply put, the effect achieved by blending two layers varies with the contents of those two layers. A blending mode compares the content of two layers and enacts changes based on the content of both layers. You'll find blending modes in many of the tools, and they can be combined with every filter.

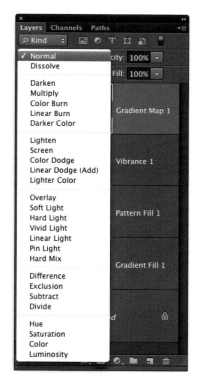

The blending mode specified in the Options bar controls how pixels are affected by a painting or editing tool. Additionally, you can set the blending mode of a layer to control how it interacts with those below it. A clear understanding of the following terms will better help you understand blending modes:

- **Base color.** The original color in the image

- **Blend color.** The color being applied with the painting or editing tool (or the color in the top layer)

- **Result color.** The color resulting from the blend

NOTE

Blending Mode Practice

For more practice with blending, open the files Ch09_Blend Modes1.psd and Ch09_Blend Modes2.psd inside the Extras folder in the Chapter 9 folder, and experiment with different modes and opacity settings.

List of Blending Modes

With 27 blending modes to choose from, keeping them straight can be tough. Fortunately, the modes are grouped together by similar function. Here are clear and simple definitions as well as a sample of how each blending mode behaves:

The colored swirl will be blended with the underlying photo to illustrate each mode. Open the file Ch09_Blended_Overlay.psd from the Chapter 9 folder to experiment with blending modes.

Normal.
The default mode performs no additional change to how layer contents interact.

Dissolve.
Creates a random replacement of the pixels with the base or blend color.

Darken.
Pixels lighter than blend are replaced; darker ones are not.

Multiply.
Is similar to drawing strokes on the image with magic markers.

Color Burn.
Evaluates each channel; darkens base by increasing contrast.

Linear Burn.
Evaluates each channel; darkens base by decreasing brightness.

Darker Color.
Uses the lowest value from both layers to create resulting color.

Lighten.
Evaluates each channel; it then uses base or blend color (whichever is lighter).

Screen.
Use a lighter color. It is useful for "knocking" black out of a layer.

Color Dodge.
Evaluates color information and brightens base by decreasing contrast.

Linear Dodge (Add). *Evaluates color information and brightens base by increasing brightness.*

Lighter Color.
Uses highest value from both layers to create resulting color.

Overlay.
Overlays existing pixels while preserving highlights and shadows of base.

Soft Light.
Effect is similar to shining a diffused spotlight on the image.

Hard Light.
Effect is similar to shining a harsh spotlight on the image.

Vivid Light.
Burns or dodges by increasing or decreasing the contrast.

Linear Light.
Burns or dodges by decreasing or increasing the brightness.

Pin Light.
Is useful for adding special effects to an image.

Hard Mix.
Enhances the contrast of the underlying layers.

Difference.
Evaluates each channel and subtracts or inverts depending on brightness.

Exclusion.
Is similar to the Difference mode but lower in contrast.

Subtract.
Looks at the color in each channel and subtracts the blend from the base.

Divide.
Looks at the color in each channel and divides the blend from the base.

Hue.
Uses luminance and saturation of the base and the hue of the blend.

Saturation.
Creates color with luminance and hue of base and saturation of blend.

Color.
Preserves gray levels. It's very useful for coloring and tinting.

Luminosity.
Is the inverse effect from the Color mode.

Blending Modes in Practice

So far you've looked at blending modes in a strictly technical sense. Although it's useful to have a clear understanding of the technology, don't lose sight of the design possibilities. Blending modes are a great way to mix layers together. Let's take a look at a stylized photo that uses blending modes to enhance its look.

1. Open the file Ch09_Butterfly.psd from the Chapter 9 folder. This five-layer document uses blending modes to create a colorful image.

2. Turn on the visibility of the Gradient Fill layer. Set its blending mode to Multiply, and adjust its opacity to 60% to create a vignette effect.

3. Turn on the visibility of the Pattern Fill layer. Set its blending mode to Divide, and adjust its opacity to 25% to create a distressed texture.

4. Turn on the visibility of the Vibrance adjustment layer. This adjustment selectively boosts the saturation in the image. Set it to Overlay mode to dramatically increase the saturation of the image.

5. Turn on the visibility of the Gradient Map adjustment layer. This adjustment tints the image. Set it to Hue mode to shift the colors in a gentle way.

Feel free to experiment with different combinations of blending modes and Opacity settings. This sample image provides just a quick glimpse into the power and flexibility of blending modes.

Blending Modes in Action

Now that you have a little practice with blending modes, it's time to explore their creative and production side in greater depth. Blending modes are part of a professional's workflow. The next three sections showcase a few different ways to better integrate blending modes for professional results.

VIDEO 57:
Blending Modes
in Action

DESIGN "RULES" FOR BLENDING MODES

RULE #1—DON'T TRY TO MEMORIZE HOW EACH BLENDING MODE WORKS. The good news is that they are grouped by similar traits. As you make your way through the list, you will notice a gradual progression through styles. The first group darkens your underlying image, whereas the second lightens it. The third set adds contrast, and the last two generate dramatic results by comparing or mapping values. Depending on your sources, some blending modes will generate little or no results. Sound confusing? Keep reading.

RULE #2—EXPERIMENT. The best way to use blending modes is to just try them out. Clicking through a long menu is boring. A much better alternative is to select the Move tool and then use the Shift++ keyboard shortcut.

RULE #3—EXPLOIT THEM. Do you need to tint an image? Place a solid or gradient on top of the image and change to Hue or Color mode. Need to drop out white in a layer? Just set it to Multiply mode. Blending modes are available for every filter (choose Fade Filter from the Edit menu) and all the Brush tools.

VIDEO 58:
Adding Spice with
Blending Modes

Instant Spice

One way to improve a washed-out or flat image is through blending modes. By blending a blurred copy of an image on top of itself, you can quickly create a visual pop. Let's give it a try.

1. Open the file Ch09_Spice1.psd from the Chapter 9 folder.

2. Select the *Background* layer in the Layers panel.

3. Duplicate the *Background* layer by pressing Command+J (Ctrl+J).

4. Significantly blur the new layer by choosing Filter > Blur > Gaussian Blur. A value of 25 pixels should do the trick.

5. Select the Move tool by pressing V.

6. Cycle blending modes by pressing Shift+=. Look for modes (such as Multiply or Soft Light) that increase saturation and add visual "pop" to the image. Adjust the layer's opacity to deemphasize the effect if needed.

7. If needed, adjust the opacity of the layer as desired. You can quickly change opacity by typing in the first number of an Opacity setting, such as 4 for 40% opacity. You can type 25 to quickly switch to 25% opacity, for example, if a more specific adjustment is required.

Original

Gaussian Blur | 25 Pixels

Soft Light | 80% Opacity

Multiply | 40% Opacity

Fixing a Shadowed Image

If an image is completely thrown into the shadows, you can turn to blending modes to shed a little light. In fact, this technique is often used by law enforcement to enhance security photos or footage.

1. Open the file Ch09_Shadow1.tif from the Chapter 9 folder.

2. Duplicate the *Background* layer by pressing Command+J (Ctrl+J).

3. Set the top layer to Screen mode. You can choose it from the menu in the Layers panel or press Shift+Option+S (Shift+Alt+S). The image should appear significantly lighter.

4. You can further lighten the image by placing another duplicate copy on top. Press Command+J (Ctrl+J) as many times as needed. Each will lighten the image further.

Applying a Rubber Stamp

You can also use blending modes to make one image appear as if it were applied to another. If you add the Free Transform command, you can make that stamp match the perspective of the photo. Let's give it a try.

VIDEO 59:
Filters and Blending Modes

1. Open the files Ch09_Boxes.tif and Ch09_Logo.psd from the Chapter 9 folder.

2. Select the Logo.psd file so it is active.

3. Choose Select > All and then Edit Copy to add it to your clipboard.

4. Switch back to the Boxes file and choose Edit > Paste.

5. Press Command+T (Ctrl+T) to invoke the Free Transform command.

To use additional transformations, right-click.

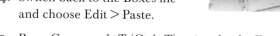

VIDEO 60:
Corner Pinning an Image

NOTE

Not All Modes Have Shortcuts

The four newest modes (Darker Color, Lighter Color, Subtract, and Divide) do not have a shortcut key.

6. Choose Distort: This allows you to corner pin the logo and match its angle to that of the box. Adjust the position so the corners of the image match up to the edge of the box.

7. You now need to scale the logo smaller. Right-click (Ctrl-click) and choose Scale. Shrink the logo so it fits better on the side of the box.

8. Set the Logo layer to the Multiply blending mode and lower its opacity to 85% to make the Logo layer appear to be stamped on the crate.

Table 9.1 provides the keyboard shortcuts to make it easier for you to use blending modes.

Table 9.1   Blending Shortcuts

Result	Mac OS	Windows
Normal	Shift+Option+N	Shift+Alt+N
Dissolve	Shift+Option+I	Shift+Alt+I
Darken	Shift+Option+K	Shift+Alt+K
Multiply	Shift+Option+M	Shift+Alt+M
Color Burn	Shift+Option+B	Shift+Alt+B
Linear Burn	Shift+Option+A	Shift+Alt+A
Lighten	Shift+Option+G	Shift+Alt+G
Screen	Shift+Option+S	Shift+Alt+S
Color Dodge	Shift+Option+D	Shift+Alt+D
Linear Dodge	Shift+Option+W	Shift+Alt+W
Overlay	Shift+Option+O	Shift+Alt+O
Soft Light	Shift+Option+F	Shift+Alt+F
Hard Light	Shift+Option+H	Shift+Alt+H
Vivid Light	Shift+Option+V	Shift + Alt+V
Linear Light	Shift+Option+J	Shift + Alt+J
Pin Light	Shift+Option+Z	Shift + Alt+Z
Hard Mix	Shift+Option+L	Shift + Alt+L
Difference	Shift+Option+E	Shift + Alt+E
Exclusion	Shift+Option+X	Shift + Alt+X
Hue	Shift+Option+U	Shift+Alt+U
Saturation	Shift+Option+T	Shift+Alt+T
Color	Shift+Option+C	Shift+Alt+C
Luminosity	Shift+Option+Y	Shift+Alt+Y

Color Correction and Enhancement

10

The primary purpose of Photoshop is to act as a digital darkroom where images can be corrected, enhanced, and refined. How do you know an image needs touch-up? You can pretty much assume every image can look a little (or even a lot) better than how the camera captured it. Whether it's adjusting the exposure, increasing contrast, or boosting saturation, Photoshop is the place to improve an image.

Learning how to spot problems and then choosing the right correction technique is an essential part of mastering Photoshop.

The left image is as shot by the camera. The right image has been refined using the Camera Raw plugin. You can open the Ch10_Major_Fix.NEF file to experiment.

Several different tools are available, some more useful than others. By analyzing the most important tools and determining in which situations they might help you, you can achieve a more thorough understanding of color correction.

Approach to Color Correction

New users often have a difficult time when color correcting or enhancing images. They generally lose sight of the goal: making the image look better while still being believable. Many users go "too far" in their quest to fix images. If the image starts to look fake or too altered, it will be distracting. Although getting it "right" requires some practice, here's some general advice to get you started:

- **Identify what's wrong.** Before you can fix a picture, be sure you have decided on what's wrong. Is it too dark? Is the sky washed out? Has the picture faded over time? Make a list and prioritize the issues you find in each image. It's easiest to fix one problem at a time, and if you identify those problems, you'll know when to stop twiddling with the image.

- **Work with a copy of the image.** Before you start to color correct an image, you should duplicate it. This way you can return to an original version if you make a mistake or go too far in your image touch-up. After opening your file, choose File > Save As and name the duplicate version that will be corrected. Color correction can be a *destructive* process, meaning that you cannot revert to the original state at a later time. By preserving an original version of the image or employing adjustment layers, you make *nondestructive* editing possible. Some users also choose to duplicate the *Background* layer at the bottom of the layer stack.

- **Edit with adjustment layers.** Adjustment layers allow you to apply most of the image correction commands as nondestructive effects. They are added as a layer above the actual image; the adjustment layer can be blended, masked, or deleted at any time. Additionally, if you select the adjustment layer, you can modify its properties in the Adjustments panel. The same modifications are available in both the Adjustments menu and Adjustments panel. You should work with an adjustment layer whenever possible because its flexibility will be important for future revisions.

- **Get a fresh opinion.** It's not a bad idea to step back and examine your work. Open the backup copy of the original image and compare it to the image you've been working on. This before-and-after comparison can be very useful. If you have a fresh set of eyes nearby, ask that person for his or her opinion.

- **Use Smart Filters.** This will open up most of the filters and several of the image adjustments including the Shadows/Highlights command and Variations. Just choose Filter > Convert for Smart Filters.

Primary Image Adjustments

Photoshop offers several image adjustments, but only a few are used most often. Commands such as Levels and Curves are used by professionals to achieve outstanding results. These professional imaging techniques may take a little time to get comfortable with, but the power they offer is worth your investment.

Levels

The Levels command corrects tonal ranges and color balance issues. With this command you can fix poor exposure. Additionally, you can perform color correction by manually identifying a white point and black point in the image. Nearly every image can benefit from making a Levels adjustment.

To understand Levels, you must be able to read a histogram. This graph works as a visual guide for adjusting the image. The Levels adjustment has its own histogram that is visible when working in the Adjustments panel. You may also want to call up the Histogram panel (Window > Histogram) and leave it open while color correcting to help you spot issues in color and contrast. You can also expand the Histogram panel by clicking the submenu and choosing All Channels View. Let's give the command a try.

> **NOTE**
>
> **Levels Beats Brightness/Contrast**
>
> A Brightness/Contrast command does exist, but the Levels adjustment lets you perform several improvements with one command. Using a single image process cuts down on the loss of quality introduced from multiple image-processing steps.

1. Close any open files, and then open the file Ch10_Levels.tif from the Chapter 10 folder.

2. Add a Levels adjustment layer by clicking the Levels icon in the Adjustments panel. Levels is also available from the Adjustments menu (Image > Adjustments), but the adjustment layer is more flexible for future modifications.

3. This photo was shot under mixed light, but you can reset the black and white points of the image to fix the exposure. In the Adjustments panel, move the white Input Levels slider to the left. This affects the image's white point and allows you to reassign where white should begin in the image.

4. Move the black Input Levels slider slowly to the right. The more you move the black slider to the right, the more contrast is introduced into the image.

5. The true power lies in the middle (gray) Input Levels slider. By moving this slider, you can modify the gamma setting. Effectively, you can use the middle Input Levels slider to change the intensity of the midtones. This adjustment can be made without making dramatic changes to the highlights and shadows, and lets you better expose an image. Move the slider to the left to add light; move the slider to the right to subtract light.

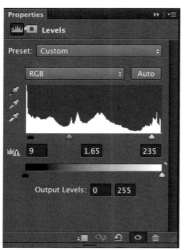

6. In the future if you need to edit the adjustment, simply select the adjustment layer in the Layers panel and manipulate the controls in the Adjustments panel.

Rinse and Repeat

If you have several images from the same camera or shoot, they may need the same Levels adjustment. The Save button allows you to save a Levels adjustment (to the folder that contains the image is a good place). You can then click the Load button to apply that adjustment to another image.

VIDEO 61:
Levels Command

Auto-Levels

When working with the Levels adjustment layer, you may have noticed the Auto button. This command button triggers an analysis of the histogram data by Photoshop that is then used to modify the individual controls of the Levels adjustment. In many cases this results in an image that is properly adjusted for color balance and exposure issues. In others it will get you closer to a corrected image.

1. Close any open files, and then Open the file Ch10_Auto_Levels1.tif from the Chapter 10 folder.

2. Add a Levels adjustment layer by clicking the Levels icon in the Adjustments panel.

3. Click the Auto button to perform an automated adjustment for the image. The image's levels and color are adjusted.

4. To refine how the automatic adjustment works, hold down the Option (Alt) key and click the Auto button again. A new dialog box opens.

5. Select Enhance Per Channel Contrast and Snap Neutral Midtones to create a very natural balance of colors for the image.

6. Click OK to close the dialog box.

7. Adjust the middle slider (gray) to refine the Levels adjustment to taste.

VIDEO 62:
Correcting Color Cast
with Levels

VIDEO 63:
Adjusting Levels
per Channel

Color cast

In the first Levels example you made a Levels adjustment to all the channels evenly. In the Auto-Levels example, you let Photoshop adjust the levels and remove color cast using an automated algorithm. The Levels command can be further isolated to a specific channel by clicking the drop-down list in the center of the Levels dialog box. This allows you to tackle color cast issues, such as spill from a background, a bad white balance, or a photo shot under mixed or colored lighting.

PHOTO BY JAMES BALL

1. Close any open files, and then open the file Ch10_Levels_Color_Balance.tif from the Chapter 10 folder. Notice how the image has a greenish tint.

2. Add a Levels adjustment layer using the Adjustments panel. You will use the Levels command to fix color and exposure issues.

3. Select the Set White Point (white eyedropper) in the Levels dialog box. Click an area that should be pure white. For this image, click a bright area in the white pillar. If you click an area that is not bright enough, the whites in the image will overexpose. (You can click the Reset button—it looks like a circular arrow—at the bottom of the Adjustments panel to reset the Levels command, if needed.) After you click, you'll see that some of the color spill has been removed.

4. Select the Set Black Point (black eyedropper) in the Levels dialog box. Click an area that should be pure black. Choose an area such as a jacket or a dark shadow. This will adjust the color balance and the exposure.

5. The image's color balance should now be better. Adjust the middle Input Levels slider to brighten the image.

Curves

VIDEO 64:
Working with Curves

Most users will either use Curves a lot or they won't use it at all. The Curves interface is more complex than Levels, which scares away many users. Although Levels gives you three control points (highlights, midtones, and shadows), the Curves adjustment allows for up to 16 control points. This can significantly open up more options when adjusting color and exposure.

Let's try the Curves command on a practice image.

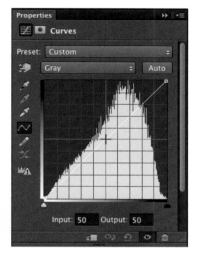

1. Close any open files, and then open the file Ch10_Curves_Practice.tif from the Chapter 10 folder.

2. Add a Curves adjustment layer by clicking the Curves button in the Adjustments panel. When you first open the Curves interface, there are two points (one for white and one for black).

3. Add a single control point in the middle of the line (click at an Input Value of 50%).

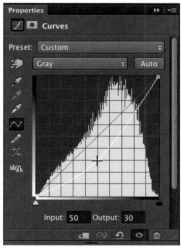

4. Pull this new control point down to lighten the image (toward the lighter area on the Y axis). You can pull the point up to darken the image. Notice that the Input and Output values update as you drag.

5. The adjustment is applied gradually throughout the entire image. Multiple points can be employed for contrast adjustments based on tonal range.

The primary advantage of Curves is that you have precise control over which points get mapped (whereas in Levels you do not). Another benefit is that Curves adjustments can use several points

NOTE

RGB Reverse

You're about to work with an RGB image; the direction of darks and lights will be reversed from the Grayscale image.

connected by a curved line (as opposed to Levels, which uses only three control points) to make adjustments. So, color correction can be applied in a more gradual manner (without the hard clipping that can be associated with Levels).

1. Close any open files, and then open the image Ch10_Curves.tif from the Chapter 10 folder.

2. Add a Curves adjustment layer by clicking the Curves icon in the Adjustments panel. The curve has only two points on it—one representing the black point; the other, the white point.

3. It's now time to add more control points to refine the curve. To do this, you'll use a Curves preset. Click the menu to select a Curves preset in the Adjustments panel. Choose the Strong Contrast (RGB) preset. Notice that the image now has more contrast in the shadows and highlights, and more visual "pop."

4. Experiment by adjusting the five control points. Try to further emphasize the shadows in the image. Continue to experiment by moving the control points (you can use the up and down arrow keys for precise control).

TIP

Easy Curves

When the Curves Editor is open, you can easily add control points. Click the icon that looks like a pointing finger, and then just click and drag in the image to modify the curve. The control points will appear in the editor.

NOTE

Pay Attention to Your Axes

When working with a grayscale or CMYK file, the axes go from light to dark. When working with RGB images, the scales are reversed. This means that pulling a control point up or down may have a different effect.

Hue/Saturation

The Hue/Saturation command lets you adjust the hue, saturation, and lightness of color components in an image. Additionally, you can simultaneously adjust all the colors in an image. This command can work in two ways:

- To adjust colors in an image that appears slightly out of phase or skewed toward a color, such as an image that appears to have a blue overcast

- To create stylistic changes by dramatically changing colors in an object, such as trying out different combinations of colors in a logo

When combined with a selection command (such as Color Range), the Hue/Saturation command can be used to selectively enhance colors in an image.

Let's give the command a try.

1. Close any open files, and then open the file Ch10_Hue_Saturation.tif from the Chapter 10 folder. You'll subtly tweak the color in the motorcycle.

2. Choose Select > Color Range and click the motorcycle body to make an initial selection. Hold down the Shift key to add to the selection. Adjust the Fuzziness slider to soften the selection. Use the Localized Color Clusters to further constrain the selection. Click OK when you have a suitable selection.

3. Click the Hue/Saturation button in the Adjustments panel to add an adjustment layer.

The Five Most Useful Image Adjustments

- Levels
- Curves
- Black & White
- Vibrance
- Shadow/Highlights

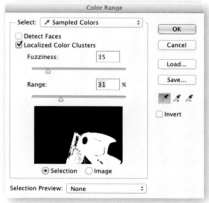

4. The two color bars at the bottom of the dialog box represent the colors in the color wheel. The upper bar shows the initial color; the lower bar shows the new color. Drag the Hue slider to the left until maroon appears under red.

5. Additionally, you can adjust Saturation (which is the intensity of the color) and adjust Lightness (which adds white or black to the image). Increase Saturation to **+15** and decrease Lightness to **−20**.

NOTE

A Better Saturation

If you need a more robust saturation control, be sure to try out the Vibrance adjustment. It offers its own saturation control that uses a different method to control saturation. It tends to produce better changes, but doesn't offer Hue or Lightness controls.

Recolor

A Hue/Saturation adjustment can be a fast way to experiment with color options. You can use it to quickly change the fill colors of an object by making a global adjustment. This works well when you are experimenting with different color combinations. Let's try it out.

1. Close any open files, and then open the file Ch10_Logo_ Adjustments.psd from the Chapter 10 folder.

2. Select the layer thumbnail of the Hue/Saturation adjustment layer to access its controls in the Adjustments panel.

3. Adjust the Hue slider to try out different color combinations.

Tinting a photo

You can also use the Hue/Saturation command to tint an image. If you are working with a grayscale image, you need to convert it to an RGB image first.

VIDEO 65:
Tinting a Photo

1. Close any open files, and then open the file Ch10_Tint.tif from the Chapter 10 folder.

2. Add a Hue/Saturation adjustment layer.

3. Click the Colorize box to tint the image.

4. Adjust the Hue slider to try out different color combinations. Adjust Saturation and Lightness to refine the tint.

   The adjustment layer automatically has a Layer Mask attached, which allows you to mask the effect.

5. Click the Layer Mask icon for the Hue/Saturation adjustment layer.

6. Select your Brush tool and press D to load the default colors of black and white.

7. With a small black brush, paint the flowers so the original red shows through. If you make a mistake, you can press X to toggle back to white for touch-up.

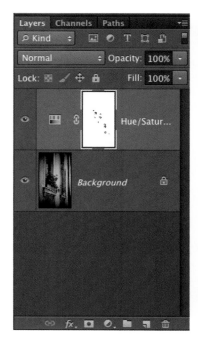

VIDEO 66: Vibrance

Vibrance

When working with photos, many choose to have very saturated and rich colors. The problem with too much saturation is that it can cause clipping (a flattening of the range of colors). To help

Original image.

with this, Photoshop offers the Vibrance command. Unlike Saturation, Vibrance only boosts those parts of a photo that are less saturated. It also respects skin tones, which means photos look more natural when pumping up the intensity of color.

1. From the Chapter 10 folder, open the image Ch10_Vibrance1.tif.

2. You'll first add a Saturation adjustment layer for comparison. In the Adjustments panel, click Saturation icon to add a new adjustment layer.

3. Drag the Saturation slider to the right until the colors in the image start to clip.

4. Discard the Saturation adjustment layer by clicking the trash icon at the bottom of the Adjustments panel. Click Yes in the dialog box that appears.

5. In the Adjustments panel, click the Vibrance icon to add a new adjustment layer.

Hue/Saturation begins to posterize the reddish areas of the image.

6. Drag the Vibrance slider to the right to increase saturation without color clipping.

7. To add a little more saturation overall (in a gentler fashion than the Saturation adjustment layer), use the Saturation slider in the Vibrance adjustment layer.

A Vibrance adjustment increased saturation selectively.

Useful Image Adjustments

Although a Levels or Curves command can usually get the color-correction job done, there are often atypical problems that require particular commands. Let's explore some other commands that have special purposes and should generally be reserved for the unique problems they address. Let's take a look at the specialty commands.

Black & White

If you want to create a dramatic grayscale or duotone effect, the most effective way is to use a Black & White adjustment layer. Unlike a simple saturation adjustment, you maintain full control over how individual colors are converted. This allows you to emphasize or deemphasize specific colors and tonal ranges. Additionally, you can tint the grayscale by applying a color tone to the image (such as a sepia tone).

VIDEO 67:
Black and White
Adjustments

1. Close any open files, and then open the file Ch10_Black White Conversion.tif from the Chapter 10 folder.

2. Click the Black & White icon in the Adjustments panel.

3. Photoshop performs a default grayscale conversion. You'll want to adjust the conversion using the color sliders. You can also apply an Auto conversion or use a saved custom mix.

You can adjust the color sliders to emphasize gray tones of specific colors in an image. Each image is unique, so you'll need to find the right balance. Drag a slider to the left to darken or to the right to lighten. Be sure to select the Preview check box so you can see the results of your changes.

TIP

Black & White Auto—A Good Start

Normally, I recommend avoiding the Auto buttons, but with the Black & White adjustment layer it works well. Auto sets a grayscale mix based on the image's color values. It attempts to maximize the distribution of gray values. The Auto mix often produces excellent results and can serve as the starting point for tweaking gray values using the color sliders.

TIP

Blended Black and White

Be sure to try out blending modes with your adjustment layers. The Black & White adjustments look great blended. Try Multiply or Overlay for this exercise.

VIDEO 68:
Creative Sepia Tones

4. With the Black & White command window open, click the icon in the Adjustments panel that looks like a pointing finger.

5. You can click on the image to sample a target. The mouse pointer changes to an eyedropper if you move it over the image. Just click and hold on an image area to target the right color slider for the strongest color at that location. You can then drag to shift the color slider for that color, thus making it lighter or darker.

6. To create a duotone effect, select the Tint option. To change the tint color, click its swatch and use the Color Picker to choose a new color that matches your needs.

Gradient Map

You can use the Gradient Map to dramatically or subtly stylize images. The effect works best when used as an adjustment layer. The command works by mapping the colors of a gradient to the image based on the luminance values of the source image. Let's give the technique a try.

1. Close any open files, and then open the image Ch10_Gradient_Map1.tif from the Chapter 10 folder.

2. Click the Gradient Map icon in the Adjustments panel.

3. In the Properties panel, click the gradient to open the Gradient Editor.

4. In the Gradient Editor, choose a loaded gradient or load a new set to taste. For more on gradients, see Chapter 6, "Painting and Drawing Tools." Click OK when you're satisfied.

5. To soften the effect, you can change the adjustment layer's blending mode. Setting it to Hue or Color creates a nice tint effect.

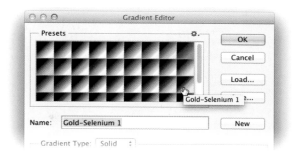

Photo Filter

Professional photographers often place glass filters in front of the camera lens. These can be used to "cool" or "warm" a picture, or to add special effects. Since Photoshop often tries to simulate or correct for steps not taken in the field, the addition of Photo Filters was a logical evolution for Photoshop.

Adobe added to the "real-time," color-correction options with the addition of 20 different adjustments. These layers simulate the traditional colored glass filters. Besides the built-in presets, you can also choose custom colors from the Photo Filter interface using the standard Color Picker.

There are three main groupings for color effects:

● **Warming Filter (85 and LBA) and Cooling Filter (80 and LBB).** These adjustment layers are meant to even out photos that were not properly white balanced. The Cooling Filter (80 or LBB) makes images bluer to simulate cooler ambient light. The Warming Filter (85 or LBA) makes images warmer to simulate hotter ambient light.

● **Warming Filter (81) and Cooling Filter (82).** These adjustment layers are similar to the previous filters but cast a more pronounced color. The Warming Filter (81) makes the photo more yellow, and the Cooling Filter (82) makes the photo bluer.

● **Individual Colors.** The Photo Filter also has 14 preset colors to choose from. These can be used for two primary purposes: to add a complementary color to a scene to remove color cast or for stylistic reasons.

VIDEO 69:
Stealing Sunsets

Let's try applying a Photo Filter adjustment layer.

1. Close any open files, and then open the file Ch10_Photo_Filter.tif from the Chapter 10 folder.

2. Click the Photo Filter icon in the Adjustments panel.

3. In the Filter area, choose Warming Filter (85) to adjust the temperature of the photo.

4. Deselect the Preserve Luminosity option to allow the image to darken.

5. Adjust the slider to taste.

   The sky and the image should be "warmer." You can adjust the Density slider to control the intensity of the effect.

Shadows/Highlights

Exposure problems often plague photos. Dark shadows may make a photo seem unusable, but Photoshop offers a powerful command for fixing these problems. The image command Shadows/Highlights is very flexible for solving problems. The command can help salvage images where the subject is silhouetted from strong backlight. You can also use the command to improve subjects who have been washed out by the camera's flash.

The Shadows/Highlights command does more than lighten or darken an image. It makes adjustments by analyzing neighboring pixels. However, when first opened, the tool is very basic. It is important to select the Show More Options check box, which adds significant control. Let's give the command a try.

1. Close any open files, and then open the file Ch10_Shadows_Highlight_1.tif from the Chapter 10 folder.

The Shadow/Highlights command is not available as an adjustment layer. You can still apply it in a nondestructive manner by first converting the photo to a Smart Object.

VIDEO 70:
Shadows/Highlights

2. Choose Layer > Smart Objects > Convert to Smart Object.

3. Choose Image > Adjustments > Shadows/Highlights. The image is brightened automatically because the command boosts the shadowed areas by default.

4. Select the Show More Options check box and be sure to select the Preview check box.

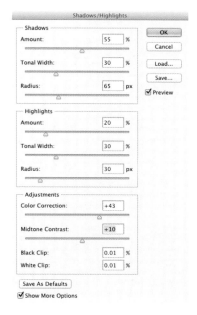

5. Adjust the Shadows and Highlights of the image:

- **Amount.** This value determines how strong of an adjustment is made to the image.

- **Tonal Width.** Small values affect a reduced region; larger values include the midtones. If pushed too high, halos appear around the edges of the image.

- **Radius.** Is a tolerance setting that examines neighboring pixels to determine the affected area.

6. Modify the image adjustments to improve image quality:

- **Color Correction.** This slider modifies the saturation of the adjusted areas. Essentially, it can counterbalance washed-out images.

- **Brightness.** If you're working on a grayscale image, Color Correction is replaced by a Brightness control.

- **Midtone Contrast.** This adjustment affects the contrast in the midtones of a photo. Positive values increase contrast, whereas negative values reduce contrast.

- **Black Clip and White Clip.** This adjustment modifies the black point of shadows and lowers the white point of highlights. This can lower the intensity of the effect.

7. Click Save if you'd like to store the adjustment to use on another photo. When you're satisfied, click OK to apply the adjustment.

If you'd like extra practice, you'll find additional images in the Chapter 10 Extras folder.

Exposure

Starting with Photoshop CS2, support was added for 32-bit images. Generally referred to as high dynamic range (HDR), these images offer great flexibility in exposure. These images can better handle re-creating the wide range of exposures found in outdoor scenes or intense lighting conditions. The Exposure adjustment is usually used on images that exist in 32-bit space and is said to be a 32-bit floating point operation (often shortened to *float*).

Creating an HDR image is a combination of shooting techniques and a Photoshop command. It requires that the camera be secured firmly to a tripod and that you be careful when triggering or adjusting the camera to not move it (or allow anything to move in the shot either). Several photos at various exposures are taken of the same scene (a minimum of three; usually five to seven is adequate). The camera should have its auto-bracket and ISO features disabled. Each shot should be about two f-stops apart. The user then harnesses the Merge to HDR command (File > Automate > Merge to HDR) to create the 32-bit image. You'll create an HDR image later in the book, but for now let's jump ahead to an HDR image that's already built.

1. Close any open files, and then open the file Ch10_HDR1.tif. If you click in your menus, you'll notice that several features are grayed out. Most image adjustments do not work for a 32-bit image. This image was taken in a very low-light environment, but by combining multiple exposures together into the HDR image, I captured a much better photo.

2. Click the Exposure icon in the Adjustments panel. This command makes tonal adjustments by performing calculations in a linear color space (Gamma 1.0) rather than the current color space. This offers extreme flexibility for future changes.

3. Three properties can be modified:

- **Exposure.** Modifies the highlight end of the tonal range with little effect on the extreme shadows.

- **Offset.** Darkens the shadows and midtones with little effect on highlights.

- **Gamma.** Adjusts the gamma of the photo.

4. Additionally, three eyedroppers adjust the image's luminance values:

- **Set Black Point eyedropper.** Sets the Offset, which shifts the selected pixel to zero.

- **Set White Point eyedropper.** Sets the Exposure, which shifts the selected pixel to white (1.0 for HDR images).

- **Midtone eyedropper.** Sets the Exposure, which shifts the selected pixel to the middle gray.

VIDEO 71:
Merge to High Dynamic Range Pro

5. Make a dramatic adjustment and click OK. Let the image blow out, because this will show you the flexibility of HDR images.

6. Apply a second Exposure adjustment and bring the image back into a more accurate exposure. Notice that the blown-out areas are restored (this is often impossible with 8- or 16-bit images captured in a single exposure because overexposed or underexposed data is discarded).

VIDEO 72:
Equalize

Equalize

The Equalize command can restore contrast to a washed-out photo. The command attempts to redistribute pixels so that they are equally balanced across the entire range of brightness values. The command works best when you sample a small area that will drive the overall adjustment. The Equalize command takes the

lightest area and remaps it to pure white, and takes the darkest area and remaps it to pure black. Let's give it a try.

1. Close any open files, and then open the file Ch10_Equalize1.tif from the Chapter 10 folder.

2. With the Rectangular Marquee tool, make a selection inside the largest cactus branch.

3. Choose Image > Adjustments > Equalize to repair the image.

4. Make sure the Equalize entire image based on selected area check box is selected, and then click OK.

5. If the image appears overexposed, you can choose Edit > Fade to reduce the intensity of the Equalize command.

Color Lookup

A new option for color grading in Photoshop CS6 is the ability to apply a Color Lookup adjustment layer. The adjustment lets you choose from several different included presets (organized into three categories: 3DLUT File, Abstract, and Device Link). Each method uses a LUT (or lookup table). The benefits of using a LUT are that color changes are absolute and work well across multiple images for consistent adjustments.

NOTE

What's a LUT?

Historically, LUTs have been used by the digital cinema industry to apply color adjustments between different applications. They work by building a new table of colors that completely remap the colors in use.

NOTE

Create Your Own LUTs?

In Photoshop CS6, LUTs are meant to be applied, not created. You can use an application like Adobe SpeedGrade to make custom LUTs or download them from many websites.

1. Close any open files, and then open the Ch10_LUT.tif file from the Chapter 10 folder.

   This image already has a few LUTs applied so you can see the results of the adjustments.

2. Click the visibility icon next to each LUT adjustment layer. Have only one turned on at a time for the best results.

3. To apply a new LUT, click the Color Lookup icon in the Adjustments panel.

4. In the Properties panel, choose a loaded preset from one of the three pop-up menus.

5. Modify the adjustment layer to taste and experiment with opacity and blending modes.

Tweak a LUT

Remember that you can adjust the opacity and blending mode for a LUT adjustment layer. This leads to several choices when designing.

Using Camera Raw

The Camera Raw support in Photoshop is enabled by a plug-in (essentially an application that runs inside Photoshop). With Camera Raw you can import and develop raw files, and then pass them on to Adobe Photoshop. Camera Raw is designed to work with the native files recorded by many cameras.

A Camera Raw file contains unprocessed and uncompressed data, as captured by the digital camera's image sensor. These native files contain much more color and exposure information than a JPEG or TIFF file. The camera also includes metadata, such as white balance, exposure, and more, specifying how that information should be treated.

VIDEO 73:
Recovering a Raw File

NOTE

What's the raw extension?

Raw files are not really a file type but rather a description for several manufacturer-specific file formats. You'll find several different file formats in use, and they will vary by camera manufacturer.

NOTE

Can I Use Camera Raw?

Not all cameras work with Photoshop Camera Raw (although the list is very long). Adobe keeps updating the plug-in to support new cameras all the time. To keep track of Camera Raw and for a list of supported cameras, visit www.adobe.com/go/learn_ps_cameraraw.

Opening a Raw File

To process a raw file, you'll need to open it with Photoshop Camera Raw. Essentially, you need to develop the file, deciding during the editing stages which information to include. The Camera Raw software interprets the metadata and raw file information to generate a new image.

The good news is that adjustments you make to a raw file are all stored as metadata. The adjustments essentially reprocess the raw file data. The Camera Raw plug-in writes to a sidecar file, which contains instructions on how to treat the raw data. In fact, you can have multiple sidecar settings for each raw image.

Let's try opening a file.

1. Close any open files, and then choose File > Open.

2. Navigate to the Chapter 10 folder and select Ch10_Mountain. NEF. Do not open the file yet.

   You can choose more than one file at a time to process with the Camera Raw dialog box.

3. Hold down the Command (Ctrl) key and select the Ch10_Recover_Raw.NEF file.

4. Click the Open button to open both images into the Camera Raw window.

   Now that you have something to look at, let's take a quick look at the dialog box and its controls.

An Overview of the Camera Raw Dialog Box

At first glance, the Camera Raw dialog box can be a little overwhelming. It's okay to feel this way, because there truly are a lot of sliders and tabs. What you'll find, however, is that the controls are fairly intuitive and very powerful. Here's a quick overview of what you'll find:

A Filmstrip. If you select more than a single image to open, the images will display here. It is possible to apply star rankings to images in the Filmstrip. You can also synchronize the settings between multiple clips. Just adjust one image, select similar images, and then click the Synchronize button.

B Toggle Filmstrip. If you don't want to see the Filmstrip, just double-click the bar. You can also drag to resize the preview thumbnails.

C Camera name or file format. The camera name and model appears at the top of the window so you know more about the file.

TIP

Clipped Warnings

As you make adjustments to the developed image, it's possible to clip data (essentially a loss of detail). In the Histogram display, you'll see two small triangles. You can click the one on the left for shadows and the one on the right for highlights. When enabled, clipped shadows appear in blue, and clipped highlights appear in red. Highlight clipping will warn you if any one of the three RGB channels is clipped (fully saturated with no detail). Shadow clipping will warn you if all three RGB channels are clipped (black with no detail).

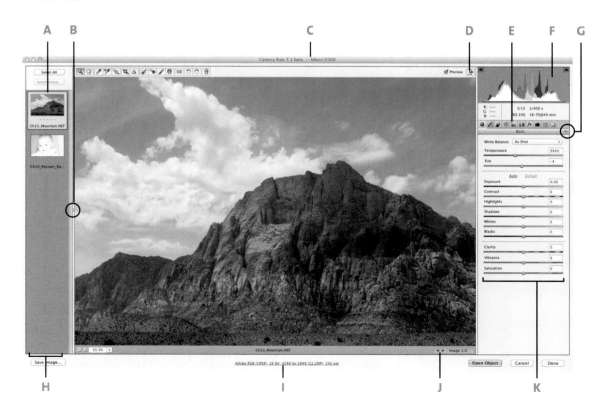

VIDEO 74:
Working with Shadows and Highlights in Raw

D Toggle full-screen mode. It is possible to maximize the Camera Raw window to see more details and a larger interface. Click to toggle between the larger and default view.

E Image adjustment tabs. There are ten tabs in total for controlling the development of Camera Raw files. More on these in the next section.

F Histogram. The Histogram displays the tonal range of the developing image. The left edge shows the shadows, whereas the right shows the highlights.

G Camera Raw Settings menu. Click this submenu to access controls for saving and loading custom settings.

H Zoom levels. You can adjust the magnification level of the image. The most accurate view is 100%, but you'll likely choose to zoom out to see the entire image in full.

I Workflow options. You can specify how images should be saved from Camera Raw and how they should be opened in Photoshop. Clicking the blue hyperlinked text lets you choose a color mode, bit depth, file size, and resolution.

J Navigation arrows. Let you switch between multiple images. These work well if the Filmstrip is hidden.

K Adjustment sliders. For each adjustment tab, you'll find a set of sliders. These controls are essential for developing the image.

Image Adjustments Tabs

The Camera Raw dialog box offers ten tabs to process your raw files. The tabs are organized by task. Normally, you'll use only some of the tabs to adjust each image. For learning purposes, let's take a quick look at each.

Basic

The Basic tab lets you make primary adjustments to white balance, color saturation, and tonality. These are the most important controls and the ones you're most likely to change.

1. Click the White Balance list and choose Auto to have Camera Raw attempt to automatically adjust white balance.

2. Let's set a different white balance. Select the White Balance tool and click on one of the clouds in the sky.

THE RAW TOOLBAR

Across the Camera Raw window is its own toolbar. You'll see several similarities to the Photoshop tools you're already familiar with:

A **ZOOM TOOL (Z).** You can click on an image to zoom into an area. You can also click and drag to make a selection for zooming.

B **HAND TOOL (H).** When zoomed, you can use the Hand tool to pan across an image. Hold down the spacebar to temporarily switch to the Hand tool.

C **WHITE BALANCE TOOL (I).** You can override the white balance settings written by the camera. Just click to select the tool, and then click on an area of the image that should be white or gray.

D **COLOR SAMPLER TOOL (S).** You can add up to eight sample points. These are useful ways to track changes in color as you make adjustments to an image. Many users will place a sampler on a white and black area of an image to track any shifts in color.

E **TARGETED ADJUSTMENT TOOL (T).** There are five different tools to choose from. Click and hold to select specific tools.

F **CROP TOOL (C).** You can crop freely or select from several preset aspect ratios. Remember that any adjustments you make are nondestructive. The cropping will be applied when the image is opened.

G **STRAIGHTEN TOOL (A).** If your photo is crooked, just select the Straighten tool. Click and drag with the Straighten tool in the preview image to establish a horizontal or vertical angle.

H **SPOT REMOVAL TOOL (B).** The Spot Removal tool lets you heal or clone imperfections in the raw file. The most typical problem you'll need to tackle is sensor or lens dust.

I **RED EYE REMOVAL TOOL (E).** If an image has red eye, select this tool and click on the center of the pupil.

J **ADJUSTMENTS BRUSH (K).** This powerful tool lets you brush in localized color and exposure adjustments. Click and brush over an area to define it, and then adjust settings with the Adjustment sliders.

K **GRADUATED FILTER (G).** This tool is similar to the Adjustments Brush except it allows you to create a transitioned adjustment gradually between two points. This is most typically used to fix areas like a sky.

L **OPEN PREFERENCES DIALOG BOX (COMMAND+K OR CTRL+K)**

M **ROTATE IMAGE LEFT (L).** Rotates the image 90° counterclockwise.

N **ROTATE IMAGE RIGHT (R).** Rotates the image 90° clockwise.

3. In the Basic controls, click Auto to have Camera Raw analyze the image and make adjustments.

4. Drag the Exposure slide to +0.35 to brighten the image.

   The image is now brighter, but some of the highlights are too bright.

5. Drag the Highlights slider to –25 to recover detail in the brightest areas.

   Let's put a little more color into the image.

6. Boost the Saturation to +45 to increase the overall color in the shot.

7. Let's bring the color in the sky out a bit more. Increase the Vibrance slider to +30 to richen the sky without oversaturating the reds in the photo.

   Now that color is correct, let's enhance Contrast. The Clarity slider is best for this. To accurately judge clarity, you'll need to change your view.

8. Double-click the Zoom tool to switch to 100% magnification.

9. Drag the Clarity slider to the right slowly. Stop when you start to notice halos near the edge of details.

   Around +45 you should notice a blooming effect; at this point you have too much clarity.

10. Drag the Clarity slider back to the left until the halos disappear. A value of 30 for this image seems to work well.

11. Click the Zoom Levels presets list and choose Fit In View.

12. Toggle the check box for Preview (near the top of the window) to see the before and after states.

13. Make sure the Preview check box is selected, and then click the Tone Curve tab.

Tone Curve

With the Tone Curve, you can fine-tune tonality in an image with controls similar to Photoshop's Curves adjustment. You can choose to use either a Parametric curve or a Point curve.

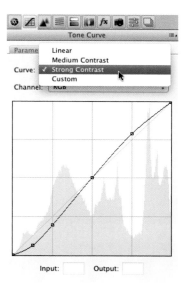

1. In the Tone Curve controls, click the Point tab.

2. From the Curve presets list, choose Strong Contrast.

   You can also click the curve and make adjustments like the Curves adjustment layer that you learned earlier.

3. Toggle the check box for Preview (near the top of the window) to see the before and after states.

4. Make sure the Preview check box is selected, and then click the Detail tab.

Detail

The Detail tab offers precise control over both sharpening an image as well as reducing noise. All raw images will need some sharpening. Noise, on the other hand, may not appear unless the image was shot with a high ISO setting or under low light.

1. Double-click the Zoom tool to switch to 100% magnification.

   It's easiest to accurately judge both sharpening and noise at a 100% view.

2. In the Detail tab, you can adjust sharpening to bring out fine image details:

   • **Amount.** Increases definition at the edges of an image. Use a lower amount for a cleaner image. When you open the file, the Camera Raw plug-in calculates the settings to use based on camera model, ISO, and exposure compensation. For this image, enter **35**.

- **Radius.** Use a low number for fine detail and a higher number if the photo lacks much detail. For this image use a lower number like **1.2** to preserve detail in the rocks.

- **Detail.** Controls how much high-frequency information is sharpened in the image and how the edges are emphasized. For this image, try a value of **50** to bring out lots of detail.

- **Masking.** Controls the edge of the mask. Using a value of zero means that everything receives the same amount of sharpening. A higher number limits the sharpening to those areas near the strongest edges.

An easy way to tell how much masking to use is to hold down the Option (Alt) key while dragging. White areas will be sharpened; black areas are ignored (masked). Try this out: Hold down the Option (Alt) key and drag slowly to the right. A value of 50 seems to be the right balance for this image.

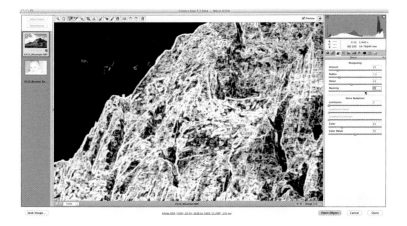

3. Noise reduction controls let you remove extra grain from the image:

- **Luminance.** Reduces luminance noise. Set this to **10** for this image (it's not very noisy).

- **Luminance Detail.** Sets a threshold for the noise reduction. Higher values preserve detail but can produce noisier results. Lower values tend to produce cleaner results but likely remove some detail. Use a value of **80** to preserve more details.

- **Luminance Contrast.** Works best for very noisy photos. A value of **80** works well for this image.

- **Color.** Reduces color noise. The default is fine for this image.

- **Color Detail.** Use a higher value to protect detailed edges. A lower value preserves more color but can result in color bleeding. The default is fine for this image.

4. Toggle the check box for Preview to see the before and after states. This image is very subtly changed.

5. Click the Zoom Levels presets list and choose Fit In View.

6. Make sure the Preview check box is selected, and then click the HSL/Grayscale tab.

HSL/Grayscale

The HSL/Grayscale tab offers fine-tuning controls for Hue, Saturation, and Luminance adjustments. The most typical use of this tab is to target a particular color or tone that needs emphasis.

1. Select the Saturation tab.

2. Drag the Red slider to the left to deemphasize the Red tones.

   Try a value of **–10** for this image.

3. Drag the Blue slider to the right to boost the sky further.

   Try a value of **+25** for this image.

   The image on the top is prior to adjustments. On the bottom, the increased saturation comes through.

Before

After

4. Switch to the Luminance tab to change the brightness of a color range.

5. Enter a value of **+15** for both the Red and Orange sliders to lighten the rocky areas of the mountain.

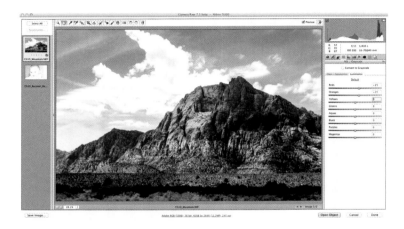

6. Toggle the check box for Preview to see the before and after states.

7. Make sure the Preview check box is selected, and then click the Split Toning tab.

Split Toning

The Split Toning controls are used when you want to color a grayscale image. It only works if you select the Convert To Grayscale in the HSL/Grayscale tab or work with a grayscale image.

Click the Lens Corrections tab.

VIDEO 75:
Lens Correction in Raw

Lens Corrections

The Lens Corrections tab attempts to compensate for defects in lens technology. The first tab lets you automatically compensate for any physical distortion based on a lens profile.

1. Click the option for the Enable Lens Profile Corrections.

Photoshop automatically removes some of the wide-angle distortion from the image. You can refine the adjustment using the third tab (Manual).

2. At the bottom, you can adjust for lens vignetting. This lets you compensate for shadows caused by the lens or hood.

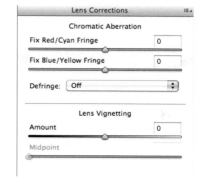

3. Click the second tab (Color) to adjust for common problems like chromatic aberration.

This particular image suffers from neither issue. Chromatic aberration shows as fringing in the color, particularly at the edges of the image. It is easiest to see aberration at 100% magnification.

4. Click the Effects tab.

Effects

The Effects tab can be used to stylize the image. It is used to add photographic imperfections that were more typical with film-based cameras. You can choose to simulate film grain or apply a post crop vignette to the edges.

1. Double-click the Zoom tool to switch to 100% magnification.

It's easiest to accurately judge grain at a 100% view.

2. Set grain to a value of **15** and a size of **35** to create a filmic type noise in the image.

3. Click the Zoom Levels presets list and choose Fit In View.

4. You can use a post crop vignette to stylize the images edges:

   - **Style.** You'll find three different options for how the vignette shades the image. The default, Highlight variety, works best for this image.

   - **Amount.** Use a negative value to darken the edges or a positive to brighten them. For this image, enter **−25**.

   - **Midpoint.** Controls how close the vignette appears to the corner of the image. Enter **60** to push out the edges.

   - **Roundness.** A positive value creates a circular effect, whereas a negative value takes on an oval shape. The default is fine for this image.

   - **Feather.** Can create a gentler transition between the affected areas. The default is fine for this image.

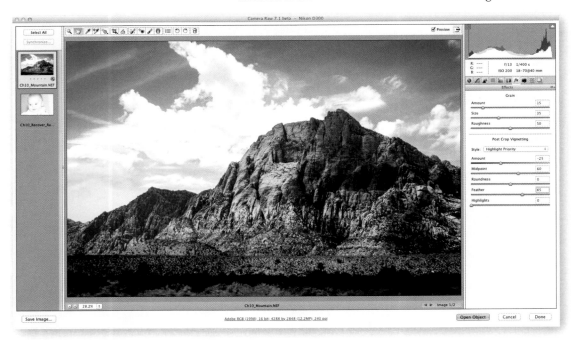

   - **Highlights.** If you're using a very dark vignette, the Highlights slider can be used to protect the brightest tones in your image.

5. Make sure the Preview check box is selected, and then click the Camera Calibration tab.

VIDEO 76:
Removing Noise
in a Raw File

Camera Calibration

The Camera Calibration tab is used to apply specific profiles to raw images. Typically, you'll use it to correct for color cast (unwanted spill) in an image. It can also compensate for unwanted behaviors by a camera's image sensor.

- **Process.** The process list lets you choose a decode technique. The newer 2010 process is a significant improvement that ships with Photoshop CS6. If you're working with raw files you've processed with an older decoder, be sure to switch and update the file for greater control and quality.

- **Camera Profile.** You'll find three types of camera profiles. The ACR options are compatible with older versions of Camera Raw. The Adobe Standard option works best for Photoshop CS6. You'll also find profiles that attempt to match the manufacturer's presets for shooting modes like neutral, standard, and vivid. In most cases (including this one) Adobe Standard is best.

  Make sure the Preview check box is selected, and then click the Presets tab.

Presets

If you like a setting you've created, you can save it as a preset, which makes it easier to reload in the future. Remember that custom presets can serve as a great starting point (especially if you have several images from the same shoot). To make a preset, just click the pad-shaped button at the bottom of the window.

Make sure the Preview check box is selected, and then click the Snapshots tab.

Snapshots

Another way to store a version of your image is to create a snapshot. Each snapshot is essentially a recording of the image's current state. You can in fact create multiple snapshots for a raw file and easily switch between them.

TIP

Other Than Raw Files?

You can in fact open TIFF and JPEG files using the Camera Raw plug-in. You need to switch to Adobe Bridge and select the desired files. Then choose File > Open In Camera Raw. You won't see any major benefits to image quality, but you can use the Camera Raw dialog box to adjust the images.

Finish the Process

When you are satisfied with the settings you've entered into the Adjustment sliders, you can decide what to do with the file. Before you open (or close) the file, you should check a few things.

1. Click the Workflow Options text at the bottom of the image.

2. Set the Depth to 16 Bits/Channel for the maximum tonal fidelity.

3. Set the resolution to **300** pixels per inch.

4. Select the Open in Photoshop as Smart Objects check box to ensure future ease in readjusting the raw processing.

5. Click OK to store the settings.

6. Select the Straighten tool (A).

7. Drag across the horizon line at the base of the mountain to straighten the image.

   When you release, you'll see a new crop box drawn on the image. If you need to reset the crop, click the Crop tool in the Tools panel and choose Clear Crop.

8. You now must choose what to do with the file. Clicking the Done button stores the Camera Raw settings in a sidecar file (or database) without opening the image in Photoshop. For this image, click Open Object to develop the raw file and send it to Photoshop.

   A new file opens in Photoshop with the raw file added as a Smart Object.

   You can now use any of the adjustment techniques you've learned in this chapter. Be sure to save the file as a layered Photoshop or TIFF file. If you need to reprocess the raw file, just double-click its thumbnail in the Layers panel to reopen the image into Camera Raw.

The image on the left is unprocessed, whereas the image on the right has had many settings adjusted.

Repairing and Improving Photos

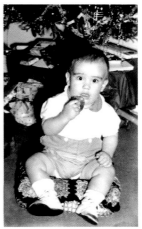

The photo on the right has had several small blemishes repaired, proper contrast restored, and a small "accident" fixed.

Damage, like fashion, is often very subjective. If you show the same set of photos to five people and ask them to comment on mistakes or damage, you'll likely get five very different answers. The reason is that people find different things distracting: A crooked photo may bother some, whereas others may dislike dust on the camera sensor. Several aspects of an image can be "wrong," but it is also impossible to have a "perfect" photo.

Because damage is so subjective, I recommend asking your clients or end customers (if possible) what needs repair. Ask them questions like, would you like anything different or can anything be better? You'll often be surprised by their answers. Sometimes a fix will be as simple as a crop or a color correction, but more often it will involve removing something from (or adding to) the picture. The world has embraced digital enhancement, and you may be surprised at how much Photoshop can do.

This chapter tackles issues like physical damage, such as rips, wrinkles, scratches, and fading as well as digital issues such as overblown skies and noise. It focuses on techniques that you can perform in less than 10 minutes. With practice you can fix 80 percent of the problems in 10 minutes; the other 20 percent you either learn to live with or spend more time on.

Image Selection

Most problems can be repaired, but not every problem is worth trying to fix. Photographers usually shoot many exposures of a subject, so they are willing to discard several that they are unhappy with. It is best to repair images that are close to their desired state; otherwise, you may spend too much time on a project (which could send it over budget in the professional world).

Working with Modern Images

The most common problems in modern photos are color or exposure issues (both of which were addressed in detail in Chapter 10, "Color Correction and Enhancement"). However, modern

photos can still suffer physical damage as well as dust on the camera sensor or lens. If the print is wrinkled or creased, it's always best to use a fresh source (either an alternate print or the negative). If the print is dusty or smudged, gently wipe it with a soft cloth, and then try to scan or rescan it. If you're forced to work with what you have (or there are issues with a digital photo), you can attempt to fix several problems within Photoshop.

Working with Historical Images

Historical photos often have more problems than modern photos. There is a much greater likelihood of physical damage. You may have to repair creases, tears, water damage, or adhesive stains (from scrapbooks). It's likely that the photos will have faded and need a boost in contrast or toning. It is generally easiest to remove color from a historical source while repairing it. The color can then be added back in during the final stages as an overlay or sepia tone.

The Retoucher's Toolbox

The process of making a photo look better is often referred to as *retouching* (while repairing damaged photos is referred to as *restoration)*. Because there are many different problems that can manifest in a photo, Photoshop offers several tools with which to respond. Knowing which tool to use is often a dilemma, but with a little bit of study and practice the process can be greatly accelerated. Let's explore how the tools work and give them a try. But first, realize that most of these tools use a paintbrush behavior. Be sure your painting tools are set to Brush size and your other tools to Precise in the Preferences dialog box (Edit > Preferences). This will allow you to better see your tools as you move them in your image.

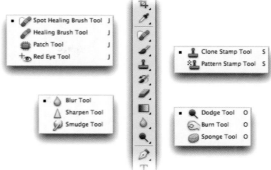

VIDEO 77:
Cloning

Clone Stamp Tool

The Clone Stamp tool works by replacing unwanted or damaged pixels with good pixels that you target. It's a popular tool that is relatively easy to use and achieves accurate results. The Clone Stamp tool allows you to set a sample point (where the good pixels are taken from), and then paint into bad areas (to cover up damage or blemishes). This technique is very powerful, because the Photoshop paint engine can use soft brushes, which can soften the stamp's edge, making the strokes more believable as they blend together better.

1. Open the Ch11_Clone.tif file from the Chapter 11 folder. You'll notice a distracting dark area in the upper-right corner.

2. Activate the Clone Stamp tool by pressing S. Roll over the tool's icon and be sure you have not accidentally activated the Pattern Stamp tool.

3. Select a soft-edged brush from the Options bar or Brush panel. If needed, modify an existing brush. A brush around 200 pixels wide works well.

TIP

Clone Across Layers

If you're working with a layered image, you can clone from all visible layers by selecting Sample All Layers. This method can be used to clone to an empty layer, which makes the cloning nondestructive. If the Sample All Layers option is deselected, only the active layer is used.

4. In the Options bar, you need to specify the alignment for the clone:

- **Select Aligned.** The sample point and painting point move parallel as you move. If the user clones and moves the cursor to the right, the sample point moves as well. This ultimately creates more variety in the cloning, which is desirable. However, it can lead to the unwanted material being repeated into the stroke.

- **Deselect Aligned.** If Aligned is not selected, the initial sample point is used (even after you stop and resume cloning). This option ensures that you are always sampling from the same pixels when starting a new stroke.

Choose the Aligned option for this image.

5. Option-click (Alt-click) within the current document (or even another open document set to the same color mode). This defines the source point for sampled pixel data. Click in the large, tan area in the upper corner.

6. Click and paint as if you were using the Brush tool. You can also try small dabs and short strokes to get a blended look. The sampled pixels are taken from the sample point and cover the unwanted pixels. Continue cloning until the entire shadow is painted over. You may need to select a new sample point to get a realistic clone. Try blending multiple strokes together and lower the opacity of the brush for the best results.

TIP

For Better Results When Cloning

- Try cloning at a low opacity and build up strokes.
- Try sampling from several different places to fill in an area.
- Experiment with blending modes.
- Clone to an empty layer by setting the Sample method to use All Layers.

Healing Brush Tool

The Healing Brush tool (J) is an innovative and powerful tool that can be used to repair blemishes in a photo. The Healing Brush tool operates much like the Clone Stamp tool. However, instead of just moving pixels from one area to another, the Healing Brush tool clones pixels while also matching the texture, lighting, and shading of the original pixels.

Because the Healing Brush samples surrounding areas, you may want to make an initial selection around the damaged area and feather it. This will give you better results on an area with strong contrast. The selection should be slightly bigger than the area that needs to be healed. It should follow the boundary of high-contrast pixels. For example, if you're healing a blemish on a subject's face, make an initial selection of the skin area to avoid mixing in the adjacent background or clothing. The selection will prevent color bleed-in from outside areas when painting with the Healing Brush tool.

VIDEO 78:
Healing Brush

1. Close any open files, and then open the file Ch11_Healing_Brush1.tif from the Chapter 11 folder.

   The photo is of a wall texture that will be used as a background layer for a composite. There is a distracting element that needs to be removed.

2. Activate the Healing Brush tool by pressing J. (Be sure to closely examine the icon and not select the Spot Healing Brush tool.)

3. Select a soft brush from the Options bar or the Brush panel.

4. Set the blending mode to Replace. This option preserves noise and texture at the stroke's edges.

5. Specify a source for repairing pixels in the Options bar. The standard option is to use Sampled. This takes pixels from the area surrounding the sample point. As the brush moves, the sample point also moves to ensure variety in the sampled source.

6. Specify the alignment option. If Aligned is selected, the sample point and painting point move parallel as you move the stroke. If Aligned is deselected, the initial sample point is Always. The Always option ensures that you are always sampling from the same area.

7. If you want to heal to an empty layer, select the Sample All Layers check box. This allows you to sample one layer, and then apply the healing to a new empty layer above. This will provide greater flexibility in your workflow. If the Sample All Layers box is deselected, only the active layer is used.

8. Add a new, empty layer above the *Background* layer.

9. In the middle of the wall, Option-click (Alt-click) on the clear brick texture.

10. Click and start to paint as if you were using a brush. Because the sampled pixels are drawn from before you click, it may be necessary to release and start over occasionally to avoid sampling the problem area.

11. After several short strokes, release the mouse to merge the sampled pixels. Before the pixels blend, you will have a visible stroke. Afterward, the stroke should gently blend.

12. Continue to heal the remaining unwanted pixels. To improve the overall blend, you can sample from a few different areas.

Spot Healing Brush Tool

The Spot Healing Brush tool was added to Photoshop as a way to harness powerful blending technology with less work (although the Healing Brush is pretty labor-free to begin with). It can quickly remove blemishes and imperfections in photos without requiring a sample point to be set. The Spot Healing Brush tool automatically samples pixels from the area around the retouched area. Let's give the tool a try.

VIDEO 79:
Spot Healing Brush

1. Close any open files, and then open the file Ch11_Spot_Healing.tif from the Chapter 11 folder.

   Look closely at the image; you'll see some acne on the child's forehead and a wet spot on her shirt. Both are easy fixes with the Spot Healing Brush tool.

2. Activate the Spot Healing Brush tool from the Tools panel.

3. Choose a soft-edged brush from the Options bar. Make the brush only slightly larger than the problem areas. For this image, a brush size of 25 pixels and a hardness of 25% will work well.

4. Set the blending mode in the Options bar to Replace to preserve noise, grain, and hair texture at the edges of the stroke.

5. Choose a Type of repair in the Options bar:

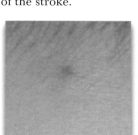

   - **Proximity Match.** Pixels from the edge of the selection are used as a patch for the selected area. This should be the first attempt at repair; if it doesn't look good, switch to the Create Texture option.

   - **Create Texture.** Pixels in the selection are used to create a texture to fix the damaged area. If the texture doesn't work, try dragging through the area one more time.

6. Click once on an area you want to fix. You can also click and drag over a larger area. After fixing the acne, touch up the wet spot on the child's shirt. If you are unhappy with the spot healing stroke, simply undo and try again with a smaller brush. You can also try stroking in different directions to modify your results.

Upon close examination, you should notice that you have healed several blemishes in the photo. If only life were so easy.

Patch Tool

The Patch tool uses the same technology as the Healing Brush tool, but it is better suited to fix large problem areas. Start using the Patch tool by selecting the area for repair and then dragging to specify the sampled area. For best results, select a small area.

The Patch tool can be used two different ways:

- **Source.** Make a selection in the area that needs repair, and then drag to an area of good pixels.

- **Destination.** Make a selection in an area of good pixels, and then drag that selection on top of the unwanted pixels.

Let's give it a try.

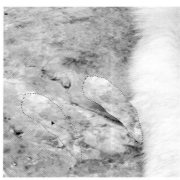

1. Close any open files, and then open the file Ch11_Patch1.tif from the Chapter 11 folder.

2. Select the Patch tool by pressing J to cycle through the tools. (It's in the same well as the Healing Brush tool.)

3. Set the Patch tool to Content-Aware. This does a superior job of removing the patched area and seamlessly blending it. The feature is new to CS6; if you're using an earlier version of Photoshop, choose Source.

4. Set the Adaptation method to Very Strict for the highest-quality patch.

5. Make a selection around the discarded cigarette butt under the cat's arm.

6. Drag into the clear area of the brick street.

7. Release and let the Patch tool blend.

8. Repeat for the remaining trash or blemishes in the shot.

TIP

Making Selections

Although you can make a selection with the Patch tool, you can always make a selection using any other selection tool (such as Marquees or Lassos), and then activate the Patch tool. The Patch tool behaves just like the Lasso tool (as far as selections go), but it may not offer the level of control you need.

Red Eye Tool

Red eye is caused when the camera flash is reflected in a subject's retinas. This happens frequently in photos taken in a dark room, because the subject's irises are open wide. There are two solutions to fixing red eye in the field:

VIDEO 80:
Content-Aware Patching

- Use the camera's red eye reduction feature. This will strobe the flash and adjust the eyes of your subject. This strobing will increase the time from when you click the camera's shutter and the photo is taken.

- Use a separate flash unit that can be held to the side or increase the distance between the lens and the flash.

Getting it right in the field is important, but you can fix it in Photoshop as well. Photoshop offers a powerful Red Eye tool that can fix flash problems. It effectively removes red eye from flash photos of people and white or green reflections in the eyes of animals.

1. Close any open files, and then open the file Ch11_Red_Eye.tif from the Chapter 11 folder.

2. Zoom into the red eye area. An easy way is to take the Zoom tool and drag around the problem area.

3. Select the Red Eye tool from the Tools panel or press J repeatedly to cycle through the tools.

4. Click in the red eye area to remove it. If you're unsatisfied with the results, choose undo and modify the two options in step 5.

5. In the Options bar, adjust the Pupil Size to a smaller number to convert a more constrained area (30% works well for this image). Adjust the Darken Pupil setting as desired to modify how dark the pupil will be after the conversion.

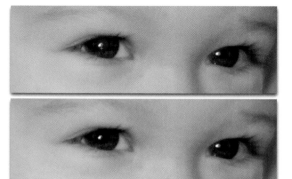

VIDEO 81:
Content-Aware
Fill/Scale/Heal

Content-Aware Fill

The Content-Aware fill option provides the ability to automatically generate new textures to fill a selected area. What happens is that Photoshop randomly synthesizes similar content to fill the area based on the source image. This is a great way to remove an object or blemish from a scene. In some cases it completes the job in one step; in others it offers a great jump start and can be touched up with a little cloning or healing.

1. Close any open files, and then open the file Ch11_Content_Aware.tif from the Chapter 11 folder.

   Before you remove the distracting items, let's straighten the image first.

2. Press C to invoke the Crop tool, and then click the Straighten button in the Options bar.

   Find a surface you think should be horizontal (or vertical). The edge of the sand is a good reference point.

3. Click and drag along a line to measure the angle.

4. In the Options bar, click the commit button to apply the new crop.

5. With the Lasso tool, make a rough selection around the woman and seaweed on the beach. Make a selection slightly larger than the woman.

6. Choose Select > Modify > Feather and enter a value of **5** pixels to blend the selection.

7. Choose Edit > Fill or press Shift+Delete to bring up the Fill dialog box.

8. From the Use menu, choose Content-Aware fill and click OK.

9. Press Command+H (Ctrl+H) to hide the selection.

   Try removing the beach chair in the lower-left corner and clean up any blemishes with the Content-Aware Fill command, Clone Stamp, or Spot Healing Brush.

This image was finished with a little additional cloning, a Levels adjustment, and a Vibrance adjustment layer.

TIP

Try, Try Again

If you don't like the first attempt Content-Aware fill generates, just choose Edit > Undo and apply another Content-Aware fill.

Content-Aware Move

The Content-Aware Move tool is the latest extension of the capabilities of cloning, healing, and Content-Aware technology in Photoshop CS6. With the Content-Aware Move tool, you can select an object, and then drag it into a new position. The original object is extracted, and its background is filled generating a new texture with Content-Aware fill technology; then the repositioned copy is blended into the image. This tool can be quite effective, especially if you adjust the Adaptation property in the Options bar to a stricter setting.

1. Close any open files, and then open the Ch11_Content_Aware_Move.tif file from the Chapter 11 folder.

   The image has some blue guides to help with composition that should be visible in the image.

2. Select the Content-Aware Move tool (J), which is in the same well as the Patch and Heal tools.

3. Drag a loose selection around the bird.

4. Choose the Very Strict Adaptation method in the Options bar to produce the most accurate blend.

5. Choose the Move mode in the Options bar to reposition the object.

The Extend mode method can be used on other images to change the apparent width or depth of an object while preserving key details.

6. Drag the bird to a new position based on the rule of thirds guides and release.

The rule of thirds guides were manually added to the image.

The image may take a few seconds to blend. Feel free to refine the blend using additional cloning or healing tools.

Blur and Sharpen Tools

Often, a photo will need a focus adjustment. Although global changes are often implemented through blur or sharpen filters, it's frequently necessary to lightly touch up an area by hand. To do this, you can use the Blur tool (to defocus) or the Sharpen tool

(to add focus or detail). Both tools are driven by brush-like settings, which allow you to change size, hardness, strength, and blending mode. Remember that if the Caps Lock key is down, brush previews are disabled.

1. Close any open files, and then open the file Ch11_Blur-Sharpen.tif from the Chapter 11 folder.

2. Select the Blur tool from the Tools panel (it looks like a water droplet).

3. Specify a brush size of approximately **120** pixels and a Strength of **50**%. The Strength settings modify how quickly the tool alters the image. Sometimes several built-up strokes are better for a subtle look.

VIDEO 84:
Blur Gallery Explored

4. Paint over an area of the edge of the white bowl to deemphasize it.

5. Choose one of the tool's blending modes. The Darken and Lighten modes are particularly useful for isolating the blurring effect to darken or lighten areas, respectively. Try the Darken mode and blur the dark floor.

6. Switch to the Sharpen tool and try enhancing parts of the image. Enable the Protect Detail option in the Options bar. The duck's bill is a good choice as well as the eyes and edges of feathers. Experiment with the Mode and Strength settings.

7. Be careful not to oversharpen the image, because it will quickly introduce visible noise and distortion.

TIP

Blur Gallery

Are you looking for another way to blur your images? You'll find three great filters for creating Field, Iris, or Tilt Shift blurs included with Photoshop CS6. Don't miss the in-depth video.

TIP

Nondestructive Tools

Both the Blur and Sharpen tools can be used nondestructively. Simply create a new layer to hold modified pixels. Then in the Options bar, select the Sample All Layers check box. The blurring or sharpening will be isolated to the selected layer.

Smudge Tool

The Smudge tool simulates dragging a finger through wet paint. The pixels are liquid and can be pushed around the screen. With the default settings, the tool uses color from where you first click and pushes it in the direction in which you move the mouse. This

tool is useful for cleaning up dust specks or flakes in a photo. Set the tool's blending mode to Lighten or Darken (depending on the area to be affected), and you'll have digital makeup to touch up the problem.

1. Close any open files, and then open the file Ch11_Smudge.tif from the Chapter 11 folder.

2. Select the Smudge tool from the Tools panel (it looks like a finger painting icon).

3. Zoom into the model's flyaway hair.

4. Experiment with the Darken and Lighten modes. These are particularly useful for isolating the smudge by pushing only dark or light pixels.

5. Smudge the edges of the hair pixels. Experiment by switching blending modes: You can always undo the smudge, and then change the tool's mode and resmudge. To quickly cycle blending modes, press the Shift+= or Shift +- shortcut keys.

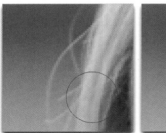
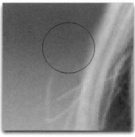

Using the Smudge tool's Darken mode lets you push darker pixels over lighter pixels.

TIP

Smudge Tool for Historical Images Too!

The Smudge tool also works great for touching up blemishes in historical photos. Rips, tears, and cracks can easily be filled in using the Smudge tool's Lighten and Darken modes. You can also try the Blur tool in a similar fashion.

Dodge and Burn Tools

The Dodge and Burn tools are known as toning tools. They allow you finer control over lightening or darkening your image. These tools simulate traditional techniques used by photographers. In a darkroom, the photographer would regulate the amount of light on a particular area of a print. These tools are particularly helpful when touching up faded photos, especially when repairing water damage. Let's try out both tools.

VIDEO 85:
Dodge and Burn

1. Close any open files, and then open the file Ch11_Dodge_Burn.tif from the Chapter 11 folder.

2. Duplicate the current layer because the Dodge and Burn tools are destructive. Closely examine the four faces. You should notice that the two on the right look washed out, and the two on the left are a bit dark.

3. Select the Dodge tool from the Tools panel. Adjust the brush to be soft and large (approximately 80 pixels). Set the tool to adjust the Midtones.

4. Paint over the shadowed faces on the left half of the picture to bring out the darkest areas a bit.

5. Select the Burn tool from the Tools panel. Adjust the brush to be soft and large (approximately 80 pixels). Set the tool to adjust the Highlights and set an Exposure setting of **20**%.

6. Paint over the washed-out faces on the left half of the picture to restore the contrast a bit.

7. Continue to touch up areas in the photos as needed. Lower exposure settings are generally more desirable.

TIP

Protect Those Tones

If you are working on color images, be sure to use the Protect Tones option for the Dodge and Burn tools. Simply select the check box in the Options bar to get more natural-looking results.

PHOTO BY JAMES BALL

Sponge Tool

The Sponge tool is very elegant and efficient. This toning tool can be used to make subtle adjustments in color saturation or grayscale contrast. It can also be used during conversion processes to prepare images for commercial printing or television. The Sponge tool allows you to gently desaturate (or saturate) areas by brushing over them.

1. Close any open files, and then open the file Ch11_Sponge.tif from the Chapter 11 folder.

2. When converting RGB images into CMYK, there is often a shift in colors. This is because RGB has a wider color gamut than CMYK, and it can display more colors. Photoshop allows you to highlight the areas that are "out of gamut" or will shift when you convert modes. Choose View > Gamut Warning. The gray areas represent out-of-gamut areas.

3. Select the Sponge tool by pressing O to cycle through the tools, or choose it from the Tools panel.

4. Adjust the brush to a large size and set it to have soft edges.

5. Set the tool to Desaturate and adjust the flow to a lower value. It is generally better to use a slower flow and make several applications.

6. Paint over the gray gamut warning areas with the Sponge tool until they disappear.

7. If needed, you can switch the Sponge tool to Saturate to boost areas. If you see a gray gamut warning, you've gone too far.

8. When you're done, you can convert the image to CMYK by selecting Image > Mode > CMYK. CMYK conversion is covered again in Chapter 16, "Printing, PDF, and Specialized File Types."

9. To complete the image, choose File > Save As, pick a new destination, and rename the file to **Ch11_Sponge_CMYK.tif**.

TIP

Gamut Warning Color

If you'd like to change the gamut warning color so it stands out more, open your Photoshop Preferences. In the Transparency & Gamut controls, click the swatch next to Color to set a new warning color.

Lens Correction

The Lens Correction filter is designed to fix common flaws in an image (such as barrel distortion, lens vignettes, and chromatic aberration). The filter can be run on 8- or 16-bit-per-channel images that use the RGB or Grayscale image mode. The filter can also correct perspective problems caused by camera tilt.

1. Close any open files, and then open the file Ch11_Lens_ Profile.tif from the Chapter 11 folder.

2. Choose Filter > Convert for Smart Filters to ensure flexibility in editing.

3. Choose Filter > Lens Correction.

   A new window opens. Look in the bottom-left corner for information about the camera and lens used for the shot (this is included in the metadata the camera wrote to the original file).

4. Choose a manufacturer from the Camera Make menu. In this case choose Nikon Corporation.

5. From the Camera Model menu, choose the correct camera model. In this case just choose Nikon D300s.

6. From the Lens Model menu, choose the correct lens. The closest match is the 17.0-70.0 mm f/2.8-4.5.

7. Switch to the Custom tab for advanced controls.

8. Click the Show Grid option at the bottom of the window.

   Let's compensate for the low angle, which is causing some keystoning.

9. Set the Vertical Perspective to −50.

TIP

Create Your Own Profiles?

If you want to create your own lens profiles, Adobe has a great utility. Visit http://labs.adobe.com/technologies/lensprofile_creator/ for full details.

VIDEO 86:
Lens Correction

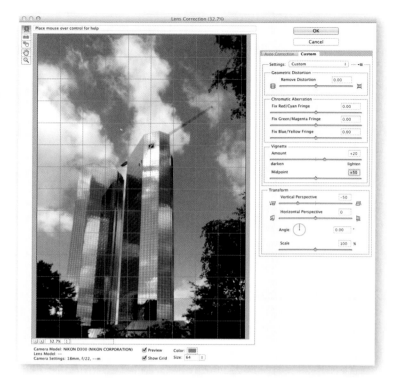

10. Set Vignette Amount to **20** to further brighten the edges.

11. Click OK to apply the correction.

You can double-click the Lens Correction filter in the Layers panel to open the Smart filter for future edits.

Adaptive Wide-Angle Correction

A common flaw caused by wide-angle lens is distortion. If you shoot with a very large field of view (wide-angle rectilinear or full-frame fisheye), the photo will often show a bending of straight lines and other distortion near the edges of the photo. The Adaptive Wide Angle Correction plug-in (new to CS6) can fix perceptible distortion. The plug-in requires only a small amount of input from a user to know which lines should be straight.

Let's try using the command on a very distorted image.

1. Close any open files, and then open the Ch11_Adaptive_Wide_Angle.tif file from the Chapter 11 folder.

2. Choose Filter > Convert for Smart Filters to ensure flexibility in editing.

3. Choose Filter > Wide-Angle Correction.

4. Choose a correction method from the pop-up menu. You can choose among Fisheye, Perspective, Full Spherical, or Auto.

   Try out the different methods to see their different approaches. For this project, Auto works well.

VIDEO 87:
Adaptive Wide-Angle
Correction

5. Select the Constraint tool in the upper-left corner of the new panel.

6. Hold down the Shift key to define a horizontal or vertical anchor.

   Draw in the center of the image to start; then you'll work your way out wider.

7. Click and drag to define a straight line along the edge of one of the buildings.

   The image updates to minimize distortion.

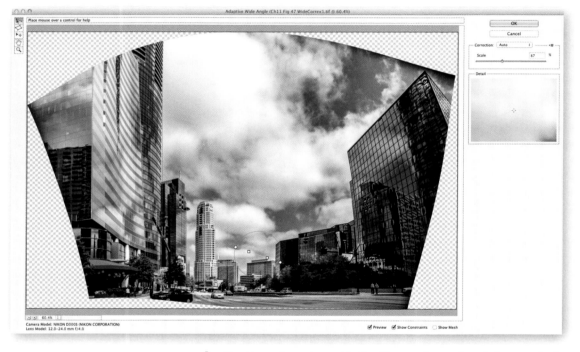

8. Continue dragging with the Constraint tool to define vertical and horizontal surfaces.

   Hold down the Shift key when dragging. The line should properly help define a portion of the image as perpendicular or vertical. You can also drag the center control points to rotate a constraint option.

9. Adjust the Scale slider to minimize the presence of gaps in the image.

10. Click OK to apply the effect.

11. Crop the image or use the Clone Stamp tool to fill in the gaps.

Restoration in Action

Learning how to fix damaged areas in photos is not a step-by-step process. Rather, it is learning how to identify problems and make strategic decisions about which techniques to employ to fix the image. Practice is the best path to becoming a skillful retoucher. However, you can expect good results if you know which tools to use. I have personally seen students become proficient using Photoshop's rich suite of tools in just a few weeks.

Soft Focus

Cameras are much more likely to generate a soft focus under low light. The Smart Sharpen filter has the most options of any sharpening filter built into Photoshop. It allows you to choose the sharpening algorithm as well as control the amount of sharpening in shadow and highlight areas. This filter can produce dramatically better quality, but do not expect results like you see in a TV police drama.

1. Close any open files, open the Ch11_Sharpen1.tif file, and zoom the document window to 100%. This will give you the most accurate view of the sharpening.

2. Choose Filter > Sharpen > Smart Sharpen and select the Advanced radio button.

3. Click and drag the image in the preview window so you can better see the wood texture.

4. Adjust the controls in the Sharpen tab:

   - **Amount.** Sets the amount of sharpening. A higher value increases contrast between edge pixels, which gives the appearance of more sharpness.

   - **Radius.** Determines the number of pixels surrounding the edge pixels that will be affected by the sharpening. A greater radius value means that edge effects will be more obvious, as will the sharpening.

Oversaturated Colors

If you sharpen a color photo and you get oversaturated colors, switch to the Lab image mode. Apply the filter only to the Lightness channel.

- **Remove.** Allows you to set the sharpening algorithm to be used:

  - **Gaussian Blur.** Is used by the Unsharp Mask filter. It works well on images that appear slightly out of focus.

  - **Lens Blur.** Detects edges and detail in an image. It provides finer sharpening of detail and can reduce halos caused by sharpening.

  - **Motion Blur.** Attempts to reduce the effects of blur caused by camera or subject movement. You will need to set the Angle control if you choose Motion Blur.

- **Angle.** Set this to match the direction of motion. It's only available when using the Remove control's Motion Blur option.

- **More Accurate.** Allows Photoshop to spend more time processing the file. It generates more accurate results for the removal of blurring.

5. You can refine the sharpening of dark and light areas—try using the Shadow and Highlight tabs. These controls should be used if you start to see halos in light or dark areas:

- **Fade Amount.** Adjusts the amount of sharpening in the highlights or shadows regions.

- **Tonal Width.** Controls the range of tones in the shadows or highlights that are modified. Smaller values restrict the adjustments to smaller regions.

- **Radius.** Controls the size of the area around each pixel that determines if a pixel is considered a shadow or a high-

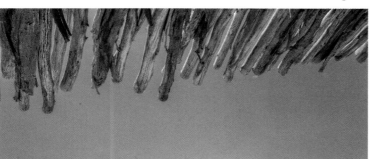

light. Moving the slider to the left specifies a smaller region; moving the slider to the right defines a larger region.

6. When you're satisfied, click OK to apply the filter.

Faded Historical Photos

VIDEO 88:
Restore a Damaged Photo

A common problem with old black-and-white or sepia-toned photos is that they fade over time. You can use a Levels or Curves adjustment, but both commands often introduce color artifacts into the image. A few extra steps are needed to get the best results.

1. Close any open files, and then open the file Ch11_Fading_Historical.tif from the Chapter 11 folder.

2. With the Eyedropper tool, sample the color tint if you want to retain it in the finished piece.

3. Leave the photo in RGB mode but strip away the color. Choose Image > Adjust > Desaturate or press Shift+Command+U (Shift+Ctrl+U).

4. Perform a Levels adjustment and restore the white-and-black points. Drag the black Input Levels slider and the white Input Levels slider toward the center.

5. Add a Solid Color fill layer by choosing Layer > New Fill Layer > Solid Color. Click OK. The Foreground color you previously sampled will load automatically.

6. Set the Color Fill layer to use the Color blending mode. Adjust the Opacity slider as desired.

TIP

Colorize Another Way

You can use a Hue/Saturation adjustment layer to tint the image. Just click the Colorize option and adjust the sliders to taste.

VIDEO 89:
Replacing Skies

Blown-out Skies

A professional photographer can spend a good part of a day waiting for the perfect sky and weather conditions. You, however, may not be as lucky. Skies will often be washed out and appear missing due to overexposure. One solution is to take pictures of the sky when it looks its best, and then use a few techniques to combine two or more images into a new composite.

1. Close any open files, and then open the file Ch11_Fix_Sky.tif from the Chapter 11 folder.

2. Use the Color Range command (Select > Color Range) to choose the sky region.

3. Subtract any stray selections in the lower half of the photo by using the Lasso tool and holding down the Option (Alt) key. Alternatively, switch to Quick Mask mode for more detailed touch-up of the selection.

4. Double-click the *Background* layer to float it. Name the layer **Boat** and click OK.

5. Invert the selection by choosing Select > Inverse or by pressing Shift+Command+I (Shift+Ctrl+I).

6. Use the Refine Edge command to improve the selection and add a layer mask to the image.

7. Click the Add layer mask button to mask the sky area.

   Let's now add a new sky. You'll find a diverse collection of skies in the Chapter 11 folder in a subfolder named Skies. Match one that has the right color and time of day for this photo (try DSC_2197.jpg). Feel free to use the others for future projects.

8. Choose File > Place and select the file DSC_2197.jpg. Press Return (Enter) to apply the placed photo.

9. Drag the sky photo behind your masked image. Use the Free Transform command to scale and position the clouds. There may be fringe on the edges that will need touching up.

10. Select the Layer Mask thumbnail in the Layers panel.

11. Open the Properties panel and click the Mask Edge button to refine the mask as desired.

12. Touch up any problem areas on the Layer Mask. Use the Smudge tool set to Darken mode to touch up the area around the trees on the right of the frame. You can also touch up the Layer Mask by using a paintbrush and black set to 20% Opacity. Brush over areas that need to be blended.

13. Blur the sky slightly so it better matches the depth of field in the image. Use the trees for guidance. You can use the Gaussian blur filter (Filter > Blur > Gaussian Blur) set to a value of 4–6 pixels.

14. To make the colors match better, you can place a second copy of the sky on top. Be sure just the blue sky is covering the photo. Set the blending mode to Overlay or Soft Light and lower the Opacity of the layer.

The completed image, Ch11_Fix_Sky_Completed.tif, is on the DVD if you'd like to examine it more closely.

TIP

Shooting Skies

The desert or the ocean is the best place to shoot the sky. This is often because the amount of environmental and light pollution is greatly reduced. Don't worry if this isn't an option for you; just keep your eyes out for a great day with beautiful skies and remember to shoot some still plates for your collection.

Remove Grain/Noise

Often, distracting noise or grain will appear in your image. This is typically caused by shooting photos with a high ISO setting on a digital camera, but it can also be caused by underexposure or a long shutter speed. A lower-quality consumer camera is also more likely to exhibit noise problems. Additionally, film grain can be picked up by a scanner and cause problems as well.

The most common type of noise is luminance (grayscale) noise where the noise does not have varying colors. This noise is usually more pronounced in one channel of the image, usually the blue channel. By adjusting for noise on a per-channel basis, higher-image quality can be maintained. Let's give it a try:

1. Close any open files, and then open the file Ch11_Remove Grain.tif from the Chapter 11 folder.

2. Activate the Channels panel and view each channel separately. Click the channel's name to isolate it. Do this for each channel.

   You should notice a large amount of noise in the Blue channel.

3. Activate all three channels by clicking the RGB composite channel.

4. Choose Filter > Reduce Noise.

5. Select the Advanced radio button to enable per-channel corrections. This allows for additional correction to be added at the channel level.

TIP

Remove Noise from a Raw File

You learned how to remove noise and grain from a raw file in Chapter 10. Go back and watch video #76 if needed.

6. Switch to the Blue channel within the filter's dialog box and adjust Strength and Preserve Details as desired.

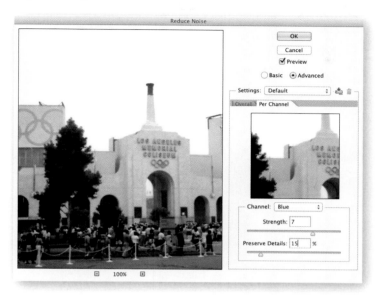

Adding Lens Blur

Selectively blurring an image can help your viewer find a focal point. Photoshop offers a realistic lens blur that also produces depth-of-field blurring. This allows some objects to be in focus while others fall out of focus. You can be very specific in regard to the blurring if you make an accurate alpha channel to serve as a depth matte. The depth matte defines how far away things are from the camera. Black areas in the alpha channel are treated as being the foreground, whereas white areas are seen as being in the distance.

VIDEO 90:
Lens Blur

1. Close any open files, and then open the file Lens Ch11_Lens Blur.tif from the Chapter 11 folder.

An alpha channel has already been added to the image. It was created using the Calculations command and Quick Mask mode (see Chapter 5, "Selection Tools and Techniques").

2. Make sure the RGB composite channel is selected.

3. Choose Filter > Blur > Lens Blur to run the Lens Blur filter.

4. Choose the alpha channel from the Source menu. You can click the Invert box if you need to reverse the blur. For faster previews, choose Faster. When you're ready to see the final appearance, select More Accurate.

5. Adjust the Iris shape to curve or rotate the iris. Photoshop mimics how a traditional lens operates. Even if you are not an experienced photographer, you can twiddle and adjust as desired.

6. Move the Blur Focal Distance slider until the desired pixels are in focus. Additionally, you can click inside the preview image to set the Blur Focus Distance.

7. You can add Specular Highlights by adjusting the Threshold slider. You must set the cutoff point for where highlights occur. Then increase the highlights with the Brightness slider.

8. Finally, it's a good idea to add a little noise/grain back into the image. Normally, the blur obscures this, but putting it back in makes the photo seem more natural as opposed to processed.

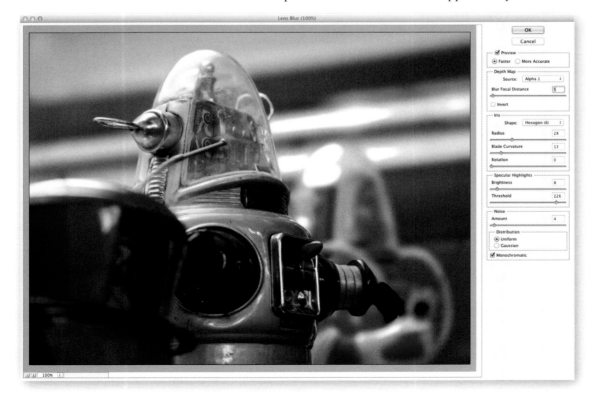

Using Vanishing Point

Vanishing Point is a special plug-in that allows for perspective cloning. Essentially, a user can identify perspective planes (such as sides of a building), and then apply edits such as painting, cloning, copying or pasting, and transforming. All the edits to the image honor the perspective of the plane you are working on; basically, you are retouching the image dimensionally. This produces significantly more realistic results, but it does take some time to set up.

1. Close any open files, and then open the file Ch11_VP.tif from the Chapter 11 folder. This photo of a sign is marred because one of the letters is burned out. With Vanishing Point you can clone or repair the sign.

2. Invoke the Vanishing Point dialog box by choosing Filter > Vanishing Point. This will bring up a custom interface for defining the perspective planes, as well as tools for editing the image.

    You must first specify planes to define perspective in the image. For this photo, you want to replace the burned-out letter O.

3. Choose the Create Plane tool and define the four corner nodes of the plane surface. You can use the edges of the sign for guidance when creating the plane. See the figure for guidance.

4. After creating the four corner nodes, Photoshop allows you to move, scale, or reshape the plane. An accurate plane means accurate vanishing point effects, so take your time. If there's a problem with a corner node's placement, the bounding box and grid turn red or yellow. You must then move a corner node until the bounding box and grid turn blue or green. This means that the plane is valid. A plane that is yellow or red is a problem plane and needs to be adjusted.

VIDEO 91:
Vanishing Point

5. Grab the left edge of the plane and extend it to the left, and then repeat for the right edge. This gives you more room for cloning. Strokes can be painted only onto the grid.

6. Zoom in so you can make a more accurate selection.

7. Select the Stamp tool in the Vanishing Point window. Option-click (Alt-click) on the illuminated letter O that is on the front of the sign. You can also experiment with the Heal option to improve the blending.

8. Position your painting cursor (using the preview for guidance) and clone the illuminated letter over the burned-out letter.

9. When you're satisfied with the perspective cloning, click OK.

Table 11.1 shows the keyboard shortcuts to make Vanishing Point easy to use.

Table 11.1   Vanishing Point Shortcut Keys

Result	Mac OS	Windows
Zoom tool	Z	Z
Zoom 2x (temporary)	X	X
Hand tool	H	H
Switch to Hand tool	Spacebar	Spacebar (temporary)
Zoom in	Command+=	Ctrl+=
Zoom out	Command+- (minus)	Ctrl+- (minus)
Increase brush size	]	] (Brush, Clone tools)
Decrease brush size	[	[(Brush, Clone tools)
Increase brush	Shift+]	Shift+] (Brush, Clone tools) hardness
Decrease brush	Shift+[	Shift+[(Brush, Clone tools) hardness
Undo last action	Command+Z	Ctrl+Z
Deselect all	Command+D	Ctrl+D
Hide selection	Command+H	Ctrl+H and planes
Repeat last duplicate	Command+Shift+T	Ctrl+Shift+T and move
Fill a selection	Option-drag	Alt-drag under the pointer with image
Create a duplicate of	Command+Option-drag	Ctrl+Alt-drag a floating selection
Render plane grids	Option-click OK	Alt-click OK
Exit plane creation	Command+. (period)	Ctrl+. (period)

Using the
Type Tool

12

Although Photoshop initially had *very* primitive type tools, its capabilities have grown significantly because many people choose to create and stylize type within Photoshop. This flexibility allows many designers to start (and even finish) designs inside Photoshop.

For many tasks, like multimedia and web graphics, Photoshop plays an important role. In fact, if raster graphics are the intended output, Photoshop offers a full suite of typographic controls. Even if you intend to use other tools for text layout, it's worth spending time learning Photoshop. With support for precision layout as well as the use of text and paragraph styles, the Photoshop CS6 upgrade takes typography to a new level.

The Photoshop text engine is the standard that Adobe uses throughout its software products. Working with type might seem foreign at first, but you'll find that type is fairly easy once you understand a few key areas of the interface.

Open the file Ch12_Colonial_Postcard. psd to explore using type in a finished design. In this case Photoshop was used to design a postcard.

Role of Type

Many people rely on pictures to tell a story, but there's just no getting around the use of type. Sure, a picture of a bus on a street sign would clue most into realizing they were standing at a bus stop, but you couldn't stop there. Without accurate use of a few letters and numbers, you'd have little confidence in the route or timing of the service. It is proper use of type that designers must rely on to communicate vital information to audiences. If you can combine this functional purpose with a better sense of style and control, you can improve the professional appearance of your designs.

Choosing Fonts

Font choice can be a very tough decision for you if you are a new designer. You can easily become overwhelmed with the sheer quantity of options. To simplify the process, you need to approach this decision with a triage mentality and consider a few guiding questions:

- **Readability.** Is the font clear to read at the size you are using it? Are all the characters in the line readable? If you look at it quickly and then close your eyes, what do you remember about the text block?

- **Style.** Does the font convey the right emotion for your design? The text on an action movie poster is very different from that advertising the latest romantic comedy. Type is a like wardrobe; picking the right font is essential to the success of the design.

- **Flexibility.** Does the font mix well with others? Does it come in various weights (such as bold, italic, and book) that make it easier to convey significance when using that font?

These are my three guiding principles, but there are other constraints at play as well that require much more analysis. It's a good idea to formally study typography if you want to work in a design field professionally. At the bare minimum, you can at least read a few books. I strongly recommend *The Mac Is Not a Typewriter* (Peachpit Press, 2003) by Robin Williams and *Stop Stealing Sheep & Find Out How Type Works* (Adobe Press, 2002) by Erik Spiekermann and E.M. Ginger. But for now, let's go over the essentials.

Serif vs. Sans Serif

A font has many characteristics, but the presence or lack of serifs is one of the easiest to identify. Serifs are the hooks that distinguish the details of letter shape. Sans serif fonts tend to be more uniform in shape. Choosing which type of font to use will greatly depend on your needs.

Table 12.1 shows the pros and cons of serif versus sans serif fonts.

Table 12.1   Comparison of Serif vs. Sans Serif Fonts

	Pros	Cons
Serif	• Increased readability • More traditional • More options available due to longer history	• Thin lines can cause problems for low-resolution printing or applications like video and Internet
Sans Serif	• More modern • Can compress more information into a smaller space • Optimal for onscreen usage	• Letter shapes not often as unique • Can be harder to read if too stylized

X-Height, Ascenders, and Descenders

You'll quickly notice that point size for fonts is a very relative measurement. The apparent size of your text will depend on which font you choose and what resolution your document is set to. Most designers look at the height of a lowercase x when deciding which font to use, because a lowercase x is a very clean letter with a distinct top and bottom. By comparing the x characters, you can quickly compare and contrast fonts. This measurement is combined with ascenders (strokes that go above the top of the x) and descenders (strokes that go below the bottom of the x, or the baseline). These three aspects provide a visual clue to the font's purposes. Heavily stylized fonts (such as those used for titles or logos) often have greater variety than those intended for a page layout, where the text must take up little space yet remain easy to read.

Font Weight/Font Families

If a font comes in several weights (such as bold, condensed, book, italic), it offers increased flexibility. These different versions of a font are called a font family. When choosing a font to use in a design, pros often look to font families. Some of the best designs use a single font family but mix weights. This allows a consistent look with the added benefit of a consistent style throughout. You'll find font families listed next to the font name in the Options bar and in the Character panel.

Using Vector Type

Now that you have a clear understanding of the basics, you can start to use text in Photoshop. Your goal should be to keep your fonts as vector type as much as possible. Type will be created as a vector if you use the Horizontal or Vertical Type tools. Vector type uses curved lines, not pixels, that can be scaled and transformed infinitely without quality loss. This allows you to make last-minute changes, like scaling the headline bigger on your print advertisement when the client requests it, and allows greater flexibility for changes throughout the design process.

Type Tool

Photoshop has two kinds of type tools that use vectors: the Horizontal Type tool and (the much less used) Vertical Type tool.

Let's try adding some text using the Horizontal Type tool.

1. Create a new document by pressing Command+N (Ctrl+N). From the Preset list choose 800 × 600 and click OK.

2. Press T (for Type) to select the Horizontal Type tool or click the Text icon (a black letter T). You can then press Shift+T to cycle through the four Type tools as needed. As an alternative, you can click and hold on the T in the Tools panel to see a flyout list of tools.

TIP

Type Tool Presets

If you have a specific kind of text combo that you use a lot (say Bawdy Bold at 45 points with a tracking value of 50), you can save it. Just enter all your text settings as desired, and then click the menu in the upper-left corner of the Options bar to add new Tool Presets (just click the pad of paper icon).

NOTE

Type Mask Tool

The Horizontal Type Mask tool or Vertical Type Mask tool is used to create a selection in the shape of the type. These selections can be used for copying, moving, stroking, or filtering (just like any other selection) on an active layer. Text created with the Type Mask tool is not editable like other text layers.

3. Notice that several options related to type are now available in the Options bar. These options are discussed in the following sections. For now, click the color well in the Options bar and specify a color that will contrast with your background.

VIDEO 92:
Formatting Text

4. Click once inside your document; a new type layer is added. Type a few words to practice. Good? OK, now you'll learn what all those newly available options mean.

5. Click the Commit button in the Options bar and leave this document open as you experiment with other typographic controls.

Point Text vs. Paragraph Text

When adding text to a document, you have two options that determine how that text behaves. Point Text adds text beginning at the point where you click and continuing from there. Paragraph Text constrains the text to a box and will wrap when it hits the edge. To create a Paragraph Text block, click and drag using the Type tool to define the paragraph area first. Which option you choose depends on your design needs.

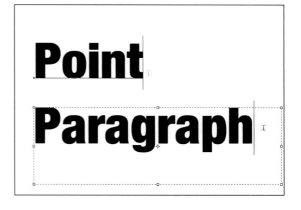

Table 12.2 shows the pros and cons of using Point Text and Paragraph Text.

Table 12.2   Point Text vs. Paragraph Text

	Pros	Cons
Point Text	• Instant results • Good for small amounts of text • More flexible when using Warped Text (see "Warped Text" later in the chapter)	• Can lead to manual reformatting, including inserting manual hard returns
Paragraph Text	• Adds column-like behavior to page layout • Allows for use of hyphenation and Adobe Every-line Composer for smoother layout (more on this option in the "Paragraph Panel" section of this chapter)	• If text is too large at the start, you may not see the text entry • Can require designer to resize text block to accommodate copy or font changes

NOTE

Number of Fonts

There are no hard and fast rules about how many fonts to use on a page, but here are a few "basics":

- Using a font family (with mixed weights/styles) is best.
- Using two fonts is good.
- Using three fonts is OK.
- Using four fonts—are you sure?
- Using five fonts or more— you're in trouble!

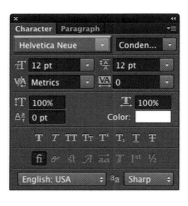

Character Panel

The bulk of your control over type lies in the Character panel. This panel gives you access to options that allow you to control the characters in your text block including basics such as font, size, and weight, as well as important advanced controls like kerning and baseline shift. If you don't see the Character panel icon in the Options bar, choose Window > Character. There are several controls here—all of them are essential, so let's take a look at each one.

Font Family

Setting the font family simply means picking the font you want to use. Nothing too complex, but navigating hundreds of fonts in your Font Family menu can be time-consuming. Here are a few tips to help you choose a font quickly:

- You can click in the Font Family field and just start typing the font name to jump through the list.

- If a text layer is active or even just selected, you can click in the Font Family field. Use the up and down arrows to cycle through loaded fonts.

- To make selection easy, you can see the fonts in their actual face. Just click the Font Family down arrow to see a font preview.

TIP

Name That Font

Are you trying to match a particular font for your design? A useful website is www.WhatTheFont.com, which offers visual recognition for type. Simply load a JPEG file with a text sample, and it will try to match the font to an extensive database.

Font Style

Certain fonts have multiple styles or weights—just look at the Font Style menu, which is to the right of the Font Family menu. Click the triangle to access the menu and choose variations like bold, italic, and condensed (as long as the font was designed to include them). This is a *much* better option than using the Type Enhancements buttons at the bottom of the Character panel. The Type

Enhancement buttons simply thicken the character (for faux bold) or skew it (for faux italic). This can produce text that is much harder to read and is generally not very elegant. It is always best to use the true bold or italic versions created by the font's designer.

Font Size

Traditionally, type is measured in points. The PostScript standard (which was developed for use by commercial and laser printers) uses 72 points per inch. However, this principle doesn't hold up very well, because different fonts will have different x-heights.

Instead of worrying about point size, just use it as a "relative" measurement. Increase the point size to make text appear larger, decrease it to reduce the size of the text. If you need to be more precise, such as designing text for the web, you can measure text in pixels.

To switch text measurement to pixels:

1. Press Command+K (Ctrl+K) to launch the Preferences dialog box.

2. Choose the Units & Rulers category.

3. In the Units area, switch Type to be measured in Pixels if you want a more precise measurement.

Leading

Pronounced "*led*-ing" as in the metal, not "*lead*-ing" as in sheep, leading is the space between lines of type. The name comes from when strips of lead were used on a printing press to space out lines of text. Adjust your leading value to improve your text's readability. Leading works best when you are using Paragraph Text. By default, the leading should be set to Auto; however, adjust as needed to fit text into your design. Just be careful to avoid setting leading too tight; otherwise, your ascenders and descenders will collide, resulting in a negative impact on readability.

Welcome

improper kerning

Welcome

proper kerning

Kerning

Adjusting the space between individual letter pairs is called kerning. So what, you say, why bother? Design pros *always* check their kerning. Adjusting the space between letter pairs produces a better optical flow. Think of each word as existing in a stream; you are trying to balance out the spacing between each letter so the water flows evenly between each letter pair.

Taking the extra effort to kern letters will produce text that is easy to read. This is especially true as your text block gets bigger. Inexpensive fonts and freeware fonts usually have the most kerning problems because it takes a lot of effort for a fontmaker to set proper kerning for every possible letter combination. Cheap or free fonts are just that–cheap or free and may have kerning issues. Although you can adjust kerning using the Character panel, here's a more "organic" method:

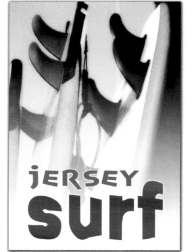

For a more artistic example of good kerning, open the project file Ch12_Surf_Card.psd to examine its construction.

1. With the Type tool, click between two letters in the file you created earlier.

2. Hold down the Option (Alt) key and use the left arrow key to tighten the spacing between a character pair, or use the right arrow key to loosen spacing.

3. Release the Option (Alt) key and then use the arrow keys to move to the next pair.

4. Hold down the Option (Alt) key and repeat kerning as desired.

tracking

loose tracking

tracking

tight tracking

Tracking

Kerning adjusts the space between pairs of letters, but tracking affects all letters in the text block or the selection. Tracking can be adjusted to fit text into a smaller space, for example, if you must fit a certain number of characters on a line without reducing point size.

Conversely, you might choose a loose track to improve readability (especially if you're using all caps). Tracking, like kerning, is subjective and can be learned best by studying professional examples and looking for inspiration and guidance.

Vertical Scale

Do you need to make the text a little taller? Perhaps you want to make the text look skinnier, or you are trying to create a stretched look. Well, you can adjust the vertical scale from 0–1000% if you are so inclined. Normally, this causes unintentional fluctuations in font appearance. If you are working on a shared computer, be sure to inspect this option and make sure it's set to 100% before designing to avoid unintentional scaling.

Horizontal Scale

You can use horizontal scale to compress (or expand) the width of text. By scaling down text, you can pack more text on a line. Increasing horizontal scale can make the text appear "fatter." Normally, this kind of scaling is less desirable than trying to find a font that better matches your design goals. Be sure to check to see if scaling is applied before designing with the Type tool.

Baseline Shift

Earlier, baseline was discussed when you learned about x-height. This is the virtual line that the characters sit on. If you need to reposition elements such as quote marks or apostrophes for design purposes, this property is useful.

Text Color

By default, text in Photoshop is black. Although black is a very functional color (a third of my wardrobe is black or a shade of black), it won't always work for your designs. Click the Color Swatch to load the Color Picker window. Click a radio button for the color model you want to work with, and then adjust the Color slider as desired. Click in the Color Field to choose the color you want. If you need to use a Pantone color (or at least a close equivalent), click the Color Libraries button (selecting colors is covered in depth in Chapter 6, "Painting and Drawing Tools").

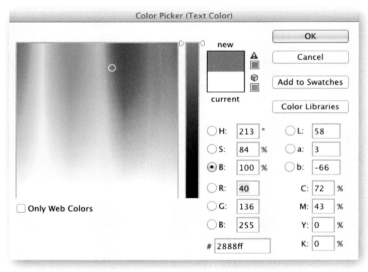

Type Enhancement Buttons

Herein lies a collection of treasures as well as several booby traps. Some of the Type Enhancement buttons are truly useful, but others are just plain bad design and should only be used in a pinch:

- **Faux Bold.** Faux is French for *fake*. Do not use a faux bold if a true bold is available within the font style you are using. This button just makes the text thicker and harder to read.

- **Faux Italic.** Same deal here: Skewing the text to the right does not make it italic. Always choose an italic version of the font you are using from the Font Style field.

- **All Caps.** Formats the text in all uppercase letters; just click this button instead of retyping.

- **Small Caps.** Works well for titles and in certain layouts. It replaces all lowercase text with a smaller version of the capital letter.

- **Subscript.** Used for scientific notation and other specialty purposes where a character is reduced in size and lowered below the baseline.

- **Superscript.** Used for specialty purposes such as showing mathematical power. This reduces the character's size and moves it above the baseline.

- **Underline.** Draws a line below the text. You may choose to manually add a line on another layer for better control.

- **Strikethrough.** Places a line through the characters to indicate text for removal.

italic

faux italic

Notice the dramatic differences between choosing italic from the Font Style menu as opposed to choosing the Type Enhancement button.

H_2O

subscript

$E=mc^2$

superscript

Ligatures

Some fonts contain additional ornamental elements. These characters can be difficult to access because they are not on standard keys. To make it easier to find them, the Character panel has special buttons near the bottom. Which options are available depends on the chosen font. These can include ligatures, fractions, swashes, ornaments, ordinals, titling and stylistic alternates, superior and inferior characters, old-style figures, and lining figures. For more details on ligatures, see the Photoshop Help menu.

Language Selection Menu

Computers should help make the design process easy, so in this vein, recent versions of Photoshop ship with a built-in spell check. Not every country is represented, but you do have obscure options like Nynorsk Norwegian and Turkish.

1. In the Character panel, select the language you are using.

2. Choose Edit > Check Spelling to invoke the spell check for all visible layers. The language chosen in this setting will also affect the hyphenation of words.

Anti-alias Menu

When designing text at low resolutions, adjusting your Anti-alias settings can improve readability. Anti-aliasing blends the edge pixels of text. This option is most needed when working with complex character shapes. You have five methods to choose from:

- **None.** No anti-aliasing
- **Sharp.** Makes text appear its sharpest
- **Crisp.** Makes text appear somewhat sharp
- **Strong.** Makes text appear heavier
- **Smooth.** Makes text appear smoothest

Smooth   None

Paragraph Panel

To complete your control over text, you'll need to visit the Paragraph panel. Even though there are not as many choices as the Character panel, you will still need these controls. The Paragraph panel, as its name implies, works best with Paragraph Text.

Alignment/Justification Buttons

The Alignment buttons attempt to align text left, right, or centered. They also add support for justification, which forces the text to align to both margins through the adjustment of spaces between words.

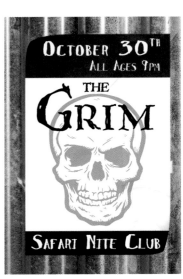

Use of the Paragraph panel results in precisely aligned text on this poster. Open the project Ch12_Concert_Sign. psd file to examine its construction.

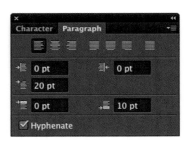

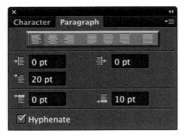

Indent Fields

The three Indent fields allow for the indentation of the left or right margins, as well as the first line of text. If you will have multiple lines of text, be sure to use the first line indentation to improve readability.

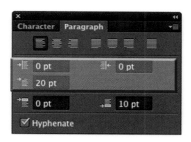

Spacing Fields

To further improve readability when multiple paragraphs are involved, use the Spacing option. You can specify how much space to add before or after a paragraph (either really works the same). This is a much better option than adding extra hard returns at the end of a paragraph.

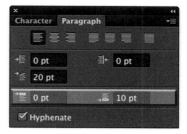

Enable Hyphenation

At the bottom of the Paragraph panel is a Hyphenate check box. If selected, it allows lines to break mid-word. Photoshop uses the selected dictionary from the Language Selection menu in the Paragraph panel. Although the Hyphenate option better fills out a text block, it is not always the best for large type. It is more acceptable for a multicolumn layout or body copy. Be sure to try the Adobe Single-line and Every-line Composer options, which you can access from the Paragraph panel submenu:

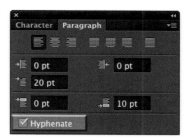

- **Adobe Single-line Composer.** Determines line breaks on a line-by-line basis. It is the default option, but it can often lead to strange hyphenation or line breaks.

- **Adobe Every-line Composer.** Examines the entire block of text and makes line breaks based on all lines of text. This option can often create a better visual flow and is generally preferable to the Single-line Composer.

Styles allow you to quickly format your text. A style can contain formatting for individual characters (such as bold or italic) or for an

Applying Styles

Styles allow you to quickly format your text. A style can contain formatting for individual characters (such as bold or italic) or for an entire paragraph (like hyphenation or alignment). They are typically used in page layout applications, but have made their way into Photoshop CS6. If you find yourself working with text a lot, using styles can add consistency and save time.

Character Styles

The Character Styles panel can be accessed by choosing Window > Character Styles. The panel is used to specify the

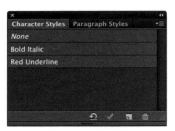

look of individual characters or words. To create a character style, simply select a character or word and modify its style using the Character panel. Then click the Create New Character Style button at the bottom of the Character Styles panel. If you want to closely see the content of the style, just double-click it in the list. You can then name the style as well as see all the properties that have been applied.

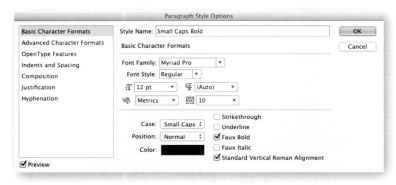

Paragraph Styles

The creation and use of Paragraph Styles is nearly identical to Character Styles. A paragraph style has all of the same styles as a character except it applies a style to an entire paragraph (regardless of what's selected). The paragraph style also allows for options to control line indents, alignment, and hyphenation. To properly use the Paragraph Styles options, be sure to double-click a style and view all of its properties (updating where needed).

Clear Overrides

If you've modified text after you've applied a style, it is considered an override. In this case, you can use it as is or click the Clear Override button at the bottom of the Character Styles or Paragraph Styles panel (both are a curved arrow pointing backwards). This will remove the additional style and reset the text to the state specified by the originally applied style.

Modifying Text

If you need to tweak your text a little more, you're in luck. Photoshop has even more options for typographic effects. The next five options discussed can truly enhance your typographic treatments.

Free Transform

Because the text you're using is vector-based, it can be sized and modified using the Free Transform command with no loss of quality. The text will "redraw" itself after the command is applied. The Free Transform command lets you rotate, scale, skew, distort, and add perspective in one continuous operation, which ensures the highest quality of your text. Let's experiment with this command.

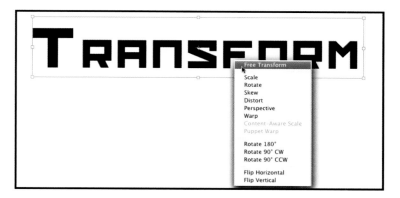

1. Select your text layer and press Command+T (Ctrl+T) or choose Edit > Free Transform.

2. Do one or more of the following options:

   - To scale by dragging, drag a handle.

   - Press Shift while dragging a corner handle to scale proportionately.

   - Press the Option (Alt) key while dragging a corner handle to scale from the center.

Reuse Styles

If you want to permanently store a style to reuse in a different document, just click the panel submenu button (in the upper-right corner of the panel). This allows you to save styles to a common library that can then be reloaded with another document.

NOTE

Simple Design Rules

- Limit total number of fonts used.
- Use heavier fonts if designing for onscreen display (web, presentations, or video).
- Make sure text is readable. Print it out or at least move a few feet away from the computer screen and take a fresh look.
- Be consistent with capitalization and justification.
- Do not overuse Layer Styles.

- To rotate by dragging, move the pointer outside the bounding border. Notice that the pointer changes to a curved, two-sided arrow. Click and drag.

- To distort freely, press Command (Ctrl) while dragging a handle.

- To skew, press Command+Shift (Ctrl+Shift) while dragging a handle.

- To apply perspective change, press Command+Option+Shift (Ctrl+Alt+Shift) while dragging a handle. You may also need to combine this option with Scale to achieve a believable perspective change.

- If you forget how to do any of the preceding options, right-click (Ctrl-click) a corner of the transform box to display a pop-up list of options.

3. Click the Commit button (the check mark in the Options bar).

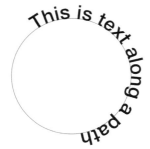

Text on a Path

Originally a job for Illustrator, placing text along a vector path allows you to make text follow a curved line or other geometric shape. Starting with Photoshop CS, this ability could be achieved in Photoshop.

1. Add a path to your document using the Pen tool or Shape tool.

2. With the Horizontal Type tool selected, move over the path until your cursor changes to a new icon (an I-bar with a curved path).

3. Click and start typing.

4. Use the Direct Selection tool to move the margin of the text for repositioning. You can also pull up or down to move the text to the inside or outside of the path.

5. Adjust the baseline and tracking as needed for improved readability.

6. Click the Commit button or press Return (Enter).

Warped Text

With names like Flag, Fish, and Wave, the Warp Text dialog box doesn't scream *useful*. However, a lot of powerful (and useful) distortions are available. These vector distortions allow you to reshape text, which is particularly helpful for advertising-style type effects:

1. Select an existing text block.

2. Click the Create warped text button in the Options bar.

3. Choose a Style for the warp and specify Horizontal or Vertical.

4. Additionally, experiment with the Bend, Horizontal Distortion, and Vertical Distortion properties.

5. Click OK when you're satisfied.

6. To modify the text effect after you've closed the Warp Text dialog box, simply click the Create warped text button again.

VIDEO 93:
Warped Text

Using Layer Styles

Text often needs a little style, and Layer Styles allow you to add a stroke, shadow, bevel, or even texture to your text. At the bottom of the Layers panel you'll see a small *f*x. This is the easiest way to access Layer Styles. But be sure to show good taste and not go wild with effects. Let's work with some prebuilt styles to see the possibilities available to you.

1. Select or create a text layer.

2. Select the Styles panel or choose Window > Styles to open the Styles panel.

3. From the panel's submenu (the triangle in the right corner), choose Text Effects.

4. Click a style's thumbnail to apply the effect; just click another to apply an additional effect.

Some of these effects are attractive and useful; many are gaudy (but that is my personal taste). The best approach is to create your own styles. Be sure to see Chapter 13, "Layer Styles," for more information.

System Performance

Having too many fonts active can impact the performance of your system by hogging RAM and slowing system boot and application launch times. Instead, use a font manager like FontBook or Suitcase to better manage your font collection.

VIDEO 94:
3D Text

Filters on Text

If you want to run a filter on text, Photoshop will rasterize the text. This process converts the text from being vector-based (and scalable) into pixel data (which cannot be enlarged without visible softening of the edges due to blowing up pixels). When you have a text layer selected and you want to apply a filter, Photoshop will warn you that it will rasterize the type and leave it uneditable. Click OK if you are sure you want to do this. I recommend making a duplicate text layer as a backup (with the visibility icon turned off) before filtering text, or try to create the effect using Layer Styles and warped text instead. Open the file Ch12_Light. psd to see an effect that combines the Radial Blur–Zoom filter with Layer Styles.

Layer Styles

13

Photoshop comes with several built-in effects: shadows, glows, bevels, textures, and strokes. These effects allow for quick changes to a layer's appearance. Layer Styles are "live" effects, which is to say that as the content of a layer updates, so does the effect. For example, if you have a bevel and shadow applied to a type layer and you change the text, the effect will be applied to the new characters. Because they update so quickly, Layer Styles have grown in popularity and are widely used by all kinds of designers.

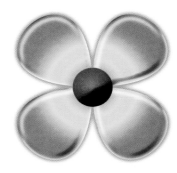

This flower was created from two basic shapes. The beveling, textures, and colorization were done with Layer Styles. Open the file Ch13_Flower_Style. psd from the Chapter 13 folder on the DVD to explore the effects.

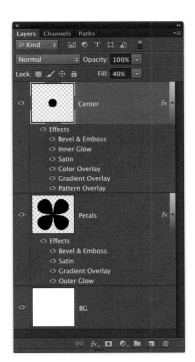

The effects that are applied to a layer become the layer's custom style. You can tell that an effect has been applied if an *f* icon appears to the right of the layer's name in the Layers panel. A layer style can be expanded by clicking the triangle icon next to the *fx* icon to reveal the layer effects in the panel. This makes it easier to edit the effects to modify the style. Let's start exploring the many options of Layer Styles and how they will impact your overall designs.

NOTE

New Order

The Layer Styles in Photoshop CS6 have been reordered. They now match the Z-order style in which they are actually applied (for example, drop shadow is at the bottom, below the other effects).

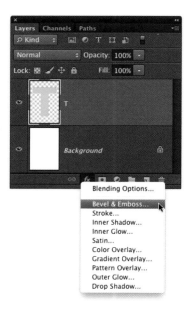

Adding a Layer Style

Photoshop offers ten effects to choose from. Each offers several options for customization and can be used to create unique and dynamic layer styles. Each effect has its own interface with many shared commonalities; however, each deserves close exploration.

1. Create a new document and choose the Photo category and the Portrait, 2 × 3 preset.

2. Select the Type tool and add the letter **T**. Use a thick sans serif font and set the point size large enough to fill the canvas. If you are not yet familiar with the Type tool, open Ch13_Layer_Style_Start.psd from the Chapter 13 folder.

3. At the bottom of the Layers panel, click the *fx* icon and choose the first effect, Drop Shadow.

4. The Layer Style dialog box opens and provides you with control over the effect.

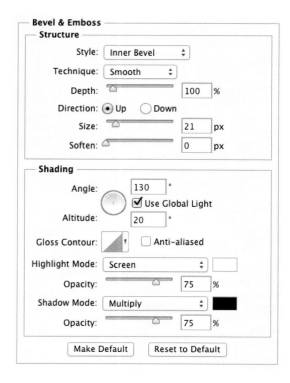

Bevel and Emboss

The Bevel and Emboss effect is very versatile, but you'll need to be careful not to overdo it. You can use bevels in combination with other effects to create realistic depth. This effect has five different kinds of edges:

- **Outer Bevel** effect adds a three-dimensional beveled edge around the outside of a layer. This bevel is created by adding a clear edge.

- **Inner Bevel** effect generates a similar effect inside the edge. Instead of a clear edge, it uses the layer's pixels.

- **Emboss** effect combines inner and outer bevels into one effect.

- **Pillow Emboss** combines the inner and outer bevel effects, but it reverses the outer bevel. This causes the image to appear stamped into the layer.

- **Stroke Emboss** must be used with the Stroke Layer Style. These two effects combine to create a colored, beveled edge along the outside of the layer.

The Bevel and Emboss effect allows significant control over the edges. You can change the lighting source and direction of the bevel, as well as the bevel's thickness, softness, and depth:

- **Depth.** Specifies how thick the bevel is.

- **Direction.** Indicates whether the bevel goes up or down to change the look of the bevel.

- **Altitude.** Allows you to set the altitude of the light source between 0° and 90°. The higher the number, the more the bevel appears to go straight back.

- **Gloss Contour.** Creates a glossy, metallic appearance. The Gloss Contour is applied after shading the bevel or emboss.

- **Highlight Mode and Opacity.** Specify the blending mode and opacity of the highlight.

- **Shadow Mode and Opacity.** Specify the blending mode and opacity of the shadow.

TIP

Bevel Overuse

Don't over-bevel. A slight bevel helps a text or logo element lift off the page or screen and adds subtle depth. Overuse, however, looks amateurish.

TIP

Like a Style?

You can easily store a custom style as the default by clicking the Make Default button below the style. To reset an applied style for the default, just click the Reset to Default button.

THE FLEXIBLE POWER OF CONTOUR SETTINGS

The least understood option of Layer Styles is the Contour setting. Most users leave Contour set to the default linear slope setting. The easiest way to grasp the Contour setting is to think of it as a cross-section of the bevel (it represents the shape of the bevel from a parallel point of view).

The basic linear contour reflects light with predictable results. However, irregularly shaped contours can generate metallic highlights or add rings to the bevel. The Contour setting is extremely powerful and unlocks many looks. Be sure to choose the Anti-aliased option for smoother results.

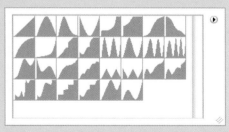

You have a few options available to modify a contour:

- Click the menu and select a preset.

- If you don't like the 12 included contours, you can load additional contours. Loading contours is similar to loading styles—just click the submenu triangle.

- You can make your own contours by defining the shape of the curve. Click the curve and add points. If the Preview check box is selected, the curve will update in near real time. This is the best way to learn how the Contour controls work. You'll find Contour controls on glows, shadows, and bevels.

You'll find an extra set of contours called UAP contours.shc in the Chapter 13 folder.

TIP

Is There a Soft-edged Stroke?

Sure—it's called Outer Glow. Adjust the size and spread for a better appearance.

- **Contour.** Provides flexibility of the Contour controls and is the bevel effect's best option. There are two Contour settings: the first affects the bevel's lighting; the second, the specialized Contour pane, alters the shape of the edge.

- **Texture.** Allows you to add texture to the bevel. You'll find several textures available in the Pattern Picker, and additional textures can be added by loading them from the Picker's submenu.

Deselect the Bevel and Emboss check boxes to remove the bevel, and then select the Stroke check box.

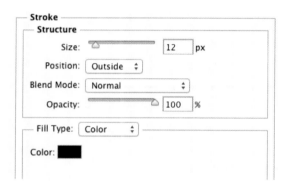

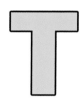

Stroke

The Stroke effect places a colored border around the edge of a layer. You can choose from inner, outer, or center strokes, as well as advanced controls such blending modes, textures, and gradients. If you'd like to emboss the stroke, combine it with the Stroke Emboss effect (within the Bevel and Emboss options).

Deselect the Stroke check box to remove the stroke, and then select the Inner Shadow check box.

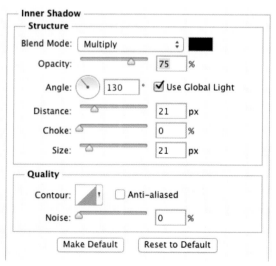

Inner Shadow

The Inner Shadow effect casts a shadow in front of the layer. This effect can be used to create a "punched-out" or recessed look. It looks best when the shadow is set to a soft setting. Inner shadows look good when used in combination with other layer styles but are distracting when overused.

The controls of this effect are nearly identical to the Drop Shadow; the only new setting is Choke. The Choke slider shrinks the boundaries of the Inner Shadow prior to blurring.

Deselect the Inner Shadow check box to remove the shadow, and then select the Inner Glow and Outer Glow check boxes.

Inner Glow and Outer Glow

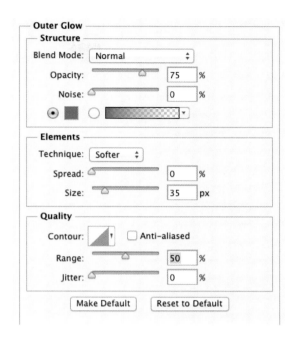

The Inner Glow and Outer Glow effects create a glow on the outside and inside edges of an object. Both effects allow you to set the color, amount, and shape of the glow. If you choose a dark glow, you might need to change its blending mode to see it.

The key difference between the two is that Inner Glow lets you set the glow's emanation, either from the edges of the layer or from the center of the layer. Inner Glows signify light coming from behind the layer. It is unlikely that you would need to apply a Drop Shadow and a glow simultaneously. Tweak Contour and Quality add a variety of shapes to your glows. Use these options to further fine-tune the effect:

- **Technique.** You can choose the Softer option, but it does not preserve as many details. Choose Precise if the source has hard edges (like text or a logo).

- **Source.** Determines where an Inner Glow emanates from— either the edges or the center of a layer.

- **Range.** Helps target which portion of the glow is targeted by the contour.

- **Jitter.** Varies the application of the glow's gradient. It affects color and opacity.

Deselect the Outer Glow and Inner Glow check boxes to remove the glows, and then select the Satin check box.

VIDEO 95:
Type Effects

Easy Bake Effects

If you'd like to permanently apply a layer style, simply highlight the layer and choose File > Scripts > Flatten All Layer Effects.

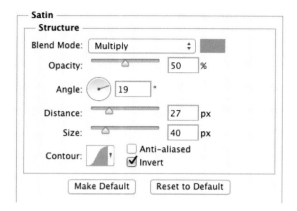

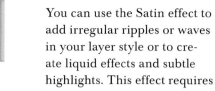

Satin

You can use the Satin effect to add irregular ripples or waves in your layer style or to create liquid effects and subtle highlights. This effect requires experimentation because its controls are very sensitive. To create different looks, experiment with different colors, contour settings, and blending modes. The Satin effect works well in combination with other effects.

Deselect the Satin check box to remove the satin, and then select the Color Overlay check box.

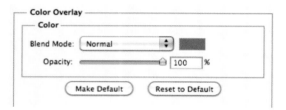

Color Overlay

The Color Overlay style replaces the contents of your layer with a new fill color. This can be a great time-saver and allows for fast design of text effects or web buttons. Additionally, you can use blending modes to create tinting effects.

Deselect the Color Overlay check box to remove the color, and then select the Gradient Overlay check box.

NOTE

Adding Soft Highlights

Satin is an underused effect that can add soft highlights to a layer.

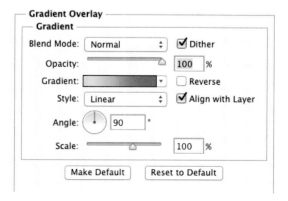

Gradient Overlay

The Gradient Overlay allows you to overlay a gradient on top of a layer. You can harness the full power of the Gradient Editor. For more on gradients, see Chapter 6, "Painting and Drawing Tools." The Dither option makes a cleaner gradient and should typically be selected for best results.

Deselect the Gradient Overlay check box to remove the gradient, and then select the Pattern Overlay check box.

Pattern Overlay

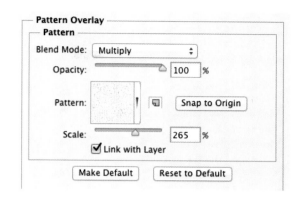

A Pattern Overlay uses photo-realistic patterns or seamless tiles. To create more believable effects, combine patterns with blending modes. Photoshop ships with several seamless patterns, and you can find several more online.

Deselect the Pattern Overlay check box to remove the pattern, and then select the Drop Shadow check box.

Drop Shadow

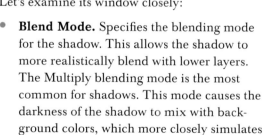

The Drop Shadow effect is straightforward and useful, and it serves as an introduction to the Layer Styles. Several of the Drop Shadows' interface elements appear in other effects. Let's examine its window closely:

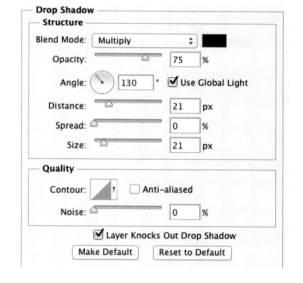

- **Blend Mode.** Specifies the blending mode for the shadow. This allows the shadow to more realistically blend with lower layers. The Multiply blending mode is the most common for shadows. This mode causes the darkness of the shadow to mix with background colors, which more closely simulates a natural shadow.

- **Color.** By default, color is set to black for the shadow. But shadows often pick up the color of the light source or background. To change the color of the shadow, click the color rectangle to load the Adobe Color Picker.

- **Opacity.** Adjusts the opacity of the effect. Opacity is the opposite of transparency: the higher the number, the less you can see through the layer.

- **Angle.** Sets the direction of the shadow.

VIDEO 96:
Photo Effects

TIP

Change the Color of Several Layers at Once

1. Apply a Color Overlay Layer Style.
2. Copy the layer style by right-clicking (Ctrl-clicking) the small *fx* icon and choosing Copy Layer Style.
3. Select multiple layers that you want to change.
4. Right-click (Ctrl-click) and choose Paste Layer Style.

TIP

Make Up Your Mind... Or Change It

At the bottom of the Layer Styles controls are two buttons. You can click Make Default to have the current settings carry forward to new instances of layer styles. In the future, just click the Reset to Default button to change the current style to the stored default.

- **Use Global Light.** Allows you to use a consistent light source for all layer effects. It's a good idea to leave the Use Global Light check box selected so that your designs have realistic (and consistent) lighting.

- **Distance.** Affects how far the shadow is cast. You can also click in the window and manually drag the shadow into position.

- **Spread.** Affects how much the shadow disperses.

- **Size.** Modifies the softness of the shadow.

- **Contour.** Most users skip the Contour settings. This is a terrible mistake. The contour is essentially a curve; it is representative of how Photoshop fades transparency. There are several presets to try, and you'll explore this setting more later on.

- **Anti-aliased.** Gives you a smoother onscreen appearance. This is important if you are creating titles for screen usage (such as Internet or video).

- **Noise.** Places noise in the shadow, which adds random dispersion to your style.

- **Layer Knocks Out Drop Shadow.** Is selected by default (and should probably stay that way). It ensures that the shadow does not bleed through partially transparent text.

LAYER STYLE SHORTCUTS

Adobe created a few useful shortcuts that increase the efficiency of Layer Styles:

- Double-click a layer in the Layers panel (except on the name) to open the Layer Styles dialog box.

- To edit a specific effect, double-click its name in the Layers panel.

- Turn off an effect's visibility by clicking the eye icon next to it in the Layers panel.

- Copy and paste layer styles by right-clicking (Ctrl-clicking) the effect icon in the Layers panel and choosing Copy Layer Style. You can then paste layer styles to other layers by right-clicking (Ctrl-clicking) and choosing Paste Layer Style.

- Move a layer style from one layer to another by dragging it.

- Option-drag (Alt-drag) a layer style from one layer to another to copy it.

Working with Layer Styles

Using Layer Styles is an important part of a professional user's workflow. The efficiency and flexibility offered by Layer Styles are huge time-savers. They can also add consistency to a designer's techniques. Be sure to fully explore all the ways Layer Styles can be useful to you.

Using Prebuilt Layer Styles

Adobe Photoshop includes some very attractive Layer Style presets to work with. Using these presets is an excellent way to learn the potential of Layer Styles. By seeing the possibilities, you can learn how to combine effects to create your own custom looks.

1. Open the file Ch13_Style_Practice.psd from the Chapter 13 folder.

CREATING DUOTONES AND TREATED PHOTOS WITH LAYER STYLES

The Color, Gradient, and Pattern Overlays are very useful when working with photos. If you're working with groups of historical sources or grayscale photos, you can use Layer Styles to create consistent tinting effects. Often, it is easiest to strip out all the color data of a historical photo before restoring it. You can then add the duotone or sepia tone effect back in as the last step.

1. Open the file Ch13_Photo_Styles_Practice.tif from the Chapter 13 folder.

2. Load the Layer Styles set UAP Photo-Styles.asl from the Chapter 13 folder as well.

3. Double-click the *Background* layer to float it. Name the layer *photo*.

4. Click the different styles to try them out.

5. Open the effect window and examine how blending modes and textures can be harnessed for powerful effects.

2. Activate the Styles panel by choosing Window > Styles. Each swatch represents a layer style. To apply a style, highlight any layer (other than the *Background* layer or a locked layer) and click a swatch.

3. If you need more looks, click the Styles panel submenu. You'll find several options built into Photoshop. When you select a new set of styles from the Preset list, you are presented with a choice:

- **Append.** Adds new styles to the bottom of the current list

- **Cancel.** Does not load anything new

- **OK.** Replaces the current list with new presets

You can also load styles that don't appear in the Preset list. Choose Load Styles from the Styles panel submenu. You'll find a collection of styles called UAP Styles.asl in the Chapter 13 folder. If you'd like these new styles to appear in your Preset list, locate the Presets folder inside your Photoshop application folder. Any Layer Style library copied into the Styles folder will appear as a preset the next time you launch the application.

You'll find these presets and 31 other styles in the UAP Styles set on the DVD.

Creating Your Own Layer Styles

It's a pretty straightforward process to create your own layer styles. You simply add one effect at a time and experiment with different combinations. Options like Contour and blending modes go a long way toward creating appealing layer styles. The Layer Styles feature is quick to learn and easy to master; just continue to experiment with many options.

Saving Layer Styles

Once you've created an original style (or even modified an existing one), you may want to save it. There are two ways to save a style:

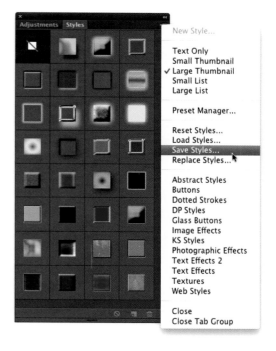

- **Embed.** Photoshop embeds the layer style information into the layered files. Be sure to save the document in a layered format (such as Photoshop Document, Layered TIFF, or Photoshop PDF). Three months from now, when your project comes back to life, you can open your source files and start making changes. Remember that layer styles will automatically update as you make edits to the layer.

- **Save as a Library.** After creating a layer style, you can add it to the open style library by clicking an empty space in the Styles window. A new thumbnail swatch is created, and you are prompted to name the swatch. It is then available to you until you load another style library.

If you want to permanently save styles, you must save a Styles library (or set) from the loaded swatches. It's a good idea to create a personal set in which to store your styles. There is no "new set" option. Simply create new styles and then delete any styles you don't want by dragging them onto the trash icon at the bottom of the panel or Option-clicking (Alt-clicking) an unwanted style. When you're ready to save, choose Save Styles from the Styles panel submenu.

You should store styles in <*Photoshop Application folder*> > Presets > Styles. Styles placed in this default location will appear in your menu when you restart Photoshop.

Scaling Styles

When you're changing the image size (Image > Image Size), specify that you'd like styles to scale proportionately.

Maximizing Filters

14

Filters are among Photoshop's most popular features. These specialized add-ons can be used to boost productivity or add special effects. Photoshop ships with over 100 built-in filters, and there is a rich array of others available from third-party developers. Filters are so popular that you'll find more tutorials online than you could ever make through in a lifetime.

Photoshop almost did not ship with filters, because many at Adobe thought they were too "gimmicky." However, John Knoll, co-creator of Photoshop, managed to "sneak" them in. Those early executives were partially right, though: When used improperly (or too often), filters can be gimmicky. Think of filters like spices: When used properly, they can add to a meal, but if they're overused, they can ruin it—and no one can live on spices alone.

Both built-in and third-party filters were run on this image. You would not normally run as many filters on a single image, but you can see just how diverse filters can be.

Filters Defined

The proper use of filters can significantly extend Photoshop's capabilities. There are filters that perform important image-enhancement tasks for removing grain or damage. Additionally, filters can be used for tasks like blurring and sharpening image details.

Filters allow you to achieve more quickly what otherwise would be time-consuming results; they can unlock options that could not be done with standard tools. Filters can often create stylized looks as well as enhance the lighting of a photo.

Gaussian Blur	⌘F
Convert for Smart Filters	
Filter Gallery...	
Adaptive Wide Angle...	⇧⌘A
Lens Correction...	⇧⌘R
Liquify...	⇧⌘X
Oil Paint...	
Vanishing Point...	⌥⌘V
Blur	▶
Distort	▶
Noise	▶
Pixelate	▶
Render	▶
Sharpen	▶
Stylize	▶
Video	▶
Other	▶
Digimarc	▶
Browse Filters Online...	

By definition, a filter must reside in Photoshop's Plug-ins folder. Besides the bundled filters that are installed with Photoshop, you'll find a few specialty filters on the Photoshop installer DVD or in the Support area of Adobe's website.

Preparing to Use Filters

Filters can save time and can be fun to use. But before you rush in and try out every filter in Photoshop, you need to make sure the image is ready to be processed. Many filters are render-intensive, so there's no reason to spend extra time on pixels you may be throwing away.

Fix Major Errors

Filtering mistakes only draws further attention to them. Most importantly, make sure the image is properly exposed with natural-looking contrast. This can be accomplished easily using a Levels adjustment (Image > Adjustments > Levels). For more on Levels, see Chapter 10, "Color Correction and Enhancement."

The wealth of third-party Photoshop plug-ins is an important aspect of Photoshop's customization. These filters range in price from free to several hundred dollars. When you're looking for filters, a great starting place comes to mind: *Photoshop User* magazine frequently reviews plug-ins. Members of the National Association of Photoshop Professionals (NAPP) often get discounts as well. Go to its site at **www.photoshopuser.com** and click the Magazine link to find out more.

The original image (left) lacks contrast. Proper contrast (center) creates an image that's ready for filtering (right).

Set Your View

Filtering an image is easiest when you can see all your pixels (otherwise, resampling occurs). For best results, zoom in 100% or choose View > Actual Pixels. You can also double-click on the magnifying glass in the Tools panel or press Command+Option+0 (Ctrl+Alt+0). The Navigator panel is useful to get a global overview and to move quickly around an image that is zoomed in. Some filters also offer the ability to view a 100% preview in the filter interface.

Check the Color Mode

You'll want to be sure that you are working in RGB mode whenever possible (Image > Mode > RGB). This will ensure that you have the most filters available. Very few filters work in CMYK mode because CMYK conversion is supposed to be the last step in processing an image. Only filters that are meant for print work have been optimized to work in CMYK mode.

If you have a CMYK image and you need to convert it back to RGB mode for filtering, go ahead. You do not have to worry about color shift when converting from CMYK to RGB. Because CMYK has fewer colors than RGB, no information will be lost.

Check the Bit Depth

It's also important to keep an eye on bit depth when working with filters, or your filter options will be limited. The vast majority of filters only run on images in the 8-bit mode. In fact, as of Photoshop CS6, only 43 of the built-in Photoshop filters will work in 16-bit mode, and only 23 of them work in 32-bit mode.

The filters designed to work at higher bit depths are primarily for image enhancement (as opposed to stylization). These filters are targeted for use with digital photography applications. Although a 16-bit image can be processed more without showing banding or posterization, you may need to work in 8-bit mode. If you can work in 16-bit mode, do so, but be prepared to lose some functionality with filters and image adjustments. If a filter is grayed out, it doesn't work in the selected bit depth.

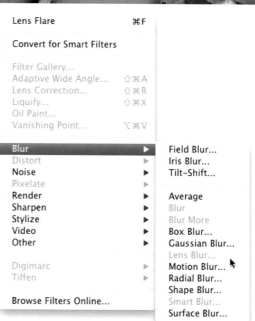

Depending on the Color Mode or Bit Depth, some filters will be unavailable. If the filter is grayed out, you'll need to choose another.

NOTE

Color-correct Before Filtering

An image should be color corrected properly before filtering. Remember: GIGO (garbage in = garbage out).

VIDEO 97:
Smart Filters

VIDEO 98:
Fading a Filter

Understanding Filter Interfaces

Because filters are designed for specialty purposes, the interface you use to control filters will vary. A few filters have no user interface (for example, Average, Despeckle, Facet). If a filter does not have an ellipsis (…) after its name, it has no user interface. These filters are fairly limited and will likely fall off your favorites list.

Most filters, however, will have some form of user interface. Some filters have their own window; others use the Filter Gallery. No matter which interface you use, consider selecting the Preview option. This allows you to see the filter's changes to your canvas before you actually apply the filter.

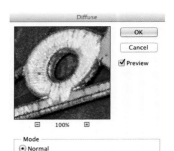

Here are a few more tips about using a filter's interface:

- Click in the preview window and drag your view to change the preview area.

- Use the + or - button under the preview window to zoom in or out. Additionally, you can zoom into the preview by pressing Command+= (Ctrl+=) and zoom out with Command+- (Ctrl +-).

- Click in the image window to adjust the center point of the preview window. (This may not work in all cases.)

- When you're in a dialog box, fully explore it. Try adjusting all the variable sliders one at a time. If there's a Load button, try loading presets that shipped with the product.

- To see the "before" state, click and hold inside the preview window. When you release, the filter preview is shown again.

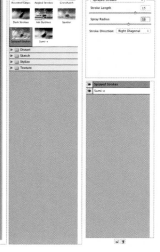

Depending on the filter chosen, Photoshop will use a different interface. Newer filters like Oil Paint have a very large preview area while older filters like Diffuse have a much smaller preview area. The Gallery Effects filters have a unique user interface that allows multiple effects to be combined into a single operation.

Getting the Best Results

Many people simply "slap" filters on their images and expect great results. This bandage approach does not usually create award-winning results. With a little bit of care, you can achieve significantly better looks.

Using Smart Filters

If you'd like maximum flexibility, you can choose to apply filters to a Smart Object. Any filter applied to a Smart Object is applied as a Smart Filter. The names of the Smart Filters appear in the Layers panel directly below the Smart Object they have been applied to. Smart Filters can be adjusted, masked, or removed at any time (even after a document has been closed and reopened). This makes using Smart Filters essentially nondestructive but can slow down your system if you're working on high-resolution images.

Let's practice with Smart Filters:

1. Open the Ch14_Well.tif file from the Chapter 14 folder on the DVD.

2. Choose Filter > Convert For Smart Filters, and click OK. If an item is already a Smart Object, there is no need to convert it.

3. Choose Filter > Sharpen > Smart Sharpen, and adjust the filter as desired.

4. Click OK to apply the filter. The Smart Filter appears below the Smart Filters line in the Layers panel beneath the Smart Object layer.

   Let's modify the Smart Filter's results.

Is There an Interface?

If a filter name is followed by an ellipsis (...), it has a dialog box that will open. If not, the filter is as-is and cannot be tweaked before application (but you can still use the Fade command afterward).

NOTE

Graphics Card Dependent

Some filters like the new Oil Paint and Blur filters may require a specific category of graphics card. This is because some new features are heavily dependent on your computer's GPU (graphics processing unit). See http://www.adobe.com/products/photoshop/tech-specs.html for more details.

VIDEO 99:
Blur Tools Combined

TIP

What Is Smart?

Almost Every filter in Photoshop (except for 4 blurs, Liquify, and Vanishing Point) can be used as a Smart Filter. Even more useful, you can apply the Shadow/Highlight adjustment as a Smart Filter.

5. Double-click its name, Smart Sharpen, in the Smart Filter list. Reduce the amount of sharpening for the filter, and then close its dialog box.

6. Choose Filter > Blur > Gaussian Blur, and apply a blur at a high value, such as **15** pixels. Click OK to apply the filter. The filter appears at the top of the Smart Filters list.

Smart Filters can also use blending modes, which opens many options.

7. Double-click the Edit Blending Options icon next to the filter in the Layers panel.

A Blending Options window opens to adjust the filter.

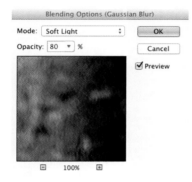

8. Set the filter's blending mode to Soft Light, and adjust the Opacity to **80%**.

9. Click OK to close the Blending Options window and update the Smart Filter.

The blended Gaussian Blur filter has nicely intensified the color in the image but has also softened the image a little too much. This can be fixed easily by adjusting the Smart Filters stacking order.

10. Drag the Smart Sharpen filter so it appears at the top of the Smart Filter list. Remember that Photoshop applies Smart Filters from the bottom up.

11. Continue to experiment with Smart Filters and add additional effects.

12. When you're satisfied, close the photo. You can save it if you'd like to a local drive.

TIP

Smart Filters Only Where You Want Them

Smart Filters automatically have a Layer Mask attached. If you make a selection before applying a Smart Filter, the Layer Mask will hide the filter's results. If you need to alter the Smart Filter after the fact, you can use standard masking techniques to paint on the Smart Filter mask. The mask applies to all the Smart Filters applied to a layer. If you need to disable the Layer Mask, hold down the Shift key and click its thumbnail.

VIDEO 100:
Masking Smart Filters

Better Define the Target Area

You spent a lot of time attaining accurate selections in Chapter 5, "Selection Tools and Techniques" (if you skipped it, reviewing it now will help you get the most out of this chapter). For the best results, you'll want to accurately select the area to be filtered. Depending on what you want to achieve, filters can be run on the entire image, a

small portion of the image, or even a single channel. Also, it's not a bad idea to test a filter first by running it on a small area.

Smooth the Edges

A hard-edged selection creates a visible border where the filter processed the image. It is absolutely essential to soften your selections. Two techniques work well (and can be combined):

- Choose Select > Modify > Smooth to round out hard corners in your selection.

- Choose Select > Modify > Feather to create a gradual edge. This is similar to the difference between a line drawn by a ballpoint pen and a line drawn by a felt-tip pen.

- Choose Select > Refine Edge to improve the overall selection intuitively.

Fade and Blend

The Fade command is a little-known secret in Photoshop. It allows you to further modify filters by harnessing the power of blending modes. Use this command to access all 24 blend modes besides Normal. It makes your filter collection 24 times larger.

You must choose the Fade command immediately after the filter has run (even before you deselect the active selection). Let's try it out:

NOTE

Smart Fade?

The Fade command is not available for Smart Filters (for that functionality, use the Blending Options icon).

VIDEO 101:
Oil Paint

1. Open the file Ch14_Butterfly.tif from the Chapter 14 folder.

2. Choose Filter > Stylize > Glowing Edges.

3. Adjust the sliders as desired until you have an image that looks much like a black velvet painting.

4. Click OK.

5. Invoke the Fade command by choosing Edit > Fade <*name of filter*>, or press Command+Shift+F (Ctrl+Shift+F). To remember this shortcut, think of it as though you want to command (or control) the shifting (fading) of the filter.

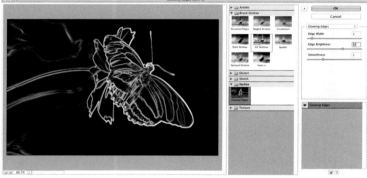

6. Try different blending modes and Opacity settings to modify the look of the filter.

TIP

Using the Fade Command

If you forget to invoke the Fade command, step backward through your History panel until the filter is removed. Then run the last filter again (with the same settings) by pressing Command+F (Ctrl+F). You can then invoke the Fade command.

The Guide to Standard Filters

Do you want to know more about filters? You'll find a detailed filter guide included in the Chapter 14 folder. The guide examines every standard filter included with Photoshop CS6.

Filters are often surprising, so the guide will help you explore them in depth. Be sure to examine the official uses for each filter as well as recommendations for new techniques. The guide is richly illustrated to help inspire new ideas.

Actions and Automation

15

Photoshop is an extremely efficient program, but you're truly missing out if you don't learn how to use its automation features. Automation is one of the key differences between Photoshop and its sibling Photoshop Elements. You'll find three categories of technology that can streamline your workflow and save you hours of work per week. These powerful commands can take the most repetitive tasks and automate them completely:

- **Actions** record a series of commands for playback on future images. They can be used to generate extremely complex results. You can also use batch processing to run an action on an entire folder of images.

- **Automate commands** perform complex production tasks (like creating panoramic or high dynamic range [HDR] images) with minimal effort.

- **Scripts** can perform tasks that are more complex than actions. Scripts have made a strong impact on complex workflow issues.

Along with automation commands in Photoshop, a few additional tasks can be easily completed using Adobe Bridge. You can use Bridge as a powerful image browsing and organization tool. Bridge also makes it simple to batch rename files or create contact sheets and Web galleries.

Actions

Photoshop's actions technology lets you record nearly every command (or better yet, a series of commands), and then play them back on another image. You can use basic actions, such as a resize or file format change, to quickly convert files at a push of a button. These simple actions can be recorded and then mapped to empty

function keys at the top of your keyboard. By using combinations of Shift and Option (Alt) as modifiers to the function key, a standard keyboard can have 48–60 customizable keys (depending on the size of your keyboard).

Meet the Actions Panel

If your Actions panel looks something like this figure, you're using Button mode. This is a useful way to access actions, but you cannot create or modify actions when using Button mode.

To use actions, let's take a closer look at the Actions panel. To toggle the visibility of the Actions panel, press Option+F9 (Alt+F9). If the panel does not look like a list, go to the panel's submenu (in the panel's upper-right corner) and make sure that Button mode is not selected.

The interface has fairly clear controls. The Stop, Record, and Play buttons behave as you might expect. The folder icon creates a new set (place) to store actions, and the page icon creates a new (empty) action. Click the trash icon to delete the highlighted items, or you can drag actions or sets onto it.

Let's practice with actions by using some of the built-in actions.

1. Open the file Ch15_Bike.tif from the Chapter 15 folder.

2. From the Actions panel submenu, choose Image Effects. This menu item adds a set of actions that will process the image to a different look using a combination of filters and adjustments.

3. Click the triangle next to the Image Effects set to display the actions contained within.

4. Choose the action Sepia Toning (layer) and click Play. The action should take very little time to process the image. The end result is a nice sepia tone effect.

5. Choose File > Revert, and then try other actions from this set to see the diversity of those actions.

You can explore the steps in an action by clicking the triangles in the Actions panel to look at how elaborate some actions are. You may be thinking that these are interesting, but they will get stale quickly because they create the same look each time.

This does not have to be the case. It's very easy to modify an action. The easiest way to do this is by turning on dialog boxes. Normally, an action will play all the way through using the original values assigned to the filters or image adjustments. However, if you click in the column next to each step, you can enable dialog boxes for a filter or adjustment (click a second time to disable dialog boxes). These dialog boxes let you enter variables and influence an action's outcome. Let's try this out:

1. Choose File > Revert, and then go back to the Sepia Toning (layer) action in the Actions panel. Click the triangle next to the action so you can expand it and see all of its steps. You may find it useful to expand individual steps to better see what command they perform.

2. The final step, Make, creates a new adjustment layer for the tinting. Click next to its name to enable the dialog box.

3. Run the action again. This time a dialog box opens for the final step so you can customize the tint effect. Click OK to create the adjustment layer. Modify the tint effect, and then click OK to finish the action.

This exercise has only scratched the surface of what's possible with actions. Actions open all sorts of options, for creative and technical outcomes.

NOTE

Different Is Good (When It Comes to Actions)

By modifying an action, several different outcomes are possible. Expand the triangle next to the action's name to see the list of steps. It is possible to turn on only some of the dialog boxes by clicking next to a specific step.

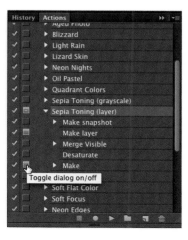

Working with Third-Party Actions

An innumerable amount of actions are available on the Internet. The Adobe Studio Exchange website (www.adobe.com/exchange)—mentioned in an earlier chapter—is an excellent starting point. Most actions are available for free; some of the most creative and useful actions are sold by small and large developers. Let's try out some third-party actions and learn how to load and use them:

1. Open the file Ch15_Spacesuit.tif from the Chapter 15 folder.

2. In the Actions panel, click the submenu to choose Load Actions.

3. Navigate to the Chapter 15 folder where you'll find a folder named PanosFX Actions. The folder contains four sets of actions from the creative mind of Panos Efstathiadis (www.PANOSFX.com). Load the action "Stamp v2 by Panos.atn."

4. Select the README first! Action, and click Play to run the action. Follow the onscreen instructions.

5. Select the !!! STAMP !!! round stamp action, and click Play.

6. Follow the detailed onscreen instructions. You can substitute the Return (Enter) key for clicking the Commit check mark if you want.

7. When the action gets to the very end, it asks you to make a choice. You can stop and preserve the high-res version or click Continue to reduce the image to a very small size for screen resolution. I recommend clicking Stop.

8. All the important layers are in a group already. You can drag this group into a new document or save it to use later.

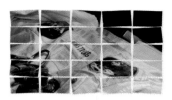  

Three more sets and a total of nearly 20 actions are available to explore in the Lesson folder. These are some wonderful samples of how powerful and devoted the Photoshop community is.

VIDEO 102:
Creating an Action

Creating Actions

By now, actions should seem pretty appealing. You've explored using built-in actions as well as loading (and finding) third-party actions. Now it's time to create your own.

You must first create a set to hold your personal actions (think of it as a folder). Sets hold actions, and there's no limit to how many actions can be placed into a set or how many sets you can load. Let's give it a try:

1. Close the previous files, and then open the Ch15_Desert.tif file.

2. Call up the Actions panel and click the folder icon to create a new set. Give the set a name of your own choosing, and click OK.

3. Click the New Action icon. You can give the action a name now or rename it later. In this case, name it **Cartoon Look**, and click Record to start recording.

4. Choose Filter > Convert for Smart Filters to make the layer a Smart Object, and if necessary click OK.

5. Run the Find Edges Filter by choosing Filter > Stylize > Find Edges. There is no dialog box for this effect.

6. To achieve the look you need to fade the filter, click the Blending Options icon for the Smart Object (it looks like a double arrow next to the effect's name).

7. In the new window, try the Overlay blending mode and adjust the Opacity slider as desired. Depending on the source image, you may need to try different blending modes. You can always remove steps from a recorded action afterward by dragging individual steps into the trash can in the Actions panel.

8. To enable flexibility, turn on the dialog box for the Set Filter Effects step.

9. In the Actions panel, click Stop.

Congratulations; you've created your first action from scratch. The preceding recipe is one of my own, but the technique works with most filter recipes. Let's try making one more:

1. Open the Ch15_Desert.tif file from the Chapter 15 folder or if it is still open from the last action, choose File > Revert.

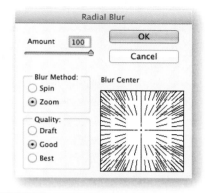

2. Click the New Action button. You can give the action a name now or rename it later. In this case, name it **Zoom Blur**, and click the Record button. The action is now recording.

3. Duplicate the *Background* layer by selecting it and pressing Command+J (Ctrl+J).

4. Desaturate the color from the duplicate layer by pressing Command+Shift+U (Ctrl+Shift+U).

5. Now you'll make the image zoom from a center point. Choose Filter > Blur > Radial Blur. Set the Method to Zoom and use an Amount of **100** at Good Quality. Move the center point by dragging within the Blur Center area in the dialog box to place it relative to the subject, and then click OK.

6. Repeat the Blur filter by pressing Command+F (Ctrl+F).

7. On the topmost layer, make a Levels adjustment by pressing Command+L (Ctrl+L). Bring the black and white Input sliders toward the center. Move the gray slider until the midtones are brighter. Click OK.

8. Change the blending mode of the top layer to Screen mode, and set it to 80% Opacity.

9. Press Option+[(Alt+[) to select the previous layer.

10. Press Command+Option+F (Ctrl+Alt+F) to run the Zoom filter again with options.

11. Set the amount to **30**, and click OK.

12. To achieve the look you need to fade the filter, choose Edit > Fade Radial Blur. Lower the Opacity of the effect to **30**%, and click OK.

13. In the Actions panel, click Stop.

Experiment and create your own looks. Virtually every menu command or button can be recorded. Starting with Photoshop CS6, even tools can (just be sure to set your rulers to percentages to get relative results—see the "Tips for Creating Better Actions" sidebar). Actions can be duplicated, modified, and deleted. Be sure to explore all the options in the Actions panel submenu. Be sure to dissect actions made by others to get ideas of what is possible. With a little practice and imagination you'll be amazed at what you can accomplish.

If you want to check out the actions you just created, compare them to a set I've saved in the Chapter 15 folder.

Saving Actions

Actions are stored in a temporary cache. If you delete the set, load a replacement, or experience an application crash, your new actions could be overwritten. Therefore, it's important to save your actions so they can be backed up and reloaded in the future.

1. Click an action set. You can use the one created in the previous exercise. You must click the whole set, not just an action in that set.

2. Go to the Actions panel submenu, and choose Save Actions.

3. The Photoshop Actions folder (inside the Presets folder) will be chosen by default. If it isn't, manually locate it in your Presets folder.

4. If you add to the set later, just be sure to resave it to the same location with the same name.

Sharing Actions

If you create useful actions, you can post them to the Adobe Studio Exchange community to share with other users (www.adobe.com/exchange).

TIPS FOR CREATING BETTER ACTIONS

Making great actions from scratch can be a bit of a challenge. You need to come up with great design ideas or useful time-savers. You also need to make sure the action is technically solid so it runs without errors. Here are a few tips to make your actions a little more tech-savvy:

- Run actions on a duplicated image or folder to preserve your originals.

- Brush strokes, cloning, and most manual tools from the Tools panel may not record properly with actions. Photoshop CS6 improves this, but realize that strokes are based upon a relative percent-based position.

- As an alternative to tools, try using options such as a Gradient Fill layer (Layer > New Fill Layer > Gradient) instead of the Gradient tool. Fill layers are easier to modify after running an action as well.

- To play a single step of an action, double-click it.

- If you make a mistake in an action, click Stop. Delete the incorrect steps by dragging them into the Actions panel's trash can. Choose Edit > Step Backward as many times as needed. Then click Record and start again from the last good point.

- Button mode lets you launch actions quickly—just click an action and it runs. You can access the command from the Actions panel submenu. You'll need to disable Button mode to access recording and editing features.

- Choose Playback Options from the Actions panel submenu. Specify that you want the actions to play back an action accelerated. Photoshop can process faster than it can redraw the screen.

- Be sure to back up your custom actions to two locations: the default location and a secondary backup location. This way a reinstall or upgrade won't blow away your custom actions.

- To create an action that will work better on all files, set the rulers to measure using percentage.

- Choose File > Automate > Fit Image to resize an image for a specific height or width.

- Photoshop records the names of layers as you select them. This may cause playback issues, because the action will look for specific names. Use keyboard shortcuts to select layers and such so that the action won't look for a specific name for that step. For more on layer shortcuts, see Chapter 8, "Compositing with Layers."

Outcome	Mac	PC
Choose layer above	Option+]	Alt+]
Choose layer below	Option+[	Alt+[
To Move the Current Layer		
Up the layer stack	Command+]	Ctrl+]
Down the layer stack	Command+[	Ctrl+[
To the top	Shift+Command+]	Shift+Ctrl+]
To the bottom	Shift+Command+[	Shift+Ctrl+[

VIDEO 103:
Batch Processing

Automate Commands

Photoshop offers several commands for speeding up professional imaging workflow. You'll explore several options available throughout this chapter. If you are working with an older version of Photoshop, you might not have some of these automation tools. Each is a significant time-saver, and you should attempt to integrate them into your workflow as often as is feasible.

Batch

If you liked actions, you'll love the Batch command. The Batch command allows you to apply an action to a group of images. This is a huge time-saver, especially for mundane tasks like resizing. You can also use it to batch process an entire roll (or card) of images and run the same Levels adjustment on each image. Let's give it a try.

Let's start by making the action "batchable":

1. Open a JPEG image from the Batch folder in the Chapter 15 folder.

2. Choose File > Save As, and save a copy to the desktop. This is a temporary copy to prepare the action and can be thrown away when you're finished.

3. Call up the Actions panel.

4. Create a new action in your custom set named **Zoom Blur Batch**, and start to record.

5. Click the Zoom Blur action, and click Play (an action can record the running of another action).

6. When the action completes, choose File > Save As. Navigate to your desktop and save the file. Select a TIFF file format, deselect the Layers box, and click Save.

7. Choose a compression option: In this case LZW is very efficient.

8. Click Stop.

> **TIP**
>
> **Batch Jams**
>
> A batch process can get stuck on file closings, especially with JPEG or TIFF compression, which asks for user interaction. You'll want to either batch convert the files ahead of time to another format (like PSD) or record the close-and-save step as part of the action. Be sure to select the Override Action "Save As" Commands option. This will ensure that your files are saved in the folder specified by the Batch command.

9. Close the open image.

10. Discard the two temp images from your desktop now (or later).

The action is now ready to be applied to a folder of images.

1. Choose File > Automate > Batch to invoke the Batch window.

2. Specify a set and an action from the set that you'd like to use. The action must be currently loaded in the Actions panel to appear in this list. In this case, use the Zoom Blur Batch action that you created earlier.

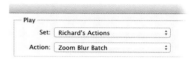

3. Choose the files that you want to process from the Source menu:

- **Folder.** This option processes all items in a specified folder. Click Choose to navigate to and select the folder. A folder can include additional subfolders as well. For your images, choose Folder. Click Choose and navigate to the folder called Batch in the Chapter 15 folder.

TIP

Batch Multiple Folders

You can batch multiple folders at once. Create aliases or shortcuts within one folder that point to the desired folders. Be sure to select the Include All Subfolders option.

- **Import.** This option processes images from a digital camera, scanner, or a PDF file. A useful batch and action would be to create an action that sets a document's resolution to 300 pixels per inch without resampling. You could then run this action on all items you import from a digital camera.

- **Opened Files.** This option processes all open files.

- **Bridge.** This option works on all selected items in Adobe Bridge. You would first select several images in Bridge, and then choose Tools > Photoshop > Batch.

4. Set processing options that guide what is and is not processed as well as how to handle errors or files:

- **Override Action "Open" Commands.** If your action contains an Open command that refers to specific filenames rather than the batched files, you'll want to deselect the Override Action "Open" command.

NOTE

Filenaming Compatibility

For filenaming compatibility, be sure to choose Windows and Mac OS to ensure that filenames are compatible with the OS.

- **Include All Subfolders.** This option applies the action to all files in the subdirectories of the specified folder.

- **Suppress File Open Options Dialogs.** This option hides File Open Options dialog boxes. It's a good idea to use this when batching actions on Camera Raw image files. Photoshop will then use the latest settings. For maximum compatibility, select this option.

TIP

Converting File Formats

The Batch command cannot convert file formats. This can easily be done in advance using the Image Processor script that ships with Photoshop. In fact, you can even add an action to the Image Processor script. It is a good idea to convert a JPEG file to TIFF or PSD before running an action. More on the Image Processor later in the chapter.

VIDEO 104:
Create a Slideshow in Photoshop

- **Suppress Color Profile Warnings.** This option ignores color profile warnings, which can cause an action to hang and wait for user interaction. For maximum compatibility, select this option.

5. Specify a destination for the processed files by choosing one from the Destination menu:

- **None.** This option leaves the files open without saving changes.

- **Save And Close.** This option saves the files in their current location. This is a destructive edit because it will overwrite the original files.

- **Folder.** This method saves the processed files to another location (this is the safest option). Click Choose to specify the destination folder. For this batch, navigate to the desktop and create a new folder named **Batch Processed**.

6. If the action you're using includes a Save As command, choose Override Action "Save As" Commands. Otherwise, the image may write to the wrong folder. For maximum compatibility, select this option.

7. If you chose Folder as the destination, you'll need to specify a filenaming convention. Several pop-up fields are available for easy filenaming. These fields make it very easy to rename files from a digital camera or to specify a serial number. Photos from multiple digital cameras often end up with the same name, so this is a very good idea because you can create more accurate and descriptive names for each image. In this case, choose the following settings:

- **Field 1.** Dinosaur Exhibit_ (manually type in)

- **Field 2.** mmddyy (date) (from pop-up list)

- **Field 3.** _ (manually type in)

- **Field 4.** 3 Digit Serial Number (from pop-up list)

- **Field 5.** extension (from pop-up list)

These settings will result in a name like Dinosaur Exhibit _052612_001.tif.

8. Set an option for error processing from the Errors menu:

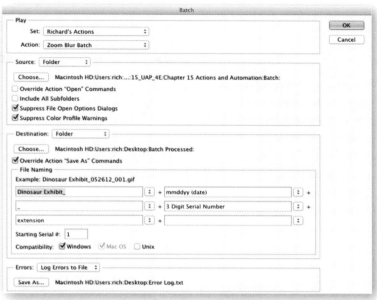

- **Stop For Errors.** This option suspends the process until you confirm the error message. Choose this option only if you will be monitoring the batch process closely.

- **Log Errors To File.** This option records each error into a file without stopping the process. After processing, a message appears indicating if any errors occurred. For this batch, choose Log Errors To File. Save a file named **Error Log.txt** on the desktop.

9. Set the file compatibility for Mac OS and Windows.

10. Click OK to run the batch. Photoshop will batch process the images. Depending on the speed of your computer, this may take a few minutes. You can abort a batch by pressing Esc at any time.

Crop and Straighten Photos

When scanning images, it's often possible to fit more than one image on the scanner bed. Scanning multiple images at once can save input time when you are loading images into Photoshop. Fortunately, the Crop And Straighten Photos command picks up and keeps the efficiency going. Let's give it a try.

1. Open the Ch15_Crop_and_Straighten.tif file from the Chapter 15 folder. If you would rather, just scan in a few images on your own scanner.

2. Choose File > Automate > Crop And Straighten Photos.

   Each image should be cropped, straightened, and moved into its own document window.

Crop and Straighten Best Results

For best results, you need to keep 1/8 inch between the images in your scan. If the Crop And Straighten Photos command does not succeed (which is rare), you should process the individual images using the Crop tool. If images are dramatically different exposures, scan them separately.

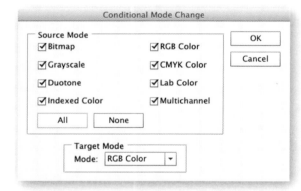

Conditional Mode Change

The Conditional Mode Change command is meant to be used within an action. It allows you to specify conditions for a mode change to occur during an action. Recording a mode change into an action can result in an error if the action is run on an image that has a different image mode. For example, if one step of an action were to convert an image from a source mode of RGB to a target mode of CMYK, applying this action to an image in Grayscale mode would result in an error. The command allows you to specify one or more source modes and a mode for the target mode.

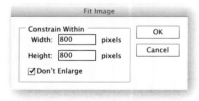

Fit Image

The Fit Image command is also meant to be inserted into an action. It allows you to specify a maximum width and height (in pixels) that the image cannot exceed. This is useful when sizing images for the screen or Internet. If you intend to use it for print resolution, you'll need to know your resolution setting and multiply by your desired print size to convert inches to a pixel-based measurement.

Photomerge

The Photomerge command allows you to merge several (adjacent) photographs into one continuous image. This command is used to make panoramic images, which was covered in depth back in Chapter 8. If you skipped that hands-on activity, flip back to Chapter 8. If you'd like another set of practice images, you'll find a folder called Photomerge in the Chapter 15 folder.

Merge to HDR Pro

The Merge to HDR command was introduced in Photoshop CS2 as a way to create technically accurate 32-bit images. It allows you to take multiple exposures (with different values) of a subject (shot from a locked tripod or camera mount) and merge them into a new image that better displays highlights and shadows. The resulting image is also a 32-bit image that allows great flexibility for adjusting exposure.

With Photoshop CS5, the Merge to HDR command got a major overhaul for stylistic purposes, and it can now create tone-mapped images that display a wider range of exposure than a traditional photo. HDR images were initially discussed in Chapter 10, "Color Correction and Enhancement." Let's create another HDR image:

1. Choose File > Automate > Merge to HDR Pro.

2. In the Merge to HDR dialog box, click Browse to navigate to the source images. You'll find a folder named Merge to HDR in the Chapter 15 folder. In the folder, Shift-click images 1–5 to select them. Select the Attempt to Automatically Align Source Images check box, and then click OK.

3. After a few moments, a second Merge to HDR dialog box opens. You'll see thumbnails for each of the images used as well as a resulting image.

4. From the Preset list, choose Photorealistic High Contrast to get a punchier image.

5. Select the "Remove ghosts" check box to remove the trailing image details caused by wind blowing items in the scene.

6. Adjust the exposure with the following values: Exposure: **−1.0**, Shadow: **50%**, and Highlight **−80%**.

7. Boost the Saturation to **30%** for richer colors.

8. Click OK to create a new HDR image.

9. Try adjusting the Exposure settings to different values to see the results of the HDR image.

The image on the left exhibits ghosting caused by slight movement between exposures. Selecting the "Remove ghosts" check box compensates for variables like wind.

Scripts

Photoshop scripting offers a more powerful automation technology than actions. Scripts allow for the execution of more elaborate tasks than what actions can do because scripts recognize conditional states like image mode and orientation. Scripting was introduced in Photoshop CS, and powerful built-in scripts automate the processing of multiple layers or layer comps.

Creating original scripts requires you to use a scripting language such as AppleScript, JavaScript, or Visual Basic. Photoshop includes a script editor and debugger for JavaScript. JavaScript is the preferred language because the scripts are cross platform. Scripting is complex; it's essentially computer programming. Plenty of resources are available for those who want to learn scripting, but be prepared to spend some time. You'll find a folder called Scripting Guide in the Photoshop application folder. In it you'll find sample scripts and a PDF with detailed information.

Fortunately, some wonderful examples of scripting are available at the Adobe Studio Exchange website (www.adobexchange.com). Be sure to look for scripts by Photoshop guru Russell Brown on his site (www.RussellBrown.com). Load new scripts by choosing File > Script > Browse. To permanently add a script to the Script menu, copy it into the Scripts folder inside your Presets folder. For now, let's explore the built-in scripts.

VIDEO 105:
Image Processor Script

Image Processor

You can use the Image Processor command to convert and process multiple images. The Image Processor differs from the Batch command in that you don't have to first create an action. The Image Processor can be used for any of the following tasks:

- To convert a set of files to JPEG, PSD, or TIFF format. You can also convert files simultaneously to all three formats.

- To process a set of Camera Raw files using the same Camera Raw options.

- To resize images to fit within a specified pixel dimension.

- To embed a color profile into images or convert files to sRGB and save them as JPEG images for the Web.

- To include copyright metadata within the processed images.

NOTE

Batch Processing

The Image Processor is another way to batch process images (and you don't need to go through the extra step of using the Save As command). The Image Processor script can be more flexible than the Batch command. The Image Processor works with PSD, TIFF, JPEG, or Camera Raw files.

TIP

Saving Settings

You can click Save to save the current settings in the Image Processor dialog box. These settings can be reloaded for a later job if needed.

TIP

Apply One Setting to All

If you need to process a group of Camera Raw files taken under the same lighting conditions, you can open and adjust only the first image to your satisfaction. In the Image Processor dialog box be sure to select the "Open first image to apply settings" check box. You can then reuse the same settings for the other images.

1. In the Actions panel, click the submenu and load the Image Effects actions.

2. Choose > File > Scripts > Image Processor.

3. Choose the images you want to process. You can use open images or navigate to a folder to choose images. Click Select Folder and navigate to the folder named called Batch in the Chapter 15 folder. Highlight the folder and click Choose.

4. Select a location in which to save the processed files. You should make and then choose a Script Exports folder on the desktop.

5. Select the file types and options you want to convert to:

   - **Save as JPEG.** Sets the JPEG quality between 0 and 12. You can also resize the image and convert it to the sRGB color profile.

   - **Save as PSD.** Sets the PSD options. You can also resize the image and select Maximize Compatibility.

   - **Save as TIFF.** Saves images in TIFF format with LZW compression. You can also resize the image.

   For this example, choose JPEG and choose to resize to **800 × 800** pixels with a compression of **10**.

6. You can choose other processing options as well:

   - **Run Action.** If an action is loaded into Photoshop, you can run it on the image during the process.

   - **Copyright Info.** This includes any text you enter in the IPTC copyright metadata for the file. Text overwrites the copyright metadata in the original file.

   - **Include ICC Profile.** This embeds the color profile with the saved files.

   For this example, choose the Aged Photo action from the Image Effects set to run on the processed images.

7. Click Run. Photoshop processes the images to the specified folder.

Layer Comps to Files

You may remember layer comps, which were covered in depth in Chapter 8. This useful design tool allows you to save different arrangements of layer visibility, position, and effects. Layer comps are very useful when experimenting with designs. Photoshop makes it easy to create an individual file for each layer comp.

1. Open an image that uses layer comps. You can use your own or the file named Ch15_Script_Sample.psd from the Chapter 15 folder.

2. A warning dialog box about the display of nonsquare pixels appears with pixel aspect ratio preview. This is a graphic intended for use in a digital video project; therefore, it uses a special pixel designed for video technology. Click OK to close the dialog box.

3. Choose File > Scripts > Layer Comps To Files to export all layer comps to individual files, one for each comp. You can choose to create BMP, JPEG, PDF, PSD, Targa, TIFF, PNG-8, or PNG-24 files.

4. Click Browse to specify a target destination. Select the Script Exports folder you created on your desktop.

5. Specify PNG-24 files as the File Type output (this will automatically embed the transparency of each layer into the file).

6. Click Run.

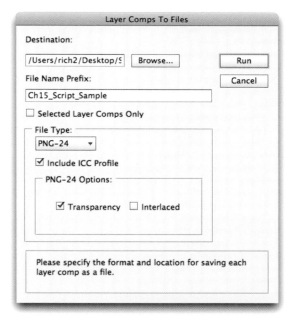

If desired, you can create a PDF file using an additional script. For even more control, use Adobe Bridge to share these files for review (these techniques are discussed later in the chapter).

VIDEO 106:
Export Layers to Files Script

TIP

Mini Bridge

A welcome addition to Photoshop is Mini Bridge. Mini Bridge lets you quickly browse and organize files. You can also click the Tools button and choose Photoshop and a list of automated tasks. Be sure to try it out by choosing Window > Extensions > Mini Bridge.

NOTE

Complex Names

If you need to do a complex batch rename, you can click the plus button (+) to add descriptive information. A preview of the new filename appears at the bottom of the dialog box. Be sure to keep the total character length low to avoid conflicts with different operating systems.

Automation with Adobe Bridge

Longtime Photoshop users will notice that certain Automation commands have gone missing. You will no longer find the Picture Package command as part of the application, and you will have to perform some tasks in Adobe Bridge. These changes were due in part to some core technology changing within the application and an effort to streamline tasks. Let's take a look at a few useful commands you'll find in Adobe Bridge.

Batch Renaming Files

One of the key functions of Adobe Bridge is organizing your digital images. As part of that organization, you'll likely rename files. This is particularly true since most digital cameras progressively number their files, which is great for counting but not organizing. Bridge makes it easy to rename several files or folders at one time; this process is called a batch.

1. If it's not running already, launch Adobe Bridge CS6 (you can also launch Bridge from within Photoshop by choosing File > Browse in Bridge).

2. Navigate to the folder named Batch in the Chapter 15 folder. Double-click to open the folder and view the nine images contained within it.

3. Press Command+A (Ctrl+A) to select all the files within the folder.

4. Choose Tools > Batch Rename. A new dialog box opens.

5. You must specify a destination for the renamed files. You can choose to keep them in their current folder, move them to another folder, or copy them to another destination. For this example, choose to "Copy to other folder" and specify a target folder on your desktop (you cannot resave files to the DVD-ROM drive).

6. Specify New Filenames using a combination of menus and a text field. For this example, choose Text and enter **Dinosaur_Exhibit_**. Then add a sequence number of **1** and specify Two Digits.

7. In the Preview section, check the New filename for accuracy.

TIP

Bridge from the Start

If you'd like Bridge to launch automatically when you log in to your computer, open Bridge's preferences and select the Advanced category. Simply select Start Bridge at Login to make Bridge readily available.

8. Specify that you want the files to be compatible in Mac and Windows.

9. In the Options section, select the "Preserve current filename in XMP Metadata" check box.

10. When you're ready, click the Rename button to complete the batch rename. The Batch command is a useful way to improve the organization of your files.

PDF Contact Sheet and Presentation Output

Another useful function of Bridge is its ability to quickly generate PDF files for selected images. Bridge CS6 includes a workspace called Output that uses the Adobe Output Module script. In just a few clicks, you can generate Adobe PDF contact sheets and presentations.

NOTE

Two Contact Sheets?

Although you'll find a contact sheet option back in Photoshop CS6, the one in Adobe Bridge is more robust and should be used in my opinion.

- **Contact sheet.** A contact sheet is a useful catalog of a group of images. You can place multiple, small thumbnail images on a large page along with caption information.

- **PDF Presentation.** The PDF presentation output lets you quickly create a multipage PDF file that you can use to display images as a slide show presentation. The PDF output also offers options for image quality, security settings, and display preferences. You can also add text overlays at the bottom of each image in the PDF presentation.

Let's go ahead and create a PDF file from a folder of images:

VIDEO 107:
Adobe Output Module & Bridge

1. If it's not running already, launch Adobe Bridge CS6.

2. Choose Window > Workspace > Output. The Bridge interface rearranges to show the Output panel at the right side of the screen. The Content panel appears at the bottom of the screen (nested with Preview); this is where you see thumbnails for the images you choose to use. The left column contains a list of folders.

3. Navigate to the Chapter 15 folder.

Contact Sheet

TIP

Custom Flow

If you want to specify an order for the thumbnails in the contact sheet, switch to the Content tab. Here you can rearrange the order of images by dragging them in the window.

The Output Module offers several contact sheet templates as starting points. You can modify these presets as needed to serve your unique needs.

1. Select all the images in the Contact Sheet folder, and then press Command+A (Ctrl+A).

2. Click the PDF button in the Output panel.

3. Click the Template menu and choose a layout option. For this example, choose the 4*5 Contact Sheet option, and click the Refresh Preview button. Bridge creates a preview layout of the first page for the PDF file. Let's customize the appearance a bit more.

4. In the Document controls, change the Page Preset to U.S. Paper and set the Background to White.

5. Select the Open Password check box, and enter **raster-vector**. A password provides security to keep a document private for only its intended recipient.

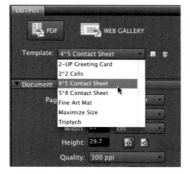

6. In the Layout controls, change the Columns to **3** and Rows to **4** to place a larger image on the contact sheet.

7. In the Overlays controls, increase the Size menu to **12 pt** and set the style to Bold.

8. Click the Refresh Preview button to see how the PDF contact sheet will look.

9. Click the Save button to create the contact sheet. Name the file and store it on your desktop. When Bridge is finished creating the file, it will open by default in your system's PDF viewer application.

Slide Show

The Output Module also offers presets for generating a PDF slide show. This is a useful way to present several images in one document. The PDF file can be emailed, posted to the Web, or used as part of a live presentation.

1. Switch back to Bridge and select all the images in the PDF Presentation folder.

2. In the Template menu, choose Maximize Size.

3. In the Document controls, change the Page Preset to the Web category and select the size of 1280 × 1024. Also, set the Background color to Black.

4. In the Layout controls, deselect the Rotate for Best Fit option. Images will then all remain oriented to the screen.

5. In the Overlays section, deselect Filename overlays.

6. Adjust Playback controls to your liking (scroll to the bottom of the list). You may want to use a longer duration such as Advance Every 10 Seconds. Feel free to modify the Transition and Speed controls.

7. Click the Refresh Preview button to see how the PDF slide show will look.

8. Click the Save button to create the PDF slide show. Name the file and store it on your desktop. When Bridge is finished creating the file, it will open by default in your system's PDF viewer application.

9. When you are finished viewing, press the Esc key to exit the full-screen slide display.

Web Gallery Output

The Web Gallery component of the Adobe Output Module is a very easy way to quickly build a website for displaying photos. A Web photo gallery uses a home page with thumbnail images and several gallery pages with full-size images. Power users and amateurs alike have discovered the power and flexibility of creating entire galleries within Bridge.

Without knowing any HTML or Flash, users can quickly create online galleries for their images. Bridge offers several customizable templates, which are well suited for different tasks like client review or online portfolios.

1. If it's not running already, launch Adobe Bridge CS6.

2. Choose Window > Workspace > Output. The Bridge interface rearranges to show the Output panel at the right side of the screen. The Content panel appears at the bottom of the screen (nested with Preview); this is where you see which images you've selected to use. The left column contains a list of folders.

3. Navigate to the Web Gallery folder inside the Chapter 15 folder.

4. Press Command+A (Ctrl+A) to select all the photos contained within the Web Gallery folder.

5. Click the Web Gallery button in the Output panel.

6. Choose the Lightroom Flash Gallery from the Template list.

7. Choose Paper White option from the Style menu.

8. Customize the gallery by entering Site Info. This information helps the site's visitors understand the photos presented (such as when and where the photos were captured). For this exercise, enter your own information into some of the fields.

9. You can change the Color Palette controls to further stylize the site. Try changing the Header color to a dark orange by clicking its swatch and using the Color Picker.

10. Customize the design of the page using the Appearance controls:

   • Set the Slideshow Size to **800** pixels.

   • Set the Gallery Image Size to **650** pixels.

   • Set the Thumbnail Size to **100** pixels.

11. Specify a destination for the generated Web Gallery (the folder will contain several pages and images). If you have a Web site, you can use the built-in Bridge FTP features to upload the Web Gallery to your server. For this exercise, click the Save to Disk button, and then click Browse and specify your Desktop.

12. Click the Preview in Browser button to simulate the site (this will only load the first ten images). Browse the Web site and try its many controls. The Web Galleries are truly versatile and elegant.

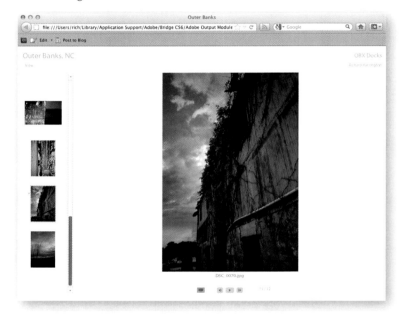

13. When you're satisfied with the preview, close the Web browser and return to Bridge.

14. Click the Save button in the Create Gallery controls to generate the Web Gallery.

Printing, PDF, and Specialized File Types

16

At some point, you'll need to send your images to an output device. Several different devices are available, including paper and film printers, plates, or a digital printing press. Whether you are printing on a desktop inkjet printer or sending your images to prepress, there are some essentials you should know. In the digital age, preparing a photo for web or video has become just as important with many devices like tablets and digital signage growing in popularity.

Understanding the core technology will ensure that your jobs go smoothly and that your images turn out as desired. The material in this chapter serves as a primer on printing and PDF technology. Additionally, you'll explore screen delivery techniques.

Professional Printing Options

Depending on the type of image you've processed, you'll need to determine the right type of printer for output. This will be a balance of budget and availability. The simplest images, such as line art, use only one color. An illustration may use several colors, and those can be printed using CMYK inks to create the different colors or spot inks that exactly match. The most complex images are photographs because they use varying colors and tones to simulate the image. These types of images are generally referred to as *continuous-tone images*.

PHOTO BY ISTOCKPHOTO.COM

Professional printing is a trade that requires a lot of experience and specialized knowledge.

Color Separation

If your multicolored image is intended for commercial output (printing on a large press), it will need color separation. This process allows for a master plate to be created for each color. Generally, the plates created are for cyan, magenta, yellow, and black—also called key—(CMYK) inks.

These plates can be created in several ways. Usually, the process is handled by a printing professional. However, let's take a quick look at how these separations can be created in Photoshop.

1. Open the file Ch16_Color.tif from the Chapter 16 folder.

2. Check to make sure that your document is in CMYK Color or Multichannel mode.

3. Choose File > Print.

4. Choose Separations from the Color Handling menu.

5. Click Print. Your printer will print separations for each color in the image.

NOTE

Separations in Multiple Locations

Depending on the printer you are using, the separation options may also appear in the Print dialog box. Under the Mac OS, use the pop-up menu in the second Print dialog box that appears. With Windows, click the Print Settings button to access additional printer driver options.

Halftoning

To simulate continuous tones in images, commercial printers break down images into dots. For those images printed on a press, this process is referred to as *halftoning*. By varying the size of the dots, the halftone screen creates the optical illusion of variations in tone.

An inkjet printer also uses dots, but it's not the same. An inkjet printer's dots are very small and uniform in size.

Quality of Detail

How clear an image prints depends on its resolution and screen frequency. Professional printing devices are often capable of high resolution. As such, they require a finer screen ruling (lines per inch). For more on resolution, you can revisit Chapter 3, "Acquiring Digital Images." It's a good idea to discuss resolution requirements with your service provider or vendor before starting a job.

TIP

How Do Laser Printers Work?

For more information on laser printing, be sure to read the information article at http://computer. howstuffworks.com/ laser-printer1.htm.

Desktop Printing Options

The majority of Photoshop users print their images on desktop printers most of the time. These printers generally fall into three categories:

- **Inkjet.** These printers are the most popular and widespread. They offer relatively affordable printing. For best results, look for inkjet printers with separate cartridges for each color.

- **Dye sublimation.** These printers allow for printing of lab quality prints. Recently, the price of these printers has plummeted. These printers do not use dots; rather, transparent film (using CMYO dyes–Cyan, Magenta, Yellow, and Overcoating) is heated and transferred to the paper. The vaporized colors are absorbed into the printer paper. This method is less vulnerable to fading over time if it uses a laminated overlay.

- **Laser printer.** Laser printers use static electricity to affix powder to the page to form the image. These printers are generally more expensive than inkjets but can usually print faster and at a higher quality.

RGB vs. CMYK

Inkjet printers use CMYK inks, but they prefer to ingest RGB images. If the image is in RGB mode, there is no reason to convert it if you're using an inkjet printer. Desktop printers are designed to do their own CMYK conversion using internal software. Sending a CMYK image to an inkjet printer will usually result in a second (and unpredictable) color

TIP

A Better Print Needs More Data

If you're printing from a Mac, you'll have the option to print using 16 bits of information. This option is best when working with a 16-bit image because it will give you the highest possible quality. The extra information really helps reproduce subtle tones like skies and shadows.

conversion. It is important to realize that the computer screen can display more colors than the printer can print. You might want to use the Gamut Warning command (View > Gamut Warning) to identify areas that need to be toned down with the Sponge tool before printing.

Printing Paper

Several specialty papers are available for desktop printers. You will not get good results trying to print on plain white copy paper. These specialty papers must be selected in the printer window. It's a good idea to identify the paper you are using so the printer driver can adjust the density of the ink coverage to match the paper stock. To conserve paper, you might want to create and print a contact sheet with several smaller images first. It is a good idea to stick with the ink and paper recommended for your particular printer. Remember that different papers and different printers will warrant very different output.

VIDEO 108:
Printing Dialog Box

Printing Commands

Several commands are associated with printers. Those specific to your printer are controlled by the printer driver, which can be clearly explained by visiting the printer manufacturer's website. Many different drivers are available, so instead of focusing on the multitude of manufacturers and hardware options, let's focus on what can be controlled within Photoshop.

Print

Photoshop offers a powerful Print command with great flexibility when printing in Photoshop. The command allows you to adjust the size of an image and its position on the page, and to specify color management policies. Learning to control the Print window will help you produce the best results.

1. Open the file Ch16_Print.tif from the Chapter 16 folder.

2. Choose File > Print or press Command+P (Ctrl+P). The Print window is divided into three areas of functionality.

3. The left side of the Print window shows you how the image will print on the current page. Notice how the photo is currently clipped because it is too large for the selected paper. To fix this, adjust the settings in the Print window.

4. Choose a Printer from the Print menu. The setting you choose will depend on which printer is attached to your computer. If the printer supports it, choose the 16-bit Data option.

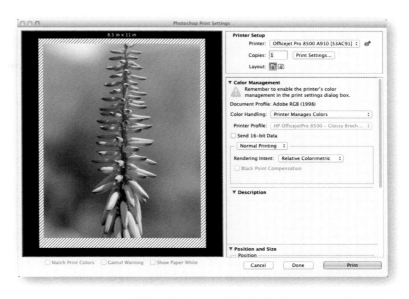

5. In the Scaled Print Size section, select the Scale To Fit Media check box. Photoshop adjusts the print resolution so the image fits on the page. If you want to permanently change the image, you'll need to exit printing and choose Image > Image Size.

6. If needed, you can click the Print Settings button to access the printer driver controls. These allow you to adjust options like ink coverage, print quality, and paper size.

7. In the Color Management area, click Color Handling and choose Printer Manage Colors. This is generally the best option for consumer-quality printers because it lets the printer use its specialty software to get the most accurate color.

8. In the Color Management area, you need to specify the Rendering Intent. This is how the colors will be converted for the destination color space. This option is useful for high-end printers that offer PostScript support; however, most consumer-oriented printer drivers ignore this option and use the Perceptual rendering intent, but there are four options to choose from:

- **Perceptual.** This method attempts to present color so it is natural to the human eye, even though the color values may change.

TIP

Your Image Is Larger than the Paper's Printable Area

When you choose to print, you might get a warning that the image is larger than the printable area of the paper. If this happens, click Cancel, choose File Print, and select the Scale to Fit Media check box.

- **Saturation.** This method tries to produce vivid colors in an image; however, it may sacrifice color accuracy.

- **Relative Colorimetric.** This method compares the highlights of the source color space to the destination and shifts all colors accordingly.

- **Absolute Colorimetric.** This method leaves colors that are in gamut untouched while clipping those colors that are out of gamut for the destination color space.

9. If needed you can select different output options, like Labels and Crop Marks, in the Printing Marks area. These are often used for separations or to identify prints by filename and additional info embedded in the file (like exposure information). For this image, the default settings are fine.

10. Once you have the print settings properly configured, you have three choices:

- To print the image, click Print.

- To close the dialog box without saving the settings, click Cancel.

- To save the printer options for later use, click Done.

COLOR MANAGEMENT CHOICES

When printing, you have to keep color management in mind. This process determines how color accuracy is maintained.

PHOTOSHOP MANAGES COLOR

In the Photoshop Manages Color software workflow, Photoshop does all the color conversion. This method works best when you have a custom ICC profile for each specific printer, ink, and paper combination. This method is more commonly used in professional printing environments when working with higher-end devices that have been professionally calibrated.

PRINTER MANAGES COLOR

The Printer Manages Color workflow approach lets the printer hardware handle the color conversion. Instead of performing the color management, Photoshop sends all the necessary details to the printer. This method is the best method when printing to inkjet photo printers because each combination of paper, printing resolution, and additional printing parameters requires a different profile. Using this option is generally best, but it does require you to set printing options and turn on color management in the printer driver.

If you're working with a PostScript printer, you can harness powerful options. PostScript color management allows for color separations and complex color management.

Print One Copy

If you are in a rush and don't need to make any additional changes in the Print dialog box, you can print one copy with your current options. Choose File > Print One Copy to output a single print using the latest settings you have loaded.

PDF Essentials

The Portable Document Format (PDF) is a file format invented by Adobe and was intended to be an extension of PostScript. A PDF can describe any combination of text, images, multimedia, and layout. It is independent of the device it was created on and can be viewed on virtually every operating system and portable media player or phone.

The PDF is an open standard, which means that the computer industry is able to create applications that can read or write PDFs without paying Adobe additional fees. This openness led to the quick adoption of PDF, and it is utilized online extensively.

The most powerful PDF authoring tool is Adobe Acrobat, which is bundled with Photoshop in the Adobe Creative Suite or sold as a standalone product. However, Photoshop has the ability to create PDFs. The PDF file format is an excellent way to send files to a service bureau or print shop because the file can be stored at print resolution with embedded vector files and high-quality output options.

Compression Options for Adobe PDF

When you choose to save artwork as a Photoshop PDF, you are presented with the Save Adobe PDF dialog box. You can choose to compress text and line art as well as downsample bitmap images. Depending on the settings you choose, you can significantly reduce the size of a PDF file with little or no loss of detail. Let's open the Save Adobe PDF dialog box.

1. Open the image Ch16_PDF.tif from the Chapter 16 folder.

2. Choose File > Save As.

3. From the Format menu choose Photoshop PDF.

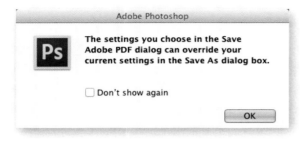

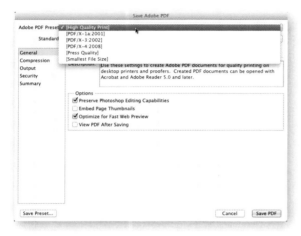

4. Target the Desktop for saving, and then click Save to open the Save Adobe PDF dialog box.

5. A warning dialog box opens to caution you that the settings you choose in the Save Adobe PDF dialog box will override settings in the Save As dialog box. Click OK to dismiss the warning.

6. In the Save Adobe PDF dialog box, you can choose an Adobe PDF Preset.

This is a fast way to specify that the newly generated PDF file is intended for commercial printing or to be distributed via email. You can also choose to Preserve Photoshop Editing Capabilities to save layers and editable text for future changes. At this point, you can click Save PDF to generate the file right away or keep modifying the settings for special purposes.

ADOBE PDF STANDARDS

You can choose to create a PDF that matches the most widely used standards for print publishing. There are three different types of PDF/X formats:

- **PDF/X-1A (2001 AND 2003).** PDF/X-1a is an industry-recognized standard for graphic exchange. Choosing PDF/X-1a requires all fonts to be embedded and for the appropriate PDF bounding boxes to be specified. PDF/X-compliant files must contain necessary information describing the condition for which they were prepared to be printed. PDF/X-1a-compliant files can be opened in Acrobat 4.0 and Acrobat Reader 4.0 and later.

- **PDF/X-3 (2002 AND 2003).** The main difference in this newer version of PDF is that it allows for the use of color management. Additionally, it supports device-independent color as well as CMYK and spot colors. Also, ICC color profiles can be used to specify color data later on in the workflow. PDF/X-3-compliant files can be opened in Acrobat 4.0 and Acrobat Reader 4.0 and later.

- **PDF/X-4 (2008).** The newest format of PDF is designed to support newer features like printing artwork with live transparency and layers. This format is designed to work within the existing Adobe PDF Print Engine. The major benefit is that PDF/X-4 jobs can print without flattening artwork or converting the file to PostScript.

For more information on PDF/X, see www.adobe.com/products/acrobat/standards.html.

Compression

The Compression area of the Save Adobe PDF dialog box offers several options for reducing file size. You do not need to downsample, but you might want to if you want to better match the output resolution of a particular printer or to reduce file transfer times.

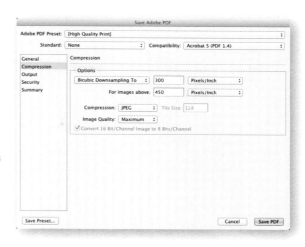

The interpolation method you choose determines how pixels are deleted:

- **Average Downsampling.** This method averages the pixels in a sample area and replaces the entire area with the average pixel color.

- **Subsampling.** This method chooses a pixel in the center of a sample area and replaces the entire area with that color.

- **Bicubic Downsampling.** This method uses a weighted average to determine pixel color. It generally yields better results than Average Downsampling. This is the slowest but most accurate method.

The Compression setting offers three compression methods:

- **ZIP.** This works well for images with large areas of single colors or repeating patterns.

- **JPEG.** This is suitable for grayscale or color images. JPEG compression eliminates data, so it usually results in much smaller file sizes than ZIP compression.

- **JPEG2000.** This is the new international standard for image data compression. Like JPEG compression, JPEG2000 compression is suitable for grayscale or color images. It also provides additional advantages, such as progressive display.

The Image Quality setting determines how much compression is applied. The settings will vary based on the compression method you choose, but they are clearly labeled.

You can select the convert 16 Bit/Channel Image to 8 Bits/Channel check box if you're working with a 16-bit image. This can significantly reduce file size but is not a good option if you're creating a PDF for professional printing. This option is grayed out if the image you are working with is already in 8-bit mode.

Output

The most common way to create accurate color when creating a PDF is to stick with the PDF/X standard. However, you can choose to modify settings in this area and embed color profiles. Be sure to check with your printer or service bureau regarding color profile settings.

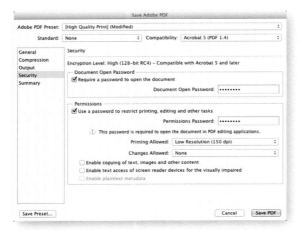

Security

The PDF format supports several different security options, which can be useful to protect the document from unauthorized viewers or to preserve copyright by blocking copying or printing functions. Here are two of the most important security options:

- **Require a password to open the document.** The viewer must enter a password to view the PDF document.

- **Use a password to restrict printing, editing, and other tasks.** Several options can be placed on the document. You can restrict printing and block modifications to the page. This is a good idea if you are posting a PDF for review purposes but do not want people to be able to print the file.

It is important to note that the security in PDF files is very strong but can be breached. These security options are useful and work well for most users. You'll also find additional modifiable options that allow the copying of text or access to screen readers for the visually impaired.

Summary

The Summary area provides a single pane view of all the settings you have used. This is a quick way to verify the options you've enabled.

When you're finished, you can click Save PDF to create the PDF file. You can also click Save Preset if you want to save the settings you've modified for future PDF creation.

NOTE

Selecting File Types

You'll find additional advice on the DVD for choosing the right file format. Look in the Chapter 16 folder for a bonus PDF with more details.

Specialized File Formats

Photoshop is a feature-rich and truly enjoyable program, but it is frequently not the end of the road for a designer or artist. Most often, professionals (and even hobbyists) will need to save their files for use in other software packages and environments. Whether it's a JPEG for a website, an EPS for a professional printer, or a PNG file for video editing, Photoshop can create it. In fact, Photoshop supports more than 20 file formats by default. Additional formats used by cameras or other software packages can be added via plug-ins. Not all formats will work with every color space or image type, but each has a special purpose. Let's explore some of the most common formats you'll encounter. Bold items in the following tables are supported features.

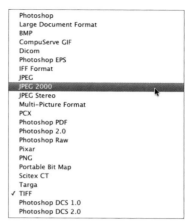

From the Save As dialog box, you can select from several file formats. Certain ones may be unavailable due to bit depth or image mode.

Photoshop (.psd)

Layers	8-bit	16-bit	32-bit
Bitmap	**Grayscale**	**Duotone**	**Indexed Color**
RGB	**CMYK**	**Lab**	**Multichannel**

Note that not all color spaces work in 16- and 32-bit modes.

Photoshop format is the default file format. This format supports all Photoshop's features. It's a good idea to save your design files in this format for maximum editability. Additionally, many other software packages recognize Photoshop layers.

NOTE

Many Formats to Choose From

If you need to explore additional formats, you'll find further information in the Photoshop Help menu.

CompuServe GIF (.gif)

Layers	8-bit	16-bit	32-bit
Bitmap	**Grayscale**	Duotone	**Indexed Color**
RGB	CMYK	Lab	Multichannel

The online service provider CompuServe originally developed the Graphics Interchange Format (GIF). This format displays 8-bit or indexed-color graphics and images in HTML documents on the Internet. You'll hear the file called both "giff" and "jiff"; both are

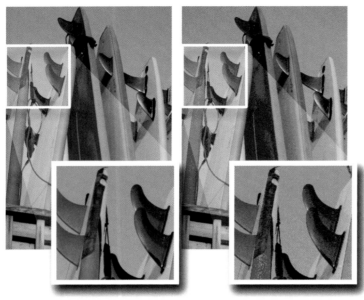

acceptable. GIFs use a color table (with no more than 256 colors total, not per channel) to represent the image. This can lead to a small file size but also banding in the image. If you need transparency in a web graphic, GIF is one of two choices (the other is PNG). There are also animated GIFs, which are GIF frames displayed one after the other to create animation. Unless you need transparency or animation, JPEG is a better option for web delivery.

Compare a JPEG (left) and a GIF (right). Notice how the GIF uses fewer colors. This format can reduce file size but often creates banding or color shifts.

Photoshop EPS (.eps)

Layers	**8-bit**	16-bit	32-bit
Bitmap	**Grayscale**	**Duotone**	**Indexed Color**
RGB	**CMYK**	**Lab**	Multichannel

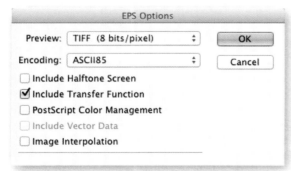

You can embed an image preview into an EPS file, which makes previewing your image easier in a page-layout program.

The Encapsulated PostScript (EPS) language file format can contain both vector and bitmap graphics. It is nearly universal and is supported by virtually all graphics, illustration, and page-layout programs. EPS format is used to transfer PostScript artwork between applications. When you open an EPS file that contains vector graphics, Photoshop rasterizes the image.

JPEG (.jpg)

Layers	**8-bit**	16-bit	32-bit
Bitmap	**Grayscale**	Duotone	Indexed Color
RGB	**CMYK**	Lab	Multichannel

The Joint Photographic Experts Group (JPEG) format is most often used to display continuous-tone images (such as photos) on the Internet. Most digital cameras use JPEG because it provides excellent compression; the maximum set-

ting provides comparable image quality to much larger file formats like TIFF. Occasionally, the print industry (especially newspapers) will use JPEGs.

The JPEG format supports RGB, CMYK, and Grayscale color modes but does not support alpha channels. JPEG is a lossy compression, which means that some data is discarded during compression of the image. JPEGs should not be used as an archive or production file format. You should generally only save JPEG files once, because resaving continues to discard data and lower image quality. If you have acquired an image as a JPEG in your camera, be sure to save the edited document as a PSD or layered TIFF file.

If you are using JPEG as a source format, be sure to set the digital camera to Maximum quality. The best way to create JPEGs for the Internet is with the Save For Web command (discussed in depth at the end of this chapter).

Notice the difference in file-size savings between the two formats. The JPEG (even at maximum quality) is almost four times smaller. File savings make JPEG a popular format for mobile phones, consumer digital cameras, and the newspaper industry.

Large Document Format (.psb)

Layers	8-bit	16-bit	32-bit
Bitmap	Grayscale	Duotone	Indexed Color
RGB	CMYK	Lab	Multichannel

FORMATS THAT SUPPORT SPOT COLOR CHANNELS

Do you need spot color channels for special printing jobs? Then you'd better stick to these file formats:

- Photoshop
- Photoshop Large Document Format (.psb)
- JPEG2000
- Photoshop PDF
- Photoshop Raw (not Camera Raw)
- TIFF
- Photoshop DCS 2.0

Large Document Format Doesn't Automatically Mean Larger Files

When comparing a file saved as a standard .psd file versus the large format .psb file, the two file sizes are virtually identical. Using the Large Document Format does not increase file size, it just allows a larger-sized file to be saved.

FORMATS THAT SUPPORT ALPHA CHANNELS

Do you need embedded transparency for use in printing, multimedia, video, or animation programs? Then you might want to stick with file formats that support alpha channels. Be sure to check your software program's manual to see which of the following formats are compatible:

- **Photoshop**
- **BMP**
- **JPEG2000**
- **Large Document Format**
- **Photoshop PDF**
- **Photoshop 2.0**
- **Photoshop Raw**
- **Pixar**
- **SGI RGB**
- **Targa**
- **TIFF**

There is normally a 2 GB file size limit in older versions of Photoshop and most other computer applications. To respond to the need for larger file sizes, Adobe launched the Large Document Format (PSB). It supports documents up to 300,000 pixels in any dimension (up to 100 inches at 300 ppi). All Photoshop features, such as layers, effects, and filters, are supported.

Additionally, 32-bits-per-channel images can be saved as PSB files. It's important to remember that files saved in the PSB format can be opened only in newer versions of Photoshop.

PNG (.png)

Layers	**8-bit**	16-bit	32-bit
Bitmap	**Grayscale**	Duotone	**Indexed Color**
RGB	CMYK	Lab	Multichannel

The Portable Network Graphics format provides lossless compression. It is increasingly common on the Internet, but not all browsers support it. The PNG format was created to be a patent-free alternative to GIF. Its major advantage is the PNG-24 file, which allows for 24-bit images (8 bits per channel) and embedded transparency. It is technically superior to GIF.

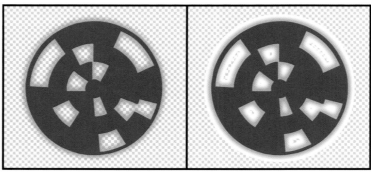

The file on the left is a PNG-24. Notice how the transparency is handled perfectly (even in the soft glowing areas). On the right is a GIF, which is an 8-bit image. Transparency is not handled as cleanly, and you will notice a white edge outside of the glow.

Targa (.tga)

Layers	**8-bit**	16-bit	32-bit
Bitmap	**Grayscale**	Duotone	**Indexed Color**
RGB	CMYK	Lab	Multichannel

The Targa format was originally designed for use on systems using the Truevision video board. The name is in fact an acronym meaning Truevision Advanced Raster Graphics Adapter. The Targa format predates Photoshop. It is a common format in the video industry (because it supports alpha channels), especially for PC users.

TIFF (.tif)

Layers	**8-bit**	**16-bit**	**32-bit**
Bitmap	**Grayscale**	**Duotone**	**Indexed Color**
RGB	**CMYK**	**Lab**	Multichannel

The Tagged-Image File Format is one of the most common and flexible formats available. It is widely used to exchange files between applications and computer platforms, and has a long legacy of compatibility. One benefit of TIFF is that it acts as a layered file within Photoshop but is treated as a flattened file by other applications. Additionally, TIFF is one of the few formats to work in a bit depth of 8, 16, or 32 bits per channel. High dynamic range images can be saved as 32-bits-per-channel TIFF files.

Adobe Digital Negative (.dng)

Layers	**8-bit**	**16-bit**	32-bit
Bitmap	Grayscale	Duotone	Indexed Color
RGB	CMYK	Lab	Multichannel

There are several competing raw file formats for digital cameras (most are proprietary to a particular manufacturer.) Adobe released the Adobe Digital Negative (DNG) file format to unify things. The concern is that proprietary formats will become obsolete more quickly due to company changes. Adobe hopes the DNG format will be the open-standard model. The specs for this format are available to camera and software manufacturers, and Adobe has had relative success getting others to adopt it. For more information, visit www.adobe.com/dng.

The DNG format offers a unified solution for camera raw images. In Photoshop you can only save a DNG file from the Adobe Camera Raw dialog box. You can also download a standalone DNG Converter for free from Adobe's website. This format is also used by many Adobe Lightroom users to store raw files.

Specialized Processes

Creating files for specific devices often requires special processing. The techniques discussed in this section are fairly elaborate, so the short overviews are meant for a clearer understanding of possibilities. The creation of specialized formats for the Internet, professional printing, or video requires a mastery of several interconnected skills. Let's take a quick look at converting to special purpose files.

VIDEO 109:
Save For Web

Save For Web

Preparing images for the web or mobile devices is all about compromise. You must learn to balance appearance with file size. If a web page takes too long to load, people will leave–which defeats the purpose of running the site. Fortunately, Photoshop provides a powerful command for compressing images and previewing the results: the Save For Web command.

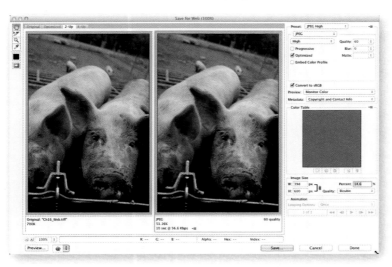

Let's give the Save For Web command a try.

1. Open the file Ch16_ Surfboards.tif from the Chapter 16 folder.

2. Choose File > Save For Web.

3. The Save For Web dialog box offers several important options for optimization and preview:

- **Tools.** If you can't see the entire image, you can use the Zoom tool to make the image more visible. Additionally, you can use the Hand tool (or hold down the spacebar) to drag and navigate around the image. Alternatively, you can click the Zoom Level menu in the lower-left corner and choose a magnification level.

- **Optimization tabs.** By clicking the four tabs at the top, you can choose to view the Original image, an Optimized view, 2-Up for two versions of the image side by side, or 4-Up for four versions of the image side by side. Being able to compare optimized images helps you choose the right format and compression settings. For this image, choose 2-Up.

- **Image Optimization Info.** The area below each image in the Save For Web dialog box gives you optimization information. You can see the current optimization applied, the projected file size, and the estimated download time based on a selected modem connection speed. Choose the JPEG High preset, and you'll notice that the file has been reduced from 32 MB to 1.055 MB (a significant savings). However, the download time is 196 seconds on a 56K modem (you can right-click the time to choose another speed).

JPEG
51K   60 quality
10 sec @ 56.6 Kbps ▾≣

4. You need to further reduce the file size for Internet delivery. The first area to tackle is the actual image size in pixels. In the Image Size field you'll see that the image is more than 4,000 pixels tall (which is much taller than a typical web page that can be displayed on most monitors). Type in a Height of **600** pixels, so the image can integrate easily into the web page (even with a screen resolution of 1024 × 768, a height of 600 would allow the image to display without scrolling up and down). Press the Tab key to exit the file and apply the resize value.

Image Size

| W: | 398 | px | Percent: | 14.6 | % |
| H: | 600 | px | Quality: | Bicubic | ⬍ |

5. The file size has been significantly reduced, but it's difficult to see the effects of the compression. Set the image magnification view to **100%**.

6. Change the amount of Compression by either changing the preset (from High to Medium, for example) or adjusting the Quality amount. You can manually enter a number or click to access a slider (you will need to release the slider for the image to refresh). Try a setting of **45** to see the results. The image is now at just over 32K, which is more than a 99.9 percent reduction in file size and a fundamental change for web delivery.

7. Toward the lower-right corner you have the ability to choose to preview the image in a web browser. If you don't see your browser of choice, just choose Edit List, and then choose Find All to add all web browsers on your computer.

8. Click Save to specify a location for the saved file. Choose your desktop and click Save in the new dialog box to process the image and save a compressed web-ready version. The original file will remain untouched, and its resolution and quality will be identical to its state when you launched the Save For Web command.

9. Experiment with other file formats such as GIF and PNG to see their benefits and limitations.

Convert to CMYK

Although CMYK conversion is an everyday process for many users, several authors and trainers have developed some useful techniques. What I offer here is a proper workflow that will work for most users, on most images, in most environments. I encourage you to continue to explore prepress production through further reading. CMYK conversion can be a very tricky process, and it is essential that you have access to the color profile used by your output device. Additionally, be sure to discuss the process with your service bureau that will do the professional printing. With all of these caveats said, let's take a look at the process.

1. Check your color management settings by choosing Edit > Color Settings or by pressing Shift+Command+K (Shift+Ctrl+K). Choose North America General Purpose 2.

2. Open the file Ch16_Gamut.tif from the Chapter 16 folder.

3. Choose View > Gamut Warning or press Shift+Command+Y (Shift+Ctrl+Y). Areas that are too bright or saturated for CMYK printing will be highlighted in gray. This is because

the RGB space can represent a wider ranger of visible colors based on the additive method of color. CMYK printing instead uses the subtractive model, and it has a narrower range. The warning is useful because it lets you identify areas that are subject to color shifting when printing or converting to the CMYK color mode.

4. Select the Sponge tool (O) from the Tools panel. Adjust the brush to a large size with soft edges. Set the flow to a lower value such as 30% and the mode to Desaturate. Deselect the Vibrance option to have greater impact on the saturated color areas. These settings will gently soak up the color in the oversaturated areas.

5. Carefully paint over the oversaturated areas with the Sponge tool. It may take multiple strokes or adjusting the Flow setting, but you'll see the gamut warning go away as you reduce the oversaturated areas. Repeat for other problem areas in the photo.

6. When all of the gamut warning has been removed, choose Image > Mode > CMYK. There should be no visible color shifting. By taking the time to manually touch up the out of gamut areas, you'll get a better CMYK conversion with less posterized edges or color clipping.

7. Save the image in a print-ready format such as TIFF.

Add an Alpha Channel

You explored saving selections as channels much earlier in the book (Chapter 5, "Selection Tools and Techniques"). The alpha channel can be used to store transparency information, and it is particularly useful for video and multimedia users. In Photoshop's Actions panel, you'll find

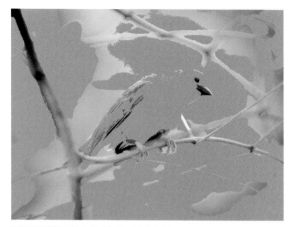

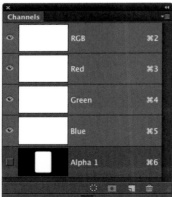

the Video actions that I co-wrote with Daniel Brown (a Photoshop expert). These can speed up certain tasks for a video workflow. Two of these actions can create an alpha channel for multi-layered graphics with transparency.

1. Make sure the Logo layer is selected in the Layers panel.

2. Call up the Actions panel and load the Video Actions by clicking the submenu. Choose the Video Actions set.

3. Choose the Create Alpha Channels from Visible Layers action. You must see Photoshop's transparency grid for it to work.

4. Click the Play Selection button to run the action. A dialog box appears with instructions. Read it and click Continue. A new alpha channel is added to the document.

5. Choose File > Save As and save the file as a PSD, TIFF, or Targa file, and then choose to embed the transparency by including the alpha channel.

There are many other issues related to creating graphics for use in video. I invite you to check out my "other" Photoshop book, aptly titled *Photoshop for Video* (Peachpit, 2010).

Include a Clipping Path

If you are preparing an image to import into a page layout program (such as Adobe InDesign or QuarkXPress), you may want to embed a clipping path. The clipping path embeds the transparency information into the file.

It's important to note that paths are vector based; therefore, they have hard edges (and do not preserve softness or a feathered edge). Features like a drop shadow cannot be preserved when creating a clipping path (but can often be added in the page layout program). An alternative to clipping paths is to use an alpha channel (which can include a feathered edge).

Photoshop offers a few ways to create accurate clipping paths; let's explore the easiest. Photoshop has a built-in wizard to help you create clipping paths.

1. Open the file Ch16_Clipping_Path.psd from the Chapter 16 folder.

2. Choose Selection > Load Selection, and then click OK to use the default properties. Photoshop loads a selection based on the transparency in the document.

3. Switch to the Paths panel and click the Make work path from selection icon.

4. Double-click on the work path to open the Save Path dialog box. Name the path Logo Edge and click OK.

5. Click the Paths panel submenu and choose Clipping Path.

6. Select the new path Logo Edge from the Path pop-up menu.

7. Leave the flatness value empty to print the image using the printer's default value.

8. Convert the file to CMYK by choosing Image > Mode > CMYK.

9. Choose File > Save As and store the file as a Photoshop EPS, DCS, or PDF format for PostScript printing or as a TIFF for use in Adobe InDesign or QuarkXPress.

This path is functioning as a clipping path. When the path's name appears outlined, it is being used as a clipping path.

End of the Road

Have you reached the end of the road? Hardly. Photoshop contains a wealth of tools. But you have now gained a firm foundation of knowledge. Many more techniques and specialized uses are worth exploring. And there is a plethora of Photoshop websites and books available to further your knowledge. A great place to start is at my blog at www.richardharringtonblog.com. You should also explore the National Association of Photoshop Professionals; be sure to check out its website at www.PhotoshopUser.com. You can also subscribe to the free Understanding Adobe Photoshop podcast on iTunes or check out advanced classes at Lynda.com. Photoshop will be a core tool as you grow into other software applications. Continue to expand your Photoshop knowledge and the investment in time will pay back greatly.

Index